W9-DAT-531

Thoughtful Teachers, Thoughtful Schools

Issues and Insights in Education Today

Second Edition

Editorial Projects in Education

Allyn and Bacon

Boston ● London ● Toronto ● Sydney ● Tokyo ● Singapore

Senior Editor: Virginia Lanigan
Series Editorial Assistant: Nihad Farooq
Design and Layout: David Kidd/EPE
Project Editor: Liz Parker/EPE
Production Editor: Catherine Hetmansky
Manufacturing Buyer: Aloka Rathnam
Cover Administrator: Suzanne Harbison
Electronic Production: MediaLink Associates, Inc.

ISBN 0-205-18496-0

Printed in the United States of America

10 9 8 7 6 5 4 3 2   00 99 98 97 96 95

Contents

W H A T   W E   W I L L   T E A C H

About Editorial Projects in Education

Since its inception in 1958, Editorial Projects in Education's primary mission has been to help raise the level of awareness and understanding among professionals and the public of important issues in American education.

A nonprofit, tax-exempt organization, EPE's first publishing ventures were in higher education. Beginning in 1958 and continuing for more than two decades, the organization published annual reports on major issues in higher education. These annual reports were bound into more than 300 college and university alumni magazines and, at their peak, reached more than 3 million readers.

In 1966, EPE founded *The Chronicle of Higher Education,* which it sold to the editors in 1978. In September 1981, *Education Week* was launched as American education's newspaper of record. And in 1989, EPE created *Teacher Magazine.* In the winter of 1993, *Education Week* and *Teacher Magazine* became available on-line through GTE Educational Network Services. More than 30 foundations have made grants to EPE in support of these ventures.

COMMENTARY AND FREELANCE AUTHORS

Clifford Adelman *is a senior research analyst at the U.S. Education Department.*

Eleanor Armour-Thomas *is an educational psychologist in the school of education at Queens College, City University of New York.*

Colette Daiute *is a professor at the Graduate School and University Center at City University of New York.*

Chester E. Finn *Jr. is John M. Olin fellow at the Hudson Institute.*

Marilyn Gootman *is an assistant professor in the department of elementary education at the University of Georgia.*

Daniel Gursky *is a communications associate with the American Federation of Teachers.*

Susan Harman *is director of evaluation for Community School District One, New York City.*

David Hill *is a freelance writer for* Teacher Magazine.

Willard L. Hogeboom *is a freelance writer and an adjunct history teacher at Dowling College.*

David W. Hornbeck *is the superintendent of Philadelphia public schools.*

Paul DeHart Hurd *is professor emeritus of science education at Stanford University.*

Mary Koepke *is a freelance writer for* Teacher Magazine.

Robert Lake (Medicine Grizzlybear) *is a member of the Seneca and Cherokee Indian Tribes and was an associate professor at Gonzaga University's school of education.*

Joseph P. McDonald *is a senior researcher at the Coalition of Essential Schools at Brown University.*

John Morris *teaches 1st, 2nd, and 3rd grades at Marlboro (Va.) Elementary School.*

Lewis J. Perelman *is the president of Kanbrain Institute.*

William A. Proefriedt *teaches philosophy of education at Queens College, City University of New York.*

Robert Rothman *is a senior associate at the National Alliance for Restructuring Education.*

David Ruenzel *is a freelance writer for* Teacher Magazine.

Elizabeth Schulz *is a Jacob Javitz fellow at the University of California at Berkeley.*

Morris J. Vogel *is a professor and the chairman of the department of history at Temple University.*

Deborah Wadsworth *is the executive director of the Public Agenda Foundation.*

Tony Wagner *is the president of the Institute for Responsive Education.*

William B. Wood *is the director at the Office of the Geographer and Global Issues at the U.S. State Department.*

A Season of Change

The primary mission of public education is to prepare people for productive work and effective citizenship. It hasn't changed in 150 years, since Horace Mann transformed local free elementary schools in Massachusetts into a public school system and instituted compulsory attendance. But though the mission remains the same, the requirements for productive work and effective citizenship have radically changed—and keep changing. And that is the essence of the crisis in public education and is behind the present efforts to reform schooling.

All of the accumulated knowledge about science in the 19th century could have fit on a few bookshelves in Thomas Jefferson's library, and he quite likely could have discoursed on it at length. As the 20th century draws to a close, vast libraries are needed to store what we know about the sciences, and information pouring forth is sometimes obsolete before it is published.

This extraordinary explosion of knowledge, the incredible advance of technology that has accompanied it, and profound demographic and economic developments are like hurricane-force winds hurling mankind into the future. We have moved further faster in the past 75 years than in all the previous years combined.

No wonder all of our social institutions are creaking and trembling under the strain. Designed in part to provide stability and continuity to society, our political, economic, legal and judicial, health care, and educational systems struggle to respond rapidly. They were designed to solve yesterday's problems.

In 1918, the Commission on the Reorganization of Secondary Education said that, to adequately prepare a high school graduate, the objectives of the school should be: "1. Health. 2. Command of fundamental processes. 3. Worthy home-membership. 4. Vocational education 5. Citizenship. 6. Worthy use of leisure. 7. Ethical character."

Workers in the 21st century will need more than elementary basic skills to maintain the standard of living of their parents. They will have to think for a living, analyze problems and solutions, and work cooperatively in teams. And responsible citizenship will entail understanding and reacting to a host of problems so complex that 19th-century Americans couldn't even have imagined them.

Moreover, to be productive workers and effective citizens, today's students will need to learn continuously throughout their lives. Most will likely have two, three, or even four different careers during their lifetimes. That is the challenge confronting public schools in the 1990s: to equip young people to cope with changes that they cannot yet envision.

Americans expect schools to meet that challenge. We have always believed deeply in the value of education; it has been called our secular religion. We credit it, with good reason, for our astonishing progress and prosperity. Not surprisingly, then, when our progress and prosperity seem to be in peril, as is now the case, we look for the fault in our schools.

This *Education Week* and *Teacher Magazine* reader offers a snapshot of American education in the midst of the most dynamic period in its history. The articles in the pages that follow were written day by day, week by week, on the scene as events unfolded. Inevitably, some of the material will be dated, but the stories are ongoing; themes echo across chapters, issues wind like sinews through the text, and voices intermingle.

Education is by no means the dry, static, systematic accumulation of facts it is often thought to be. It is a dynamic process involving values, politic, and aesthetics. And it is, first and last, a human endeavor—a matter of relationships among people, of hope and aspirations, of personal success and failure.

Those who become teachers in the next decade will have the opportunity to be in the vanguard of a movement to redirect the course of American education and, through it, the course of the nation. No previous generation of teachers has faced problems and issues as complex as those facing us today.

The domain of tomorrow's teachers must go well beyond the classroom; to have some control of your own destiny and that of your students, you must be able to see and understand the entire terrain of education—the structure of the system, how power and money flow, the politics, the dynamic relationships between the players. The most enduring impact of the school reform movement may well turn out to be the empowerment of teachers as true professionals.

The philosopher Alfred North Whitehead wrote that, on occasion, powerful forces combine in "driving mankind from its old anchorage." "Sometimes," he said, "the period of change is an age of hope, sometimes it is an age of despair. When mankind has slipped its cables, sometimes it is bent on the discovery of a New World, and sometimes it is haunted by the dim sound of breakers crashing on the rocks ahead."

Whether this season of change will be one of hope for America or one of despair may depend on how well our education system can adapt to new demands. ■

—*The Editors*

Who We Will Teach

"This nation cannot continue to compete and prosper in the global arena when more than one-fifth of our children live in poverty and a third grow up in ignorance. And if the nation cannot compete, it cannot lead. If we continue to squander the talents of millions of our children, America will become a nation of limited human potential."

—Report of the Committee for Economic Development, 1987

1.

America's Changing Students

Today's students are different from their predecessors, and they pose formidable challenges to schools and teachers.

Demography is destiny. And nothing has had more impact on America's schools than the profound demographic and behavioral changes in the nation's population. The challenge of nurturing, educating, and socializing the young was once shared by the family, the church, and the community. Increasingly, that responsibility has passed disproportionately to the schools.

University of Chicago sociologist James Coleman wrote that public schools came into their own when America began to industrialize and men had to leave the farm in search of work and could no longer take responsibility for teaching their sons. Now, he noted, we are living through an equally significant sea change as women leave the home to work and our public schools struggle to adapt.

The majority of women between the ages of 17 and 44 are working full time; more than 80 percent of children under the age of 18 now have working mothers. An increasing number of women are living alone, and more and more of them are raising children. Some 6.6 million households are headed by single women raising some 13.7 million children.

Clearly, the family—the backbone of American society—has been undergoing major upheaval. Only about 6 percent of families today fit the description of the "traditional" household: a working father, a mother at home, and two or more school-age children. In 1965, about 60 percent of the nation's households matched that image.

Studies indicate that in the 1980s the nation lost ground on almost all measures of child well-being. There were more children living in poverty, more births to unmarried teenagers, more latchkey children, and more young people involved with the criminal justice system. Said one report: Shifts in the econ-omy, changes in "the routines and realities" of family life, and the failure of institutions to respond to those realities have severely hampered "the capacity of typical families to raise their children well."

Not surprisingly, the children who enter school in this decade will bring with them a heavy burden:
- 1 out of 4 will be from families who live in poverty;
- 14 percent will be the children of teenage mothers;
- 15 percent will be physically or mentally handicapped—often the result of low birth weight or drug use during the prenatal period;
- 15 percent will be immigrants who speak a language other than English;
- 15 percent will be children of unmarried parents;
- 40 percent will live in a broken home before they reach 18;
- 10 percent will have poorly educated, even illiterate, parents;
- Between one-quarter and one-third will be latchkey children with no one to greet them when they come home from school;
- 14 percent will be without health insurance; and
- a quarter or more will not finish school.

Obviously, the majority of American students will not live in poverty, will not be special education students, will speak English and come from two-parent, middle- and working-class families. But even these more fortunate young people will not be as easy to teach as their counterparts in previous generations. They have been reared on television and movies, during an age when standards of public morality and ethical behavior often seem to have slipped badly.

More than half of all high school students report on surveys that they have had sex. Moreover, a substantial proportion engage in behaviors that place them at risk for HIV infection—such as having intercourse with multiple partners and not using condoms.

A 1992 survey of some 9,000 teenagers and adults by the Edna Josephson Institute of Ethics found that an "unacceptably high" number are willing to lie, cheat, and steal. Some 61 percent of high school students admitted to having cheated on an exam during the past year, and 83 percent said they had lied to their parents during that time. A third said they had shoplifted, and a third said they would lie on a résumé or job application if necessary to get the job.

Materialism and selfishness are too often the motives for students to work part time. According to the 1992 report by the National Safe Work Institute, 5.5 million high school students have part-time jobs. The average 15-year-old worker works 17 hours a week in addition to a 32.5-hour school week. Sixteen- and 17-year-olds work 21 hours a week on average.

That kind of work schedule offers students little time for studying. And students working late at night may be coming to school too tired to learn, the report says. That may account, in part, for the consistently poor showings of American students on academic achievement tests.

Under pressure to conform, to achieve, and to make money, an increasing proportion of American students are suffering from problems of stress. The suicide rate for adolescents ages 15-19 has quadrupled over the past four decades, from 2.7 per 100,000 in 1950 to 11.3 in 1988. Two percent of high school students, or 276,000 young people, sustained medical injuries while attempting to commit suicide during the past year. According to the federal Centers for Disease Control, approximately one in four students acknowledged thinking seriously about attempting suicide during the past year.

Not surprisingly, a disproportionate percentage of the most troubled young people are from racial minority groups. Surveys of youth deviance consistently reveal minority students in the most endangered brackets. Minority students are also particularly at risk of dropping out of school.

About one-third of the nation's students are from racial minority groups, and the proportion is growing. They tend to be concentrated in, but by no means limited to, the larger inner-city schools (and scattered throughout rural areas, particularly in the South). Within 15 years, the student bodies in a number of our most populous states will have a majority of minority students.

National Indicators of Child Well-Being

Indicators	From		To		Difference
Percent low birth-weight babies	1980	6.8%	1989	7.0%	+0.2%
Infant mortality rate (per 1,000 live births)	1980	12.6	1989	9.8	-2.8
Death rate, ages 1-14 (per 100,000 children	1980	39.5	1989	32.4	-7.1
Violent death rate, ages 15-19 (per 100,000 teens)	1984	62.4	1989	69.3	+6.9
Percent all births that are to single teens	1980	7.5%	1989	8.6%	+1.1%
Custody rate, ages 10-15 (per 100,000 youths)	1985	142	1989	156	+14
Percent graduating high school	1982	69.7%	1989	69.6%	-0.1%
Percent children in poverty	1979	16.0%	1986-90	19.5%	+3.5%
Percent children in single-parent families	1980-84	21.3%	1987-91	24.1%	+2.8%

Source: Center for the Study of Social Policy; Annie E. Casey Foundation

Behind all of these numbers are real children, and you will find them in your classrooms. Indeed, teachers will bear the brunt of trying to find ways to reach these young people and help them forge the tools they will need to survive and succeed in a changing world.

It will not be easy. The majority of teachers responding to a 1992 survey by the Metropolitan Life Insurance Company expressed dismay and frustration over their students' lack of readiness for school; they worried that they are ill-equipped to deal with the range of problems their students present.

Among teachers citing student preparedness problems, 65 percent pointed to a lack of parental support as a serious hindrance to students. More than 40 percent cited poverty as a major problem, while 32 percent identified parents' drug or alcohol use as a cause of trouble. Teachers mentioned physical and psychological abuse, poor nutrition, student drinking, violence, language difficulties, and poor health as serious obstacles to teaching and learning.

In the face of such problems, teachers said that they often feel stymied and do not know how to help their students. More than two-thirds thought that their own education and training had not prepared them well to deal with these social problems.

But if such social and demographic forces have made teaching much more difficult, they have also made it more crucial to the welfare of the nation. As one teacher said during an open discussion at a national meeting of educators: "We as teachers may lament and resent that we are being asked to cope with problems that schools are not organized to deal with and we are not prepared to solve. But these are America's children, our students. We cannot turn them away or walk away from them. We cannot exchange them for students with less baggage. We must accept them as they come to us and do our best to help them learn and succeed. We owe that to them, we owe it to ourselves as teachers, and we owe it to this country." ■

2.

Getting Ready for School

The first national goal may be the hardest one to reach—and the most important.

By Deborah L. Cohen

The success of the six national education goals hinges to a great degree on the first: ensuring that, by the year 2000, all children enter school ready to learn. If children are already at risk when they enter school, it will be that much harder to meet the other five goals—raising high-school graduation rates, boosting students' competency in key subjects, making U.S. students first in the world in science and mathematics, ensuring that all adults are literate, and ridding schools of drugs and violence.

But the readiness goal itself may be the most difficult one to meet. It will require overcoming a complex set of obstacles and implementing a set of interventions far more comprehensive than anything now in place. Consider some of the obstacles:

There is still no broadly agreed-to definition of the age group, range of services, or outcomes that determine readiness—though most agree that readiness must include health, support and education for parents, and good early-childhood care.

The readiness goal involves three objectives:
● Ensuring that all disadvantaged and disabled children have access to high quality, "developmentally appropriate" preschool programs;
● Seeing that all parents get the support they need to act as their children's first teachers and spend time each day helping their preschool children learn; and
● Improving access to prenatal and other health care to reduce the number of low-birthweight babies and

ensure children get adequate nutrition and health care.

One fundamental problem with the goal, many maintain, is how it is worded. While the goal is most frequently associated with the preschool period, some experts have begun to advance a definition that extends beyond the earliest years. Advocating that the health, social, and emotional needs of families and children don't go away when a child enters school, top scientists in the field recently proposed abandoning the concept of school readiness and substituting continued readiness to learn. Experts have also proposed expanding Goal 1 to ensure that "every child comes to school every day ready to learn" and that "every school is ready for every child."

The goal's wording troubled early-childhood experts from the outset, some said, because it implied that a child didn't do any learning prior to school, and that any difficulties they encountered were their own fault. Teachers' differing expectations of what constitutes readiness could also unfairly pressure or penalize children or foster inappropriate classroom practices. Some school programs, for example, have been making kindergarten more stringently academic, a trend that has predisposed a number of children to unhappy experiences.

The National Association for the Education of Young Children argues for teaching approaches and policies that respond to the wide variations in young children's development, help compensate for inequities in their early-life experiences, and shift the onus to schools to be "ready" to meet young children's needs.

There is uncertainty about how to assess progress toward universal readiness. And that's important because the measures used to assess readiness will in part determine the strategy used to achieve it. In addition to perpetuating a narrow definition of readiness, some experts fear that Goal 1 could encourage testing practices that they consider unreliable for young children.

"Just using the word has the potential of inviting more readiness tests," said Lorrie A. Shepard, a professor of education at the University of Colorado. Ms. Shepard has collected data suggesting that children held back or tracked into special classes based on readiness tests do not fare better than those of similar capacity who enter 1st grade on time—and may actually suffer harm. Readiness, she said, "is so evocative of the misuse that we've been seeing of school districts giving tests to decide if kids are ready and either not letting them in or relegating them to two-year kindergartens if they are not."

One of the biggest problems in testing readiness is that schools tend to reflect middle-class values and knowledge systems, automatically setting poor children at a great disadvantage. Measuring readiness, in fact, has been one of the thorniest issues faced by the National Education Goals Panel.

When the group last year was unable to identify an acceptable readiness test, panel members divided

> # One of the biggest problems in testing readiness is that schools tend to reflect middle-class values and knowledge systems, setting poor children at a disadvantage.

along party lines over whether the first progress report on the goals should instead include data on prenatal and child health, preschool enrollment, family life, and other factors affecting a child's ability to learn.

An advisory group to the goals panel issued a report in the fall of 1991 proposing an in-school assessment process to gather data on children during their kindergarten year. Using parent and teacher observations, individually administered profiles of skills and knowledge, and a portfolio of children's performance, the assessment would gauge children's physical well-

being and motor development, social and emotional development, approaches to learning, language usage, and cognition and general knowledge.

To avert "potential misuse," the report "assiduously avoids" the term readiness. It also stresses that results should not be used to "label, stigmatize, or classify" individual children or groups. Some early childhood activists charge that the whole education-goals-panel activity has concentrated on how to measure progress rather than on how to achieve the goal.

Others believe the key to achieving Goal 1 is more resources. "There's just one obstacle," says Keith Geiger, the president of the National Education Association: "money."

Increasing numbers of states are investing in initiatives—from preschool programs to parenting education—that target high-risk groups or address pieces of the problem. But the cost of making full-day, high-quality preschool programs universally available makes the goal elusive.

Some, like Mr. Geiger, say federal, state, and local resources should be tapped to fund preschools through the public schools. In the past, there has not been the willingness to invest that kind of money. Even with the additional funding Head Start has received in recent years, it still falls far short of serving all the disadvantaged preschoolers who are eligible.

The funding gap is also impeding expanding children's access to health care, improving youngsters' nutrition, and ensuring that all children are immunized. "It's an outrage that we don't use the knowledge we have to assure the physical and emotional health of children when they enter school," says Jack Shonkoff, the chief of developmental and behavior pediatrics at the University of Massachusetts Medical School. "For preventable, treatable, or curable problems to appear at the schoolhouse door is unacceptable."

But as fiscally strapped states cut programs ranging from welfare benefits to school aid, advocates of early services will be doing well just to hold their own.

There is a complex group of players whose support and collaboration will be needed. "It just isn't a mystery in terms of what we ought to be doing," says one expert. "The problem is, how do you wrap it up so it's a coherent program?"

The problem is compounded by a lack of an "infrastructure" for reaching children from birth to age 5. "There is no one institution or set of institutions that has access to all of those families, so it's a hit-or-miss proposition," says Douglas R. Powell, the head of the department of child development and family studies at Purdue University. "It takes time to work through all those layers of bureaucracy."

Meeting the goal's objectives—especially in the current fiscal climate—will require unprecedented coordination among health, education, and social services agencies and also among groups that are fragmented.

The link between health and school success, for example, could be made by placing a medical professional on the search committee for a school superintendent, or education people on a public-health advisory committee. Easing the funding restrictions that keep agencies from pooling and coordinating resources could also help cut across old lines that block progress toward Goal 1.

Educators can also play a key role in helping make progress toward Goal 1. Schools could begin by:
● becoming more adaptable to the range of children entering school and what they bring with them;
● minimizing retention and early categorization of children by responding to developmental and cultural differences among children;
● establishing non-traditional mixed-age grouping and team-teaching practices;
● recruiting, hiring and training early-education staff members; and
● promoting programs that ease the transition between Head Start and school, to sustain the gains made by children in preschool.

Teachers could benefit from a human-development framework that would highlight the need to involve parents and meet kids' needs beyond mastering skills.

Researchers are also calling for interdisciplinary training to ensure that professionals across sectors have a broad perspective and can pool their expertise.

Teachers, for example, could benefit from a human-development framework that would highlight the need to involve parents and meet children's needs beyond mastering skills. In addition to curricular reforms, though, schools' role must be redefined and facilities revamped to make them the primary contact point for the referral or delivery of a wide range of services to families. And for such efforts to succeed,

many agree that parents must play a pivotal role.

Rather than focusing on counting to 10 or knowing the alphabet, advocates say, interventions should help parents bolster children's social and organizational skills and zeal for learning. "Readiness is really civilizing people," says Dorothy Rich, the president of the Home and School Institute Inc.

For disadvantaged families in particular, intervention with a child is much more effective if it causes a positive change in the parents' behavior as well. Ideally, family intervention would help some parents improve their literacy skills, education, or training, which would bolster their self-esteem and greatly enhance the readiness capability of their children. But many agree that creating the ideal conditions for a generation of young children to succeed will require large-scale societal change.

Besides ensuring families access to the support and services they need, says one skeptic, "You wouldn't have any homeless children, any unimmunized children, or children not covered through health insurance. No child would be living in poverty.... Even in affluent homes, you wouldn't have exposure to horrible, violent television or bad care. You would have highquality child care for all who needed it. And then you would still have to make sure that what schools expected was appropriate."

But perhaps the most daunting challenge in the effort to achieve universal readiness is marshaling the "political will." Early-intervention activists complain that Goal 1 has not been made part of the political agenda; often, businessmen understand the need for early services better than politicians. Moreover, the United States is way behind other industrialized nations in offering support for young children in the form of child care, preschool, and paid family leave.

The broader public needs to start seeing young children as a priority and needs to understand that readiness is everyone's business. Such political, economic, and social obstacles make some experts skeptical about achieving the readiness goal. But they say they see it as a rare chance to spotlight the early years. Having readiness as a national priority gives the opportunity to launch initiatives that are good for states, regions, and localities. In the words of one expert: "We want to seize the moment!" ■

From Education Week, *Feb. 12, 1992*

3.

Breaking the Language Barrier

Hispanic special-education students prove that their deficiency lies not with them, but with the traditional curriculum.

By Lynn Schnaiberg

Carlos, a 3rd grader, reads softly to himself in Spanish from *Los Trucos de Clifford*, his index finger carefully tracing each word as he sounds it out, syllable by syllable. Carlos is doing what most other 3rd graders are doing: learning to read, with Clifford, the ubiquitous, oversized red dog. But that is the very thing that his teacher and school psychologist's assessment said he wasn't supposed to be able to do. Not even in his native Spanish—the first language of many students at Murchison Street Elementary School, which sits in a predominantly Hispanic neighborhood in east Los Angeles.

Labeled a "nonreader," Carlos was sent to Eleanor M. Vargas' special-education class in September 1993. Each morning for about 2 hours, when the other students in his mainstream class are in language arts, Carlos and other students with mild learning disabilities are getting the special attention they need to learn to read.

"When he picked up a book, he just couldn't do anything with it" at the beginning of the year, says Beatriz Carreon, Carlos' mainstream-classroom teacher.

Under a brightly colored banner that reads "Seeing Is Believing" hangs the work of another student, Joselito, whose teacher said he could not write and generally did not participate in class before he came to Vargas' class. "I play SEGA, the game I play, NBA jam I play, wet my fins, I play at my hous," it reads.

Vargas knew that what she was doing in her classroom was working when the parents of one of her students, in a show of gratitude, came in one weekend to blanket her cracked, lime-green classroom walls with a fresh coat of white paint.

In fact, many parents and teachers at Murchison Street Elementary call Room 51, Vargas' class for bilingual learning-disabled students, "a miracle."

In a nation where the vast majority of special-education students never leave special education—and limited-English-proficient students are disproportionately represented among its ranks—Vargas' class appears to be an anomaly.

Under state law, special-education classrooms like Vargas' can't enroll more than 28 students. In such classrooms, researchers say, an average of 1.7 Hispanic students per class return full time to their mainstream classes each year.

In the 1992-93 academic year, Vargas sent four students back to their mainstream classrooms. Her students' reading scores shot up by as many as five grade levels in the same year.

None of this happened by accident. Three years ago, researchers chose Vargas' classroom as one of two pilot sites for their OLE, or "optimal learning environment," project. The other site, a rural elementary school in northern California, has a large migrant student population. Six other schools have since adopted elements of the OLE project in their classrooms.

More than half of Murchison Street Elementary's 1,050 students are limited English proficient.

Each year, Vargas, a 20-year veteran special-education teacher, welcomes some 30 students into her classroom, about half of whom are limited English proficient.

About 85 percent of the school's students live a few short blocks from the school in one of L.A.'s oldest housing projects, Ramona Gardens. Some students come from families that have spent three generations living within the clusters of gray-blue, cinder-block buildings, Principal Robert S. Bilovsky says. Roughly 98 percent of the student body participates in the federal government's free lunch program.

OLE is a "theory busting" experiment to make special-education classrooms look and work more like those for gifted students, says Richard A. Figueroa, the head of the California Research Institute on Special Education and Cultural Diversity in Sacramento and OLE's lead researcher.

The project also tries to move away from the traditional, medical approach to special education. That model, Figueroa and others argue, allows schools to explain underachievement as a result of an often unidentifiable student flaw instead of the school's poor instruction for students whose language needs don't "fit" into the general-education program.

There is no way to "prove" that a child has a learning disability, which usually manifests itself in problems with reading, spelling, or writing. In fact, researchers have documented many cases of LEP students being misassessed as learning disabled. In these cases, special-education evaluators unfamiliar with the second-language acquisition process have misinterpreted as learning deficiencies typical characteristics of the language-learning process.

For example, students who remain silent for a long period of time may be diagnosed as having aphasia (the partial or total loss of the ability to articulate ideas as a result of brain damage). But this so-called "silent period" is often a normal stage for a child absorbing a second language.

Estimates on the number of LEP students in special-education classrooms nationwide range from roughly 228,000 to one million, according to a report from the U.S. Education Department's office of special education, an indication of how thorny just identifying these students can be.

To compensate for these diagnostic difficulties, the OLE project sets out to place students in a classroom environment that gives them the chance to show that their deficiency lies not within them, but within the curriculum.

"The simple handshake of bilingual education and special education just doesn't work," concludes Figueroa, who speaks from personal experience.

Eight years ago, prodded by frustration with the program serving his 1-year-old daughter Elena, who is deaf, Figueroa and his wife decided to experiment at home with teaching principles that would later grow into the foundation for the OLE program. Since kindergarten, after numerous negotiations with the district, Elena has attended totally mainstreamed classes in the Sacramento schools.

Comprehensive results on OLE student performance will not be available until the end of the year. But initial findings from the two California sites where the OLE program has been fully implemented point to a model that could drastically change the way bilingual special education works, observers note.

In fact, Los Angeles plans to expand the model to 10 other elementary schools to serve more learning-disabled students this fall.

"When we first got into bilingual special education, we assumed that the special-education delivery system was OK and all we had to do was make it accessible in two languages," says Leonard M. Baca, a pioneer in bilingual special education and the director of the Bueno Center for Multicultural Education at the University of Colorado at Boulder.

"What we've learned from this project is that that model is in serious trouble," he says.

Attitude Adjustment

The OLE program flies in the face of the conventional wisdom upon which traditional special education is based: that students need a highly centralized program that focuses on remediating isolated skills largely through repetition and watered-down instructional materials.

The typical, prepackaged special-education program runs totally counter to what researchers have said bilingual students need, Figueroa maintains. In response to those needs, the OLE classroom is student-driven, using the student's home language, whole language, rich literature, and group learning.

For many LEP students, their home-language support stops the minute they enter traditional special education, adds Nadeen T. Ruiz, one of the project researchers and an assistant professor of education at California State University at Sacramento.

So the OLE model also takes into account the fact that many language-minority students often have fewer chances than their English-speaking peers to use their native language outside the home, making learning in school more difficult.

It took Vargas and her assistant, Angélica D. Beltrán, almost two years to make the full shift into using the OLE principles. They started by locking away the Buffy and Max basal readers, prepackaged teachers' manual, word lists, and weekly spelling tests that they had relied on for years.

Then they replaced the publisher's laminated ABC chart above the chalkboard—"which no one ever looked at," Vargas says—with a student-made version. The letter A, which used to represent "apple," now stands for "avion" (airplane) and "anillo" (ring).

Charts, drawings, and stories—all student creations—now plaster the walls.

"It took a total change in attitude," Vargas says. "We had to back off a little so students could discover things themselves."

Before launching the OLE program, Vargas and Beltrán would work individually with four or five students in a class for 50 minutes a day. Now, they have about 15 students each morning during their mainstream classrooms' language-arts time on a three-week-on, three-week-off rotation throughout the school year.

English- and Spanish-speaking students used to work side by side in the same class, "just with different worksheets," Vargas says. Now, Vargas and Beltrán separate the youngsters into two groups so they can tailor instruction to their needs and students can work in groups more efficiently.

The research behind the project, which began in 1989, is funded by the University of California at Davis and the state department of education. Frustrated with the overrepresentation of LEP and minority students in special education, Shirley A. Thornton, the department's deputy superintendent of specialized programs, wanted to develop an alternative.

"Regular education can fail you a lot cheaper than this," Thornton says, noting that California spends about $3 billion a year on special education. "To me, the best special education is the one that gets kids back to their mainstream classes."

And that's just what Vargas intends to do. What's more, by bolstering literacy in her students' primary language, she can help ease their transition into English (which begins around the 4th or 5th grade in California), the OLE researchers say.

Interactive Storytime

"Grab whatever book you want, in English or Spanish, it doesn't matter," Vargas shouts in Spanish as her 15 LEP students stream down the hall of the pale yellow stucco building and into her classroom.

She encourages her students to choose freely between English and Spanish when they speak, write, and read in class. She used to reserve English for one block of time or activity and Spanish for another.

Although many of the students in this class are predominantly Spanish speakers, Vargas says more and more of them are starting to take risks by using English. A similar trend has emerged at OLE's San Francisco-area site.

Two 5th grade boys read "Batman" comics in Eng-

lish while a bespectacled girl pulls out a laminated book, *Los Dos Amigos,* that some of her classmates wrote in Spanish. Vargas plops into a black leather chair, taking on the role of classroom emcee. "So what did everybody do over the weekend?" she asks.

Hands fly up. Eric explains in English that he went to a friend's birthday party. Rene talks in Spanish about going to Shakey's pizzeria with his family.

"Ay no me digas, and how was it?" Vargas asks, effortlessly switching between the two languages. Aware of the gap that often exists between the experiences language-minority students read about in standard schoolbooks and what they have actually lived, Vargas is careful to let her students guide their discussions and writing.

A poster hanging off a small table in the front of the classroom reads, "What We Want To Learn About." Cooking, dinosaurs, computers, writing, English, and making books—topics the students voted on at the start of the year—fill out the list of studies.

In a seamless transition from their discussion, Vargas asks her students to pull out their "interactive" journals. A key OLE feature, the journal exercise encourages students to write without fear of being corrected. Students write anything from one paragraph to an entire page, in Spanish or English, using the discussion as a launching point for their compositions.

Carlos, gripping a newly sharpened pencil in his fist, writes about going to Mexico and riding horses on his relatives' ranch. Beltrán sits with him, reads his entry, then writes questions about it, talking to Carlos the entire time.

Sometimes, the journals may even offer an explanation for why a student may be falling behind. One of Vargas' former students wrote about a cousin who had just died of AIDS. Another wrote about his father's truck being firebombed during a gang shootout.

"If you can get through that," Vargas says, "reading and writing is a piece of cake."

On a recent morning in Room 51, Ana, a 5th grader, is putting the finishing touches on the cover of her first solo book in Spanish: *The Day I'll Never Forget.* Other bound books—all written and illustrated by Vargas' students—such as *Have You Seen My Rabbit?* and *Vacaciones a Hollywood y Tejas*—spill out of a plastic basket.

Ana's mainstream-classroom teacher, Hilda Maldonado, says that before Ana joined Vargas' class, she was afraid to call on her. She knew Ana had reading problems and didn't want to embarrass her.

A few weeks ago some students chose Ana to read a passage aloud. "I sort of cringed and thought, 'Oh no,'" Maldonado recalls. "But she stood right up and read without any problem."

Maldonado shakes her head slightly. "I thought to myself, this is truly incredible." ∎

From Education Week, *June 15, 1994*

4.

'A Quiet Crisis'

In the competition for resources, programs for the gifted are losing out to programs for special-needs students.

By Debra Viadero

Once educators in his community decided he was gifted, Marcus Simpson began to do wonderful things in school. He created inventions, spent hours working on complex problems, and visited with a local television station to find out how weather reports are produced. He gave a presentation on meteorology to his classmates and spoke for more than half an hour, without notes, because the subject excited him so much.

Marcus lost some of his enthusiasm for school, however, after the local school board voted to eliminate his gifted-and-talented program. Back in his regular classes, his mother noticed, Marcus began to grow restless. Last fall, six weeks into the 8th grade, he transferred to a private school.

"You're watching your child just sort of becoming bored and unmotivated," Marcus' mother, Janney Simpson, says. "It's hard to decide to make a transfer six weeks into the year."

Experts in the field of gifted education say Marcus' situation may become increasingly commonplace in the future—not only because funding for such programs is scarce, but also because school reformers consider gifted education a form of tracking.

Some education reforms have called for schools to move away from the traditional practice of grouping students according to their ability in favor of more heterogeneous classroom settings. And that trend, along with such other reform-minded innovations as site-based management and cooperative learning, has put traditional gifted-education programs in jeopardy.

"We believe that the field of education for the gifted and talented is currently facing a quiet crisis," two researchers in the field, Joseph S. Renzulli and Sally M. Reis, wrote in a recent paper, "and that this crisis is directly related to the educational-reform movement in America."

'Rich Get Richer'

To a large degree, school programs for gifted students have always been engaged in a struggle for survival. Despite a boom in support for gifted education in the 1980s, the programs have long been criticized as elitist or unnecessary.

"Every time the legislature deals with this issue, the first question is: Why should the rich get richer?" says Lee Sheldon, a consultant in gifted-and-talented education to the California Department of Education.

Gifted-education advocates worry that that attitude will erode their programs even further. They point to recent developments in several states. For example:
● The number of towns with programs for gifted students in Connecticut, Marcus Simpson's home state, has declined by 20 percent over two years as state reimbursements for the programs have dried up. And Gov. Lowell P. Weicker Jr. has proposed eliminating state support altogether.
● State funds for gifted programs in Massachusetts have been reduced from a high of $1 million two years

ago to zero last year. Michigan, Vermont, and New York have also reported cuts in their gifted programs.

● New Hampshire lost its only state coordinator for gifted programs last year in a budget-cutting move. Gifted-education advocates in the state say that loss, along with the elimination of a state-grant program for gifted education, has also prompted a college in the state to drop its teacher-training program for instructors of gifted students.

"It's been disastrous," says Reis, a principal investigator for the National Research Center on the Gifted and Talented at the University of Connecticut. The center, the first of its kind, was established in 1990 with a $7.5 million federal grant.

There were so many programs being cut and so many people losing their jobs that the center decided to change the direction of its research to focus on how gifted children are faring in their regular classrooms. Those studies, three of which were released in early 1992, "paint a pretty sad picture," Reis says.

They found that gifted pupils in regular elementary school classrooms typically receive the same curriculum as academically average students and that they are usually asked to revisit material they have already learned. The researchers concluded that gifted students would be better served if they were freed from covering up to 70 percent of the standard curriculum or were grouped by ability.

"They spend years and years learning what they already know, and, sometimes by 3rd or 4th grade, their affective feelings about school have already changed," Reis says.

Pamela Thompson, the mother of another gifted student in Marcus Simpson's town, agrees. Her daughter had spent her time in gifted classes honing her writing skills. After the program was cut, however, her daughter, who was then in 6th grade, spent some of her spare time in study hall learning to knit.

"If she's bored now, I really fear what's going to happen in the future," Thompson says.

Eighty-five percent of the parents of gifted pupils in that community said the loss of the program had had a negative effect on their children, according to another University of Connecticut study. The researchers declined to reveal the name of the community. Nearly half of the parents had, like Simpson, considered putting their children in private schools after the program was cut.

Researchers and advocates say that gifted programs are particularly vulnerable to budget cuts because 24 states do not mandate them. In Connecticut, for example, schools are required to identify gifted students but not to serve them. The programs are more vulnerable because they benefit only a small number of students—usually 3 percent to 5 percent of schoolchildren in most states.

JOHN LIGOS

Marcus Simpson decided to leave the public schools after his gifted-and-talented program was eliminated.

Faced with a decision of whether to increase class sizes for all students or reduce gifted programs for a few, many local school boards may be right in choosing the latter, some gifted-program supporters concede. But, in some states and communities, the motivation to do away with gifted programs also has something to do with changing educational philosophies and practices.

In the early 1980s, when the reform movement was beginning to stress economic competitiveness, gifted programs experienced a small boom. Both state and federal support for programs meant to nurture the "best and brightest" increased for virtually the first time since the Sputnik era. Now, however, a number of education reforms have called for an end to traditional classroom practices of grouping students by ability.

Both the National Governors' Association and the Carnegie Council on Adolescent Development have, for example, issued reports that have been critical of such practices. The problem with ability groups, some reformers say, is that students get locked into a particular academic track at an early age.

While higher-ability students may continue to thrive in homogeneous classroom settings, pupils in lower-level tracks are less fortunate. Studies show that such students get fewer classroom resources, inferior teachers, a less challenging curriculum, and fewer opportunities than do the better students. Moreover, in many communities, these pupils are disproportionately poor or members of minority groups.

"There is a strong recognition that, when we separate off the top 5 percent or 10 percent of kids in an attempt to give them special programs, we lose sight of what happens to the education of the other 90 percent of kids," says Jeannie Oakes, a professor of education at the University of California at Los Angeles.

"Most of us see any kind of whole-class grouping and most pullout programs as simply another form of tracking," she adds.

Advocates of gifted education say, however, that schools should draw a distinction between tracking, in which students are homogeneously grouped in every subject and for every grade level, and ability grouping, in which students may be with students of similar ability in some subjects but not in others.

"We are anti-tracking," says Peter D. Rosenstein, the executive director of the National Association for Gifted Children. "However, though children are born deserving equal opportunity, they're not born with equal potential."

Some parents of gifted students also complain that their children tend to fare poorly in the kinds of cooperative-learning groups that characterize instruction in many of these new mixed-ability classrooms. These groupings usually involve children of varying academic abilities who work together on a project or a complex problem. Teachers evaluate pupils both individually and as a team for their work in these groups. Parents of gifted pupils say, however, that, in practice, their children often end up doing all the work in the groups or teaching their less able peers.

However, Robert Slavin, who has led much of the research on cooperative learning, disputes such contentions. Preliminary statistics from his own studies indicate that gifted and higher-ability pupils in properly run cooperative-learning groups gain as much from the group interactions as do lower-achievers. Slavin notes, however, that in the classrooms he studied, the more academically advanced students were permitted to do some accelerated work in reading and math.

"I don't see any reason at all to provide separate gifted programs at any level," says Slavin, who is the co-director of the elementary school program at the Johns Hopkins University's Center for Research on Effective Schooling for Disadvantaged Students.

"The main thing to do is accommodate the rate of learning for these kids," he argues. "If that means grouping within a class, where they go at different rates, OK." He adds: "If it's letting a 6th grader take math with the 7th graders, I think that's reasonable. But if you're given a stark choice, if someone's going to provide $1,000 for an additional enrichment program for gifted kids, I would say $1,000 worth of one-to-one tutoring for a kid struggling to learn to read can make a big difference."

Partly as a result of such criticisms of gifted education and partly because of new theories of "multiple intelligences," advocates in recent years have taken steps to "open up" their programs. In an effort to bring more minority, non-English-speaking, and special-education students into gifted programs, for example, researchers have begun looking for ways other than traditional IQ tests to determine if a student has gifted abilities.

"We believe that our field should shift its emphasis from a traditional concept of 'being gifted' [or not being gifted] to a concern about the development of gifted behaviors in those youngsters who have the highest potential for benefiting from special-educational services," Renzulli and Reis wrote in their paper last year in Gifted Child Quarterly.

Some newer models of gifted education also strive to provide schoolwide "enrichment," with gifted-education teachers acting as resources for regular classroom teachers. Such models include projects or activities in which a wide range of students can participate.

"To a good degree, gifted education is good education," says James Delisle, the president of the Association for the Gifted of the Council for Exceptional Children. "If we're guilty of anything, it's probably being too isolated in a resource room on the corner."

Many educators of the gifted maintain, however, that their pupils still need a certain degree of separation from regular classrooms. "One mind sharpens off another," White of Connecticut says. Moreover, he adds, gifted children often feel pressured to "hide their light under a bushel" in the regular classroom because of the social stigma associated with giftedness.

Coordinators of gifted programs in several states also see a threat to their programs in the movement toward site-based management, in which more of the control for how schools are run is placed in the hands of teachers and principals.

In California, for example, schools using such management arrangements can often obtain waivers from state education-department rules, including those governing gifted programs.

"Usually, when a district goes to site-based management, one of the first casualties is the district-level person who coordinated the GATE [gifted and talented education] program," Sheldon says.

It is too soon to tell how much of the retrenchment in gifted-education programs is the result of changing educational philosophies and how much is the result of limited resources. In many locations, education reforms are coexisting peacefully with gifted-education programs. Concepts currently at the heart of education reform—such as hands-on learning and the use of authentic databases and information in classroom instruction—have been a part of gifted-education programs for years. To abandon the field now, in order to embrace some other reforms, some say, would be like "throwing the baby out with the bath water."

After all, says White: "These kids will be our future leaders, discoverers, and great performers." ■

From Education Week, *March 18, 1992*

5.

Kids Just Ain't the Same

Teachers say students are becoming apathetic, impatient, self-centered, overwhelmed, and harder to motivate.

By Mary Koepke

If anyone is in a good position to determine how students have changed over the years, it's Allen Weinheimer. The 65-year-old has been teaching calculus at the same suburban Indianapolis high school for 36 years. And if anyone has a good chance of giving today's kids a thumbs up, it's Weinheimer. His students—the type who take the challenging, elective math course—are considered to be among the most highly motivated in the school, and his school—North Central High—is considered one of the best in the country.

Yet here is what the popular math teacher has to say: "Kids don't have time to do assignments. They seem to be satisfied to make a C. It's a waste of talent. They know that to do any better will require more effort, and they are at the limit. They don't have any more time or effort to give." Weinheimer isn't alone. He expresses a concern that many experienced teachers are voicing about student motivation.

As 25-year Ohio veteran Chris Hayward puts it, "It's harder for teachers to be teachers."

These aren't the teachers of inner-city teens plagued by urban violence and poverty; everyone knows that their jobs have gotten tougher. Weinheimer and Hayward are the teachers of kids who attend model schools, who live in suburban communities that are relatively safe and still fairly homogeneous. The students about whom they're talking are not the small percentage who drop out, or fail. They are the ones who succeed.

Increasingly, these teachers say, their students are becoming apathetic, impatient, self-centered, overwhelmed, and harder to motivate; they demand more, yet aren't willing to work for it. According to a recent poll of more than 21,000 teachers by the Carnegie Foundation for the Advancement of Teaching, 71 percent of teachers agree that students in their school "want to do just enough to get by."

Charlotte Huggins, who has been teaching English at New Trier High School in Winnetka, Ill., for the past 27 years, watched in horror recently as a cheating scandal unfolded at her nationally respected school. A group of students, who clearly did not need to cheat, had been stealing material from a teacher's file over a period of time. "Fifteen years ago, you wouldn't have seen this. You were still getting neck-craning, shouted whispers—the sorts of things kids were ashamed of when caught," says Huggins. "Now they're not even ashamed. They're only sorry that they got caught."

Although the unfortunate drama did not occur in Huggins' classroom, she has her share of frustrations. "What I see in this school is that kids aren't willing to accept lower grades," she notes, "but they aren't willing to work harder to raise them." After midterm grades have been sent to colleges with applications, she watches sadly as the vast majority of her seniors lose interest in their studies. "Of course, to some extent you saw that before," she admits. "But it's getting worse."

Private schools aren't immune, either. High school art teacher Chris Hayward at the Cincinnati (Ohio)

Country Day School has similar problems. Recently, a gifted student in Hayward's video class decided it wasn't worth the effort to finish a meaningful longterm project. "She is not alone," says Hayward. "Students are losing sight of their priorities."

Compared with the challenges faced by some inner-city teachers, these problems may seem minimal. But as the nation reels with more and more bad news regarding its schools, as the reports about poor test scores flood in, to think that even the kids with all the advantages are sliding into mediocrity is depressing. It symbolizes the overall concern that America is losing its edge.

But, wait a minute—is there really something wrong with the typical suburban teen or are teachers just idealizing the past? Something *is* wrong, according to David Elkind, child psychiatrist and author of *The Hurried Child* and *All Grown Up and No Place to Go*.

"Of course, in one respect, kids and teenagers really haven't changed," says Elkind. "I mean they still go through puberty and all those things." And there is some truth to the notion that every decade of adults feels compelled to ask, what's the matter with kids today? Rewind a couple of thousand years, and you'll even hear Aristotle whining about the laziness of the youth in his day. "Even though children have been here forever," Elkind explains, "they are always new for each generation."

But Elkind and researchers who have been studying adolescent behavior and development understand why teachers are frustrated by students' behavior and performance. Today's teenagers are different from previous generations in many ways—in their attitudes, their values, and their behavior. Considering the changes that have reshaped society in the past 50 years, it would be miraculous if kids hadn't changed.

So how are young people different? And what does it mean for teachers? Are kids collapsing under the weight of societal pressures? Or are schools remiss in placing too much emphasis on rote learning and superficial test scores? Who's the culprit? Bad kids? Bad parents? Bad schools? Too much television? A combination of one or more of the above?

Although opinions and theories vary, one common word pops up in all the explanations for why kids are acting the way they do: stress. It is harder these days for teachers to be teachers; but that's because it's harder these days for kids to be kids. The world is changing more rapidly and more dramatically than ever before; and it's becoming a more stressful place for young people—even those children of reasonably affluent families who seem to have it so easy.

Young people today seem to have lost some of the natural optimism that has always been characteristic of youth. Only 17 percent of high schoolers feel that life in America will get better 10 years from now, according to the 1992 Scholastic Poll of American Youth.

"Kids used to be basically optimistic," says Elkind. "But there isn't this sense of progress that was once present. We don't see the world progressing, necessarily." News of global warming, the deterioration of the environment, the increasing problems of homelessness, racial intolerance, violence, AIDS, and teenage pregnancy abound. With recent innovations in video and television technology, bad news reaches us faster and in more graphic detail.

Hayward can practically monitor the increases in societal stress by looking at the topics of her school's recent assemblies. "One of our alumnae was date-raped; she came in and talked to students," says Hayward. "Last week, we did a thing on AIDS. Three weeks ago, we did one on drugs. And tomorrow night, 75 students have signed up to learn how to defend themselves against aggressors."

The bad economic situation and the growing national debt aren't exactly relieving any of the pressure. This generation senses that it will be harder to "make it" in the new world. And as the media constantly point out, a bachelor's degree or even a graduate degree is no longer a guarantee to good jobs and prosperity. "Kids are not stupid," says Elkind. "They see that no matter how hard they work, they still might not find jobs."

But the heart of the problem lies much closer to home than the ozone hole and the economy. Psychologists believe that the messages that kids are getting from society—particularly parents—are adding pressure to the pot. On the one hand, we expect too much from adolescents, and on the other hand, we don't expect enough. It may seem paradoxical, but the two notions are not so far apart.

We send them the message: Don't just be all that you can be; be perfect—and be grown up about it.

One of the most fundamental changes in society is that we now believe that life ought to be perfect, argues Glen Elliott, head of Child and Adolescent Psychology at the University of California, San Francisco, and co-editor of a definitive text, *At the Threshold: The Developing Adolescent*.

Teens are bombarded with the message that perfection is not only attainable but also a must. Television tells them that they should have the perfect body and wear the perfect clothes. It's not enough to own a pair of sneakers for the basketball court. You have to own a pair of sneakers perfectly designed for playing basketball.

And society is setting standards that are intrinsically impossible for most people to meet. "Take sports, for example," explains Elliott. "We have this extraordinary value for certain kinds of sports figures. Starting in about the 5th grade, we have created a structure that promises kids that if you're at the very, very top, you're worth millions. But if anything happens to you—if you're not that good or if you get injured—then you're not worth anything."

This message is especially devastating to teens. "Kids don't know how to process that," explains Elliot. "All of those things speak to the very fears that adolescents have to begin with, i.e., 'I'm not perfect.'"

Today's teenage girls face particularly difficult standards, notes Cornell historian Joan Jacobs Brumberg, who has been studying girls' diaries from the past and present. "Girls face a particular anxiety about appearance and have serious body-image concerns," she writes about in her book, *Fasting Girls: The History of Anorexia Nervosa.*

And teens are not just getting these messages from the 3 hours of sitcoms and MTV that they supposedly watch each day. Parents have a lot to do with it, too. Harold Stevenson, psychology researcher and co-author of *The Learning Gap: Why Our Schools Are Failing and What We Can Learn from Japanese and Chinese Education,* believes that American parents are sending their kids the wrong message.

Today's parents don't just want their kids to be good students, they want them to be everything. Parents value education, but the problem is that they also place as high a value on lots of other things. "The demands on youth have increased greatly," says the University of Michigan researcher. "Kids are supposed to do well in school and be popular, help around the home, look better, do better in sports." And on top of all that, get jobs. Kids in the United States are working at paying jobs more now than they used to and are working more than kids in other countries, according to Stevenson.

Teacher Allen Weinheimer hates to ask how many of his algebra students work 20 or even 40 hours a week in addition to carrying a heavy academic load. He can spot them anyway by seeing whose heads are down on the desk first thing in the morning. "Sometimes you think that students have gotten lazier," explains Weinheimer. "But priorities are changing. School used to be number one, but now it isn't."

Kids get caught up in so many other things that they're stretched to the limit. Weinheimer recalls the smart senior boy who was failing his calculus class—not because of a lack of ability, but because, with a 40-hour-a-week job, he simply didn't have time for his schoolwork. Did he have to work to support his family? "No, he said it was important that he work because he wanted to buy a car," says Weinheimer, frustration still audible in his voice.

In extensive cross-cultural studies of students in the United States and other countries, Stevenson found that over 70 percent of U.S. students felt stress once a week or every day. The surprise here is that U.S. kids scored higher on the stress tests than Asian kids; meanwhile U.S. educators have been criticizing Asian education for being too stressful. We've assumed that such high academic standards must drive kids crazy.

The reason that Asian countries produce good students who are not totally stressed out, Stevenson says, is because everyone there still believes that school is the student's number one priority; school is the student's job. In interviews with parents, Stevenson hears the same message repeated in many different variations. "An Asian mother said, 'I don't expect my child to do chores. It would break my heart because it would take my child away from his studies,'" he recalls.

Not expecting 14-year-old Jack and Jill to mow a blade of grass or wash a dish might seem a bit extreme to suburban moms and dads. They find nothing wrong with the good old tradition of wanting kids to help around the house. It is also normal for them to want their kids to be well-rounded individuals who can play a tune on the piano as well as tell you the

---

In the 1960s, educators became excited about the idea that IQs could actually be raised with early intervention—a good notion that has led to all kinds of miseducation.

---

difference between an atom and a molecule.

But a change in attitude toward children has caused us to go overboard, says Elkind. In the 1960s, educators became excited about the idea that IQs weren't fixed but could actually be raised with early intervention—a good notion that has since led to all kinds of miseducation, in Elkind's mind. Now, too many parents believe and expect that if they teach a subject or task early enough, their children can become Einsteins at anything. "It used to be that you wanted your kids to be normal. Precocity was looked upon as irregular: Early ripe, early rot," Elkind explains. "Now, everybody wants their children to be gifted."

As a result, parents push their kids into more and more activities at an earlier age. According to Elkind, it's much more prevalent today than 15 or 20 years ago.

Consequently, by the time kids get to high school, some of them burn out. "For example, we see a million fewer kids going out for sports in high school, and I think that has to do with the fact that so many kids have been in competitive sports since the age of 5," he notes. "At a time when their bodies are physically able, and they could really do well, they get turned off." And some very good students, if their parents would let them, would prefer to postpone college for a year or two in order to try something else; they feel like they've spent their whole life in school.

The root of the problem, as Elkind sees it, is that adults are putting their own needs above the needs of children and young people. Ever since those tumultuous '60s, a shift has slowly worked its way into the fabric of our everyday lives. The shift is to value autonomy, the individual needs of self-realization and achievement, over those of the family and community.

It's not all bad, Elkind notes. There are healthy and beneficial aspects of self-realization. Before, the individual was too submerged in the family, but now we've swung the balance too far in the other direction; sufficient attention isn't given to the needs of children. "Parents and society as a whole have abrogated their responsibility to young people," says Elkind. "And the kinds of things that we're seeing from young people is a response to that."

Before, children were typically seen as being in need of adult guidance and protection. Society, overall, took much more responsibility. Adults watched what they said and did around young people; Hollywood made sure that messages on film and television were appropriate for all ears; advertisers didn't attempt to sell 11-year-old girls cosmetics and other accoutrements of adult life. But things have changed. Busy, self-realizing adults perceive children to be much more mature and independent than they really are. "Children have come to be seen as competent, ready and able to deal with all of life's vicissitudes," says Elkind. "And teenagers are seen as sophisticated and knowledgeable about everything from computers to sex and so on."

Children are expected to make more decisions. At the same time, the number of choices has increased dramatically. Everyone—adults and children—has more options before them now than ever. In some ways, that's good; social prohibitions were constricting. But something that is beneficial for adults is not necessarily good for kids. Too many options are not healthy for young people, insists Elkind. "They get overwhelmed by all these choices."

Parents and society need to take more control, giving children stronger guidance with larger issues. At the same time, parents need to avoid taking too much control over the daily activities that their kids get involved in. If children don't have time just to play without pressure to perform, they can explode when they hit their teenage years. If pushed and pushed, kids can become resentful. "Kids feel that they've been doing all these things to meet adult needs, and their own needs haven't been recognized," says Elkind. "One of the things that happens is to say 'To heck with it, I'm going to do what is right for me, I'm not going to play this game anymore.'"

Another message is broadcast to children and teens. It goes like this: You don't have to work hard to be successful. All it really takes is a good set of genes, and either you have it, or you don't.

In his cross-cultural studies, Stevenson found that Japanese parents rate "hard work" as being the most critical determinant for success in school. In contrast, American parents cite "innate ability" as being the most important factor. "Society is saying that innate ability is a very important modifier," states Stevenson. "If you are highly able, you don't have to work hard—you'll get it."

As Stevenson conducted interviews, this new American motto kept rearing its ugly head. When he asked mothers of young children to say when they thought students were ready to be given college entrance exams, Asian mothers gave their kids time to get smart through hard work and years of study: They said the 11th or 12th grade seemed an appropriate time for testing. American moms, on the other hand, didn't believe little Jill needed time to study or years of academic preparation to determine whether or not she should be Harvard-bound: They thought she was ready to test by the end of elementary school.

And Jill seems to be getting the message. When Stevenson asked students to identify the most important thing that helps them do well in school, Japanese and Chinese students said, "to study hard." The answer chosen most often by American kids was, "the teacher."

In other words, Asian kids believe that diligence makes all the difference. American kids believe that the intelligence that they need to succeed is ready and waiting right inside of them, and they just need a good teacher to bring it out.

Society is in denial. And it's not just kids. Parents are as outraged as their children when their children don't get the grades or treatment they believe they inherently deserve. More often than not, many teachers say, parents complain to the teacher rather than the child about their child's grades. And that goes for discipline as well. In suburban Virginia, parents at one school opposed a new attendance policy for being too tough while at another school parents of students caught with water balloons protested the punishment—school suspension—saying it was too severe.

"It used to be that the teacher was right," says Weinheimer. "I'm not sure they always were. But parents supported the teacher. If I called home to talk about a problem, the parents used to say, 'Gee, what can we do?'"

The structures teachers once relied on are simply no longer there. And the lack of structure undermines the teacher's job. "If teachers set down rules, and it turns out that the parents don't support them, then the system no longer works," says Elliott. "You've got a serious problem."

Part of the problem, according to Elliott, goes back to the fact that society has set higher stakes for success. Parents know that grades and test scores are important for their children to succeed. So, they place more emphasis on what scores their children get than on how their children get the scores. Add to that the fact that high school has become a minimal expectation. A high school education is no longer seen as a valuable thing in and of itself, for this population. College attendance and success is all that really matters.

When the cheating scandal erupted at Charlotte Huggins' school, parents were not exactly pushing for serious penalties. "At one time, we could depend on families to be just as horrified as the school system," says Huggins. "Now, all they do is worry about whether the colleges will find out."

The other thing that happens is that today's parents are simply too overextended themselves to take an active, participatory interest unless a crisis occurs. Fifteen years ago, on "Parents' Night," Weinheimer's room would have been overflowing. Last year, there were plenty of empty seats. "Parenting is much more complicated," agrees Elliott, father of two. "Because of the consuming nature of our jobs, school is seen as a way to get kids out of our hair."

The bottom line is that kids are growing up with the belief that they don't need to work too hard or follow all the rules in order to make it. Put this message along with the "perfection is attainable" message and you've got a particularly confusing brew. Kids learn that life ought to be easy and painless; that they should be able to succeed at everything without putting in too much effort.

But, what about the fact that more students have jobs? Isn't that helping to teach a meaningful work ethic? Unfortunately not, says Elliott. The kinds of jobs at which kids are employed today, such as fast-food service, offer few valuable interactions with adult role models and little responsibility or challenge.

The dilemma many teachers face is perplexing: How can you expect very much of students at school if they are so overextended and stressed? But, at the same time, how will they ever learn the value of hard work if you don't expect a lot of them?

Elkind emphasizes the value of talking with kids about the pressures they face. "It's important not to lay the blame on kids but to show how a lot of the things they are feeling are part of a social system."

But if we blame everything on society and parents, then aren't we teaching students not to accept responsibility for their own behavior? The healthy response is to talk with students about the societal baggage that they carry, but also to give the firm message that they have to work hard in order to succeed.

"It's critical to acknowledge the problem," says Elliott. "But also to say that the solution is for them to take responsibility."

Educators who lower their standards only contribute to the problem, says Stevenson emphatically. Overly concerned with building and maintaining a positive sense of self-esteem in their students, teachers often reward kids for easy work. "Too many teachers have such a hollow response to children," says Stevenson sadly. "When children read three words, teachers say, 'That's wonderful!' And then the children go on to the next grade, and everyone laughs at them."

The best dose of self-esteem comes when students work hard to reach a tough goal, the psychologist says. Teacher Charlotte Huggins agrees. "I haven't given up. The integrity of classroom standards is the heart and soul of the school," she says.

But just because the English teacher hasn't changed her standards doesn't mean she hasn't changed as a teacher. She continually works to make her curriculum relevant to the experiences of today's students.

Teachers who expect kids to sit still for a dry lecture pulled directly from a 20-year-old lesson plan will be frustrated by the results. No doubt, some of the apathy and unwillingness to work that some teachers see in their students is a direct result of an archaic teaching style or curriculum. "Teachers who are unwilling to adapt," says veteran Weinheimer simply, "lose their effectiveness."

When art teacher Chris Hayward realized her students were changing, she realized that she had to change, as well. In Hayward's own experience, learning was an intellectual venture; but today's kids expect learning to be a visual adventure. "Kids want you to do more of a song and dance than you did 15 years ago," she insists. "The impact of the media and new technologies has given them immediate access to everything. And they want you to bring all the technologies into the classroom."

Hayward worked hard to create an unconventional art curriculum that met her own standards and the needs of her students. Far from seeing the change as selling out, she sees the transformation of her classroom as positive. "It's been a trip to Candy Land, for me," she exclaims. "Getting into video and media has advanced my ability to teach. It's been another way to show my students the world."

In spite of some of the negative changes, teachers do see some positive changes in their students. Kids today are more communicative about their problems, more willing to talk about a variety of topics in class. They are more globally aware, more in tune with nature and environmental concerns. Some teachers say that lately kids have become more interested in community service, in reaching out to help others.

"It's important to remember that our times are bad, it's not the kids," says Hayward, who is also a mother. "There are times when you want to grab them around the throat. But the goodness is still there." ∎

Written for this book by Mary Koepke, a former associate editor of Teacher Magazine

6.

The Baggage of Abuse

Teachers can help their students overcome the trauma of mistreatment.

Commentary by Marilyn Gootman

Millions of children in our country carry more than their book bags to school each day. They also haul into the classroom the baggage of abuse. What do they unpack? Pain masquerading in the wraps of misbehavior and underachievement. And who gets blamed? Teachers. When troubled children misbehave and underachieve, their teachers are often accused of incompetence. Feeling like failures, teachers also blame themselves when they are unable to reach these children.

Teachers are not to blame. Standard classroom management techniques do not work for these children the way they do for children who misbehave and underachieve for reasons such as immaturity, lack of motivation, and attention deficit disorder. The baggage that abused children bring to school is too heavy.

Even after teachers report suspected abuse, they still have to contend with the leaden contents of this baggage on a daily basis. In the classroom, many abused children act out their searing pain because they cannot express it in words. They act out this pain in disruptive, annoying, and frustrating ways— through aggressiveness, hypervigilance, and spaciness and by hurting others without seeming to care. Of course, not all children who behave this way have been abused, so these behaviors should not be used as the sole criteria for reporting suspected abuse. But if any of these behaviors appear in children who are known to have been abused, teachers must stop blaming the children for the problems. Instead, they should view the behaviors as a signal for help. By understanding their causes, teachers can help teach these students socially acceptable coping strategies.

Can teachers who see these students for just a few hours a day for less than a year really make a difference without devoting their full attention to one child or becoming therapists? Absolutely. Alice Miller, author of several books on abused children, argues that teachers, among others, can be "enlightened witnesses" for abused children. By believing that there is a core of goodness within each child and that children are not to blame for their abuse, teachers can help these students overcome the trauma of mistreatment.

Trust, empathy, and patience plant a healthy seed within these children that will flower in the future. The key lies in acknowledging that these children are not at fault, understanding the nature and origin of their behaviors, and then using direct teaching strategies to counterbalance the situation.

Following are several of the more common dysfunctional behaviors manifested by abused children in the classroom.

●*Aggressiveness:* Abused children often spill their rage over their mistreatment on "safe" targets, such as classmates and teachers, rather than on those who deserve it. Many are aggressive and rarely hesitate to hit when angry. They seem to be bullies who pick fights for seemingly trivial reasons. These children carry the aggressiveness they have learned at home into the classroom. They can and must be taught how to deal constructively with their anger. A teacher who remains calm yet firm when angry can replace the aggressive parent model and become a constructive source of identification for children. Staying calm does not mean ignoring inappropriate behavior; it just means "keeping your cool" when dealing with it. Children who act aggressively can be taught how to recognize that they're getting angry, how to cool down, and how to put their feelings into words.

Some abused children are terrified of re-experiencing the feeling of utter helplessness and powerlessness they suffered when being abused. When they fear that their safety or self-esteem may be threatened again, they try to replace helplessness with power and become aggressive and lash out in the process. The key to helping these children lies in giving them a positive sense of power and control over their own destiny. They need to be allowed to make choices about their own work. With the other children in the class, they need to be involved in determining classroom rules. When a rule is broken, they should help decide an appropriate consequence.

●*Hypervigilance:* Abusers are impulsive and often lash out unexpectedly with no rhyme or reason. Their victims, therefore, never know when they are going to "get it" next and, as a result, have to remain constantly on guard. Many abused children remain on guard in the outside world lest an event occur that might trigger the same feelings of helplessness and panic. In school, these children may seem fearful and suspicious, on the lookout for potential dangers. They are acutely sensitive to mood, tone of voice, facial expression, and bodily movement. Often they are afraid to express their own ideas. A predictable school environment is essential for these children. Clearly stated routines, rules, and consequences that are consistently followed can gradually help reduce their hypervigilance. These children also benefit from teachers who remain calm and do not explode in unpredictable outbursts.

●*Hurting others without seeming to care:* Many abused children are hurt so often that the only way they can tolerate it is by suppressing their feelings so they are no longer aware of them. Children who cannot feel their own pain do not know that others feel pain. Therefore, they may hurt others without seeming to care that they have done so. They seem cold, hard, and unfeeling. Such children must be directly confronted and told that they are hurting others: "Stop that. When you poke Billy with the ruler, it hurts." Because they have numbed themselves to

pain, these children often don't even know when they have been hurt. They may, for example, act totally unaware of an injury, such as a cut or a bruise. Saying, "that must have hurt when you fell off the swing," helps them acknowledge their own hurts. Once they feel their own pain, they will learn to acknowledge the pain others feel, as well.

●*Spaciness:* Many abused children dissociate or hypnotize themselves to escape overwhelming thoughts, emotions, and sensations they experience during abuse. In school, they may become spacey, forgetful, and frequently daydream if they experience an echo of their painful experience. Even a seemingly innocuous story in a reading book can trigger such a reaction. Teachers can bring such children back by gently touching them or softly calling their name. They should not reprimand these youngsters for dissociating. Instead, they should privately help these children become aware of what is happening: "Billy, I notice that when ..."

Teachers can also help students identify and sort out feelings, such as sadness, anger, and happiness, and become aware that thoughts and feelings are not the same as actions. Reassurance that nobody will punish or reject them for their thoughts and feelings is important.

Often teachers solicit parents' help when their children are being disruptive in the classroom. It certainly makes sense for parents and teachers to work together to solve problems. If you suspect, however, that parents may be abusing their children, don't make demands on them or ask them to help you with the disruptive behavior. This could generate further abuse. Instead, try to be as positive as you can when talking with them about their children.

The baggage that abused children bring to the classroom poses a challenge to the best of teachers. Their behavior is often exasperating, but it is important to remember that it is a direct result of the weight they must carry. An enlightened witness can do a great deal to ease the burden. ■

Marilyn Gootman teaches early childhood education at the University of Georgia and has written two brochures for the National Committee for the Prevention of Child Abuse.

From Teacher Magazine, *September 1992*

7.

Past Imperfect

A former teacher realizes that giving in to uncertainty is the essence of good teaching.

By David Ruenzel

The best class I ever taught was the one I ruined. It was a class of seven junior girls, all of them animated, intelligent, ambitious. Some were friends and some were not, but they had, in an almost literal sense, what's called "chemistry." I'd give them a book or writing assignment and all sorts of interesting reactions would occur. I'd walk into the classroom, and they'd be arguing about whether Hester Prynne in *The Scarlet Letter* was an early feminist or whether Macbeth was a self-pitying murdering fool and not—as they thought they were supposed to think—some sort of tragic hero. The exchanges were alternately curt, contemplative, and sardonic; their fingers were always walking through the text to find the passage that would provide some corroborating evidence.

Once, a visitor from another school happened to observe this class. Amazed, he asked afterward, "Is it always like this?"

"Yes," I said, shrugging my shoulders. I was bemused because it didn't seem as if the girls' scintillating discussions had anything to do with me.

Didn't have anything to do with me. This was the problem—or I should say *my* problem, for it was clear that the girls were doing just fine without me. Why I finally gave in to a compulsion to intrude certainly had something to do with male ego. I wanted to be the one to make the scintillating remarks. I suppose I wanted admiration more than I wanted a good class. There was also an element of succumbing to what I

thought was my duty. I had been hired to teach the class, and that I was going to do, come hell or high water. But my own voice, unlike theirs, was flat and monotonous—that of privilege asserting itself for no good reason.

That same year, I was drafted to teach an elective creative writing class. At the onset, I told the students I would have no time to prepare; they could write pretty much whatever they liked and read the result to the class, if they cared to. I did little more than provide the students with writing prompts, such as: "Describe a lake as perceived by someone who has just committed a murder." They would write frenziedly for 15 minutes and then take turns reading aloud what they had composed. That was pretty much it. At the end of the semester, I apologized for having left them so much on their own. The students sat dumbfounded, and I didn't know why until one of the boys—a computer wizard who now works at Microsoft—said, "But Mr. Ruenzel, this is the best class I ever had."

I taught these two classes, along with freshman and senior English, for two years at University Lake School, a small K-12 independent school of 250 students, 90 of them high schoolers, in Hartland, Wis. The school, which serves the sons and daughters of affluent lawyers, doctors, and executives, is set in the middle of 100 acres of wilderness. From classroom windows, I would occasionally catch sight of a deer, a fox, a soaring hawk. It was a gloriously pristine setting, though my two years there, 1988-90, were anything but serene. I might have been inhabiting one of those fairy tales in which the characters are lost in the woods, for I never quite knew what I was doing—though I admitted that to no one. So much seemed to work backward, contrary to expectations. Classes for which I was most well-prepared would be the most stale, exhausting for me and the students. Classes for which I "winged it" would catch fire, a casual remark sometimes igniting a spark. Following the curriculum would lead to a dead end; departures would invigorate, like a jog through an unexplored landscape.

A decade earlier, at a school in Indianapolis where I had begun my teaching career, things had seemed to fall into place. I wielded my grammar book, my red pen, and my English literature anthology with authority. In 10 years, the only thing I had apparently achieved was uncertainty.

Over the years, I met teachers at conferences who seemed to know exactly what they were doing. These teachers amazed me. Did they possess some sort of methodological key? Were they simply "natural born" teachers? Or were they, for all their earnest confidence, in truth as uncertain as I was?

These teachers sometimes had a beatified glow about them, so cocksure were they about the efficacy of process writing, cooperative learning, whole language, and the like. It wasn't that I disparaged any of these things; it was rather that, when I applied them, they seemed every bit as awkward and tentative as anything else I had ever tried. They didn't diminish any of my uncertainty.

Once, I was teaching a poem with perhaps two dozen difficult allusions, some of which I did not understand myself. I was about to sort the students into cooperative learning groups—each group responsible for a certain number of allusions—when I had another simpler idea. I told them to find out the meaning of each of the allusions using any method they wanted: the library, a parent, a history teacher. It didn't matter how they got their answers; it was impossible to cheat. If they could con one of their hardworking brethren to provide them with ready-made answers, that was fine. I didn't have to know.

The next day, all of the students had all of the answers. They were full of smiles. I thought the experiment a great success, though now I'm not so sure. Maybe the smiles were, in truth, duplicitous grins, a collective smirking at a facetiously simple task.

This past summer, in an attempt to understand if not dispel my sense of uncertainty, I contacted a number of my former University Lake students, all of them 1990 graduates. In that class, there were 21 students, two-thirds of them boys. They had me for two years as an English teacher. We sometimes drove each other crazy. As a class, they struck me as unusually talented, nice kids. But they were somewhat spoiled, as well. They were accustomed to getting what they wanted, and they disliked—perhaps even more than most teenagers—being told what to do. It was a tug of war, and I sometimes tugged when I should have let go and let go when I should have tugged. Many of their parents could be described as nouveau riche and had a pragmatic view of education that conflicted with the faculty's. I once overheard a mother, frustrated with her daughter's lackluster grades, tell a fellow teacher that "there wasn't going to be any new sailboat for that girl."

I wanted to learn from my former students what I on my own could not know: How valuable had they found their schooling? Was the work they had done truly meaningful? How significant were the relationships they had had with their teachers? What were the best and worst aspects of their high school education? And what, if anything, did they wish their teachers had done differently?

Not surprisingly, my own predictions of what students would say did not stand up very well. Students, for example, who had exuded discontent for University Lake now expressed gratitude for what the school had given them. The past, it seemed, was a story subject to constant revision.

Andy Saiia was an example of an apparently unhappy student who now expressed gratitude. Despite his obvious gifts as an artist, musician, and thinker, Saiia had sometimes appeared sullen to the point of despondency. (The caption under his yearbook photo reads, "Not happy unless depressed.") He slouched in class and walked slowly down the hallways. During his senior year, he took my philosophy seminar, which, he told me on a number of occasions, he hated, though he could never say why.

"I was missing the point of that class and was completely frustrated," he told me when we met at the almost abandoned school this past summer. "I have to tell you, though, that I did learn a lot from that class, whether I enjoyed it or not, because I remembered it when I came across certain things later. Once, a professor was talking about the Platonic conception of something or other, and I remembered how you, when we were talking about Plato, put a chair in the middle of the room and asked what made the chair a chair. I also remembered the idea of a Socratic dialogue—the whole idea of not just asserting things but having a discussion to get at the truth."

Saiia, who had dropped out of several colleges and worked at a convenience store before finding satisfaction at a Milwaukee art institute where he is now a design student, traced his lifelong anxiety about school to a single incident back in kindergarten. The other kids were singing and playing "London Bridge," but he refused to participate. The teacher called his mother, telling her she feared her son was antisocial. "I know it sounds weird to put so much emphasis on something that happened so many years ago," he said, "but that's when my fear of school started. I wasn't a conformist, and, on an intuitive level, I knew, even then, that school was about conforming."

After a harrowing two years at a Catholic high school where students were force-fed textbooks, he transferred during his junior year to University Lake School. While fear of failure prevented him from exerting himself to the fullest, he insisted that he is profoundly indebted to his teachers, who "cared about the way I was thinking about something, not just that I learned a lot of information."

He singled out history teacher Valija Rasmussen for praise. "She made it clear that history was about interpretation, not just about who was fighting some war. She was the first one, I think, who taught me that writing was about connecting our own ideas with the material, not repackaging somebody else's ideas. I remember writing an essay comparing ancient Rome with our own civilization and thinking, this must be what history is all about."

Saiia made a point that would later be amplified by so many of the other students that it became a kind of grand motif: namely, that students absorbed as much from teachers' off-the-cuff remarks and idiosyncrasies as they did from the "official" curriculum. Here he mentioned David Bielot, a bearded hulk of an art teacher famous for his chronic cantankerousness.

While students were working on art projects, Bielot would pace around the room, griping about everything from Reaganomics to the abysmal state of mass culture. "I learned a lot of important things just by listening to Mr. Bielot complain about the world," Saiia said. "Once, while he was complaining about something or other, he suddenly told us about this artist who was under attack for putting a crucifix in what appeared to be a jar of urine. Then he raised an intriguing question: Could such a thing ever be considered art? He just raised the question; he didn't try to answer it."

Saiia was relaxed and reflective during our conversation, and after I put away my tape recorder, we continued to talk. "You know," he mused, "I wonder what would happen if a teacher just gave kids books with no expectations—if you just let them read the books and tell you what they think."

"But would they read the books?" I asked.

"That's the question," he said. "But I would say, 'If you don't want to read, fine, leave.' Besides, if someone doesn't want to learn, it's not going to happen no matter what the teacher does. There's no formula, no method."

Saiia had gotten up from his chair and was about to leave when he paused to ask me a question. "There's something I've always been curious about: Are teachers just teaching or are they trying to learn something for themselves when they teach? I think this is an important question."

Are teachers trying to learn something for themselves when they teach? This seemed to be a crucial question, for it also was mentioned, however indirectly, time and time again by my former students.

Their comments about favorite teachers being "engaged," "committed," and "intense" were not just recycled cliches; they indicated, rather, a realization that teachers they most admired worked with them on "ground level," wanting to discover along with their students what is important.

They talked about physics teacher Mark Nowakowski "bringing out all kinds of stuff and playing with it," about history teacher Daniel McCarthy becoming so worked up during class discussions that he would end up soaked in perspiration even on the coldest days, and about math teacher Rick Peterson working with them on producing art posters based on complex geometrical patterns.

These teachers were able to interest their students, it seemed, not because they were entertainers or because they seduced and cajoled but because they were "co-learners." They were willing, as one student put it, "to get off the pedestal."

After Saiia left, I met with Alex Clar, a former student with a Grinch-like smile and a sense of humor that was acute if somewhat acerbic. In high school, Clar had dreams of attaining great wealth. His yearbook caption reads, "Divine wish is to get name in *Forbes* or to get indicted by the SEC." But now, having received his college degree, he was about to spend a year traveling in the Far East.

> I wanted to learn from my students what I on my own could not know: Was the work they had done truly meaningful? And what did they wish their teachers had done differently?

Clar complimented University Lake School for having prepared him well academically and then compared his experience there with advanced placement classes he'd observed for several days at another school as part of a college education course. "What I noticed," he said, "is that everything was much more rigid; the teachers felt they had to structure all the activities. There was a constant stream of handouts in which teachers set out exactly what they were going to do. If I remember correctly, it was a freer discussion at ULS; you teachers would come up with a discussion topic, and the students would throw out things. But at the public school I observed, discussions never got deep. The teacher would ask a question, but it was clear he already knew what the answer would be; it was an open-and-shut question. There were also quizzes every other day just to make sure that the reading was done.

"The teachers at ULS were eccentrics, even unstable," he laughed gleefully, "but from them we learned we couldn't take what we read or saw at face value. I particularly learned this from McCarthy, who kept asking us, 'Why do you think that?' 'What's the purpose of the writer writing like that?' He questioned whatever opinions we had. We'd give our opinions, and he wouldn't condemn or condone but would say, 'Why?' And then he'd give a counter-argument. He'd say to us, 'OK, I'm going to play devil's advocate now.' Then he'd challenge us to defend our views, which often, as it turned out, were based on sheer bias."

I met with Carrie Grange, an undergraduate at the University of Wisconsin at Madison, in the UW student union. Like Clar, she lauded ULS for the pervasive atmosphere of intellectual challenge. Too many high schools, she said, patronize students by treating them as simpletons, incapable of dealing with intellectual complexity. This she had gleaned not from personal experience but from discussions with students from other schools.

Grange, who had taken a hiatus from her university studies to live in Israel, said college hadn't been as difficult or as challenging as high school. In some ways, college had actually been a regression; it was so impersonal, with its vast lecture halls and the separation between students and professors. At ULS, students and teachers were inescapably close. While this created inevitable friction, it created intellectual excitement, too. "The teachers just didn't care much about the hierarchy, the pecking order," she said. "They weren't interested in talking at us and having us just sit around. Instead, they just kind of threw all different things at us and let us grapple with them. What we'd learn in history would, for instance, overlap with English class, so you'd see how the threads would come together. What I loved most about my classes was the flexibility, the sense that anything was fair game."

I flinched a bit when Grange talked about flexibility; as a teacher, I sometimes feared I was engendering disorder by "throwing" all different kinds of things at my students. As the years passed, I became, without any intention of becoming, almost haphazardly eclectic. It was, I think, purely a matter of impulse and intuition. More and more, I simply taught what I felt like teaching. One day, we'd be talking about a current movie, and the next day I'd bring in a movie review from *The New Yorker*. Once, on the spur of the moment, I decided to spend a few days having my students study several pages from Freud's *Civilization and Its Discontents*; for some unfathomable reason, I wanted my students then and there to understand the notion of sublimation. I always felt a bit guilty about this capriciousness, wondering if I was depriving my

students of the kind of deep understanding a more formal, systematic presentation of material might bring. When the headmaster asked teachers to prepare a detailed scope and sequence, I felt downright fraudulent, knowing I would never follow it.

The sense that the curriculum at University Lake School was a rather intriguing grab bag patched together by eccentric individuals was shared by many of the students. But this was almost universally perceived as a good thing. If the teachers followed their interests and those of the students, how could the curriculum be anything but in never-ending transition?

"Going to ULS was one of the best things I ever did for myself," said Dalynn Wade, whom I visited at his parents' home in Milwaukee's inner city. "It didn't even seem like a school, it was so different. The teachers were offbeat, weird, but highly analytical. You had to learn how to pick up and criticize someone's main point. Never at the public schools I attended before ULS did anyone teach me how to do that. But they taught that at ULS, and it's stayed with me. My brain works differently because of it. I'll listen to the news or just someone talking in the street and understand what they're really saying—the message behind the message."

Wade, who has been sporadically attending the University of Wisconsin at Milwaukee as finances permit, said it wasn't easy being the only African-American student in a school of wealthy whites. He always felt as if he were supposed to be "the black representative," called upon to express "the black point of view." But the difficulties he had at ULS paled beside those he was having these days in his dangerous neighborhood. Drugs, and the money and insidious excitement surrounding them, were constant temptations. When he was a kid, he and his friends had crab-apple fights; now there were gun battles right up the street. A few of his friends were in prison, others dead.

This lament seemed to make Wade nostalgic for his high school days. "A lot of learning went on there behind those trees," he said. "The teachers were smart, especially McCarthy. I've never had a better teacher, before or after ULS. He taught me not to take all I read as fact."

I told Wade that I remembered a heated dispute he had once had with McCarthy over an essay he had written.

"Yeah, but you can't take any of that stuff personally," Wade said. "The point is that he was never intimidated by me at all. He just showed me what was wrong and how to fix it."

Many students, even those who had little interest in the humanities, mentioned McCarthy as a teacher who had a positive and lasting influence upon them. This was understandable, for McCarthy had some remarkable gifts. For one thing, he had an uncanny ability to expatiate upon a topic at great length, in the process welding seemingly conflicting ideas into a grand synthesis. One student told me that when Mc-Carthy expounded upon a topic with the feverish intensity he sometimes generated, she virtually forgot she was in the classroom, so mesmerized was she by his talk. "It was like I was inside of his head," she said. "Outside of myself."

McCarthy was warm and charismatic, too. Chit-chatting and joking with students in the hallways or cafeteria were easy for him, and he developed lasting personal relationships with some students.

But McCarthy, we faculty knew, also infuriated students as perhaps no other teacher did. He was impulsive, tempestuous, and if his students were unprepared or indifferent, he would lash out or sometimes simply storm out of his classroom, refusing to teach. This was no act designed to motivate; he was truly furious, and I remember him, face flushed, pacing about

> ## As days and months pass, relationships with students flourish or erode, making it difficult for the teacher to see just how well things are going at any given moment.

the faculty lounge, wondering aloud if teaching were truly worth it. He alternately scared the hell out of students and enraged them. Tara Sander, now a lab technician who hopes to go to medical school, said she would often be fuming after McCarthy's class. "I remember walking out of there absolutely furious on a number of occasions. We resented the pressure he put on us."

This said, she quickly added that she had been greatly impressed by the broad range of things she had to learn in McCarthy's class and the intensity with which she had to learn them. "He really made you think," she said. "Demanding as he was, he made you come to your own conclusions. It wasn't like one of those courses that are so structured you just learn the system and get a handle on it."

The more I listened to the students talk, the more I realized they were willing to forgive a teacher almost anything—foibles, tantrums, inconsistencies—if that teacher evidenced a transcendent concern for the learning of his or her students. Moodiness, rashness, peevishness could be absolved as long as there was nothing counterfeit about the teacher's commitment to the students.

Alex Clar, the student with the Grinch-like grin,

perhaps put it best. "McCarthy," he said, "just got really unhappy when he felt the class wasn't learning anything. He'd get really upset. I was really impressed by that. His discontent actually created a high level of respect because it conveyed a feeling that he really cared."

Once, after Clar had been particularly supercilious over a number of days, McCarthy and I pulled him into an empty classroom and told him we'd had enough; it was time for him to "cool it." Clar surprised me by weeping, and I felt afterward that we had bullied him. Did he remember that encounter? He said he did and that he had been resentful over it for some time. Clar hesitated and then mentioned another time I had "nailed" him. "Before class, when you were out of the room, I wrote, 'Rodgers-Hammerstein presents Rapunzel-Ruenzel' on the chalkboard, along with a cartoon of you in a wig. You walked in, got furious, and gave me a work detail on the spot. I thought your reaction was harsh because it was intended as friendly kidding, not as an insult."

I told Clar I had but a hazy recollection of the incident, which surprised him since it had disturbed both him and his classmates, and it took some time before the bitterness dissipated.

Clar began to go on, paused, and then asked if he could speak frankly.

"Of course," I said.

"With you, more than with any other teacher, there seemed to be a dilemma as to the amount of distance you felt you should keep as an authority figure interacting with his students."

"Too much distance?" I asked.

"Not exactly. It was more like you were uncertain as to how much distance you should have. Sometimes it seemed that there was the kind of friction you might get between officers and underlings; you thought kids were taking too many liberties. You had a problem, I felt, deciding the level of interaction you should have with us. The distance wavered; you'd be hard-assed, or you'd let things slide.

"Students had particularly strong opinions of you and McCarthy, pro and con, and even now I'm sure they have strong feelings. They'd say, 'Ruenzel was really good,' or 'I really hated Ruenzel.'"

Hearing this stung a bit. What Clar had said was true, though I never thought of it quite that way. University Lake School was a small school where casual relationships between students and teachers were common, and I was never quite comfortable with that. (I had, after all, cut my teaching teeth at a very formal college preparatory school.) Shamefully, I remembered how I had once asked a disrespectful student to leave my classroom. When she momentarily refused, I threatened to bring in the headmaster.

But Clar was generously forgiving.

"We students," he said, "as irritated as we sometimes were, realized we weren't just taking a class. We

25

were taking a Ruenzel or McCarthy class, getting the full-packaged flavor. So even though some may have had some strong feelings against you, they still got something out of it. It was a common experience coming out of your class that someone would have something strongly negative or positive to say. But in terms of whether we learned something, the answer was a definite yes. You threw out a lot of strange, interesting ideas that got our attention. The negative part was when you tried to rein things in, to gain control—to make it clear to the class that you were the authority.

"You guys always kept me off-balance, on my toes. I liked your classes, I really liked them." Clar said, chuckling, his grin at full mast. "But you guys were really different."

Finding out how others really perceive you can be painfully unwise. Nevertheless, for all of its inherent discomfort, listening to others talk about you is undeniably enlightening. As my former students, without solicitation, talked about their perceptions of me and my class, I had the strange sensation of looking at an old photograph of someone much younger and clumsier. "That can't be me," you think. But then you look closer and see that it is indeed you, flaws and all.

Students, I kept thinking during our conversations, know more about us teachers than we think. But their perceptions, acute as they were, didn't much diminish my sense of uncertainty. Just how good a teacher I was depended upon whom I talked to.

Tara Sander, the lab technician, said, "I'm so glad to hear from you because I know you were the best English teacher I ever had. I learned so much from you, and I remember you constantly pushing me to improve my writing." Others praised me for teaching good writing skills and maintaining a high level of classroom discussion. But it was impossible to stay flattered for long. Others clearly felt otherwise, though they exercised tact. Two students, for example, enumerated all the teachers they admired, the list including almost everyone but me. Another student offered a perspective undoubtedly shared by others when he said, "I'm not sure teachers are really that important to students. I think students are important to each other."

I still don't know just how effective I was as a teacher and perhaps never will. There are countless intangibles in the life of any teacher. Almost invisibly, as unremarkable days and months pass, relationships with students flourish or erode, making it difficult for the teacher to see just how well things are going at any given moment. It is hard to mark a spot in the road when the road itself shifts underfoot.

But I do know now that I would have been a better teacher had I been able to accept uncertainty, which I now perceive as the nature of teaching. Every mistake I made—the meaningful ones, not flaws in presenta-

tion or organization—had to do with my attempt to rescue teaching from the necessary morass of uncertainty, to place teaching upon a bedrock that must always crumble to sand. I wish I had realized when I taught what I think I understand now: that uncertainty is not shoddiness but is in fact surprise, insight, epiphany—all the things that are the lifeblood of genuine teaching. When students praised their teachers' intensity, their passion, I think they were in truth praising the teachers' ability to surrender themselves to the unpredictable moment.

Eric Stein was the closest thing University Lake had to a school radical. He liked to dress—as much as one could within the confines of the dress code—in punk garb and proudly announced that he was an anarchist. He published a sort of underground newspaper which, as I recall, was both clever and somewhat obscene. As with Clar, I had my run-ins with him and was surprised when he expressed regret for a long-ago incident: He had laughed while I read one of my own poems to the class. "I was way out of line," he told me during our conversation at UW-Madison, where he had just finished up a degree in anthropology and philosophy. "What I did was very offensive, and I remember it to this day. I was incredibly rude, though I didn't realize it at the time."

I would have figured Stein as one of the students who would be most critical of his high school experience, but this wasn't the case at all. Although at the time he had felt suffocated by the smallness of the school—everyone was into everyone else's business— he said he now greatly appreciated the small classes and the teachers' attentiveness. "Teachers paid close attention to what I was doing so that I couldn't get away with being sloppy," he explained. "You were intense, and I really appreciated that. Going to ULS and respecting my teachers has made me want to become a teacher myself."

Like Wade, Stein sounded nostalgic. He spoke with an almost wistful gentleness that made me wonder if I had ever really known him. "Everything here at the university is politically correct. Suddenly, we're no longer talking about the gatekeeper at the end of *The Trial* but about the feminist themes behind such and such a book. I've never been asked my opinion about a given work; basically, it's tear this down and tear that down until there's nothing left. I wish there'd be someone you could have a conversation with on his or her own free time."

"If you had to do it over again, would you go to ULS?" I asked.

"I'd do it again, for eternity," he said, and for a moment I felt the same way about my two very short years there. ∎

From Teacher Magazine, *October 1994*

How We Will Teach

"If you don't confront students' ideas and show where they're

adequate and where they're inadequate, those ideas are going

to remain there. They're going to pounce like a Trojan horse as

soon as the children escape from the schoolroom."

—*Howard Gardner, Harvard University*

8.

The Mystery of Learning

Cognitive research is shedding new light on how we learn and raising questions about how we teach.

As the industrial revolution forever altered the modern workplace, a "cognitive revolution" now holds the potential to transform America's schools. In the past 20 years, cognitive science—which includes research from such fields as computer science, anthropology, linguistics, sociology, and psychology—has emerged as a powerful source of knowledge about how the human mind works. This research has begun to illuminate the mystery of how we learn and has produced some startling and controversial conclusions.

For example, research now indicates that people of all ages actively construct meaning of their world based on constant interactions with their environment. (Indeed, some cognitive researchers suggest that the ability to solve problems cannot be separated from the cues, tools, and people that individuals have available in their environment.) The experiences and beliefs that young people bring with them to school—as well as their individual learning styles—strongly influence both what they learn and how they learn.

Such findings are in stark contrast to the theories of behavioral psychologists like B.F. Skinner who have influenced educational practice for more than half a century. These psychologists argued that all human—and animal—behaviors arise from reactions to external stimuli in the environment. Children, like pigeons, repeat actions that are rewarded and drop those that are not.

Behaviorists viewed internal thought processes as unobservable and, therefore, largely irrelevant in explaining learning. Language development, for example—like maze-running for mice—was attributed to the steady accrual of rewarded behaviors that became increasingly complicated over time.

In the behavioral approach to education, skills were decomposed into hundreds of individual subskills, and their mastery by students was carefully examined and chronicled. Such research often translated into programmed, lock-step curricula, through which students were expected to progress to ever higher levels of understanding.

The educational programs of most of the nation's schools continue to be organized and operated on the basis of such behaviorist theories.

Researchers began to challenge these views in the late 1950s, and the real breakthrough came in a 1972 publication entitled *Human Problem Solving*. In that book, Allan Newell and Herbert A. Simon, two social scientists at Carnegie-Mellon University, argued that human thought processes could be investigated with positive results. To prove it, they outlined computer models that simulated what went on inside the brain.

"I didn't accept the behaviorist premise that one shouldn't develop theories about what goes on inside the head," Simon recalls. "Cognitive theories dominant today are very much concerned with what goes on between the stimulus and the response."

Unlike the earlier research, which focused on the acquisition of discrete pieces of behavior, this new generation of research began by asking how humans solve problems, why experts perform so much better than novices in a variety of disciplines, and whether more comprehensive models of learning could be developed.

One of the most fundamental findings of this new line of research is that students do not passively absorb information like so many sponges. Instead, people of all ages acquire knowledge through regular, active explorations of their environment. Soon after they are born, children begin to form powerful theories about their world based on their experiences.

By the time children enter school, they have formed

robust and complex (but not always correct) theories about a variety of phenomena. In fact, the ideas that young children bring to the classroom are so powerful and entrenched, cognitive researchers have found, that they often survive years of formal education. Harvard psychologist Howard Gardner argues that the naive and misleading notions formed in childhood can greatly interfere with learning if they are allowed to go unchallenged.

For example, many students who have studied astronomy, history, and biology continue to believe that seasons are caused by the earth's distance from the sun and that evolution is an orderly progression toward perfection.

Because schools often dismiss these misconceptions and do not encourage youngsters to explore their "common sense" understandings in any meaningful context—where they can be rejected or modified—children cling to their firmly held beliefs after they leave the classroom.

Students' learning is also hampered by what they perceive as lack of relevance in their studies to their lives outside of school. Their inability to connect what they learn in school with any real-world applications leads to what cognitive scientists call "inert" knowledge—information that is stored in the head but never used in real life. They complain that mathemat-

---

> # Skillful readers tend to stop in the middle of a text to ask themselves what the author means and to conjecture about what might come next.

---

ics, physics, history, and other subjects—as taught in schools—bear very little resemblance to their use by practitioners.

Cognitive scientists have also concluded from their studies that what students can learn depends to some degree on what they already know. Put another way, students have to be able to make sense of a situation or a textbook or an activity in order to learn from it. This theory is what prompts some teachers to encourage students in kindergarten and primary school to write and talk about their experiences and to move—through "research"—from those personal "stories" about things they know into new areas of knowledge.

Some cognitive researchers theorize that, in addition to bringing a unique set of experiences and be-

liefs to the classroom, students also bring their own particular approach to learning. Howard Gardner complains that schools often treat students as if they all learn in the same way at the same rate. On the contrary, he argues, there are different learning styles and at least seven different kinds of intelligences. Human intelligences, he says, include: language, logic-mathematical, spatial, musical, kinetic, interpersonal, and intrapersonal.

It is through these intelligences, Gardner explains, that people are able to know the real world. "Where people differ," he says, "is in the strength of these intelligences ... and in the ways in which such intelligences are invoked and combined to carry out different tasks, solve diverse problems, and progress in various domains."

One traditional school practice that may impede learning is the practice of separating "basic skills" instruction from more complex problem-solving. Recent research has found that even very young children, in their attempt to make meaning of the world, pose questions, test hypotheses, and engage in other complex reasoning skills.

Previous generations of psychologists, such as Swiss researcher Jean Piaget, focused on what children do not know. "Now we are asking what can do at each stage," says Robert Glaser, co-director of the Learning Research and Development Center at the University of Pittsburgh. "We can take advantage of the wonderful skills children have, have them participate in learning, discover that they do know a lot, and be excited."

"The most important single message of this body of research," writes Lauren Resnick, co-director of the Pittsburgh center, is that "complex thinking processes—elaborating the given material, making inferences beyond what is explicitly presented, building adequate relationships, analyzing and constructing relationships—are involved in even the most elementary mental activities."

When schools force children to master "basic skills" or long lists of isolated subskills instead of engaging them in these much richer analytical processes, learning is hampered. Thinking and problem-solving and the acquisition of substantive knowledge proceed simultaneously.

Research has also found that successful thinkers of all ages actively monitor their own thinking processes. One reason that experts are able to solve problems so much more effectively than novices is because experts employ a number of sophisticated thinking strategies that novices do not. Skillful readers, for example, tend to stop in the middle of the text to ask themselves what the author means and to conjecture about what might come next. They also employ useful strategies to help them confront difficult passages—such as paraphrasing and restating passages they find puzzling or re-reading other sections that might help illuminate the passage. In contrast, poor readers simply read the passage again and again or read it "harder."

The self-questioning or self-regulating behavior of successful thinkers is often called "metacognition" because it involves keeping track of one's own thoughts. And it is now assumed to be crucial to the thinking process. Early attempts to train students in self-monitoring activities have produced promising results. But, according to Resnick, researchers do not understand precisely why this occurs, since many of the same skills appear to be either highly automated or nonexistent in the reasoning processes of experts.

'Eventually, we should have a basic science in education that would contribute as much to education outcomes as molecular biology contributes to medicine.'

In their search for skills and strategies that might prove useful to students, cognitive researchers are exploring other "generic" thinking skills that students could transfer from one subject to another—or from the classroom to the outside world. But Carnegie-Mellon's Simon admits that it will not be easy: "Transfer is an extremely difficult, subtle area. The issue is, since each domain has its own knowledge base, is there an abstract variable that can apply across fields?"

Such variables may be hard to find. In a study of high school and college students, those taught algebra were able to notice that physics problems could be solved the same way. But those taught physics were unable to see any connections between the two sets of problems. A closer examination revealed that students were able to transfer their abilities only when the concepts involved in the problems were similar.

In looking to the future of cognitive science, many researchers call for more applied studies. Alan Schoenfeld, professor of education and mathematics at the University of California at Berkeley, says: "We need fine-grained studies of what really works. We need case studies of successful instruction, what makes them tick, the attributes of teachers that enable them to create the right kind of classroom environment." He adds: "We're talking about a very different kind of practice; we don't know enough of the dimensions of success."

For one thing, Schoenfeld notes, it is very hard to measure the effects of experiments designed to improve students' thinking. The kinds of educational assessments now available—which measure students' ability to regurgitate bits and pieces of information or to perform minute skills out of context—do not reflect the more comprehensive and applied kinds of problem solving emphasized by the new research.

Eventually, says John T. Bruer, president of the James S. McDonnell Foundation in St. Louis, which supports cognitive research, "we should be in a position to have a basic science in education that would contribute as much to education outcomes as molecular biology contributes to medicine." ■

9.

Thinking About Thinking

Educators are embracing the lessons of cognitive studies and encouraging children to construct meaning from their own experiences.

By Debra Viadero

Students at the Benchmark School in Media, Pa., spend part of each day writing in journals. Their best entries are later "published" in books that are shared with the rest of the class. At the Key School in Indianapolis, children undertake semester-long projects tied to a schoolwide theme. The results are videotaped to form part of a student portfolio that will trace each youngster's progress through the year.

In Victoria Bill's classes in Pittsburgh, elementary school students draw on their intuitive understanding to develop their own mathematical "language."

And in James Minstrell's physics classrooms in Mercer Island, Wash., students arrive at formal physics equations by debating their own hypotheses and then testing them out in experiments.

Each setting looks remarkably different. But all have something in common. They are taking new findings about how the human mind works and trying to apply them in schools.

According to the psychologist Howard Gardner, one of the leading scholars in the field of cognitive science, all of the new theories about how people think and learn "are Rorschach tests, and people can come up with all different kinds of schools based on interpretations of theories." Nonetheless, the vision underlying these schools has a certain unity.

In places where educators are taking new findings about cognitive research seriously, children are taking more responsibility for their own learning and constructing meaning based on their experiences.

In many of these classes, students are encouraged to work together and to learn from each other. Rigid adherence to textbooks has been replaced with "hands on" activities and greater use of technology. Teachers lecture less and serve more as models, co-learners, and coaches. And traditional paper-and-pencil tests have been ousted in favor of student portfolios, notebooks, and projects.

Today, cognitive science is still a long way from providing blueprints for learning. But researchers say new understandings about how children think and develop can contribute markedly to education.

"We know a lot," says Lauren B. Resnick, a co-director of the Learning Research and Development Center at the University of Pittsburgh and a leading proponent of some of the newer cognitive theories. "We know what not to do in global terms."

"We just can't be terribly prescriptive yet," she adds.

But state and national efforts to rethink student testing are finally bringing ideas gained from cognitive research into the center of the debate over school reform.

Until now, many proponents of cognitive theory note, the education-reform debate has concentrated on issues that they view as largely peripheral to learning: new incentives for teachers, site-based management, more homework, a greater emphasis on basic skills.

"There is no question that cognition and education reform should go hand in hand," says John T. Bruer, president of the James S. McDonnell Foundation, one of only a handful of foundations funding research on cognition around the country.

"This romantic notion that site-managed schools are empowering teachers to come up with solutions on their own is really foolish," he asserts.

Agrees Barbara Preseissen, who helps translate scientific theory into practice as director of national networking at Research for Better Schools, a regional education laboratory: "I don't think we'll restructure anything in education unless the classroom becomes the dynamo for the kind of change we're talking about."

Encouraging Students To 'Construct' Meaning

One of the most noticeable shifts in classrooms modeled on cognitive theories is that youngsters are encouraged to "construct" knowledge for themselves—based on hands-on activities and experiences—instead of having information fed to them.

In addition, students are encouraged to draw on their previous understandings and beliefs to make sense of new information.

In his physics classroom at Mercer Island High School, for example, Minstrell routinely begins a new unit by giving students a nongraded quiz. If a one-kilogram ball and a five-kilogram ball are dropped from the ceiling at the same time, the test might ask, which would hit the ground faster and why?

He then scans the written explanations and writes the students' predictions on the blackboard. The pupils debate their ideas and then test their theories in an experiment.

Through repeated experiments, performed under varying conditions—heavy and light objects might be dropped from higher up or in a vacuum, for example—the students gradually begin to see the limits of their own understandings of the physical world.

"Then we can focus on the contexts in which that knowledge does apply," Minstrell says, "and work toward constructing the formalisms."

Magdalene Lampert, a researcher at Michigan State University, maintains her methods for teaching mathematics to 5th graders are derived more from "good mathematics teaching" than from cognitive science. But to leading researchers in cognitive science, her approach echoes the same fundamental concepts.

Lampert structures her classes to enable students to arrive on their own at key ideas about how exponents work. For example, the students might be asked to look for patterns among the squares of numbers ranging from 1 to 100. Like the high school students

in Minstrell's class, the 5th graders offer their thoughts and debate them.

"I disagree with so-and-so's hypothesis," a child might say, adhering to a conversational format he or she has been taught. In Pittsburgh, Resnick of the Learning Research and Development Center and Bill, a local parochial school teacher, have been working to create classrooms in which students can also "leapfrog" into the formal system of mathematics by building on their intuitive understandings.

According to Resnick, Bill never teaches any formal procedures, like computation. Instead, she poses a problem for students, discusses it with them, and then breaks them into groups to work out their own solutions. The researchers have found that, by using such an approach, children as early as kindergarten can even begin writing simple equations.

Over the past two years, the students in Bill's 1st-to 5th-grade classes have shown dramatic gains in computational skills and in problem-solving abilities, even though she does not explicitly teach such skills, Resnick says.

Another noteworthy—but still somewhat controversial—feature of many of these classrooms is the social nature of the learning process. Students are encouraged to work together, pose questions to each other, and learn from one another. According to a number of cognitive scientists, such group-based activity is much more reflective of learning in the real world.

Carl Bereiter, a researcher at the Center for Applied Cognitive Science at the Ontario Institute for Studies in Education, plans to apply the principle in a study he is conducting this year in Canada.

In his project, Bereiter will study high-school students whom he has asked to work together to construct a knowledge base about the Aztec and Mayan cultures.

At the beginning of the unit, students might be asked to enter questions about these ancient cultures into a networked computer system. They might ask, Bereiter says, "Were the shamans' dreams for real, or were they just smart people?" The students will form work groups based on their interest in particular areas of inquiry and devise plans for finding answers to their questions.

The written reports resulting from their efforts can then be designated as "candidates for publication," which means that classmates will review the work and decide whether it makes a "definite contribution" to the class's growing body of knowledge.

Elementary school children being taught by the Reciprocal Teaching method, pioneered by Annemarie Sullivan Palincsar and Ann Brown, both educational researchers, also work cooperatively to develop an interpretation of written texts.

Children read together, take turns posing questions about and summarizing the materials, and quiz one another on their understanding. They predict what will happen next or ask for a clarification.

Studies have found that children who participate in this teaching method exhibit improved performance—not only on tests of reading, but also on tests of science and social-studies comprehension.

According to Robert Glaser, a co-director of the Learning Research and Development Center, "a social context for learning elevates thinking to an observable status."

"As students participate," he explains, "the details of various problem-solving procedures, strategies of reasoning, and techniques for accomplishing goals become apparent."

Classrooms based on cognitive theory are also moving away from "drill and skill" exercises and toward more meaningful, hands-on activities that are embedded in everyday experiences.

Cognitive researchers often refer to these tasks as "authentic" activities to distinguish them from the kinds of fragmented, artificial exercises often found in schools.

This shift is based on several findings from cognitive research. For example, studies have found that teaching knowledge and skills far removed from any real-world context decreases the chance that youngsters will apply such understandings outside the classroom. In addition, research suggests that attempts to separate "basic skills" from more advanced problem-solving may actually inhibit learning.

The result has been an attempt to design classrooms and lessons in which students are encouraged to engage in more holistic activities, to answer questions of their own devising, and to complete long-term projects.

In Palo Alto, Calif., for instance, high-school students are preparing video documentaries that they will use to propose to the local city council a new use for a redevelopment area in their community.

The project, part of a study being conducted under the auspices of the Institute for Research on Learning, shows how students can learn valuable lessons but still work with a genuine purpose in mind, researchers say.

'Natural Way' To Learn

In a project being conducted in elementary-school classrooms in nine states by researchers at Vanderbilt University's Learning Technology Center, teachers use entertaining video stories to pose the equivalent of complex, mathematical word problems to students.

In one such program, students must find a way to help Jasper Woodbury, a teenager on a fishing trip in a remote wilderness area, rescue a wounded eagle.

Among the questions students must answer in order to solve the problem are: How far can an ultra-light plane fly on five gallons of gasoline? Can the plane carry the pilot, the eagle, and the gasoline? And where would the plane refuel?

The information needed to answer these questions is embedded in the story, much like clues in a mystery novel.

"Stories are the natural way for people to learn," says John D. Bransford, the Centennial Professor of Psychology at Vanderbilt University and a co-director of the center. "They are much easier for people to understand because they are linked to human events."

Through experiments, performed under varying conditions, students gradually begin to see the limits of their own understanding of the physical world.

Other researchers have argued for the creation of "cognitive apprenticeships" in schools, patterned after more traditional craft apprenticeships.

Such apprenticeships would enable students to watch teachers engaged in the kinds of real-world thinking undertaken by mathematicians, historians, or writers; work with them in solving problems; and be coached and empowered to take on increasingly complex tasks themselves.

Apprenticeships were "the predominant way education took place until the innovation of schooling," observes Allan Collins, a researcher at Bolt, Beranek, and Newman Inc., who has been largely responsible for this notion.

Collins sees the "cognitive apprenticeship" model at work, for example, in the reciprocal-teaching approach to reading pioneered by Brown and Palincsar.

The method is based on research on the kinds of questions good readers ask themselves to check their own understanding of reading material.

Under the approach, the teacher models those once-invisible strategies, aloud, for the class. Better students are called on to continue that modeling process until eventually every student can easily pore over the reading material and pose questions, make predictions, summarize, and ask for clarification.

The technique of making thinking processes visible and building an awareness of one's own thinking processes is called "metacognition." That concept, says Preseissen of Research for Better Schools, is "the real boon of the cognitive movement."

"So often we hurry and go through the thought processes ourselves and just expect students to understand," says Sue Derber, a teacher who uses the Reciprocal Teaching method. "This makes it all clearer for them."

For example, Linda Flower, a professor of rhetoric at Carnegie-Mellon University and co-director of the Center for the Study of Writing there, uses tape recorders to help students become aware of the metacognitive processes involved in writing. She pairs students up for a writing task and then tape-records their conversations as they discuss how to go about it. The recordings are played back for the benefit of both students and teachers.

"It's not only a way for teachers to listen to students talking, but it's also for students looking at their own thinking—letting them in a new picture of themselves as thinkers," she adds.

Finding New Roles for Technology

In many instances, as in the Vanderbilt project, educators are also drawing more heavily on videodisks, computers, and other new technologies to provide youngsters with the kinds of rich, hands-on activities that cannot be gained through textbooks.

"I don't know if textbooks would continue to exist in the world that I'm talking about," Collins of Bolt, Beranek, and Newman says. "I think technology is going to play a big role in education in the future."

Referring to the potential of multimedia approaches to education, Collins says, "Hypermedia would become a major aspect of things—text, film, animation, simulation."

In contrast, he asserts, textbooks represent a passive form of learning in which minimal interaction is required of students. Most textbooks provide too much information for students, instead of focusing on true understanding, he adds.

From his classroom at Mercer Island High School, Minstrell offers a more moderate view on the usefulness of written texts. Over the course of his teaching career, he says, the role of textbooks has evolved from that of a framework for his courses to a source of "background reading" for his students.

"I might say, 'Those of you who would like to read more about it should read chapter 8,'" he says.

But Minstrell cautions that, "in looking at other schools, they're going to need a story line, something they can hang the activities on and see where they're going."

Some textbook publishers are already trying to rewrite their publications to reflect the new findings from cognitive research.

"I think any publisher is well aware these are important concepts to be capitalized on in terms of fostering learning," says John Ridley, a vice president

and the editor-in-chief of the elementary division of Houghton Mifflin Publishing Company.

A 1991 reading series published by his company, for example, incorporates some of the strategies embedded in the Reciprocal Teaching approach—predicting, summarizing, clarifying, and questioning.

And texts published by Houghton Mifflin and other companies are increasingly making use of what Ridley calls a "metacognitive trail"—questions placed in the white spaces of margins that are designed to help students monitor their own comprehension of the material as they are reading it.

Although some cognitive researchers think that educational technology could ultimately supplement textbooks, others question whether it needs to be an integral part of classrooms based on cognitive theory.

"The real bottleneck is not the technology, but figuring out what are the good instructional strategies and designs and materials that really come up with better ways to get students to think," says Jill H. Larkin, an associate professor of psychology at Carnegie Mellon and a senior scientist at the school's Center for the Design of Educational Computing.

In an experiment she is conducting with colleagues, for example, Larkin set out to design a computer program for teaching physics, only to abandon the idea after deciding that the technology was "irrelevant."

Instead, the scientists have designed a workbook of laboratory experiments. "When the time is right," Larkin says, "the instructor stops the class, and they take out their equipment and do an experiment."

But in a field that has grown up in part as a result of advances in artificial intelligence, a number of researchers see technology as the essential glue binding their ideas together.

They talk about creating entire learning environments, not unlike those in Bereiter's classrooms, that are based on children's interactions with computers and among themselves. In these settings, one researcher says, "the teacher would occasionally look in to see where the students are."

Whatever the orientation, one point is clear: The kinds of uses to which technological innovations would be put in these new classrooms would be a far cry from the kinds of "drill and practice" exercises now found on most classroom computers.

Rather, technological innovations would be used as a "jumping-off point" and a source of motivation for students.

A few computer software programs already on the market, for example, are designed to anticipate students' preconceptions about math or science and assist them in building their own knowledge base.

One such program anticipates that students who know that congruent triangles are equal in area might also conclude incorrectly that triangles that are not congruent cannot be equal in area. The program seeks to confront that kind of misconception by randomly drawing triangles and asking students to measure them and repeat the process with triangles of varying sizes.

"It's very likely they will stumble upon a situation that's going to [challenge] their knowledge and, therefore, they will build new knowledge," says Eleanor Arita, a director at Sunburst Communications Inc., the company that produces "The Geometric Supposer" software program.

Sunburst and other companies also offer computer databases from which students can construct their own "snapshot" of a particular period in history.

One such database, compiled from facts and figures relating to the experiences of immigrants coming to the United States, provides information on hourly wages at a particular point in time, the kinds of jobs available, and living conditions, for example. Students

---

> 'So often we go through the thought processes ourselves and expect students to understand,' says one teacher who uses the Reciprocal Teaching method.

---

can draw on the information to craft their own views of what life was like for immigrants at that historical juncture, rather than hearing a lecture or reading a textbook.

Hands-On Approaches

Gardner of Harvard University also sees cause for optimism in the kinds of technologically inspired, hands-on approaches to learning commonly found in children's museums. Such experiences allow children to "see" how things work in ways that textbooks or traditional classroom media cannot, he says. And, he adds, "these could easily be yoked to the more formal institutions of schools."

The question, according to John Seely Brown, the Xerox Corporation vice president who helped found the Institute for Research on Learning, is: "How do you construct computer environments where the purpose is to foster a kind of collaborative learning, where what's on the screen is meant to foster conversation among students?"

In a somewhat different vein, Minstrell is collaborating with Earl Hunt of the University of Washington to develop a Hypercard program that "diagnoses" the kinds of misconceptions or preconceptions about physics that students bring to school.

"There are some things technology can do a heck of a lot better than I can, like keeping track of where all 120 of my students are in their understanding," Minstrell says. "But the pat on the shoulder, the encouragement, the 'let's work one on one'—a lot of human sorts of qualities—are what will allow us to really teach more to individuals."

But if teachers are at the heart of good instruction, as Minstrell maintains, cognitive scholars caution that their roles will have to change markedly in classrooms based on the new research.

Rather than serving as mere conduits for information, these researchers assert, teachers of the future will have to become role models, co-learners, and coaches.

Using textbooks as more of a resource and less of a framework for the curriculum, for example, requires teachers to have a greater understanding of their subjects. In addition, teachers must understand how children think about academic disciplines and be willing to place more of the learning process into the hands of students.

"The teacher changes from an information-giver to someone who can say, 'Let's find out how to find out,'" Bransford of Vanderbilt says.

Preseissen of Research for Better Schools calls this new kind of teacher a "gadfly" or a "guide on the side."

"The teacher has to become a thinker," she adds. "If teachers can't think themselves, how are they going to teach kids how to do it?"

Finding, signing on, and cultivating these kinds of teachers, however, presents a major challenge for cognitive theorists. Few teachers come out of teacher-education programs prepared to teach in these new ways, according to researchers in the field.

"I think that the things that cognitive science imagines should be happening in the classroom will require a much more sophisticated teaching force than now exists," says Lampert, an associate professor of teacher education at Michigan State and a practicing elementary school teacher.

Moreover, teachers themselves, faced with the prospect of turning control of learning over to their pupils, may be skeptical. As one educator put it during a January conference on thinking sponsored by the U.S. Education Department's office of educational research and improvement, "One of my concerns is that the classroom will break down into a Phil Donahue or Oprah Winfrey show."

Indeed, some of the teachers now using cognitive-based approaches to teaching concede, their classrooms may appear "unruly." It is not uncommon for students to spend class time debating possible solutions to mathematical problems or arguing over the outcome of a physics experiment.

But "we know we're talking about math, arguing about it," Bill of Pittsburgh says. "I have succeeded if [students] feel comfortable enough to be wrong."

The apparent familiarity of some cognitive findings also tends to inspire wariness in some teachers, researchers say. Much of what is touted as new in cognitive theory, they note, sounds much like good teaching, born of intuition and experience. Researchers sometimes call that spark of recognition in veteran teachers "tacit knowledge."

They contend that teachers may "know it when they see it," but that they may not actually be putting that intuition to work in classrooms. The problem, they say, is that teachers may lack self-confidence or are constrained by school-district regulations.

"What the theorists can do is make tacit knowledge explicit," Bransford of Vanderbilt says.

Researchers concede other cognitive concepts echo successful educational programs already in place in classrooms, such as Reading Recovery, the popular remedial program imported from New Zealand, or cooperative learning, an approach in which children work in groups of peers. Neither strategy is based on cognitive theory, but both contain aspects of some of the same ideas.

Students can draw on the database information to craft their own views of what life was like for immigrants at that historical juncture.

"We often see stuff happening, but nobody quite sees why it's working," Brown of Xerox says. "What we have to have is this new perspective, to view the mind as part of a social setting, learning in context, and leveraging on content to help [students] learn."

Another cause for confusion among educators seeking to inspire their students to think more analytically has been the profusion in recent years of prepackaged programs designed to teach "higher order" or "critical thinking" skills. Researchers contend that these programs fall short of their goals because they teach thinking skills in isolation, not in the context of academic disciplines. Students tutored under such methods tend to do well on questions related to those they have already encountered, but fail to apply their newly acquired thinking skills in other

areas, research has found.

"You can talk thinking skills from the central office forever," Preseissen of Research for Better Schools says. "Lots of teachers think they're teaching thinking—and that may well be—but they really need to look at it, to examine it."

Another reason for skepticism on the part of teachers, Bransford says, is that researchers have failed "to package [their theories] in a way that makes sense to" teachers. "There's still a gap between the general theoretical framework and specific implications for instruction," he says.

In addition, researchers and teachers at the forefront of the "cognitive revolution" point out, teaching approaches based on cognitive research may be a hard sell because they require a great deal of effort on the part of teachers.

Despite the laissez-faire appearance of some classrooms and the lack of a step-by-step curriculum, many such approaches to learning require careful planning.

"The kind of teaching cognitive science is pointing to is a lot harder to do than traditional teaching," Lampert of Michigan State says. "Neither the teacher nor the learner can sustain intense engagement of the subject matter if they have only 45 minutes of math or 45 minutes of reading."

"There's no doubt about it," says Alice Gill, a 3rd grade teacher from Cleveland who is applying cognitive theories in her classroom and training others to do the same, "this takes a lot more time."

"But whatever the time," Gill continues, "I think every one of us here would shout from the rooftop that it was worth it."

Gill is one of five mathematics teachers participating in a project sponsored by the American Federation of Teachers designed to make new research on cognition more accessible to their peers. The first product of their efforts, volume 1 of a teacher-written series, "Thinking Mathematics," was released in the fall of 1991.

At the Benchmark School, a private school for children with reading problems based almost entirely on research in cognition, Irene W. Gaskins, the school's principal and founder, requires the teachers she hires to keep abreast of educational research, attend monthly in-service sessions, and work without the aid of teachers' manuals.

Teachers applying to work at the school are requested to first work six weeks at the school's summer program.

"One year I had five applicants for one position, and all five turned down a job at the end of the summer," Gaskins says. "They all said, 'I can't work this hard all year long.'"

Even if teachers are sold on the research, they sometimes feel hemmed in by school district rules requiring that they follow a closely prescribed curriculum or by pressures that their students score high on standardized, multiple-choice achievement tests. "If you expect teachers to pay attention to how children think and understand things, but you don't treat teachers as people who think and understand, you're in for a major gridlock," Lampert says.

Agrees Gaea Leinhardt, a professor of education at the University of Pittsburgh: "You can't say the learner constructs and makes meaningful knowledge, and then give a teacher a booklet and say, 'Here's what to do.'"

In contrast, Lampert says, teachers engaged in a cognitive approach to learning must be able to "move around freely" within the curriculum and to deal with fewer topics in greater depth.

In the Thinking Mathematics project, notes Lovely H. Billups, who oversees the program as director of educational research and dissemination for the AFT, "the children could talk about one word problem for 10 minutes, when 10 problems could be done in that time."

Gaskins of the Benchmark School says parents also raise questions when they learn that their children are not memorizing formulas, periodic charts, or historical facts.

"They'll tell their kids, 'I don't care what she says about constructing your own knowledge, just memorize it and get an A on the test,'" she says.

Indeed, many cognitive scholars view current forms of assessment as one of the greatest stumbling blocks to bringing about real changes in classrooms. New ways of teaching and learning call for new ways of assessing children's progress, they argue. Standardized, multiple-choice tests, which often rely on simple recall of facts and formulas, do little to foster higher-order thinking and may actually impede it, according to these researchers.

"It's not that the questions are bad," Bransford of Vanderbilt says. "It's the kinds of things they don't ask, and, if they don't ask them, they tend not to be taught."

Whether their motivations were influenced by cognitive research or by dissatisfaction with existing measures of student learning, at least 40 states are shifting from traditional, multiple-choice tests to performance-based assessments.

These new alternatives to machine-scored tests seek to take a deeper look at how students learn through the use of portfolios of student work, essay questions, and long-term projects.

Individual sites—like the Key School in Indianapolis, which is based on Gardner's theory of multiple intelligences—are also experimenting with video portfolios, student journals, and the like as an alternative to more traditional assessments.

At the national level, one of the leaders in cognitive research, Resnick of the University of Pittsburgh, is spearheading efforts to develop an examination system for all students that would focus more on "high level" skills and on the application of knowledge to real-world problems.

Under the proposal, students could complete a series of performance examinations, portfolios, and projects over a period of time in order to graduate from high school, enter college, or apply for a new job.

Although Resnick characterizes the effort as the sum total of her work, she says it does not represent a way to put her theories into practice.

"It is accumulated wisdom—if you want to call it wisdom rather than a direct application of any one piece of research," she says.

Collins of Bolt, Beranek, and Newman also sees an expanded role for technology in assessing student learning.

"The qualities needed for a good scientist or historian—being able to formulate questions, to listen, to explain—there's no way that paper and pencil can test those kinds of abilities," he asserts.

"But if you use other technology, like video or computers, you can have people form hypotheses, do diagnoses, give them a microworld where they're trying to design an electric circuit to do something or a system for running a government," he says.

All of these researchers view assessment as a potentially powerful lever for bringing about curricular change because, in the words of one scholar, "what gets tested tends to be taught."

For the same reason, however, they worry that tests, taken in isolation from other education reform efforts, could exert undue influence on the curriculum.

"We believe exams done in certain ways are a privileged point of leverage," Resnick says. "If done alone, they can be a disaster." ∎

From Education Week, *Oct. 9, 1991*

10.

Designing Woman

Ann Brown has drafted a blueprint for schools of tomorrow. Her vision: turning students into lifelong learners.

By Elizabeth Schulz

You would never know by looking at the John Swett School that groundbreaking work is going on inside. A high chain-link fence surrounds the half-dozen or so portable classrooms that make up the Oakland, Calif., elementary school. The compound is completely paved, and bare pipes run along the sheltered walkways that connect the buildings. From a little distance, the enclosure looks more like an isolated army base than a school. Only the jungle gym, strewn with yellow police tape, betrays its true identity.

Yet it is here that University of California psychologist Ann Brown has come to create what she calls "a community of learners." Working with teachers at John Swett, a predominantly African-American inner-city school, Brown is engineering change and simultaneously studying its effects in the classroom, a real-world interplay of research and reform.

Three decades ago, when Brown entered her chosen field, her laboratory was far removed from the everyday reality of students and schools. Like most behavioral psychologists of the day, she studied children as if they were mice or monkeys, using the Wisconsin General Test Apparatus. Designed to observe how animals respond to stimuli, the apparatus looks like a confessional, with a one-way mirror separating the experimenter from the subject.

In the 1950s and '60s, behavioral psychologists used this device to study children because they believed that the same basic laws of behavior held true for every species—humans included.

With a kind, round face, topped with fine curly brown hair, Brown doesn't look like someone who would ever isolate children in such an impersonal contraption or run them through what now seem like meaningless tasks. She leans forward on the dark leather couch in her Berkeley home and explains why she did.

"I am a psychologist; I have always been a psychologist of sorts," she says, implying that this was simply the way things were done back then. "I started my academic career 30 years ago studying learning, and I'm still doing that. But what I did then and what I do now are as distinct as night and day."

What she does now is delve directly into the messy realities of classroom life. Researchers have long studied the individual aspects of schooling—curriculum, instruction, technology, and assessment—but few have examined the interplay among them. This is what Brown does, and it has given her a unique perspective on teaching and learning. It has helped her see how misguided traditional schooling is, and it has given her clear ideas about how classrooms should operate, ideas she has been testing at the John Swett School and, more recently, at Sequoia Elementary School, also in Oakland.

What Brown envisions is an elementary classroom in which students take individual and communal responsibility for their learning; a classroom where constructive discussion, questioning, and criticism are the mode rather than the exception; a classroom where students are encouraged to develop their interests and strengths and conduct research. Unrealistic? Brown doesn't think so.

What schools should be doing, she insists, is teaching kids how to be lifelong learners. This is what she and the teachers at John Swett and Sequoia are trying to do. "We aim to produce a breed of intelligent novices," Brown writes in a 1993 anthology on cognitive studies, "students who, although they may not possess the background knowledge needed in a new field, know how to go about gaining it."

Brown's vision relies heavily on her own research in the cognitive sciences, much of it conducted in school classrooms. Cognitive revolutionaries, Brown among them, have discovered that people learn best when actively constructing knowledge rather than passively absorbing another person's expertise. They've found that students have knowledge and feelings about how they learn and that the most effective learners have control over the learning process. They have also come to see that, while people can learn almost anything if they put their minds to it, most learn some things more easily than others because of their individual interests.

"If you have theories that are based on what kids can actually do when they are challenged and interested and motivated," Brown says, "then you have a completely different concept of what curriculum and assessment should look like. The theories of learning that are coming out now from psychologists who are interested in schools are more complicated but more real and have more direct application to classrooms because they were developed by studying children in classrooms."

Noted author and Harvard University psychologist Howard Gardner first came across Brown's work in the 1970s. She was among the first to study students' own reflections about their thinking and learning, an area of psychology that has come to be known as metacognition. Gardner says that in the 1980s, when many psychologists began turning their attention directly to education, Brown's work stood out "because, unlike almost everything else in this field, it was actually useful."

Brown's current work designing classes that capitalize on children's natural learning processes is unparalleled, according to Gardner. By drawing on both psychological theory and classroom experience, and by offering models of what can be done in regular classrooms with regular teachers, Brown, Gardner says, is having "more impact than any other psychologist of her time."

Ann Brown was born in an air-raid shelter in Portsmouth, England, during World War II. Her mother was Irish, her father English. At age 11, Brown remembers thinking that college was not in the cards. She attended a rigid Catholic elementary school, governed by ruler-toting nuns. In those days in England, children had to pass an exam to get into college-preparatory schools. Only one in four made it over the hurdle. Brown, who was dyslexic and, as a result, a very late reader, was not among them.

Brown's mother wouldn't let her go to the local non-preparatory school because it wasn't Catholic. The only other option was an expensive parochial school that the family couldn't afford. But the school took Brown anyway because her mother did a lot for the church. The first thing the nuns did was teach Brown to read. She proved to be clever and a good student. Seeing an opportunity to improve the school's reputation by sending a graduate on to college, the nuns hired tutors to help Brown pass university entrance exams.

At 18, as Brown was preparing to attend the University of London to study history, she saw a documentary on how animals learn in their natural environments. "I was so fascinated," she recalls, "that I looked up animal learning in my handy guide to universities and found that in order to study learning, I needed a degree in psychology." Because of her late educational development, she had a poor background in math and science, prerequisites for the study of psychology. With little hope, she set up an interview with the head of the psychology department. Coincidently, the professor was an expert on 18th-century litera-

> 'I started my academic career 30 years ago studying learning, and I'm still doing that. But what I did then and what I do now are as distinct as night and day.'

ture—Brown's high school specialization. They discussed poetry for hours, and Brown left with a scholarship to study psychology.

But rather than researching animals in their natural habitats, Brown focused on lab animals—rats, mice, pigeons—that were learning things they were never intended to. In retrospect, Brown believes that the learning theories of the behaviorists she studied back then—B.F. Skinner and Edward Tolman, among them—all share common features that make them less than ideal models for educational practice. "All derived their primary database from rats and pigeons learning arbitrary things in restricted situations," she says. "By studying the behavior of pigeons in arbitrary situations, we learn nothing about the behavior of pigeons in nature." And even less, she adds, about the behavior of children.

Even as a University of London psychology student, Brown was not comfortable with the behaviorists' view of learning. "I questioned it," she says, "but I was very good at it. The trouble with academics is that if you are good at a subject, you go on doing it." So Brown continued conducting behaviorist experiments at the University of Sussex, where she landed her first teaching position.

In 1968, Brown headed off to the United States on a two-year sabbatical. It was a chance to make a new start. She had officially been trained as an experimental psychologist but had begun working with children in the area of cognitive development. Once in the United States, this is what she decided to focus on. Brown liked her new identity and her new home better than the old. "It was a much more exciting place and easier to get grants, so I decided to stay," she says. She was offered a post at the University of Illinois at Urbana-Champaign.

During the 1970s, Brown's work focused on human memory. She found that children could be trained to use simple strategies to improve their memories, but she also noted that they tended not to use the strategies they learned unless prompted to do so. She wondered why. Was it that they didn't realize the strategies were useful or simply that they didn't care? In trying to answer these questions, Brown came up with the concept of metacognition: the idea that children can learn better when they are aware of how they learn. "I was completely struck by the fact that you could get students to improve, but if you walked away, they just didn't do it anymore," she says. "The reason they didn't do it anymore is because they didn't understand why they were doing it." Many children, she discovered, especially those who are disadvantaged, don't think to orchestrate, oversee, plan, and revise their own learning activities.

Her next thought was that maybe children could be trained to take part in their learning. She found, however, that this was no easy task, especially in the laboratory setting, where children were being encouraged to learn material for no purpose other than to please an experimenter. She began to question the whole lab approach to studying children. Gradually, she was drawn into the classroom.

This migration to the classroom was frowned upon by some of her peers. The first grant proposal Brown wrote was rejected when anonymous reviewers accused her of abandoning her experimental training and conducting "pseudo-experimental research in a quasi-naturalistic setting."

Around the same time, Brown turned to the study of reading, something she had never thought she'd do given her own personal struggles as a youngster. "Having been such a poor reader myself, it's the last thing in the world that I wanted to do," she says. But

when a colleague wrote a grant proposal to launch a center for the study of reading and needed a developmental psychologist for his research team, Brown let him use her name. After the center opened, the funders requested a book chapter on what was known about metacognition in reading. "When I wrote the chapter," she recalls, "I soon realized that all the interesting questions had not been asked. I got pulled more and more into that work."

At the time, teachers commonly taught reading skills using basils and workbooks rather than real literature or whole texts. If a teacher wanted students to learn how to summarize, he or she might ask them to summarize paragraphs on a work sheet. Brown's col-

'[Brown] has taken ordinary kids, often disadvantaged, and shown that they can think, that they can be miniature scholars, doing the kinds of things scientists do.'

laboration with Annemarie Palincsar, a teacher and graduate student in special education at the University of Illinois, fundamentally challenged that teaching approach.

Although Palincsar and Brown come from different backgrounds, the two shared an interest in helping disadvantaged students learn reading-comprehension strategies. Both were also drawn to the Russian psychologist Lev Vygotsky's theory that children learn best in a real social setting with a wide range of learning opportunities available to them. Together, Brown and Palincsar developed a remarkably simple technique: Students read a particular text and then take turns leading small group discussions to help the others better understand what they've read. They called the approach Reciprocal Teaching.

During a typical session, one student reads a passage aloud while the others read along silently. The children, guided by the leader, then ask each other questions about the text. They may ask for clarification of a word or phrase they don't understand or a more general question about the subject matter. They also summarize aloud and predict what might happen next.

Brown and Palincsar tested the approach using reading groups at a number of schools in Springfield, Ill. Almost immediately, evidence that the method worked began trickling in. Students who started out scoring only 40 percent on daily reading-comprehension tests raised their scores to 85 percent after only 20 sessions. The program was adopted by the local school district and later endorsed by the state of Illinois. Over a 10-year period, more than 800 teachers have been exposed to the teaching method.

Still, it bothered Brown that the approach was being used almost solely to teach reading in a reading-group setting. "I realized that it would be better if students didn't read to prove they could read," she says. "It is important for students to read in the service of learning, which is what you and I do. I read because I want to know about something or for pleasure. I wanted to turn reading from a school task into a learning task." It was at this point that she began to envision a classroom in which students read for the purpose of learning meaningful material and spent time discussing and writing about what they were learning.

This shift in focus coincided with a move west. Tired of the rural setting in Illinois, Brown landed a professorship at the University of California at Berkeley. It was a rocky transition. Two days after she and her husband, psychologist Joseph Campione, moved into a yellow stucco house in the Berkeley hills, the Loma Prieta earthquake struck. "It's a nice place to live," she says, "but you have to have the ability to put your head in the sand."

As an outsider, she also had trouble finding a local school that would let her turn its classes upside down. After a year of following leads only to have them turn into dead ends, Brown heard about a 6th grade teacher and Berkeley graduate student who wanted to make significant changes in her classroom and then study the results. "Why, that's what I want to do," Brown remembers saying. That teacher, Martha Rutherford, became Brown's foot in the door at the John Swett School.

Guided Discovery

Inside Jill Walker's 2nd grade classroom at John Swett, students are conducting research about animals. Several have compiled a list of questions about defense mechanisms. Are animal babies born with the same defense mechanisms as their parents? Why do different animals have different mechanisms?

Where did the questions come from, one student is asked. "From our heads," she says. "When we read books, we're going to find out the answers."

Walker's students work together in small groups. One group is engaged in Reciprocal Teaching, but others are conducting research or working on computers. This aspect of classroom design was the result of collaboration with teachers. When Brown first became involved at John Swett, she impressed upon Martha Rutherford that it was important to design the class so that the students would communicate with each other and build knowledge among themselves. But Rutherford knew that young children need structure. So they came up with the idea of rotating groups of children through regular activities; the children are free within a given structure. "It was a negotiation of needs and theory," Rutherford says.

Much of the activity in this bustling classroom goes on without direct intervention from the teacher. But Walker does spend some time "guiding" each group. She approaches one table, for example, where students are supposed to be reading and taking notes about swamps. Not much is happening.

Walker first asks which student is the leader. A girl named Sharon (the children's names have been changed at the request of the school) comes to life, posing a question for the group: "What do we want to write in our journals from this book?"

"Trees," someone offers.

The students are clearly on the wrong track. Although the challenge for the teacher is to guide without taking over, that is not always possible, so Walker interrupts: "Do we want to write about trees? We're studying habitats. Which habitat is this about?"

A student says "swamps" and then falls silent.

Walker tries to turn the conversation back to Sharon. "I'm not going to facilitate this conversation," the teacher says firmly.

Guided discovery is difficult to orchestrate, Brown admits. It takes sensitive clinical judgment to know when to intervene and when to leave well enough alone. "A major problem with guided discovery," she writes in a recently published anthology on classroom practice, "is the load placed on the guide, the official teacher. Invoking comfortable metaphors such as 'teacher as coach' does not tell us how and when the teacher should coach.

"Consider the position of a teacher who knows something that the students do not. Here she is in the position of making a judgment call about whether to intervene or not. She must decide whether the problem centers on an important principle or involves only a trivial error that she can let pass for now. Consider the case of the teacher who does not know the answer, or one who may share the students' puzzlement or misconception. In this case, she is first required to recognize this fact (which she might not be able to do) and, after admitting puzzlement or confusion, find ways to remedy it."

The challenge to teachers is compounded by the fact that students given reign to discover in the classroom are apt, at times, to develop misconceptions. Last year, during a discussion on the use of DDT and other chemicals to combat malaria, a student informed the class that AIDS, like malaria, can be spread by mosquitoes. The child used analogy, theory, and technical language to support his point. "It's the same as with needles," he explained. "Infected blood gets into the needles and then spreads AIDS to another needle user. Mosquitoes bite an infected host and then bite a healthy person—the blood commingles." The dilemma facing the teacher in this situation is how to praise the boy for his impressive analysis and logic but also warn the other students against the misinformation.

Across the room, a simple exchange between two students demonstrates what Brown sees as the upside of guided discovery. "I want to show you something," 7-year-old Adria says to a classmate. Both are huddled around a Macintosh computer. Adria highlights a word and clicks on a boxed capital B on the tool bar. "See," she says. "The text gets bigger and bolder, so it stands out." One student has a bit of information and is sharing it with another.

Brown recognizes that youngsters develop talents and interests at different times. Traditional classroom practice doesn't acknowledge this, she says. Children of a particular age are all expected to grasp a certain amount of material in a fixed amount of time. This, she contends, runs against nature. In the Community of Learners program, students pursue a wide array of topics and subtopics at any given time. Students who develop an interest and expertise in a particular area pass it along to a peer. "No one is an island," Brown says of this kind of classroom. "No one knows it all. Cooperative learning is not just nice—it is necessary for survival."

Last year, during a unit on animals, for example, a student fixated on the amounts of food various animals have to eat to survive. He noticed, for example, that sea otters, though relatively small, require vast quantities of food. He hypothesized that because the otter lives in the cold sea but has no blubber, it needs to eat a lot to produce the energy to keep warm. When someone else mentioned that tiny hummingbirds also require a lot of food, the student latched on to something akin to metabolic rate. He kept coming back to the concept time and again in class discussions. In Brown's terminology, the boy "seeded" the idea of metabolic rate, which quickly "migrated" through the class.

The learning process is only part of the picture. Unless students have meaningful lessons to learn, Brown says, the process and the classroom structure will amount to little. Although there is clearly room for students to pursue areas of interest in her Community of Learners, Brown does not simply leave it up to students to decide what they will study. Instead, she and the teachers select a number of broad classroom topics and themes and revisit them often, each time pushing students to higher levels of understanding.

The classroom model also meshes Reciprocal Teaching with another cooperative learning technique known as the "jigsaw method." Students studying a particular topic in small research groups are assigned responsibility for one of five subtopics. The students research their subtopics and then share what they learn with the rest of their group; as the pieces come together, the whole picture emerges, just like with a jigsaw puzzle. When appropriate, the groups read books related to their research topic and then discuss them using the Reciprocal Teaching approach; the student who is the "expert" on the particular subtopic under discussion leads the group.

The Reciprocal Teaching session in the corner of Walker's classroom is slow-going at first. A teachers' aide sits with three students: Tyrone, Katie, and Kendra. Each holds a book new to the group. They start by scrutinizing the title. Tyrone, the designated teacher, reads it aloud: "Read About Animals That Live in Shells." He pauses, unsure of what to do next.

The aide prompts him, "What are the strategies we can use?"

"Summarize, clarify, and question," he says. "Does anyone have any questions?"

When no one speaks, the aide asks, "What are shells?"

The students have been studying the topic, and their areas of expertise quickly become apparent. "They are coverings for animals with soft bodies," Katie says. "Snails are a good example."

Tyrone asks the others to predict what kinds of things might be in the book. "I think the book will have animals with shells, like trilobites," Katie says.

With visible surprise at Katie's use of technical language, the aide inquires, "Why trilobites?" As if stating the obvious, Katie replies, "Because they are early animals that had shells."

Tyrone pipes in, "I think the book will have some animals that live in the water. I know that not all animals with shells live in the water, but some do."

As Tyrone reads the next section, Kendra and Katie help him with difficult words, such as "exoskeleton."

The aide pushes them to think. "The reading says that animals had soft bodies and then developed hard bodies. Why did they develop hard shells?"

Katie answers, "Because they need protection from predators."

"They need protection from the weather," Kendra chimes in.

Katie runs with that idea. "Yeah, in a stormy sea with waves crashing, the animals might get knocked against the rocks."

Tyrone asks if any words need clarification. "What are exoskeletons?" Katie asks.

"Skeletons are bones inside," Tyrone says.

"*Ex* means *non* or *not*, so maybe it means *no skeleton*," Katie suggests.

"Good guess, but that's not the answer, so let's keep digging," the aide says. "What is the topic we are reading about? What makes sense?"

Katie summarizes what they've read then gasps, "Oh! I think it means skeleton on the outside!"

After about an hour and a half, all the students in

the class return to their desks, and Walker asks them how their research went that day. Some students complain about problems that arose in their groups, while others talk about what they learned. Walker wraps up the session with a few encouraging remarks. "It's only our third day of research topics," she says. "There were some conflicts, but that's normal; that's just the nature of working in groups. We will be able to look back and realize that even though it was difficult in the beginning, we've come a long way."

On the door outside of Laurie Wingate's 5th grade classroom at Sequoia Elementary School is a big orange sign that says: "Caution. Construction Zone: Work in Progress." The work under way today is what Brown refers to as a "benchmark lesson." This is a common activity that closely resembles a traditional lesson, with an adult leading the class. But even here, dialogue is valued.

Today, Wingate turns the class over to biologist Doris Ash and takes a seat in the back of the room. The students sit at desks in a large circle. Ash begins by saying, "I'm going to talk some, then I am going to let you talk. We're on a search for a big idea, an idea so big that you can use it in Oakland, in Borneo, in the ocean, and on all the continents."

She asks what students know about the food chain. A small boy starts to offer a rather technical definition. Ash tells him to define his terms. "A herbivore, an animal that eats plants, gets eaten by a carnivore, which eats meats," he says. "A decomposer eats what's left over after everything dies." When he finishes, he calls on a girl across the room who adds that scavengers also eat dead things. This process, what Brown calls "handing off," allows students to have some control over the conversation and encourages them to talk to each other instead of always directing comments to the teacher.

Ash asks for examples of the kinds of animals mentioned so far. As the students give her some, she draws a simple food chain on the board: A mountain lion eats a deer, which has eaten grass. A student takes it further, noting that when the mountain lion dies it is eaten by worms, which are then eaten by insects. But he doesn't stop there. Insects, he adds, are eaten by mice, which in turn are eaten by cats and owls.

Ash is visibly excited. "Look what happened," she says. "We were drawing a nice straight chain, but we can't put all you know about food into a chain. It's more like a web."

The class explores the difference between a food chain and a food web. During the ensuing discussion, children make lengthy, sometimes complex, points. When several try to give a short answer, Ash pushes them to elaborate. The students begin to see that the web concept encompasses more complex relationships between organisms than the food-chain idea.

Taking off on a student's comment, Ash poses a hypothetical question: "If most frogs suddenly died, what would happen to the food web?"

A student who hasn't yet spoken postulates that if a lot of frogs die, flies would flourish because of the demise of one of their natural predators and worms would have a tough time because all the flies would eat them. He hands off to another student, who points out that animals that eat frogs will also be affected.

Later, when the discussion shifts to the subject of scientific evidence, Ash asks what students might do to confirm that falcons are scavengers. One student suggests that they examine falcon scat for mouse bones. But another student points out that even if they found bones in the droppings, they still wouldn't

Students develop expertise in a particular area and pass it along to a peer. 'No one is an island,' Brown says of this kind of class-room. 'No one knows it all.'

know whether the falcon ate the mouse when it was dead or alive. Another student suggests asking a ranger. "Consulting an expert," Ash interjects. "That's a good strategy."

After the benchmark lesson, the students are scheduled to work on computers. But Wingate makes an on-the-spot decision to postpone the computer work and have the students read and work in research groups instead.

Each group receives a packet of articles on a chosen topic. The articles have been selected to help the students begin to frame research questions. "You can read out loud or to yourselves," Wingate tells the groups. "If you need to ask your neighbor for clarification, that's fine. You can make notes, but remember the notes are for you and should be structured to be helpful to you."

Some of the articles are easy to read; others are quite challenging. After glancing at his packet, a boy in one group suggests, "I think we should read these by ourselves and take notes and ask each other questions as we need to."

A girl in the group disagrees. "I think we should read them together so we are sure we all understand, so that no one feels bad about asking questions." The group decides to take this tack.

One of the students volunteers to start as the leader and calls on another to read aloud. She reads about a DDT controversy in Michigan. It seems that salmon in that state are still showing signs of contamination long after companies stopped using the pesticide. A group member asks for clarification. "What does *contamination* mean?"

"It's like something bad is added," a student says.

"What does *persistent* mean?" another asks.

"It means it just keeps happening again and again, like a pattern," one girl in the group says. She did not say anything during the benchmark lesson but seems right at home in her research group. When someone asks what *hatcheries* are, she explains, "It's like a place where you raise birds, but you are raising fish."

Questions that they can't answer among themselves, they note in their research journals. Later, they will either look up the answers or ask Wingate or Ash for help.

Frustrated with what seems to her a plodding pace, one girl in the group declares, "This isn't working. Let's just read on our own." But the others demur, and the discussion continues.

Neither Jill Walker's class at John Swett nor Laurie Wingate's 5th grade class at Sequoia are perfect. As in all classes, some students don't do their work, some monopolize the discussion, some are obstinate. But with all their rough spots, these classes, like others at the two schools, are giving inner-city students an opportunity to take part in serious and rewarding discussions and to conduct real research. They are not only learning to read, write, and discuss but also how to solve problems and think.

Reciprocal Teaching has become standard practice for many teachers, but Brown is not as sanguine about her Community of Learners program. She believes that Reciprocal Teaching caught on because it is an adaptation of an already popular classroom technique—reading groups. "With the Community of Learners," she says, "we're asking teachers to do something much more complicated."

Brown has resisted the prepackaged-curriculum approach to dissemination. As Martha Rutherford of the John Swett School puts it, Brown is "not interested in having [her] work put into a glossy box like a coffin."

Instead, Brown hopes that a network of teachers who have successfully implemented the program in their classrooms and understand its underlying principles will carry it to others. She believes a wide range of teachers will become interested if they get a chance to see what the Community of Learners approach can accomplish.

Brown and her colleagues have collected information that she believes demonstrates the program works. During the 1992-93 school year, for example, the reading-comprehension scores of Walker's 2nd graders at John Swett increased by 34 months. Half of the class ended the year scoring at the 5th grade level or above on standardized reading tests.

But the more impressive evidence, Brown says, can be seen in the students' attitudes toward learning, not in their test scores. Children in her Community of Learners understand that it is not enough just to get a right answer, she says; they know they need evidence to back it up.

Harvard's Howard Gardner, one of Brown's biggest boosters, puts it this way. "She has taken ordinary kids, often disadvantaged, and shown that they can think, that they can be miniature scholars, doing the kinds of things scientists do." ■

From Teacher Magazine, *August 1991*

11.

After Dick and Jane

Whole language is more than a way of teaching. It's about empowering teachers and students.

By Daniel Gursky

For more than 100 years, public schools in the United States have operated on the theory that children learn by mastering the component parts of complex material before grasping the entire subject. In the current system, a carefully sequenced curriculum from kindergarten to graduation is determined largely by experts outside the schools. Within that curriculum, teachers and textbooks transmit information to students, who spend most of their time as docile recipients. They study structured textbooks containing drills and exercises that reinforce skills and knowledge they often perceive as having no relevance to the world outside the classroom. Emphasis is on the memorization of facts rather than on problem solving and creative thinking. And students are tested, drilled, and retested regularly to make sure they have learned the facts and absorbed the information.

The theory that prevails in the traditional school contends that learning is hard work and that students must be persuaded to undertake and stick with it. A system of external rewards and punishments provides the incentive for students to achieve. Learning is viewed largely as an individual activity, and students are discouraged from collaborating with each other; working together is often viewed as cheating. Since children naturally dislike hard work and would rather be playing than learning, or so the theory goes, the main challenge to the teacher in the traditional school is to maintain order and to control the students so that teaching and learning can take place.

There is a certain logic and coherence to the theory, and it has surely demonstrated a tenacity to survive and a resistance to recent research findings on how children learn. But the growing number of teachers, school administrators, and scholars who have become part of the whole language movement believe the traditional school not only doesn't encourage learning but also often obstructs it.

Proponents of whole language subscribe to the theory that children are eager to learn when they come to school, that learning is not work but rather an effortless process that goes on continuously without their even trying. Children do not learn by first mastering the smaller parts of the whole, but by constantly developing hypotheses about the world around them and testing those hypotheses. Whole language advocates point out that children arrive at school already having learned an enormous amount without the benefit of formal schooling. The average 1st grader, experts say, has already acquired a vocabulary of 10,000 words and assimilated many of the rules of grammar without trying.

Whole language is an entire philosophy about teaching, learning, and the role of language in the classroom. It stresses that language should be kept whole and uncontrived and that children should use language in ways that relate to their own lives and cultures. In the whole language classroom, the final product—the "answer"—isn't as important as the process of learning to define and solve problems.

Whole language advocates believe that the ideal classroom is a child-centered one in which students enjoy learning because they perceive that the material has meaning and relevance to their lives. The teacher is not an authoritarian but a resource, coach, and co-learner who shares power with the students and allows them to make choices. Learning in such a classroom is a social act, and children learn from and help each other. The challenge to the teacher is to adapt the curriculum and activities to the interests and talents of the children, to provide a content-rich environment, and to assure that they are constantly engaged in learning. When children are not learning, whole language teachers say, they become bored and restless, and control becomes a problem. The common techniques of whole language teaching—daily journal and letter writing, a great deal of silent and oral reading of real literature, and student cooperation, to name a few—are the philosophy in action.

It is hard to imagine two schools of thought more diametrically opposed in their view of how children learn than the behavioral psychology approach and whole language. Frank Smith, a leading authority on reading, writing, and children's literacy, finds the two views so contradictory "that they would appear to refer to two entirely different kinds of mental activity." But they share two points:

● Human learning begins with the learning of language: first, listening and speaking; then, reading and writing.

● Success in learning language is vitally important because it largely determines how well a child will do in school and in life.

The Great Reading Wars

Because children already know how to speak (and presumably to listen) when they come to school, their formal instruction in language begins with reading. As a result, the battles between the proponents of the divergent theories of learning are fought mainly over the way reading is taught in the primary grades.

These battles, known as "The Great Reading Debate," haven't been limited to intellectual jousting in obscure academic journals and at professional conferences. The war is regularly waged in the mass media and in statehouses and in school board chambers across the country. The adversaries skirmish in courtrooms as well as classrooms.

Although the debate is ostensibly over the most effective method of teaching reading, it goes much deeper, raising profound questions about pedagogy, the nature and purpose of schooling, and the role of teachers, students, parents, and administrators. It follows logically that a society will establish a pedagogy, and structure its schools, to conform to the theory of learning that it subscribes to.

In the United States, the traditional theory of learning became institutionalized with the beginning of mass schooling in the 19th century. Its intellectual rationale was later drawn from the work of experimental psychologists such as Edward Thorndike and, subsequently, behaviorists such as B.F. Skinner. The theory is based on the belief that children learn a complex skill such as reading by first making sense of the smallest components of the language (letters) and then progressing to larger components (sounds, words, and sentences). Children learn to read by learning to

> # Baseball fans who read the paper to see how their team fared easily pick up the nuances of yesterday's game because they already understand the game.

decode the language; understanding follows after the code is broken and the component parts are mastered.

Traditional American education, therefore, begins with lessons that focus on phonics (letters, combinations of letters, sounds, and rules), tightly controlled vocabulary, and short basal reading passages, followed by numerous skills exercises, each with only one correct answer, typically delivered by the teacher to a group of students using the same textbook.

Constance Weaver, a professor of English at Western Michigan University, calls this the "transmission" model of teaching, with teachers serving essentially as "scripted technicians" who pass on a curriculum established by people outside the classroom.

"Learning typically is broken down into small parts that can be taught, practiced, tested, retaught, and retested," Weaver says. "Some things can be transmitted, of course. But many things are likely to be forgotten because the learner hasn't necessarily connected to the material."

In other words—as assessments of student literacy point out all too clearly—we can't assume the student is learning just because the teacher is teaching. The 1988 National Assessment of Educational Progress found that about 70 percent of 17-year-olds could read well enough to get the overall message or specific information from a text, but only 42 percent could read and understand complicated passages, and fewer than 5 percent could comprehend the specialized material prevalent in business and higher education. Estimates of the number of functionally illiterate American adults, who read so poorly that they can't cope with the basics of everyday life, are even more shocking. Some figures range up to 60 million—more than one-third of the country's adult population.

But even allowing for the possibility of gross exaggeration, these figures show that the current system doesn't work for millions of students—and particularly for nonwhite and disadvantaged students. Nonetheless, inertia reinforces the dominance of the traditional model of schooling. Most people were "taught to read" that way, and most teachers have been trained to function in such a system. "It takes a revelation for teachers to even ask whether it's possible that students don't learn that way, whether language isn't acquired that way," says Patrick Shannon, head of Pennsylvania State University's language and literacy education department.

But more and more teachers are asking those questions. Sometimes with the support of their administrators, but more often on their own, teachers are embracing a holistic, meaning-first learning theory. Some do it consciously, with a solid theoretical base, while others seek new methods out of dissatisfaction with the status quo. Whole language, which has mushroomed in popularity in recent years, is by far the most widespread manifestation of this theory.

The Deep Roots of Whole Language

Although the formal label only dates back a dozen years or so, whole language has deep roots both inside and outside of education circles. As one leading expert puts it, there have always been whole language learners—but there haven't always been whole language teachers.

Whole language owes its intellectual heritage to John Amos Comenius, a 17th century educator who believed that learning should be pleasurable and rooted in students' real lives; to John Dewey's theories of progressive education; to Friedrich Froebel, the founder of kindergartens, which have a lot in common with ideal whole language classrooms; to Russian psychologist Lev Vygotsky, who emphasized the social aspects of learning and the role teachers and peers play in supporting or thwarting it; to Dorris Lee and Lillian Lamoreaux, whose language-experience approach encourages teachers to use students' stories as classroom reading material; and to Donald Graves, a writing scholar and pioneer of "process writing," who encourages both teachers and students to write more. Recent theories and research in the relatively new field of psycholinguistics have provided whole language with a more scientific base.

Psycholinguists argue that, almost from birth, children engage in a search for meaning, structure, and order. They reject the idea that decoding the smallest components of written language is an effective way for children to learn to read. Instead, they argue, language proceeds from meaning as the learner draws on his or her own experience, culture, and previous knowledge to understand the text and extract information from it. Learning and understanding are inseparable.

Smith, whose 1971 book, *Understanding Reading,* was a milestone in psycholinguistic theory, says that this view of learning has been accepted as common sense for at least 2,000 years—by everyone except educators. He suggests that most learning is as inconspicuous as breathing; both teacher and student barely realize it's happening. "Learning is continuous," he says. "It requires no particular effort, attention, conscious motivation, or reinforcement." People are constantly learning without even realizing it, from street signs, conversations, headlines, movies, and other hardly noticed events in their everyday lives.

Learning only becomes difficult, Smith argues, in contrived circumstances that are disconnected from a person's immediate interests and experiences, such as teaching children to read by asking them to study and memorize individual letters that have no meaning or isolated words that lack context.

In his book *Reading Without Nonsense,* Smith makes the point by inviting readers to glance at the texts in the following boxes and ask themselves which is the easiest to understand and remember:

JLHYL PAJMRW KHMYO EZSXPE SLM
SNEEZE FURY HORSES WHEN AGAIN
EARLY FROSTS HARM THE CROPS

Smith and whole language advocates believe that the meaning is "in the head," not in the text. One cannot read (and learn) about a subject that one does not already understand to some degree. Baseball fans, for example, who read the morning paper to see how their team fared easily pick up the nuances of yesterday's game from the written report because they already understand the game. The same article would be almost incomprehensible to a reader who knows (or cares) nothing about baseball.

To demonstrate that meaning is in the head rather than in the surface structure of language, Smith invites the reader to determine the meaning of a number of sentences: "Visiting teachers may be boring." "The chicken was too hot to eat." "She runs through the sand and waves." "The shooting of the hunters was terrible." Obviously, all of these sentences can have more than one meaning.

The point, says Smith, is that "neither individual words, their order, nor even grammar itself can be appealed to as the source of meaning in language and thus of comprehension in reading. Nor is it possible to decode from the meaningless surface structure of writing into the sounds of speech in order to find a back route into meaning. Instead, some comprehension of the whole is required before one can say how individual words should sound, or deduce their meaning in particular utterances, and even assert their grammatical function." In short, the more one knows about, or is interested in, the subject one is reading about, the more information one is likely to glean from the text.

Furthermore, Smith sees learning as social rather than solitary. "We learn from the company we keep," he explains. "We learn from the people who interest us and help us to do the things they do." As a result, children learn to read not from methods but from people. In a sense, they apprentice themselves to people who know something that they want to learn— teachers, parents, peers, and authors. Apprenticeships were a common and successful form of learning and teaching long before the advent of formal schooling.

The Politics of Reading Instruction

For years, the debate over reading instruction focused on the relative merits of phonics vs. the "whole word" method, which holds that words, rather than letters, are the most effective unit for the teaching of reading. There were countless studies, heated arguments from supporters of both sides, and even insinuations of communist conspiracies. During the 1950s and '60s, many people came to identify phonics with political conservatives and the whole word method with liberals. The rhetoric was often malicious. Rudolph Flesch, author of the 1955 polemical bestseller *Why Johnny Can't Read,* raised the stakes by blaming whole word advocates for many of America's woes, while at the same time politicizing and oversimplifying the issue of teaching reading.

In many ways, Flesch's legacy persists today, with the past attacks on the whole word methodology now aimed at whole language, whose proponents squirm with anguish at being confused with the whole word approach. They insist that the whole word method is much like the phonic approach in that it emphasizes components rather than language as a whole, memorization of individual unconnected symbols (words), and drill and practice.

Nevertheless, deliberately or inadvertently, traditionalists' attacks on whole language echo Flesch's McCarthy-era tirades against the whole word method. Sidney Blumenfeld, for instance, in a recent edition of his "Education Letter," calls whole language "an important part of the left's social agenda. Whole language is a lot more than just a new way to teach reading. It embodies a leftist messianic vision, which may account for the fanaticism found among whole language visionaries."

In recent years, fundamentalist religious groups have latched onto phonics, with its focus on skills and literal comprehension. They denounce whole language as secular humanism, atheism, and even satanism because of its emphasis on real literature rather than value-neutral basals and because of the introspection, inquiry, and multiple interpretations of texts encouraged by whole language teachers. Not surprisingly, lobbies have sprung up around the country to influence textbook-selection committees and to persuade legislators and school boards to mandate phonics as the only acceptable method of teaching reading.

Phonics-first advocates got a boost in September 1989, when a U.S. Senate Republican Policy Committee released a document titled "Illiteracy: An Incurable Disease or Educational Malpractice?" Citing a massive study supported by the U.S. Department of Education and carried out by the Center for the Study of Reading at the University of Illinois, the document called for "the restoration of the instructional practice of intensive, systematic phonics in every primary school in America."

For whole language teachers, however, arguments about the role of phonics and other methods of reading instruction miss the point: Whole language is a theory about how people learn; phonics is a method of teaching reading based on a totally different learning theory. Whole language teachers may draw upon a number of traditional methods, including phonics, but they use them only in specific situations when they think a student would benefit; the methods are not the whole language teacher's central approach to teaching literacy. "No one's suggesting that phonics isn't involved in learning to read and write," says Kenneth Goodman, University of Arizona education professor and a leading proponent of whole language. It

> # Fundamentalist religious groups denounce whole language as secular humanism, atheism, and even satanism because of its emphasis on real literature.

is the reliance on phonics as the main or sole approach to teaching literacy, he says, that whole language proponents resist.

In fact, whole language is about much more than instruction in reading and literacy. It's about empowerment and the role of teachers, students, and texts in education. In short, it's about who controls what goes on in the classroom. Will educational decisions be made by teachers and students or by administrators, curriculum developers, textbook publishers, and policymakers?

Consequently, in addition to rethinking their attitudes about learning, many whole language teachers have found it natural—indeed necessary—to develop a broader consciousness about social and political issues. "Teachers need to think about what they're doing when they decide to teach one way or another," Penn State's Shannon says. "What does [their method of teaching] mean for teachers and their students, not just in terms of language development but in their own lives? When they ask those questions, they acknowledge the politics of their work."

John Willinsky of the University of British Columbia agrees. "To give students expression is a political move," he says. "It empowers them."

Literacy as a Threat to Kings and Popes

Literacy has always been about power. The way reading has been taught for the past 500 years has more to do with religious and secular authorities trying to preserve their power than with learning theories. When Johann Gutenberg invented movable type and printed the Bible in 1455, reading was a skill largely limited to the clergy, royalty, and scribes. The authorities quickly saw the dangers inherent in widespread literacy. To prevent the spread of reading to the masses, they levied special taxes on printers, regulated the production and distribution of publications, and simply banned books and broadsides.

But even kings and popes could not withstand the inevitable, so the ruling establishment switched from trying to prevent reading to controlling it. And in some ways, as Daniel Resnick of Carnegie-Mellon University points out, the educational traditions established to control literacy during the Reformation remain stubbornly intact in modern-day American schools. Catechism-style teaching, Resnick notes, with its authoritative texts, established questions and answers, and repetitive lessons, sought to produce believers rather than thinkers. And that legacy persists. Future efforts "to move literacy expectations beyond a rudimentary ability to read, write, and calculate," he writes in the scholastic journal *Daedalus,* will be "constrained by the practice of earlier centuries: modest instructional goals, textbooks in the form of religious primers, language used primarily to create a civic culture, and mass schooling mainly for the primary years."

Basal readers, designed for specific grade levels, became the modern catechism by the 1920s, as common as pencils in the hands of primary and middle school students across the country. Shannon traces the development of the modern basal to the late 1800s, when America's growing faith in science and industry was applied to reading. Basals were intended to "ra-

tionalize" reading instruction in order to overcome the lack of good children's literature and teachers' relatively low education levels at the time. Standardized tests, which developed roughly during the same period, reinforced the use of basals.

The belief was, Shannon says, that teachers were behaving scientifically—according to psychological "laws of learning"—if they were faithfully following the directions in the manual. At the turn of the century, he notes, basal publishers apologized for 18-page teachers' manuals that accompanied all six reading levels. Today, publishers unapologetically produce manuals the size of city telephone books for each level. Textbook publishers, editors, and authors, Shannon says, have reduced teachers to managers of commercially produced materials; the best teachers are frequently considered those who explain the material well rather than those who help their students become independent learners.

In essence, the basal system has solidified into textbook form the traditional skills-based model of learning. And if the basals are something of a modern catechism, they're followed religiously by American

> # Whole language is about empowerment and the role of teachers, students, and texts in education. It's about who controls what goes on in the classroom.

teachers. Surveys show that more than 90 percent of teachers use basals to teach reading, and the vast majority of their students' class work and homework comes straight from the basal. In addition, many states require the use of basals, and teachers in some districts face fines for disobeying the mandate.

A system built around basal readers and standardized textbooks takes away from teachers and students key decisionmaking power about classroom materials. It's not surprising, then, that many teachers who are attempting to change the structure of their classes often start by limiting the use of textbooks or shelving them completely.

"For teachers," Shannon says, "whole language is about having the right and responsibility to choose what methods they use, the materials offered in class, the ways in which they assess students." Given the tradition of outside control, he argues, the thought of taking responsibility can be both frightening and exhilarating to teachers. "The possibility of control and choice has never really been offered to teachers," he says. "They thought they were supposed to fit into a scheme in which they apply someone else's material."

Weaver, of Western Michigan University, points out that many teachers prefer the safety of the basal to the unpredictable vagaries of whole language.

"You can give some teachers all the power in the world and they will use the same old traditional curriculum," she says. And even if they decide to abandon their basal readers, it may not make a big difference. "If teachers haven't made the shift in models of learning," Weaver says, "they're going to take nice trade books and do all the awful things that have been done with basals," namely, use the literature to teach isolated skills.

The basal, skills-oriented approach is also easier for teachers. They are following a preset curriculum, their lessons are planned in advance, and they can reasonably anticipate how the class will proceed. Whole language teachers, on the other hand, are constantly adapting as classroom events unfold; they guide rather than control; they watch for teaching opportunities and improvise. Whole language teachers acknowledge that while their new role is far more fulfilling than the traditional role, it is also far more demanding.

Because there are so many teaching strategies associated with whole language—journal writing, book "publishing," free reading, etc.—some teachers simply implement a few strategies and call themselves whole language teachers. "A lot of different activities plucked out of whole language and put in traditional settings can seem to be the same," says Goodman of the University of Arizona. "But they lose their significance when the reasons for the activities aren't there." Smith notes that many teachers mistakenly see whole language as just another method, rather than an entirely new approach to teaching. "They still do not trust children to learn unless their attention is controlled and their progress monitored and evaluated," he says.

Many publishing companies exploit teachers' misconceptions about whole language. "Publishers see the markets for traditional materials being eroded, so they start relabeling things and saying that if you buy their materials, you're doing whole language," Goodman says. "That's predictable, and that's a danger." Some efforts by publishers to capitalize on the movement's popularity have produced seeming anomalies—whole language basals packed with skills exercises, for example, and workbooks that are simply repackaged and billed as "journals."

There are now enough committed whole language teachers in the United States to constitute a full-fledged national movement, complete with conferences, workshops, newsletters, more than 100 support groups, and a massive whole language catalog, containing information on almost every conceivable topic related to the subject.

These whole language educators take heart from the success of their counterparts abroad, particularly in New Zealand and Australia. "Essentially, what appears as a current revolution in this country," Goodman says, "was a relatively calm evolution in other countries." In New Zealand, for example, holistic theories of learning have guided many schools since before World War II. Some whole language proponents find it more than coincidental that New Zealand and Australia rank at the top of international comparisons of literacy, while the United States barely rates a spot in the top third.

Closer to home, Canada has also become a leader in whole language, with many of the provincial educational authorities adopting the philosophy for all their schools. Extensive resources for staff development and new materials have been allocated to help with the transition.

In the United States, whole language has been a grass-roots movement, spreading classroom by classroom, as one or two teachers—rarely more than a handful—in a school change the way they teach.

Although the great debate over how children learn (and thus learn to read) seems destined to continue indefinitely, it hasn't really become a dominant issue of the current school reform movement. With a few notable exceptions, most of the efforts to improve the nation's schools seem to accept as a given the traditional theories of learning on which American public education is based. Those who would "fix" our schools have largely concentrated on issues such as increased teacher accountability, more high-stakes standardized tests, higher academic standards, more rigorous curricula, and more and better teacher training. In recent years, the emphasis has shifted somewhat to school restructuring, site-based management, and parental choice. But there has been little mention in the school reform discussion about how children learn.

Whole language advocates want to change that. They would like to focus the public discussion on classroom learning and a theory of literacy that would inevitably change the way teachers teach and the way schools are organized. As Jerome Harste, professor of education at Indiana University, has written: "Whole language inquirers want the politics of literacy made explicit. Politics, they argue, is the language of priorities. They understand that not to take a position is to maintain the status quo—to keep both those who are currently well-served and those not so well-served in place. From this perspective, curriculum is not just a new set of standards to be taught, nor even an unfinished agenda, but rather a vehicle for interrogating past assumptions as well as creating a better world. There is no neutral position." ∎

From Teacher Magazine, *August 1991*

12.

A Course of Action

In a new program, students work together for weeks trying to find solutions to complex and often controversial 'real world' problems.

By David Ruenzel

The Illinois Mathematics and Science Academy in Aurora, a distant suburb of Chicago, looms over a street dotted with industrial parks. A massive concrete structure with no apparent windows, the main facility—partially burrowed in the ground—has a severe, somewhat secretive, air. Important work, one surmises, goes on here. At the doorway, a sign reads, "A Pioneering Educational Community." Inside, past a security checkpoint, looms a cavernous lobby with a flourish of artwork on the expansive white walls. Gray carpet stretches in all directions. Students in jeans and visitors in business suits pass to and fro. No matter where I stand, I can hear the hum of the brilliant lights.

Established in 1985 by the Illinois General Assembly to address a perceived shortage of outstanding science and mathematics students, the academy is a three-year residential public high school governed by an appointed board of trustees. Its 1991 class had a mean math SAT score of 714. The school's 500 students, drawn from across Illinois, represent diverse ethnic, racial, and socioeconomic backgrounds. Admission is highly competitive. Nearly 30 percent of its faculty members hold doctorates. Equipment, ranging from a ProQuest computer system to satellite telecommunications, is state of the art.

Clearly, IMSA seems a futuristic educational outpost. Yet, if Bill Stepien is right, problem-based learning, the methodology that drives much of the school's curriculum, can help revolutionize even the most an-

tiquated public schools. As director of the academy's Center for Problem-Based Learning—he's also a history teacher—Stepien is devoted to making sure that problem-based learning finds its way into elementary and secondary schools both in the Chicago area and across the United States.

A wiry, intense man in his mid-50s, his gray hair combed straight back and down over his collar, Stepien speaks of problem-based learning with an almost prophetic intensity. "We think," he says, "that humankind is wired, inside the brain, to pay attention to dissonance, to things that don't seem to fit. We think human beings have a mechanism that demands that they try to resolve such dissonance. If you find problems that engage that hard wiring, I don't think kids will be able to resist it."

While many American schools still proceed as if knowledge were the memorization of contextless information, practitioners of problem-based learning insist that information, if it is to be transmuted into knowledge, is best acquired in the solving of a meaningful problem. "Meaningful" is the key word here; for if the problem doesn't compel students toward a genuine if less-than-ideal resolution, or if the problem is unauthentic in the sense that it would never be encountered in the "real world," then students are merely playing at inconsequential problem solving.

Stepien makes clear the distinction between problem solving and solving problems: "Problem-solving courses are too often, like, 'Let's brainstorm today, let's talk about fallacies tomorrow.' And the problems are often dinky, like, 'How does the straw man get from behind the house to the front of the house in the least number of steps?' What does that have to do with anything? I mean, let's pose a problem and brainstorm, OK. But let's make sure it's a significant problem."

In the world of the typical American school, which emphasizes the inexorable if tedious coverage of material, problem-based learning, with its emphasis on timely discovery of information, may seem highly novel. In truth, though, problem-based learning has strong roots in the pragmatism of philosopher John Dewey, who at the turn of the century began to criticize traditional teaching and learning on several fronts.

For one thing, Dewey said, children must realize the reason for acquiring knowledge if they are truly to secure it; they must be faced with a problem they truly feel a need to solve. For another thing, information—no matter how relevant it may seem at the time—quickly becomes obsolete. Schools, therefore, must spend less time imparting information and more time helping children acquire thinking skills that will enable them to solve the problems of experience. As Dewey wrote, there is a "necessity of testing thought by action if thought is to pass into knowledge." Dewey put this into practice at his own Laboratory School by having children, for example, learn mathematics as they constructed a model farm.

Idea Borrowed from Medical Education

While Dewey's theories were much discussed, they never, with some notable exceptions, much altered the American school. Schools placed too much of a premium on control to tolerate the freedom the new pedagogy demanded. It should come as no surprise, then, that it was a medical doctor—not an educator from within the system—who resurrected Dewey's ideas and pioneered problem-based learning.

During the early 1980s, Howard Barrows, assistant director for educational affairs at Southern Illinois University School of Medicine, was becoming increasingly disturbed by what he observed in medical education. "Students," he tells me, "were given a tremendous amount to memorize in the first two years of medical school. When they got into their clinical clerkships and began caring for patients, they couldn't remember much of what they'd learned. What they could remember they couldn't appropriately apply, so they had to relearn everything."

Barrows' discouragement with the status quo led him to a development that is revolutionizing medical education: the use of standardized patients—volunteers who are so thoroughly trained to simulate real patients that medical students usually can't tell the difference. In order to diagnose and treat such patients, students must retain not isolated facts but be able to apply knowledge integrated from such fields as anatomy, physiology, and chemistry. And they are evaluated on their ability to do so successfully. They also have to learn to work together, seeing each other as resourceful allies rather than as competitors.

As I listen, all of this sounds well and good. But Barrows was, after all, working with highly motivated medical students. I tell him I can't imagine the approach working very well with ordinary students.

Without hesitation or apology, Barrows assures me that I am completely wrong. For several months, he had been traveling across the country trying to incorporate problem-based learning into the curriculums of public high schools. He says it grabbed even the poorest, most disadvantaged students. "Everyone," he insists, "is motivated by real-world problems."

Content Versus Process?

My conversation with Barrows reminds me of a seminar I recently attended at which educators continually referred to teachers as "content people" and "process people," as if they were two necessarily alien factions. "Content people" imparted information; "process people" taught thinking skills. Neither group was apparently much interested in presenting to students real-world problems. Problem-based learning seems to be trying to eliminate this dichotomy between content and process by claiming that genuine knowledge always involves thinking upon information discovered in pursuit of a solution to a problem.

When I mention this to Stepien, he grabs my notebook and sketches a pair of scissors. One blade he labels "knowledge," the other "process." "You've got to have knowledge and process working together as the blades of a scissor," he says. "I don't know why we spent so many years arguing about who was going to teach knowledge and who was going to teach process. Hell, in real-problem solving, you're going to have to teach both."

Shortly after my arrival at the Illinois Mathematics and Science Academy, I am seated in a small office off the lobby with two other visitors, scientists from Israel, listening to Stepien explain the background behind the problem we are about to watch unfold. While he and another teacher designed the problem, it's based—as are all the problems the students tackle—on an actual case.

Two weeks ago, he informs us, the seniors in his "Society, Science, and the Future" course learned of an apparent August outbreak of pneumonia in the fictional town of "Centerville." Causing one death in a few days, the illness had not responded to treatment with antibiotics, arousing suspicion that the pneumonia was in fact Legionnaires' disease. The students, acting as officials in the county Department of Public Health, must determine the best course of action.

Analysis of the problem had begun, as it always does in problem-based learning, with a blackboard divided into three columns. The first column—labeled "What do we know?"—was necessarily short, essentially a list of people who had gotten sick and their symptoms. The second column—"What do we need to know?"—was lengthy: Students knew virtually nothing about the sickness and how it was transmitted. The second column was crucial, for the third column—"What should we do?"—could not be broached until vital information was considered. Because the disease initially appeared to be so much like pneumonia, the students quickly filled the second column with questions, such as: How much pneumonia could be expected in August? What would be the expected mortality rate? Exactly what is pneumonia, and how is it transmitted? Who is most susceptible?

How the students go about answering the questions they have generated is an important part of problem-based learning. The goal is to make students probing, self-sufficient learners. In this problem, because the students were under severe time constraints—more

> As the students ask narrowing questions, the problem acquires a rich multidimensionality that may compel students to re-examine original assumptions.

and more people were falling ill—it was particularly essential that they gather information in a highly systematic, efficient manner. To prevent unnecessary duplication of information, groups of students took responsibility for answering specific questions, later sharing the data they discovered with the rest of the class.

According to Stepien, true collaborative learning should require students to bring together disparate bits of information. "In a typical classroom," he says, "students collaborate for about 60 seconds; the rest of the time they're discussing weekend plans. The problem is that kids are all holding the same information so there's really no need to collaborate."

Of course, the critical information wasn't tidily bound up in a textbook. The students, under the tutelage of their teacher, had to become creative, persistent researchers. Seeking answers to the pneumonia questions, they searched school and local libraries, scouring through medical texts. Various groups also contacted epidemiologists as well as the county public-health officer.

A Vision of School as a Think Tank

In problem-based learning, one of the goals of requiring such extensive research is to propel students far beyond the boundaries of the classroom. Indeed, at its core is a vision of the school as a kind of think tank, inextricably linked to a community of experts who act as mentors. Because students must proceed as professionals—in this case as health officials—they had to seek out "real-world" sources: doctors, scientists, and government officials.

Once the students analyzed their pooled research and eliminated pneumonia as a cause of the epidemic, Stepien intervened, presenting the students with an "autopsy report" that clearly indicated Legionnaires' disease. Once again, in a recursive process that typifies problem-based learning, the students returned to the three columns, the items in each column shifting as the problem came into greater focus. Among the new questions were: What is the source of Legionnaires'? How is it transmitted? How is it best treated? These questions, in turn, sent students back through the cycle of research. Later, under the "What should we do?" column, the students wrote, "Survey the 22 infected subjects to see if the illness can be traced to a common source."

A well-structured problem demands that students, in striving toward a resolution, take multiple factors—social and scientific, for example—under consideration, and that was the case here. Although the students, in the aftermath of the outbreak, managed to confirm the presence of Legionnaires' and released a bulletin encouraging residents to see a doctor should symptoms occur, they have neglected, Stepien now tells us, critical public relations functions.

Earlier this morning, he released to the students a stern memo from the director of the state Department of Public Health—this actually created by Stepien—demanding to know why the county officials have neglected to communicate with his office. The memo also asked them why they have not communicated with an increasingly exasperated press, producing "an awkward and potentially panic-producing gap."

As Stepien briefs us, then, the seniors are, on very short notice, preparing for a press conference. Dave Workman, a physics teacher who will, along with the school's public relations person, play a reporter, walks in wearing a hat with a placard labeled "press" tucked into the brim. "Let's go," Stepien says. "The press is waiting."

On the stage of another corporate gray room called "The Pit," a girl, flanked by two colleagues, reads a prepared statement. She's composed, making eye contact with the "press" and a video camera sitting in a recessed area beneath the stage. So far, she says, Legionnaires' has resulted in two deaths; 15 or 16 others have come down with the disease, and 22 others have symptoms. But the public need not panic. Centerville's water supply has been deemed safe and Legionnaires', caught in its early stages, can be successfully treated with the drugs erythromycin and rifampin. Furthermore, the county is doing everything possible to locate the source of the bacteria.

The "reporters" begin to inquire. At first their questions, informational in nature, are easily handled; only when they become more interpretative do the students begin to vacillate.

"Why, if the county knows that bacteria often originate in old air-conditioning towers, has it not shut down businesses with those towers?"

"That might cause a panic," a boy says. "Furthermore, it would be unjust to penalize businesses whose towers may not be contaminated."

"Isn't it your duty, as a health officer, to consider public health above all else?"

"Yes, which is why we encourage anyone who shows symptoms to see a doctor immediately."

"Is that enough to tell, say, an 80-year-old man?"

The students look at one another and shrug.

"What specific precautions can the residents take?"

"There's nothing really specific people can do," the girl says. She thinks for a moment and adds, "Just stay healthy."

At the debriefing session that follows, the "reporters" and teachers evaluate the students' performance. Coming in for particular criticism is the "just stay healthy" remark. In the midst of what may be a burgeoning epidemic, the comment, all agree, seems

> ## 'We don't want to indoctrinate students, but we do want them to consider all the arguments out there—just as they must in the real world.'

superfluous and even cynical; what is needed to reassure the public is constructive action.

Here the whole class joins the discussion, trying to sort through a problem that is becoming increasingly complicated and multidimensional. Much of the debate hinges on whether it would be appropriate to close down targeted businesses or to disinfect the air conditioners, or both, raising scientific, social, and eco-

nomic issues. To peremptorily close down businesses, the more vociferous students believe, may impose economic hardship and subject the board to lawsuits, and to disinfect the air conditioners may obliterate all traces of bacteria, meaning they'll never find the source. "We'd look like dorks," a boy says.

As the class ends, the students make several decisions. They'll consult with a lawyer, for one thing, to see if they have the authority to close businesses; for another, they'll see if there isn't a way to disinfect the air conditioners without extirpating the bacteria.

During the discussion, a girl has quietly made what seems a most sensible suggestion: "Perhaps [we] could simply persuade businesses to shut off the air conditioners until the bacteria is discovered." But this suggestion is passed over; the students are focused on the issue of shutting down businesses.

Later, Stepien tells me that one of the things students must learn in problem-based learning is that the loudest students in a group aren't necessarily the ones who should be followed.

When 'Ill-Structured' Means 'Well-Structured'

The Legionnaires' problem is typical of those found in problem-based learning. In the parlance of problem-based learning educators, it is "ill-structured." In a strange twist of words, it is the ill-structured problem that is well-structured for learning. "Ill-structured" simply indicates a problem that changes form as it is worked on; good problems, such as those in the real world, are necessarily slippery, hard to get a handle on, and as students gather new information they must form new hypotheses to match altered conditions.

A history problem Stepien designed is indicative of this ill-structured nature. Students—acting as military, scientific, and diplomatic experts—receive a memo from Secretary of War Henry Stimson, dated July 18, 1945, informing them that President Truman would like their counsel on a strategy "to force the unconditional surrender of Japan and provide for a secure postwar world."

Initially, students may be predisposed to see the problem in absolutist moral terms: Is it right or wrong to unleash the power of the atomic bomb on innocent Japanese civilians? Such a question, asked in isolation, can only result in unwieldy, even sanctimonious, debate. But as the students ask narrowing questions, the answers to which they will spend days researching, the problem acquires a rich multidimensionality that may compel students to re-examine their original assumptions. What do we know about the Japanese mentality and the conduct of warfare? How successful has our blockade been in slowing the Japanese war effort? Does America have an invasion plan? If so, what may it cost in lives?

The answers to these questions demand a constant

realignment of thought, an easing of doctrinaire positions. While dropping the bomb may seem abhorrent, students also realize that, considering Japanese intransigence, to refrain from doing so would prolong a brutal war. Finally, as is typically the case with the ill-structured problem, students must come to accept the fact that there is no ideal answer; whatever resolution they come to—launching an invasion, for example, or waiting for the Russians to join the Pacific war effort—will be tainted with ambiguities, both moral and otherwise.

Getting students to tolerate ambiguity isn't easy. "A lot of kids," Stepien says, "have the conception that when you come up with a solution, you make the problem go away, and that's untrue. We talk about making something unacceptable more acceptable. Improvement through solution, not rectification, is what we're looking for. The point is that students inevitably must

> # If problem-based learning is going to find a permanent place in American schools, teachers as well as students will have to unlearn certain behaviors.

act, regardless of their doubts. What they've discovered has to be put to work in resolution."

Perhaps no problem poses more difficult moral ambiguities to students than "Jane's Baby." The problem, thoroughly documented in IMSA's literature, involves a woman carrying a fetus that has just been diagnosed as anencephalic—a disorder that invariably results, the students discover, in the death of the infant soon after birth. The students, here in the position of heads of pediatrics at a large city hospital, must decide how they should advise Jane Barton and her husband, Ralph, played by school faculty members.

The students begin by carefully structuring questions: Is the test for anencephaly highly reliable? Is abortion possible in this case? Do the personal and religious beliefs of the Bartons permit abortion? What is the law on abortion in this particular state? Further complicating the issue is the fact that tissue or organs from the fetus could be donated to research. Later, the students, cast in the role of members of Congress, will try to push legislation overturning President Reagan's executive ban on the use of fetal tissue from elective abortions.

As the students gather information, they realize, as in the case with the atomic bomb, that the problem is inherently ambiguous and even confounding. Ideally, it leads, as a realistic problem, not to purely speculative debate about the rightness or wrongness of abortion but to an eventual course of action derived from a careful consideration of the many messy particulars. The hope, as the academy materials put it, is that the "ill-structured problem will lead students to a reiterative process of speculation, problem definition, hypothesis formation, information gathering, analysis, and problem redefinition several times before the problem is resolved." In short, the problem should lead to all the things that catalyze thinking and rethinking rather than rote memorization.

It seemed controversial, even risky, for the school to ask students to tackle the abortion issue. Because the problem demanded that students act as consulting doctors, they were placed in the awkward position of perhaps having to suggest a course of action that could contradict their own deeply held beliefs. Was it fair, I ask Stepien, to demand that students face such a knotty problem?

Stepien thinks for a moment. "We don't want to indoctrinate students," he finally says, "but we do want them to consider all the arguments out there—just as they must in the real world. Now, if it's a case of moral belief, we would rather have their church or philosophical system handle it. If the students want to bring their belief system to the problem, there's no way we can avoid that.

"In the 'Jane's Baby' problem, the kids each had to meet the Bartons, to do a consultation. When the patients asked, 'Are you suggesting we have an abortion?' students said, 'Talk to your clergy, to your family.' The students felt patients should make the call.

"We had one student who never mentioned the abortion option; he simply didn't believe in abortion, across the board. Other students felt they had to tell patients of the abortion option, even as they felt there were better alternatives. The point is that morality has to come in; it's part of life. But we want a rigorous discussion of morals to take place, not indoctrination."

Still, it was apparent that bringing certain problems into certain schools is a risky proposition. Stepien wouldn't want to bring an affirmative-action problem into a recession-savaged industrial city where white ethnics were being laid off, would he?

"Of course not," he says. "But you could do something else, like with the northern spotted owl in Washington State. Is it worth protecting no matter what, even though it may cost loggers their jobs and way of life?"

Innate Desire To Learn

Problem-based learning advocates, like a variety of progressive educators, typically operate on the assumption that all children have an innate desire to learn. Those with a less sanguine view of human nature—those who think that even the more conscientious children must occasionally be pushed and prodded into learning—may take issue with educators who think that children simply need to be faced with challenging problems.

Still, teachers using problem-based learning with diverse groups of students seem uniformly enthusiastic about its results. Ira Rosencrantz, a teacher at DeWitt-Clinton High School in Bronx, N.Y., incorporated problem-based learning into a biology curriculum for "slow" 9th graders. Although he was initially apprehensive about giving students the freedom to explore on their own, he found that there was a lot more participation and constructive activity in class. "You can't just get up in a room and tell these students, 'This is the lecture for today: topic, infectious diseases,'" Rosencrantz says. "The good thing about problem-based learning is that everyone must become actively involved."

Bill Orton, who uses problem-based learning extensively in his 2nd grade classroom at Rawls Byrd School in Chickahominy, Va., says that his students were so taken with solving problems that they even had their parents buy them chalkboards so they could visually represent the challenges. "Of course, when kids have to learn things like the multiplication tables, they just have to sit down and learn them," Orton says. "But when critical thinking is the goal, kids, not teachers, must be at the center."

The types of problems Orton uses are reminiscent of those Dewey attempted at his Laboratory School decades ago. One problem has 2nd graders learning the rudiments of algebra by designing and building a geometric dome that will act as an observatory. Another problem, designed to teach students about metamorphosis in caterpillars and butterflies, has students creating a wildflower garden that will attract butterflies. Long before the children begin to plant the garden, they must determine which flowers and geometric arrangements are most suited for their purpose.

Of everyone I talked to about problem-based learning, perhaps no one was more zealous about its potential than Shelagh Gallagher, who, as former associate director of the Center for Gifted Education at the College of William and Mary in Williamsburg, Va., helped develop a K-8 problem-based science curriculum that a number of schools are using.

"If we had problem-based learning from kindergarten through 6th grade, we'd have a most powerful group of learners," Gallagher says. "If, instead of hand-holding children, we expected them to be responsible learners, they'd accomplish amazing things. They'd have not only improved cognitive abilities but also an improved ability to function, to get things done."

She talks about a problem-based learning project for 2nd graders that she was involved in. "I must admit, I walked into this 2nd grade project with trepidation because both teachers and students were using a wholly new approach. Yet, I discovered that the 2nd graders were almost the best—open to the notion that they had a problem to solve. This particular problem involved the dying ecosystem of Planet X; the students were mission specialists trying to save it. They started asking questions right away. What's wrong with the planet? Can we grow plants that will thrive there? What kind of pH levels do we need? How can we transport them?

"As well as these 2nd graders did, they still had to learn and even unlearn a number of things. They had to learn not to expect that the teacher was going to answer all the questions. They had to learn not to raise their hands at every juncture. And they had to learn to take risks and to consider many ideas that aren't necessarily all right or all wrong."

If problem-based learning is going to find a permanent place in American schools, teachers as well as students will have to unlearn certain behaviors. Problem-based learning demands, for instance, that the teacher substantially relinquish the role of expert in favor of becoming a kind of metacognitive coach who helps students become attentive to how they're lea ing as well as to what they're learning. And, to a mu greater extent, teachers must be willing to allow students to pursue their interests, even if it takes them beyond the confines of the curriculum. As Gallagher says: "If pH comes up, teach pH. You don't have to wait until the third month of the 7th grade chemistry curriculum."

Of course, there's no guarantee that schools will be willing to change even if teachers are; many will have to be pushed into providing teachers with the flexibility that problem-based learning requires. Furthermore, constructing sound problems is arduous and time-consuming. Clearly, teachers will have to be provided with both materials and intensive training in how to use them.

Still, working to bring problem-based learning into the schools seems worthwhile, despite the many obstacles that will have to be overcome. ∎

From Teacher Magazine, *January 1993*

13.

Kids Learn When It Matters

Students will take formal schooling seriously when they can see that it relates to their own lives and experiences.

Commentary by Morris J. Vogel

This spring I watched my 15-year-old son study for his final exams. In science, as in several of his other courses, studying meant memorizing lists of hundreds of words and their accompanying definitions.

By the time he took the exam, he was able to spit back dictionary identifications of terms ranging from saturated carbohydrate to degrees Kelvin. This exercise reduced science to an interminable series of facts devoid of context, and struck him—and me—as pointless. Few of these words held any real meaning for him. He no more knew the workings of science or its purposes at the end of the process than he did when he began to "learn" the subject. He would have been as well served by memorizing strings of nonsense words drawn from Lewis Carroll or generated by computer failure. And yet he—like most of the students in his academically oriented suburban high school—is mastering the words and the courses.

There are lessons aplenty in why some of our nation's children succeed in high school, and go on to college, careers, and productive lives. Examining these successes may even teach us why our high schools are failing many of their students.

Those content with superficial explanations may simply note that students who work hard master whatever their schools demand. If we hold this position, we can wish away our education crisis by insisting that children apply themselves and memorize the required facts. Former Secretary of Education William

J. Bennett long advocated this view, even identifying specific facts as prerequisites for informed citizenship. Our anxious fascination with Japan's success has led us to note similarly that Japanese schools emphasize rote learning through endless, repetitive drills.

But before we impose lock-step curricula, national exams, and a back-to-basics approach on our less successful high schools, we might consider further why the children of our privileged suburbs—and Japanese children—learn and do well in school. Might it be that these children correctly understand school as a hurdle to be jumped, an obstacle whose mastery brings them parental love, social approbation, and the prospect of adult success? There is little need to examine what these schools teach, because what their students learn often has no intrinsic value; the extrinsic rewards learning brings matter most. Learning happens because students understand that it is consequential in their own lives.

To leave matters at that is to risk failing the poor and often minority children of our inner cities. To say that schools succeed and students learn if their parents are involved, if their peers are similarly engaged, and if their culture values education is to say that schools work when society works. But society doesn't work that way for many of our children. We can't provide urban high schools with a mind-numbing curriculum and then blame broken and discouraged families for not motivating children to study it. We can't tell city children that mastering high school coursework will bring them the good life when all around

FRANCIS WASHINGTON

them the culture of despair teaches them to minimize their expectations—and to connect few of their hopes with staying in school and getting a formal education.

This is not to say that schools can't make up for some of society's shortcomings. Indeed it means we have no choice but to transform schools in order to promote student success. We can make high schools smaller so that they resemble extended families in offering students emotional support; we can link the curricula of these smaller schools-within-schools to rewarding careers, and reinforce that message by regular exposure to real-world settings in which students see adults from backgrounds similar to theirs holding meaningful and well-paying jobs. The burden of proof is on us if we are to convince disadvantaged students that learning is consequential.

We can also apply what we know about consequential learning to the very core of education. We can make learning matter—in and of itself—in the lives of our students. We have only to look at the early primary grades—in cities as well as suburbs—to see children enthusiastic about learning and about exploring their expanding intellectual skills. Most 1st and 2nd graders feel good about school—and just as importantly, about themselves—because they know that they are acquiring mastery that matters in the real world. They feel empowered as they learn to read, to

add, to subtract, and to figure things out for themselves. This is learning with a consequence; this is learning that happens because children understand that it matters in their own lives.

We ought to imagine this kind of learning in our high schools, urban and suburban alike. Why not build a curriculum that teach essential skills by allowing students to actively explore their own worlds? Why not teach American history, for example, by focusing on questions about the society in which students live? Why not root biology courses in the life experience of human communities, in relations between recognizable organisms and familiar environments?

A curriculum thus connected to the immediate and the specific can command the attention of students as it proceeds to the distant and the abstract. A curriculum that takes seriously the experience of students offers a real prospect of having otherwise unconnected students take formal schooling seriously.

The alternative is a curriculum that commands students what they ought to know and national tests that tell us that they haven't learned it. ■

Morris J. Vogel is a professor and the chairman of the department of history at Temple University.

From Education Week, *Sept. 25, 1991*

14.

The Unschooled Mind

Teachers need to address the flawed theories that children bring to school, argues Harvard psychologist Howard Gardner.

By Daniel Gursky

Ask a 5-year-old why it's hot in the summer, and she'll probably say it's because the Earth is closer to the sun. Ask a high school senior the same question, and the chances are good you'll get the same answer. Both are wrong; seasons result from the angle of the Earth on its axis as it orbits the sun. The high school senior, like the 5-year-old, is responding on the basis of powerful, instinctive ideas about the world that everyone develops early in life. Through experience, the child learns that the closer one gets to a source of heat, the hotter it is; using a child's logic, the same must be true of the Earth and the sun.

Such intuitive thinking is fine for a preschooler, but not for a high school senior. Hasn't more than a decade of formal instruction made any difference in the student's thinking? Not as much as most people believe, nor as much as it should have, says Harvard University psychologist Howard Gardner. In his new book, *The Unschooled Mind: How Children Think and How Schools Should Teach*, Gardner argues that inside every student—indeed, inside every person—there's a 5-year-old "unschooled mind" struggling to express itself.

"Just as Freud stressed the degree to which the adult personality harbors within it the complexes and strivings of the Oedipal child," Gardner writes, "I maintain that students (and non-students) continue to be strongly affected by the practices, beliefs, and understandings of the 5-year-old mind."

Children, Gardner explains, come to school with robust, but often flawed, theories about themselves, about other people, and about the world. Instead of challenging and building on these theories, schools ignore them and proceed to teach a new set. Even though these theories may be contradictory, they can coexist in the child's mind. In school, the student may be able to feed back information to the teacher on request, using the theories taught in the classroom, but the flawed ideas haven't been abandoned. As a consequence, Gardner argues, once outside the school, the student reverts to the theories of the 5-year-old mind when confronting new situations.

This startling theory is the latest work in Gardner's prolific and diverse career. He's best known for his theory of multiple intelligences, but his dozen books run the gamut from a psychology textbook to works on topics as varied as children's scribbling, brain damage, and China's educational system. Whatever the subject, his work attracts attention. And *The Unschooled Mind* promises to add more variety and complexity to the growing national debate about teaching and learning.

"I think Howard's one of the freshest, most original minds working in this area," says Jerome Bruner, a psychologist at New York University and one of Gardner's former teachers at Harvard. "His contributions have been major, not only by making us aware of the different forms of intelligence but also in terms of following through with what he has learned and coming up with interesting curricular ideas."

William Damon, chairman of Brown University's education department, expects *The Unschooled Mind* to have a powerful impact on education. "The book," he says, "is very innovative but at the same time very careful and responsible. It really sets out a new direction for how to approach education."

Gardner's Harvard office is a classic academic's space: crowded, strewn with papers, and dominated by large filing cabinets. The 48-year-old psychologist is dressed in the casual attire befitting a professor: light blue shirt with sleeves rolled up, olive-green pants, no tie.

Seated in a rocking chair in front of a computer, Gardner argues that the problems with schools are much more extensive than most educators realize. "While everybody knows there are problems with many schools," he notes, underscoring the point with broad hand gestures, "I think most people assume that our best schools are fine." Not so, he says. Even in schools with the highest test scores, students who master the material adequately enough to perform well in class and on exams don't really understand what they're being taught.

Howard Gardner with son (left) and friend

In *The Unschooled Mind*, Gardner writes about a phone conversation with his daughter, Kerith, that brought this point home. When Kerith—who had done well in high school physics—called from college, distressed about her physics class, Gardner offered some fatherly advice: Don't worry so much about the grade, he told her, just try to understand the material. "You don't get it, Dad," Kerith replied. "I've never understood it."

Kerith has plenty of company. Many top students at elite universities exhibit fragile understanding, at best. In one study Gardner cites, engineering students were asked, "What forces are acting on a coin tossed straight up that has reached the midpoint of its trajectory?" Some 70 percent of students who had taken

a mechanics course answered, incorrectly, that two forces—gravity and the original force of the hand that tossed the coin—were at work. In fact, only gravity is present.

Such misconceptions about physics provide the most striking evidence of Gardner's thesis, but he spends a good deal of his new book detailing common—but incorrect—thoughts and stereotypes that show up in other academic disciplines, as well. In math classes, for example, most calculus students can competently plug numbers into equations, but even the best students flounder when problems are phrased a little differently or applied to real-life situations. In the humanities and social sciences, people tend to respond to issues on the basis of dominant images and stereotypes, even when faced with contradictory evidence. During the Persian Gulf war, Gardner points out, huge numbers of Americans saw the conflict solely in terms of good guys vs. bad guys, demonstrating the same level of sophistication as that of a young child watching a car In reality, the comp. history, culture, and economics of the Middle East make such Hollywood-like analyses inadequate.

Why does this happen? Because the 5-year-old mind reasserts itself when a person confronts difficult questions outside school. "You should talk to 5-year-olds," Gardner says. "They're very smart. They've got very powerful theories about how the world works, and they've got very powerful theories about how people work. They're very serviceable theories." Unfortunately, however, they are often flawed.

The problem, Gardner says, is that schools ignore the strongly held notions of their young charges; teachers treat students as if their minds are empty and need to be filled with new information. "If you don't confront students' ideas and show where they're adequate and where they're inadequate, those ideas are going to remain there," he argues. "They're going to be ready to pounce like a Trojan horse as soon as the children escape from the schoolroom."

Every parent can cite examples of child logic. Gardner offers one from his 6-year-old son, Benjamin: "I can tell Benjamin that the Earth is round and he'll repeat that. But then, if I say, 'Where are you?' he'll say, 'I'm on the flat part.' He repeats the information, but he converts it to something that makes sense to him. The Earth doesn't look round to him."

Students of all ages do the same thing. They may be able to provide the expected response on homework or a test, but that rote answer offers no guarantee that they understand the material. This disparity between teaching and understanding distresses Gardner because he sees "genuine understanding"—understanding that goes beyond repetitive learning and short answers—as the fundamental goal of education. "No one ever asks the further question, 'But do you really understand?'" Gardner writes. "The gap between what passes for understanding and genuine understanding remains great."

Gardner doesn't hesitate to propose his own solutions for promoting genuine understanding. *The Unschooled Mind* goes beyond description and analysis; it outlines his most explicit prescription yet about how to reform schools. He proposes an education system suffused with individual and group projects, particularly apprenticeships and the hands-on experiences offered in children's museums, because he believes projects can restore the context sorely missing from students' school experience. As often as possible, Gardner asserts, students should work with and learn from adult experts in their fields.

Outside of education, people's lives basically revolve around projects. But that's still a "blind spot" in schools, Gardner explains. "I often hypothesize that people probably learn more from the few projects they do in school than from hundreds and hundreds of hours of lectures and homework assignments," he says. "I imagine that many people end up finding their vocation or avocation because they stumbled into a project and discovered they were really interested in it." By the same token, once they're immersed in a project, students might realize they're not really interested in a subject.

Schools, Gardner believes, should pay more attention to helping students discover subject areas that interest them. By focusing on basic skills, schools risk suppressing the positive aspects of children's minds—adventurousness, flexibility, creativity—as well as their natural enthusiasm for learning.

"To declare oneself against the institution of the three R's in the school is like being against motherhood or the flag," he writes. "Beyond question, students ought to be literate and ought to revel in their literacy. Yet the essential emptiness of this goal is dramatized by the fact that young children in the United States are becoming literate in a literal sense; that is, they are mastering the rules of reading and writing, even as they are learning their addition and multiplication tables. What is missing are not the decoding skills, but two other facets: the capacity to read for understanding and the desire to read at all."

In *The Unschooled Mind*, Gardner suggests ways teachers can help students confront their misconceptions and flawed theories in order to develop deeper understanding. One way is through what he calls "Christopherian encounters," named for Christopher Columbus because Columbus challenged the conventional wisdom of his day that the Earth was flat.

In such encounters, students' intuitive ideas are validated or proved false by comparing them with more sophisticated theories about how the world works. For example, a computer simulation that allows physics students to manipulate such forces as velocity and acceleration on an image on the screen might challenge the students' assumptions about the influence of gravity. Or history students might reconsider their beliefs about the causes of World War I by examining conflicting accounts of the same event. The key, Gardner explains, is for students to contemplate and analyze material from as many different angles as possible.

"When I talk about Christopherian encounters," he says, "the point I'm trying to make is that the only way to transform our conceptions is for these things to become a major agenda of schools from the very first years. It's got to be something that's done over and over again."

These notions about the mismatch between the way schools teach and the way students learn will undoubtedly challenge people's assumptions about learning in the same way Gardner's 1983 book, *Frames of Mind*, forced people to question their assumptions about intelligence. That book stirred controversy among educators and academics and fueled many cocktail party conversations. In it, Gardner argues that instead of having one all-encompassing mental aptitude that can be measured by an IQ test, people have at least seven separate and distinct intelligences:

● Linguistic: A sensitivity to the meaning and order of words and the ability to make varied use of language; translators or poets exhibit this intelligence.

● Logical-mathematical: The ability to handle chains of reasoning and recognize patterns; mathematicians and scientists exhibit this intelligence.

● Spatial: The ability to perceive the visual world accurately and re-create or transform aspects of it based on those perceptions; sculptors and architects, for example, exhibit this intelligence.

● Musical: A sensitivity to pitch, melody, rhythm, and tone; composers and singers exhibit this intelligence.

● Bodily-kinesthetic: The ability to use the body and handle objects skillfully; athletes, dancers, and surgeons exhibit this intelligence.

● Interpersonal: The ability to notice and make distinctions among other people; politicians, salespeople, and religious leaders exhibit this intelligence.

● Intrapersonal: The ability to understand one's own feelings and emotional life; therapists and social workers exhibit this intelligence.

Gardner categorized these intelligences by reviewing studies of a range of people: prodigies, gifted people, brain-damaged patients, idiot savants, individuals from diverse cultures, and experts in various lines of work, as well as typical children and adults. Support for his belief in distinct intelligences comes in part from cases of people who lose their ability to speak but can paint beautifully, or from autistic children who can sing dozens of songs perfectly.

People possess every intelligence in varying strengths, giving everyone a unique "profile" of intelligences, Gardner says. Unfortunately, most schools and teachers emphasize the linguistic and logical-mathematical perspectives at the expense of other areas.

"It's important to recognize that there are many people who could make wonderful contributions to the world who don't happen to have that particular blend," Gardner says. "And if we are concerned with those individuals' lives, we cannot ignore this fact."

Not everyone buys into Gardner's theory. Some leading psychologists, including Yale University's Robert Sternberg, have argued that Gardner has

---

Gardner wrote his book *Frames of Mind* for psychologists and educated lay readers; teachers, however, provided the most enthusiastic response.

---

merely described various talents, not intelligences. Sandra Scarr, a psychologist at the University of Virginia, has called Gardner's ideas on multiple intelligences a theory "in which everything good in human behavior is called intelligence." Other skeptics have said the that theory provides a convenient excuse for almost any poor performance by students, who can plead inferior intelligence whenever they encounter difficulties.

Still, many teachers find the notion "immediately liberating," Gardner says. But, he adds, that doesn't automatically translate into better teaching. "To get teachers to think deeply about their strengths, their students' strengths, and how to achieve curricular goals while taking those strengths and different profiles seriously is a huge job," he says. Teachers can't be

expected to become "multiple intelligence mavens," as he puts it, but they should know where to send students for help in, say, music or dance.

Furthermore, an awareness of multiple intelligences can suggest to teachers various ways to present the same material. "So long as one takes only a single perspective or tack on a concept or problem," Gardner writes, "it is virtually certain that students will understand that concept in only the most limited and rigid fashion."

Gardner's ideas about learning and intelligence aren't just the theoretical fancies of an Ivy League academic. For more than 20 years, he has put them to the test at Harvard Project Zero, an interdisciplinary research group that conducts various small-scale studies with teachers and students at different Massachusetts schools. Gardner is co-director of the project, which began in the mid-1960s with a focus on arts education. While he retains a special interest in the arts and artistic creativity, the group has expanded its focus to cover a wide range of topics relating to curriculum, teaching, and assessment.

Not surprisingly, the projects usually require teachers and students to rethink some long-held ideas. Gardner says most people, teachers included, endorse the same view of education they had when they were 5 years old: Schools are authoritarian, punitive institutions in which somebody smart stands in front of a room and tries to pass information on to large groups of students.

Project Zero's undertakings bear little resemblance to this vision of traditional schooling. One of its early childhood programs, for example, attempts to provide young children with a more rounded education than most typically experience. Preschoolers and primary students in Project Spectrum, as this study is known, explore a range of different learning areas, such as the naturalist's corner, the storytelling area, and the building corner, to name just three of the dozen or so areas that are available. Teachers at Project Spectrum form an impression of the children's strengths and weaknesses by watching them participate in the various games and activities. At the end of the year, they recommend specific activities that parents can do at home or around that community to stimulate the child's learning.

In *The Unschooled Mind*, Gardner writes about one 6-year-old boy who was doing so badly in a regular school that he seemed certain to be held back. In Project Spectrum, the boy proved himself best in the class at assembly tasks, such as taking apart and putting together doorknobs, food grinders, and other common objects. Building on his success in this area, he went on to improve his overall school performance. Once the boy saw he could succeed and realized he had abilities valued by other people, he gained the confidence to do better in other areas, Gardner says.

Gardner's ideas have also provided the framework

for the Key School, a public elementary school in Indianapolis that operates on the principle that each child should have his or her many intelligences stimulated every day. "Practically everything we do is put through the filter of multiple intelligences," says Patricia Bolanos, the magnet school's principal.

All Key School students participate in computing, music, and body movement and spend part of each day in one of a dozen apprenticeship-like pods, working with peers, teachers, and other professionals on skills ranging from architecture to gardening to making money.

> Only when teachers acknowledge the assumptions made by a 5-year-old mind, Gardner says, will students internalize the lessons taught in school.

During each 10-week term, the curriculum focuses on a theme; students complete a project dealing with some aspect of the theme, often working with other students or members of the community. They then present their projects to classmates, who ask questions and help the teacher and the presenters assess the work. The presentations are recorded on videotape, so students accumulate a video portfolio over the years.

Although Gardner has no official role at the school—he's an informal consultant—Bolanos says the school's six-year association with him has helped establish its credibility. Word of the school has circulated nationwide. As a result, Bolanos and her staff have received hundreds of requests over the past few years from educators and others wishing to visit.

Teachers at the Key School aren't the only ones flooded with requests from people who want to know more about multiple-intelligence theory and how it applies to schools. Eight years after the publication of *Frames of Mind*, Gardner still can't keep up with all the letters and calls he receives requesting information about his theory. Gardner admits that the book

received the sort of publicity most authors—and certainly most psychologists—only dream of. Still, the acclaim wasn't entirely new: In 1981, Gardner was selected as one of the first MacArthur Foundation Fellows, a distinction that included a five-year "genius" award of $196,000 and a lot of attention.

But his prominence spread far beyond academic circles with the publication of his theory of multiple intelligences two years later. Today, the theory has attained pop-culture status; *Washington Post* political reporter Lou Cannon even examined Ronald Reagan through the multiple-intelligence lens in his recent book *Ronald Reagan: The Role of a Lifetime*. Last year, Gardner's work on intelligence earned him another prestigious honor, the Grawemeyer Award in education from the University of Louisville; the award came with a $150,000 stipend.

"I could lead one life just giving workshops and speeches to people who are interested in knowing more about multiple intelligences," Gardner says. "There are about a dozen books already out on the topic and half a dozen people making a living giving workshops on it, none of whom I have anything to do with. I could lead another life just answering all the mail I get for requests for information about it."

Gardner has resisted offers from publishers who would like him to capitalize on this interest and write more "popular" books—something like *The Seven Smarts*, as he puts it. He wrote *Frames of Mind* for psychologists and educated lay readers; but, as it turned out, teachers and other educators provided the most enthusiastic response. With *The Unschooled Mind*, Gardner hopes to reach teachers again, this time with his theories about the 5-year-old mind.

"I think the new book will strike a chord among good teachers," Gardner predicts, "because good teachers will say, 'I've been assuming all along that what I teach is getting across. Here's a guy who seems to know what he's talking about saying that, in fact, what I teach has very little impact, especially after my students leave the classroom.'"

Gardner doesn't want teachers to merely read the book and put it down; he would like them to think about their teaching and embrace approaches to education that focus on genuine understanding. Only when teachers acknowledge and build on the assumptions made by the 5-year-old mind, he says, will students internalize the lessons taught in school and be able to apply them outside the classroom. ∎

From Teacher Magazine, *November/December 1991*

15.

Play Is Part of Learning, Too

Play is an effective learning strategy that children use to advance their skills and make sense of their world.

Commentary by Colette Daiute

School is back in session, and children are supposed to get serious. They have had time to play during the summer, and now it is time for them to work. While such reasoning is familiar to most of us, this dichotomy between play and work is one of the greatest myths of education—a dangerous myth that often leads to leaving children out of the educational agenda and ignoring the quality of their life in school. Testing, longer school days, and parental choice all resonate with the theme of increasing the work children do in school, yet play is a powerful learning process. Clearly, there is work children have to do in school, and some structure is necessary when many people are sharing resources, but given the freedom to work on challenging tasks in the company of their peers, children devise purposeful and ingenious lessons for themselves in the context of their classroom play.

Young children do some of their most important learning through play. "Peekaboo" helps them learn that the world exists independently of themselves and is often predictable. "Pat-a-cake," a cooperative game, enhances physical and social development. And children make one of the most dramatic of human accomplishments—learning language—by playing with sounds and meanings from the time they are born.

After kindergarten, though, children are abruptly expected to think and to express themselves like little adults, even as they continue to make discoveries and develop their talents by playing. I have seen, in my re-search, how play supports children's literacy development—even up through the 5th grade, when play is all but banned from the classroom.

The transcript of a brief conversation between Andy and Russ, two 3rd graders in an urban school, shows how children do difficult work such as figuring out the spelling system of English—when they have the freedom to explore academic material on their own terms. When asked to write a report for the class newspaper on events during the Renaissance, Andy and Russ engaged in an effective spelling exercise as they played with the sounds of Christopher Columbus' name:

Andy: Yea, I spelled it right! I think.
Russ: N, no.
Andy: Oh *(raspberry sounds)*, oops, I forgot one L. I didn't look at that. Forgot the L.
Russ: Challenged Christopher Columbus and his crew.
Andy: This was a great challenge for.
Russ: Chrissy.
Andy: Chrissy? *(Laughter)*. This is a great challenge for Chris.
Russ: For Mr. Columbus *(Laughter)* ...
Andy: It's shorter! *(Laughter)*.
Russ: Put Mr. Columbus.
Andy: Mr. Columbus.
Russ: Columulumbus.
Andy: Colum, Columbumps *(Laughter)*.
Russ: Colum.

Andy: Colummus? Colum, Clom, Come, Columbus?
Russ: Lumberjack *(Laughter)* ...
Andy: Colombos, Columbus. Columbus ...
Russ: Colummmmbabababababb. Ohhew. B U S. I think that's how you spell it ...
Andy: Col-um-bus. Ya, you're right.
Russ: Christopher Columbus. Collumm.
Andy: Ya, where ... Columbus, Columbus. The Spaniard Christopher Columbus discovered Amer ica. Now do you know how to spell the last three letters of Christopher Columbus? Oh, I already asked you. Forget it.
Russ: Actually, he rediscovered America.
Andy: No, U S.
Russ: And he even made friends with some Indians.

While this play may seem capricious, it is actually rule-governed. Breaking down the sounds of unfamiliar words, as Andy and Russ did, helps children with the task of writing about challenging material. After rejecting the temptation to shorten Columbus's name to make it easier to spell, Andy and Russ played with the name—"Columulumbus," "Columbumps," "Colummus" which involved analyzing the sounds of the word, testing a variety of sounds, and eventually coming up with the right spelling.

Although these same students might groan when given a spelling test by the teacher, they have challenged themselves to explore the rules of spelling and to use these rules as they composed a complex piece of writing—the way that expert authors do. In fact, rather than goofing off when allowed to work together, Andy and Russ, like other children, played around material they had not yet mastered, seizing an opportunity to advance their skills.

While play may seem silly, it is children's way of making sense of the world. Just as younger children take some control over their lives by playing doctor or Mommy and Daddy, older children can take control of intellectual material by playing with it in relation to personally meaningful themes. When children play, they may appear to stray from the topic, but what they are doing is exploring the topic in relation to their own knowledge, needs, and talents. Since new knowledge is learned only when it relates to prior knowledge, playing is a sound way to create bases for new learning.

Allowing children to use their own knowledge as a springboard for learning is also a way to build the curriculum on diverse strengths. Education may be failing in our country because too little attention has been given to making sure that lessons make sense to the diverse population of children in our schools. So finding ways to support children's play around their schoolwork is worth more effort than reforms that repeat past failed attempts at telling children what is supposed to make sense.

Play is also an effective learning strategy because it allows children to take risks—which is essential when studying challenging material. Trying out a new word or using unfamiliar concepts is easier for children to do with a friend in jest than with a teacher who evaluates them and expects to see them at their most competent. In formal lessons, only the most confident children take such risks, but in the safe context of play, even low-achieving students take on intellectual challenges, examining and using academic materials as they would their toys, and they improve their performance in this process. Allowing play in the classroom means supporting children's ownership of intellectual material, and such ownership is the right of all children.

Finally, the laughter in Andy and Russ's lesson is also one of the reasons why it leads to growth. Laughter provides social and emotional support to intellectual development, providing links between the mastery of skills and the ability to use skills during the course of life. The positive feelings evoked during play give children courage to propose and test hypotheses, such as the probing ideas Andy and Russ began to explore about Columbus: Was he really the one who discovered America? What about the people who were there before him? By having the chance to say what they think rather than only what they are supposed to think, children advance their critical-thinking skills.

Through play, children spontaneously design activities that involve them in taking responsibility over

> # When children play, they appear to stray from the topic, but what they are doing is exploring the topic in relation to their own knowledge, needs, and talents.

their own learning. It is difficult to think of a more sound educational goal. Yet, reforms continue to propose options that put the power elsewhere—with parents, in tests, in school restructuring—not with the teacher. Clearly, the job of becoming literate, knowledgeable, and critical does not end with exploring the logic of the English spelling system or social issues. But the kind of analysis, sense-making, and hypothesis-testing children do when they play in school sets a firm basis for their intellectual development.

Yet, even when play is properly understood as an effective learning process, several misconceptions keep it out of the classroom. One concern about play is whether it creates chaos. On the contrary, play flourishes in classrooms where teachers provide structure and guidance. For example, the teacher creates a meaningful task such as writing a class newspaper, asking children to work together and to use facts and concepts they have been studying. The collaborative process and the common goal provide the structure. And far from being chaotic, children's play in school is remarkably on-task.

Another concern raised recently is that when teachers allow children to play in school, they may be depriving students of the benefits of instruction. While this could happen, play and formal instruction work best when they work together. Teachers can offer pre-

> # Through play, children design activities that involve them in taking responsibility over their learning. It is difficult to think of a more sound educational goal.

cise guidelines on spelling, vocabulary, facts, and the rules of classroom discourse. But these rules are likely to be more useful to children if they can appropriate them in their own ways. If children write reports with a classmate, for example, they can practice using school rules in their own language, lingering over aspects that interest or challenge them. In this way, children have a hand in designing the curriculum as they adapt it and introduce new elements. Creating classrooms in which children own the goals, contents, and

strategies through spontaneous processes like play means providing all children with points of access and control.

There is great concern that schools in the United States are lax in comparison with those in other countries whose children score higher on achievement tests. Since a major cause of the problem is reported to be that our schools do not require children to work as hard or suffer as rigorous exams as children in other countries, allowing children to play in school might be last on the list of reforms. Yet, far from being antithetical to work, play is children's way of working. Children use play to challenge themselves, design their own lessons, and test themselves. When children in other countries do better, we should explore the culturally relevant ways of making schoolwork meaningful in those countries. Play may provide a rationale for learning that we have not otherwise conveyed to our students.

The schools and classrooms where playful learning occurs are structured with children in mind. They are schools where children are respected as special and unique and where institutional and pedagogical structures invite children to express themselves and to participate in planning—albeit in subtle ways. For young children, play is learning. Play means making sense, taking control, creating mastery. When we listen to children's play in the classroom, what we hear are their designs for education. Given a meaningful task, children as young as 8 use play as a way to stay on topic—not veer from its challenge themselves—not avoid their work—and make discoveries that are more profound than silly.

Yes, learning should be fun, and finding ways to bring learning alive to children in classrooms should be on the educational agenda. ■

Colette Daiute is a professor at the Graduate School and University Center at City University of New York.

From Education Week, *Oct. 2, 1991*

16.

The Dangers of Inclusion

Educators say federal laws are tying their hands on disciplining students with disabilities.

By Lynn Schnaiberg

At the start of his kindergarten year last fall, Jimmy sometimes ran around the classroom and yelled when his teacher tried to present a lesson. But by the winter, Jimmy P., as he is called in court documents, had become more violent, according to officials at the Ocean View school district in Huntington Beach, Calif.

School officials said the 6-year-old, who weighs slightly more than 100 pounds, hit and bit his teacher, threw chairs and desks, hit his classmates, and kicked staff members at Circle View Elementary School.

They suspended Jimmy for a few days, but when he returned, his behavior worsened, said James R. Tarwater, the district superintendent.

By the end of the school year, Jimmy's teacher and a classroom aide, both citing severe stress, had taken medical leaves.

Concerned that Jimmy's behavior was endangering his classmates and school personnel, district officials wanted to remove Jimmy from the class.

But, under the law, they could not.

Jimmy has a communicative disorder and is protected by a federal law that says students with disabilities cannot be moved from their current classroom placements unless their parents agree.

And Jimmy could not be suspended long term because of a 1988 U.S. Supreme Court decision that effectively put a 10-day cap on suspensions of disabled students.

Educators such as Tarwater say federal laws are tying their hands on disciplining students with disabilities and putting schools at risk for lawsuits from parents of other students who fear for their children's safety.

At the annual meeting of the National Association of State Directors of Special Education in Grand Rapids, Mich., this month, a special-education lawyer called on the state directors to "get out a memo on discipline, and get it out damn fast" to school districts. The lawyer, Lynwood E. Beekman, said districts across the country are vulnerable to discipline-related suits.

Educators say the rules create a double standard in the classroom. Students with disabilities are treated one way and students without disabilities another.

Situations such as Jimmy P.'s at Circle View Elementary have brought growing attention to the issue of discipline and students with disabilities—an issue that in many cases is wrapped up in the movement toward "full inclusion" of students with disabilities into regular classrooms in their neighborhood schools.

The American Federation of Teachers, a vocal critic of the full-inclusion movement, points to similar situations across the country. Union officials say teachers are being asked to go through too much in the name of what they see as "political correctness."

Proponents of full inclusion say that more inclusive school environments offer students realistic preparation for life and that segregation stigmatizes and isolates students with disabilities.

In many cases, the discipline issue has become a

lightning rod for educators who say they are frustrated by special education's cost, litigiousness, and regulation.

Father Disputes Risk

In the case of Jimmy P., his father did not want the boy moved from his regular classroom, so the district sought an injunction from a state court to override him. The injunction was granted, but a federal judge reversed the state court, saying the injuries to others in the class were not serious enough to warrant removing Jimmy.

Jimmy returned to his classroom this past spring while his father and school officials decided where he should go to school.

Parents such as Janet Edwards started pulling their children out of Jimmy's class and eventually picketed the school.

"My son told me, 'Mommy, I'm scared to go to school.'" Edwards said. "There was no way I was letting him go back there."

Superintendent Tarwater said that he was "stunned" by the federal court's ruling and that officials were "put in a really tight box" by the federal rules.

But Jimmy's father, James Peters, said that his son was not a danger and that the school set up Jimmy for failure.

"They made him out to be a monster," Peters said.

Jimmy had attended preschool in a class with other disabled students at Circle View Elementary School. But district officials had agreed to move Jimmy into a regular classroom for kindergarten.

To prepare for Jimmy's arrival, district officials said they sent his teacher and a full-time aide to workshops on inclusion and behavior-intervention strategies.

After the federal judge's ruling, Peters removed his son from the school, saying officials were not making an effort to accommodate Jimmy.

For now, a special-education teacher and a speech therapist visit Jimmy at home a few times a week, and he goes to school twice a week for adaptive physical education.

Messy Battle Looms

Lawmakers in Congress have moved over the past year to modify some of the federal rules on students with disabilities to give educators more leeway in moving those students out of the classroom. A provision in the recent bill that reauthorized most federal programs in K-12 education allows schools to place in an interim educational setting for up to 45 days a student with a disability who brings a firearm to school.

Many disability-rights advocates criticized such moves, arguing that such changes would unravel the web of civil-rights and educational protections granted to disabled students.

Many advocates charge that schools are using students with disabilities as scapegoats for the larger problem of school violence.

They say officials are looking for an easy way to get "problem" students out of the classroom—harkening to a time before the landmark 1975 Individuals with Disabilities Education Act passed, when one in eight children with disabilities was excluded from public schools.

And they wonder whether classroom crises are being exacerbated by a lack of training and supports for special-education teachers.

"I think that if there were more appropriate interventions, we wouldn't be seeing the problems we're seeing now," said Judith E. Heumann, the U.S. Education Department's assistant secretary for special education and rehabilitation services.

But many observers say that if the discipline issue is not tackled soon it could endanger the protections

> # To prepare for one student's arrival, the teacher and full-time aide were sent to workshops on inclusion and behavior-intervention strategies.

currently afforded such students by stoking a backlash against special education.

And many are looking to resolve the issue in what advocates and policymakers agree promises to be a messy battle when Congress begins work next year on reauthorizing the IDEA.

Meanwhile, parents, teachers, and administrators are navigating the system alone.

Legal Hoops To Jump

Although there are no solid data on how many of the nation's 5.17 million students with disabilities have been violent or have engaged in "life-threatening behavior," Congress has mandated that the department collect exactly such information.

Most observers say that the number of cases that pose serious problems for districts is small. "It's really a tiny proportion of kids, but you only need one," said Bruce Hunter, the senior associate executive director of the American Association of School Administrators. "Every district has at least one apocryphal story."

In 1988 the U.S. Supreme Court ruled in *Honig* v. *Doe* that school officials could not suspend for longer than 10 days students whose behavior problems stemmed from their disabilities. Many educators and legal experts, however, have interpreted the ruling to block long-term suspensions for all students with disabilities, regardless of the reason for their behavior.

Going beyond 10 days, the Court said, would violate the IDEA's so-called stay-put provision, which mandates that students stay in their educational placement until parents and school officials agree on how to change that placement.

After those 10 days, the student must return to his current placement. During the 10 days, a team of experts, usually teachers, administrators, and psychologists, determines whether the student's behavior is a manifestation of the student's disability. That often falls into such a gray area that schools tend to err on the side of connecting the two to avoid legal complications, legal experts say.

If the behavior is not disability-related, the schools can discipline the student as they would a non-disabled student. But, according to the Education Department, they can never deny him educational services—an issue Virginia education officials are battling over with federal officials.

In any case, schools can go to court to seek a temporary injunction to keep children out of the classroom, over their parents' objections, while they seek a more appropriate placement—sometimes outside the school.

But to win such an injunction, schools have to prove that the student is a danger to himself or to others—a relatively high threshold, legal experts say.

A Call for 'Common Sense'

Kathy Boundy, a co-director of the Center for Law and Education in Cambridge, Mass., said she has seen fewer than a dozen cases of courts handing down an injunction since the Honig decision.

Many observers say that the policies surrounding the disciplining of students with disabilities are too divorced from the classroom's daily realities.

"No court is better at deciding these things than a teacher or principal," argued Bill Honig, a former California superintendent of schools and the named plaintiff in the 1988 Supreme Court case. "We need to get back to common sense."

The U.S. Education Department has proposed alternative disciplinary methods for disabled students—such as the use of study carrels or "timeouts" from class.

According to Gwendolyn H. Gregory, the deputy general counsel for the National School Boards Association, "It's just not that easy to put a 210-pound, 6-foot-tall high school student into a carrel. There's a lot of wonderful theory until you try to carry it out."

Connie Rickman, the assistant principal at Stadium High School in Tacoma, Wash., said that she needs more flexibility in making disciplinary decisions about students in special education.

Schools can seek a temporary injunction to keep disabled children out of the classroom, over parents' objections, while they seek appropriate placement.

"We're not giving them any skills to help them deal with their behavior if we treat them with kid gloves," Rickman said.

She said courts do not take into account how difficult it is to educate some students. In one year she went through four teachers for the same class of students with behavioral disorders.

"It's getting harder to be creative in terms of finding alternatives to suspensions," she said. "I've got 1,700 students to think about."

While she understands that parents want the best for their children, Rickman said there are cases in which no matter what services the school provides, the student poses a threat.

"Parents love their kids so much," she said, "that sometimes they don't want to believe the extent of their children's problems, so they look for something else to blame it on."

A Parent's View

But one parent, Judy Evans, said she does realize the extent of the problem.

Her 15-year-old daughter, who is mildly mentally retarded and has attention-deficit disorder, was suspended so many times from her Susquehanna, Pa., school last year that Evans had to quit her job because she was leaving work so frequently to pick her up.

Last fall her daughter moved from a special school for disabled students to her neighborhood school with a full-time aide.

Her teacher wanted her to stop grinding her teeth and shuffling her feet, both common with ADD, because she found it distracting, Evans said.

Sometimes her daughter lashed out physically in class, but Evans thinks it stemmed from her frustration with an education plan that has not been adapted to meet her capabilities. Her daughter brings home F's from most of her classes, Evans said.

"I do expect her to be disciplined, but not for something she can't control," Evans said.

And when her daughter is punished she is getting exactly what she wants, Evans argued: attention and a ticket out of her classroom.

'They Don't Understand'

Stephen Griffen, who teaches students with severe behavior disorders at Cleveland's Paul Revere Elementary School, said suspensions are a way to get some "breathing space" from some of his most difficult students.

Because of budget cuts, Griffen shares an aide with another class. Recently, one of his students exposed himself in the school cafeteria. It took several adults to restrain the student.

"He can totally destroy a room and turn it upside down," Griffen said.

"You're always on the edge; every kid is capable of a sudden explosion," he said.

Acknowledging that sometimes he feels more like a babysitter than a teacher, Griffen said some of the regular-education teachers occasionally ask him why he is unable to do more with his students.

"I say, 'I am. I'm taking them out of your class so that you can teach,'" Griffen said. "They don't understand what it takes."

Hillsborough County school officials in Tampa, Fla., recently persuaded a federal judge to remove an autistic student from Jenna L. Hodgens's class at Chamberlain High School.

Hodgens has spent 11 years in special education, working with emotionally disturbed students.

Her classroom of 10 is populated by autistic and developmentally disabled students, but this 17-year-old autistic student proved to be a challenge, even with a full-time aide.

According to officials, the student hit Hodgens and other school staff members and punched classmates on numerous occasions.

"I was scared for myself and my other kids—the whole air of the classroom is so unpredictable," Hodgens said. "Nobody goes to a job expecting to be hit. It should never be OK."

Learning About Diversity

Back in Huntington Beach, Calif., where the federal judge rejected the district's attempt to remove Jimmy P., Edwards is upset.

When Jimmy first started in her son Dallin's class, she said, she was looking forward to having her son learn about diversity.

Edwards said she would be willing to give full inclusion another shot—with her 3rd-grade daughter—but not with Dallin.

"My son had his kindergarten year wrecked, and he won't get it back," she said. "What about a fair and safe education for my son?" ■

From Education Week, *Nov. 30, 1994*

17.

Wired for the Future

Important as it is, connecting to the digital networks is just the first step in joining the information age.

By Peter West

From an aged armchair in a converted 1920s-era school building, Larry Arrington tosses out words and phrases like "T-1 lines," "modems," and "ISDN" with abandon as he describes the future of communications that lies just over the horizon for the Montgomery County, Va., public schools. He spins a vision, larded with the jargon of the "information age," about the district's plan for a "virtual school system" in which the lines of demarcation between home and school, between the information-rich world outside the classroom and the information-poor environment inside, will largely disappear, thanks to the telecommunications revolution.

For a system of only 8,900 students, nestled in the Blue Ridge Mountains, the district already has made some prodigious leaps into the digital age.

Each of the district's 20 schools is equipped with high-speed modems and has access to the Internet, the global information network of computer networks. A recently approved technology plan spells out in detail exactly how the district hopes to catapult from the era of the printed page to the age of the computer screen by equipping schools with broadband telephone lines.

"Eventually, what we hope to have is a seamless network of interactive-video-equipped classrooms," says Arrington, the district's technology coordinator.

The school system has not always been so forward-looking. "We are one of those systems that has not done well in preparing for the future," Arrington con-

cedes. "Not to bad mouth anybody, but our past superintendent was not a computer user. Never would be."

The district had the extraordinary good fortune, however, to be located within a few miles of what is arguably one of the most "wired" communities in the United States. A short drive west on Route 460, in the small town of Blacksburg, Bell Atlantic of Virginia, Virginia Polytechnic Institute & State University, and the municipal government are engaged in an ambitious cooperative venture to provide ordinary citizens with immediate access to the so-called information highway.

Whether they're at the public library, or in the privacy of their homes, Blacksburg residents are just a local telephone call away from the Internet—and the global communications network it supports. And the system is commonly used for everything from electronic mail to advertising.

"This is a massive social re-engineering project," asserts Andrew M. Cohill, the director of the Blacksburg Electronic Village. "We've created the electronic front porch."

The project aims to extend that electronic community to the Montgomery County district's schools and eventually to link schools and homes.

With the advent of a new school administration, and armed with grants from the National Science Foundation and Bell Atlantic to further upgrade its infrastructure, the school district is poised to act as a test site for educational applications of advanced telecommunications.

Highway to Hype

When Vice President Gore challenged the telecommunications industry last January to wire every classroom in the nation for access to the "information superhighway," it's likely he envisioned the kind of links that are available today in Blacksburg.

Yet, despite their many advantages in the race to merge onto the information highway, officials here, with the help of experts at Virginia Tech, still are pondering how ubiquitous access to telecommunications might fundamentally change the way that schools do business.

From deciding what content is appropriate for grade school students, to figuring out how to train teachers to use the networks effectively, to retrofitting aging buildings for the electronic age, the district is grappling with questions that other school systems haven't even begun to think about.

What's clear so far is that connecting to the network is just the first step schools must take.

"There's more to it than dropping computers into the classroom," says Roger Ehrich, a professor of computer science at Virginia Tech. "The whole school system was brought up without networking technology of this type."

Since the Clinton Administration took office two years ago, a seemingly endless stream of news stories about the information superhighway, its potential benefits and hazards, has filled the newspapers and airwaves.

"We've started to call it the 'information hypeway,'" says Glenn Kessler, the director of media services for

---

The cost of wiring every school in the nation to the 'information superhighway' could be in the hundreds of billions of dollars.

---

the Fairfax County, Va., public schools.

Most people, however, would still be hard-pressed to define just what the term "information highway" means. And even fewer could accurately say what the Vice President's challenge implies for the way that public schools operate.

"I think it means something different to everybody," says Cheryl Williams, the director of the technology-programs department at the National School Boards Association.

Kessler, for example, notes that in Fairfax County,

an affluent Washington suburb, the information highway is structurally in place. The district operates its own cable-television system and satellite, students can download materials from any library in the state, and trials are under way with various firms to provide Internet access and "video-on-demand" to every school.

Yet, for the average school district, the information highway remains just a vague and shapeless concept.

Montgomery County officials have agreed that access to the information highway means access to the Internet. Many educators, especially those with some experience with telecommunications, would agree with that conclusion.

K-12 educators have increasingly used the Internet in recent years. In part, that's because its government subsidies make the Internet essentially free to users.

Clinton Administration officials, however, are quick to point out that the Internet is just one component of a vastly upgraded national communications network that should be available to every classroom.

Many in the telecommunications industry, meanwhile, argue that the Internet model is not at all what they have in mind when they talk about connecting homes to the information highway. Instead, they expect that subscribers will one day be able to shop or call up the latest hit film through a computer-like device atop their television sets—services they hope will generate healthy revenues. The television set model, they believe, is perfect for the large number of people who are not computer literate.

Other observers contend that the information highway phenomenon is an extension of the microcomputer revolution that began roughly a decade ago. The development of universal access to telecommunications networks, they say, simply increases the power of the personal computer as a productivity tool.

The reality is that the information highway will probably combine all of these elements. But which of them, if any, will be of value to educators is far from clear.

Beyond Commercialism

Although Gore has not spelled out what educational access to the information highway would look like, Administration officials largely reject the commercial model, arguing that it has little to do with the Vice President's vision.

"If people think of it as the 500 channels of television that are going to deliver entertainment or home shopping, then, in fact, they ought to be dismayed," says Linda G. Roberts, the special adviser on education technology to U.S. Secretary of Education Richard W. Riley.

She notes that in several recent national surveys, respondents gave the highest possible rating to the idea that the information highway should carry interactive educational programs.

"This is phenomenal," she adds. "It says to me that the public as a whole has really got it right. The information superhighway has the potential to bring the best of our world to our classrooms."

No two educators, technologists, and other telecommunications experts could agree on exactly how the development of the information highway will affect education.

Gordon Ambach, the executive director of the Council of Chief State School Officers, for example, argues that it will be impossible for the nation to meet its education goals unless students have relatively widespread access to telecommunications.

The jobs of the future, he predicts, will require that all workers know how to use telecommunications and how to access information by computer.

> ## The jobs of the future will require that all workers know how to use telecommunications and know how to access information by computer.

Moreover, because advanced telecommunications allows global electronic conversations and ready access to information, it has the potential to radically reform instruction, Ambach says.

"The technologies now, I believe, are actually transforming the ways that people learn," he says. "The potential of that for reshaping pedagogical design is extraordinarily powerful. I don't know where it's going to take us—but I think we need to think very carefully about it."

Many would agree that applications being tested in Montgomery County give some idea of how telecommunications could be applied in the classroom.

Here, students are developing a multimedia magazine that is posted on the Internet's Worldwide Web; Virginia Tech graduate students are helping high school physics teachers post student papers on the "Net" for peer-review by experts around the globe; projects are under way to link home and school via voice mail; and teachers are encouraging students to use the Internet as a massive research library.

Even so, notes John Yrchik, a telecommunications analyst at the National Education Association, at the national level there is as yet no guiding vision for

what universal access to the information highway should imply for educators.

"We're a long way from a consensus," Yrchik says, "or even a very clear direction, about where we want to go."

High-Stakes Battle

Part of the confusion stems from the fact that the information highway is actually an interrelated series of technological, regulatory, economic, and societal changes that were set in motion long before Gore challenged the industry to bring schools on board.

And for the most part, educators have been, at best, peripheral players in the game.

A central concept undergirding the phenomenon is "convergence," or the ability to convert voice, video, graphics, and computer data into digital signals and to transmit information over newer, and faster, high-volume transmission media.

Fiber-optic cables, for example, allow huge quantities of digital signals to be transmitted as pulses of light along hair-thin glass wires at high speeds over great distances. Both the telephone and cable-television industries propose to upgrade their networks with such "broadband" capability.

But the cost of replacing existing copper telephone wires with fiber-optic cables is estimated to be in the billions of dollars, causing the phone industry to argue that it must be allowed to carry such services as video-on-demand to support the costs of upgrading the network.

Yet, those same digital signals can also be transmitted by a new generation of satellites to remote or mountainous locations where laying cables would cost too much.

How the signals are carried is not as important as the rich variety of information that the networks can make available to anyone, almost anywhere.

"People confuse the delivery system with the content," notes Cohill of the Blacksburg Electronic Village. "It's much more important to be connected at low speed than to say we're going to wait for a broadband connection."

The race to build the information highway is also a high-stakes regulatory battle, played out in deadly earnest in the halls of Congress, over who should be allowed to transmit what kinds of information and in what markets.

In the rapidly changing telecommunications field, some of the major players obviously include the cable-television and telephone industries. But many utility companies also have begun to weigh the idea of using fiber-optic cables that they already use for internal communications to send programming to homes and to offer such services as automated monitoring of heating and cooling systems.

73

In the unlikely event that all federal communications regulations were to be abolished tomorrow, the cable-television industry would likely offer customers telephone service over its lines, and the local telephone company would offer video-on-demand and home-shopping services in addition to regular telephone service.

But the Communications Act of 1934, the primary federal telecommunications measure that remains largely unchanged since the heyday of radio, sharply delineates the markets open to the cable industry, the Bell regional operating companies, and other players.

A bill designed to revamp the law and ensure access for schools was withdrawn in the last session of Congress. But House Speaker Newt Gingrich reportedly is weighing as a blueprint for reform a "Magna Carta for the Information Age," drafted by a group of well-known futurists for the Progress and Freedom Foundation, a conservative think tank in Washington.

The most recent draft of the document does not address the idea of connecting schools to developing telecommunications networks, though it does call for sweeping deregulation of the industry.

Other conservative think tanks argue that the federal government should essentially get out of the business of regulating the telecommunications market, including oversight of educational access.

"There should be no federal policy on this issue," argues Adam Thierer, a telecommunications policy analyst with the Heritage Foundation in Washington. "Instead, states and municipalities should determine what their needs are and create an open process that allows all carriers to compete for service."

Thierer argues that requiring access for schools and other public entities could slow development of the information highway by placing unfair burdens on providers that would eventually limit competition.

The one role that the federal government should play, he adds, is to insure that individual networks conform to an "open data" standard so that information can be conveyed over a variety of systems. The National Research Council endorsed that concept in its report on telecommunications called "Realizing the Information Future."

And while complex questions about "cross subsidies," regulations, and "barriers to competition" may seem abstract to education policymakers, the fact is that in places like Montgomery County, school administrators are faced almost daily with competing claims of the telecommunications companies as they jockey for market share.

"We just had that discussion in our technology committee about which is the best carrier," reports Arrington. "The cable companies are a lot more aggressive than the phone companies about this."

The Vice President's challenge to the industry, observers note, has helped spur several major telecommunications firms to pledge to wire schools for the information age.

"It seems to me there's enormous power just in the idea, and just that Gore said it," Yrchik of the NEA contends.

Gore's remarks also alerted the telecommunications industry to a huge new market.

Unfortunately, few educators are aware of the potential impact of the regulatory and technological change swirling around them.

"We're changing communications patterns, the way people access and retrieve information," says Connie Stout, the past chair of the Consortium for School Networking, a nonprofit umbrella organization. "It is very important that we be at the table to participate in discussions."

Unless schools get guaranteed access, it is virtually certain that homes will be connected first. Parents who can afford access to the on-line educational services available will be able to purchase them for their children, thereby widening the educational gap between economic classes.

Public schools, argues John Phillipo, the executive director of the Center for Educational Leadership and Technology in Malborough, Mass., can either take advantage of the opportunity to "get into the learning business" and act as a broker for educational services for students of all ages or run the risk of becoming even further removed from the technological mainstream of society.

Unfortunately, Williams of the NSBA says, such ideas do not rank high on the list of local policymakers' priorities.

"I think you've got a group of people who don't get it," she laments.

No matter how the debate in Washington over telecommunications policy turns out, many problems unique to education must be resolved if schools are to take full advantage of digital communications.

Estimates vary wildly, for example, as to what the costs of wiring every classroom will be, how it will be paid, and by whom. At the low end, Secretary Riley has estimated it will cost $10 billion to wire every school. High-end estimates range in the hundreds of billions of dollars.

"What we really need now in education are specific and credible proposals to fund the National Information Infrastructure," says Yrchik, "and that's what we don't have."

The Administration has provided some seed grants through pilot programs at such federal agencies as the Commerce Department's National Telecommunications and Information Administration and the NSF. And they have made technology grants a part of the Goals 2000 reform legislation.

And the Vice President recently endorsed a suggestion that money raised by the auction of the public airwaves for advanced cellular communications should be used to help defray the costs of wiring schools. But, for the most part, the Administration has said it will rely on private industry and local government to underwrite the costs.

The costs for providing access to every classroom will vary widely depending on what blend of technologies and level of service is deemed necessary to support instruction.

And while some states are experimenting with taxes on video rentals and other schemes to raise money for technology upgrades, "I don't think anybody has a clue as to the magnitude of investment we're talking about," the NSBA's Williams says.

Meanwhile, few educators are aware of the costs associated with using telecommunications once the connections have been made to individual schools. Although regulatory bodies in some states, such as Texas, offer special rates for educational use of telecommunications, in most states, schools are charged relatively high business rates. Such costs can put even the Internet out of reach.

The Last Mile

Another major stumbling block to achieving the goal of universal classroom access is bridging the so-called "last mile" between the advanced networks and the nation's relatively old stock of school buildings, many of which require major modifications to accommodate even the most basic technologies.

According to one reliable estimate, for example, fewer than 4 percent of public school classrooms have access to telephone lines, making classroom use of telecommunications virtually impossible.

"There isn't a technology base out there," stresses Kathleen Fulton, a senior analyst at the Congres-

---

Public schools can either enter the 'learning business' or run the risk of becoming even further removed from the technological mainstream society.

---

sional Office of Technology Assessment, which plans to release a study this spring on teacher training in technology. "It's amazing to me how people outside of education have no idea how teachers still have to line up outside the teachers' lounge to use the telephone."

Only a handful of states, meanwhile, have begun to allocate the funds needed to wire schools for telecommunications.

Florida has spent roughly $74 million over the past three years to help retrofit schools so they can use the statewide Florida Information Resources Network. The competitive grants average $225,000 per school. Officials predict it will take six or seven years and $675 million to bring every school in the state into the network.

Kentucky expects to spend $80 million just to develop the wiring and other infrastructure to connect the state's 1,370 schools to a statewide network developed under the state's landmark 1989 reform law. To cut costs, one district required the contractor to hire students to help wire its buildings.

"We run it on a shoestring," admits Lydia Wells Sledge, who oversees the network's development. "But to implement at the speed that we want to, we do have to create time and services out of nothing."

Technology an 'Option'

Yet, outlets and cables are only part of the needed infrastructure.

The NEA's Yrchik estimates that 80 percent of classroom computers are incapable of handling multimedia software or receiving high-speed data, two key telecommunications functions.

Roughly half of the computers in schools, according to recent data, are Apple II's, a machine that was first introduced in the 1980's. While still adequate for some tasks, the discontinued Apple II simply does not have the features or computing power of newer machines.

Ronald E. Anderson, the editor of "Computers in American Schools 1992: An Overview," a survey of technology inventories and usage released by the CCSSO, says that schools have made progress in upgrading their equipment. He notes that since the 1992 survey was conducted, the percentage of schools with at least one modem has grown from 40 percent to 55 percent. The number of schools with access to cable television has risen from 55 percent to 75 percent. Meanwhile, the number of computers in the nation's schools has grown from 3.5 million in 1992 to about 5 million today.

And a recent report compiled by Quality Education Data, a Colorado-based market-research firm, found that 70 percent of school districts with enrollments greater than 25,000 reported having at least one school with Internet access.

Nonetheless, Anderson says, "it's still going to be quite a while before all of the schools are hooked up to external networks."

A related hardware problem is that few schools employ the technical support staff to effectively run a technology program. "Our problem here is manpower," Arrington says. "It's much easier for schools to buy computers than to 'buy' people."

Unlike many businesses, and even some government agencies, schools generally do not recognize the need for technical-support personnel, adds Jesse Rodriguez, who heads the division of information technologies of the Tucson (Ariz.) Unified School District.

"I can't pay a competitive rate to an individual who has the skills I need," Rodriguez says. "There's no way I can pay the technician $50,000." Instead, the district purchased the state-of-the-art telecommunications system that allows him to troubleshoot many problems from his office.

But too often, he says, districts designate a science or mathematics teacher as the resident "technology guru" leaving that individual to run the computer program. "You might as well take a man off the streets who happens to speak Spanish and make him a bilingual teacher," he says with chagrin. "I think a basic problem is that districts are not looking at what the real costs of what managing information systems are going to be."

Finally, experts note, the vast majority of teachers has never been encouraged to use technology or provided with the support to integrate it effectively into the curriculum.

"It does not take much to excite a teacher about telecommunications," notes Norman Dodel, a professor of instructional technology in the college of education at Virginia Tech in Blacksburg. "But when they leave a place like this and go to a place where the technology is just not available, it is very likely those people will put that vision on the shelf."

Although she won't discuss the findings of the upcoming OTA report, Fulton says that, in general, most teachers who use telecommunications today are self-taught. Few education schools effectively incorporate technology into their programs, she says.

And teachers, notes Melissa Matusevich, the supervisor of programs for gifted students with the Montgomery County schools and an avid user of the Internet as a classroom teacher, are not given any incentives to learn.

"We are one of the few professions that sees technology use as an option," Matusevich says. ■

From Education Week, *January 11, 1995*

18.

The Parable of 'Scubation'

An undersea parable illustrates how bureaucracies inherently imperil innovation.

By Lewis J. Perelman

To grasp the link between technology and politics, consider this parable: Suppose that long ago humans had so effectively pioneered working and living at the bottom of the ocean that, over a long time, they had forgotten that they had ever lived differently. In this deep-sea society, scuba gear obviously was of such overarching importance that the provision and regulation of scuba gear was uncritically accepted as one of the essential functions of government.

The ministry of scubation incorporated a vast bureaucracy of credentialed experts to administer and carry out every facet of scuba provision: mining air from seawater, filtering and compressing it into bottles differentiated to match the breathing capacity and requirements of each age group and vocation, and compulsory scubation of the young to guard against the possibility of parents' providing inadequate air for their children. Local scubation districts were chartered and funded with taxes to pump air into the captive youths in specially constructed neighborhood buildings—called "schools," perhaps because of the way children were herded into them like bunches of fish. An elaborate testing bureaucracy also was formed to accredit the scubation "schools" and to continually measure the breathing ability of the young against sea-world standards.

Naturally, scubation was such a vital function for social well-being that it could not be left to the whims of private enterprise; so the government owned, oper-ated, and regulated virtually the entire scubation enterprise. And all this was accepted as normal and reasonable by a general public that could neither remember nor imagine that air could be supplied any other way, and that simply took it for granted that breathing and scubation were just different words for the same thing.

Then, somewhere in this undersea society's march of technological progress, scientists and engineers came up with a wondrous invention they might have called a balloon or dirigible or even "airship"—a vessel filled with gas cells that allowed it to rise upward to explore the higher reaches of their liquid world. In due course, these explorations led to a revolutionary breakthrough: The scientists discovered an altitude at which the atmosphere suddenly was transformed from all water to all air. The earth in many places rose above this boundary, providing islands and continents where people could go work and live free of the encumbrance of gas tanks and hoses and face masks.

At this point, of course, the technological revolution spawned a political crisis. The bloated, rich, and powerful scubation ministry faced a lethal threat to its hegemony. Once enough pioneers came back from the frontier to tell of the new all-air environment, the public would eventually figure out that scubation—which, for as long as most people could remember was accepted as vital—had suddenly become not only unnecessary but actually an obstacle to human progress. For those who moved to the new world of universal, free air, breathing could simply be taken for granted as a normal activity of everyday life, and the very word "scubation" would fall into such general disuse that it would be remembered at all only as a historical oddity.

There being no heaven on earth, the pioneers of the air world recognized that their new society would need new technologies to keep the air clean, and even some new government roles and agencies to guard against dangerous pollution of the atmosphere. But the archaic empire of scubation had no role, experience, or knowledge relevant to these new challenges—it was simply obsolete. Worse, the huge scubation bureaucracy, with its vast demands on the public treasure, its sprawling waste of human resources and time, and its kelp forest of regulatory snares, worked only to undermine the pioneering of the new world of free breathing. The scubacracy thus threatened to squander the rich opportunities for freedom and prosperity the air world offered.

The crisis eventually compelled cities and states in the ocean-bottom society to confront inescapable political choices. In most places, the scubacrats fought back to prevent the liberation of the lung from dependency on the bureaucratic air hose: They used their political clout to get local governments to outlaw the commercial development of airships; or, failing that, they imposed regulations requiring that all airships be owned or at least effectively controlled by the scubation bureaucracy itself.

The scubacracy used its finances to counter the threat to its survival with self-serving propaganda: First they tried to deny the existence of the air world altogether. As the scientific proof of the air-filled environment eventually became public knowledge, scubacrat propaganda claimed that airships were an unproven technology that required years of further research; that travel to the ocean's surface would cause crippling, even lethal attacks of the bends; that people never could learn to breathe on their own without the careful regulation of a respirator; and that children left to run wild in the open air would hyperventilate and die of oxygen poisoning. People who advocate replacing "schools" with airship transport to a new world of free air, the scubacrats proclaimed, are greedy capitalists out to destroy our sacred institutions of public respiration.

In a few visionary communities, political alliances overwhelmed the scubation establishment's resistance, and redirected the community's resources to construct the airship fleets needed to transport everyone to the new environment of open air. In these communities and some others, a large number of more farsighted scubacrats realized that their ultimate mission was the provision of air not scuba gear—they helped the effort to phase out the obsolete scubation bureaucracy and to make the pilgrimage to a world of universal free breathing. These vanguard communities eventually became the stars of a new civilization.

But other communities of the undersea society fared not as well.

In many, business and other civic leaders were diverted into "partnerships" aimed at "saving the schools" by raising taxes to build new, expensive pipelines to the surface of the ocean in a costly and vain attempt to pump more air into the traditional public respiration structures. In these cities and states, and others where the scubacracy's clout stymied even the semblance of progress, better-off families bought their way onto airships, or acquired their own. They abandoned the bottled-air "schools" to the poorest and most disadvantaged citizens, who were deprived of the technology needed to escape from the bureaucratic iron lung by the same self-serving bureaucracy that owned the iron lung.

In some places, the squeeze between sinking economies and rising fiscal demands of a self-protecting scubation bureaucracy, whose product grew ever more stale and toxic, ultimately set off furious rebellions of people demanding their equal opportunity to breathe free. But some provinces of the sea-bottom society simply imploded, and sank into the mud. ■

Lewis J. Perelman is the president of Kanbrain Institute in Washington, D.C.

From Education Week, *September 14, 1994*

What We Will Teach

"The most fundamental requirement for a democracy is an educated citizenry capable of informed judgment on public issues. Participation in self-governance will require a higher standard of scientific literacy, a deeper understanding of history, and a greater capacity to think critically."

—Report of the California Commission

on Teaching as a Profession, 1985

19.

Focusing on Outcomes

A system of national standards and assessments would give teachers a much greater say in choosing what to teach.

The idea of a system of national standards and assessments is one of the most powerful and provocative to emerge from the 10-year-old school reform movement. It has become the "wedge issue" in the drive to overhaul America's schools. And its advocates see it as the crucial first step to systemic reform.

Pushed by the Bush and Clinton administrations and the National Governors' Association and widely endorsed by educational, political, and business leaders, the idea has moved to the top of the reform agenda. It has also sparked a vigorous debate and divided people who tend to see eye to eye on other educational issues.

The national standards and assessments movement begins with the assumption that all students can learn at significantly higher levels. It proposes to change the focus of the present educational system from "input" to "outcomes." At present, most states seek to accomplish their educational goals by determining what goes into the system—everything from the amount of money spent to the content of each course taught. An outcome-based system would focus on results—determining the levels of performance expected and holding schools accountable for achieving them.

The key components of a performance/outcome system are these:
● Content standards that define what students should know and be able to do—what is to be taught and what is to be learned. At their best, the standards would be specific enough to inform the curriculum, but general enough to provide a wide latitude to teachers in implementing them.
● Assessments that will measure students' progress toward the desired outcomes. Norm-referenced stan-

dardized tests are totally incompatible with a performance-based system. At the heart of such a system is the idea of setting tasks for students that will engage them, inform them, and encourage them to think and reason. The assessments must be rich enough to measure whether students are mastering the standards.
● Instructional strategies and technologies necessary for schools and teachers to enable their students to perform at high levels. The role of the teacher changes from imparting information to passive students to mentoring students who are responsible for their own education. In a standards-driven system, the gap between curriculum and assessment virtually disappears as testing becomes integrated into the teaching process. "Teaching to the test" is desirable in this kind of system because students know up front what they are expected to know, and they collaborate with their teachers and fellow students to accomplish that.
● Consequences that will undergird the standards and motivate schools and students to achieve them. Critics of the present system argue that expectations are low, and academic achievement counts for little. Students have little motivation to excel. In a performance-based system, admission to college or getting a job would be tied to mastery of standards.
● Delivery standards that will assure every student an opportunity to learn and perform at high standards. In the present system, there are gross inequities, and the quality of education is often determined by where a student lives. Advocates of a performance-based system stress that high stakes must not be attached to mastery of standards until all students are guaranteed the quality of education necessary to achieve them.
● Professional development of teachers that enables them to implement content standards and curricular frameworks and carry out newly developed perfor-

mance-based assessments. A new system would radically change what goes on in classrooms and the roles and relationships of students and teacher. Most teachers are not prepared to function effectively in such a system and will need training and assistance.

Proponents of voluntary national standards and assessments argue that their adoption will transform schools and the teaching profession. Teachers will be deeply involved in decisions that affect teaching and learning, the allocation of resources, and the uses of time and space. Students will be challenged to learn and will assume much more responsibility for their own education. The present system operates as though all children learn at the same rate and in the same way. The curriculum is divided into time slots and students move from one to the other, whether or not they have learned the material. Time is the con-

> # Freed from lesson plans, work sheets, and standardized tests, teachers will have both the fulfillment and the responsibility of true professionalism.

stant and learning is the variable. In a performance-based system, learning becomes the constant and time becomes the variable. The school schedule will be flexible so that students could take different amounts of time to master the standards.

The movement toward standards and assessments has progressed with astonishing speed. In 1994, the U.S. Congress passed Goals 2000: The Educate America Act, the first school reform bill in history, creating mechanisms to develop voluntary national standards and assessments and encouraging states to adopt them. A number of states, national organizations, and professional associations developed standards and assessments that states are incorporating into their standards and curriculum frameworks. The New Standards Project—a consortium of 17 states and half a dozen school districts that accounts for nearly half of the nation's students—is well along in the development of "world class" national standards in several subject areas.

Despite such widespread support for the idea, it has its critics. The issues of contention are these:

- *Top-down vs. bottom-up.* A significant number of prominent reformers argue that standard-setting should be left to local communities. They fear that mandates from on high will stifle creativity and lead to the kind of uniformity, rigidity, and bureaucratic constraints that hamper the present system.
- *Breadth vs. depth.* With various groups at work developing content standards, it is inevitable that each discipline will claim a substantial part of the curriculum. As one wag puts it: Everything will be fine as long as social studies, language arts, science, mathematics, geography, and the arts each get 30 percent of the curriculum. Something will obviously have to give, and this could lead to fierce turf battles. Multicultural tensions will also surface in the debate. Indeed, the "less is more" attitude that standards developers bring to the task is likely to intensify the multicultural issue in the arguments over what gets put into the curriculum and what gets left out.
- *Quality vs. equality.* Many fear that states and districts will implement content standards, performance standards, and assessments, but, because of costs, renege on delivery standards. That would put the neediest children at an even greater disadvantage.
- *Administrator vs. teacher.* Putting a performance-based system in place will shift power—mostly downward to the school site. Teachers and students, in particular, would be empowered. Administrators would find themselves sharing power, building consensus, facilitating.

Finally, some parents are also likely to be suspicious of an outcome-based system. Those whose children already have an advantage may be wary of leveling the playing field. Others, particularly fundamentalist Christians, are protesting the shift away from a basic-skills curriculum and arguing that efforts to foster higher-order thinking is an attack on their values.

The question of what to teach is one that will be paramount in the 1990s. It is a question made more difficult by the extraordinary accumulation of new knowledge, particularly in the sciences; the increasing diversity of the society; and the longstanding practice of calling on schools to teach mandated curriculum units that address an array of social needs—units on AIDS, drug prevention, and driver education, to name just a few.

If the performance-based system succeeds as it is now conceived, teachers will have far more freedom in designing their own classroom curricula. But they will also find that teaching is a much more demanding profession when detailed scope and sequence arrangements are gone. Freed from lesson plans, work sheets, and a plethora of standardized tests, teachers will have both the fulfillment and the enormous responsibility of true professionalism. ∎

20.

Running Out of Steam

Just when the standards movement is beginning to deliver the goods, many fear it has lost its momentum.

By Karen Diegmueller

If schools nationwide would only raise their expectations for all students by setting rigorous standards, the premise goes, then learning and achievement would surely blossom. To that end, thousands of educators and policymakers have been laboring since the late 1980s to craft voluntary standards that will promote academic excellence and equity. At the national level, the movement began with an effort in the mathematics community to redefine radically how that subject is taught. But it quickly gained momentum and swept across the disciplines. Along the way, it picked up federal funding and support and—to some observers—became more of a federal than a national effort.

The movement also picked up opponents. Some fear the development of a national curriculum and excessive intrusion by the federal government into matters of state and local control. Others question whether the emerging standards really meet the needs of all students.

Today, just as most of the multimillion-dollar efforts are nearing completion and final or draft documents are widely available, the movement has begun to show signs of slowing. Even its most ardent supporters question how useful the standards ultimately will be. They say that while some districts and states appear determined to adopt rigorous academic standards, others seem bent on maintaining a status quo that will deprive many children of a first-class education. "Some of the expectations were unrealistic to begin with," acknowledges Christopher T. Cross, the president of the Council for Basic Education. Setting standards for the core subjects is a much more complex enterprise than many had imagined.

But Cross believes that the idea of standards remains "as vital and powerful today as it has ever been. Standards are the bedrock of making major improvements in our schools."

Building Blocks

The work of designing standards began with content standards. Essentially, these describe what students should know and be able to do in a given subject area by the time they complete the 4th, 8th, and 12th grades. For several years now, a dozen groups have been developing these standards. Half the groups have completed their work, four are in the last draft stages, and two have yet to release drafts. Some of the resulting standards, such as those in health, offer general descriptions. The arts standards, on the other hand, are very specific in laying out what is expected of students. Content standards were to be the foundation on which excellence and equity would be built. Once schools had content standards in place, other pieces were to follow—new assessments, professional development, new textbooks and other appropriate resources, and policies to reinforce the expectation of academic rigor.

Such a design bears a striking resemblance to the way school systems are structured in other industrialized nations, where students often outperform U.S.

students on international assessments.

Albert Shanker, the president of the American Federation of Teachers, likes to point out that France, Germany, and Japan have an interlocking system of curriculum, teacher training, textbooks, assessments, and consequences. Students are tested on curriculum that is based on national standards. And those who perform well are rewarded with entree to institutions of higher education and better jobs.

"They have a connected system," Shanker says. "We have a system that doesn't count."

But in these other nations, the national governments generally have a hand in setting academic standards, a concept that is anathema to many in the United States.

Not that the federal government has kept out of educational affairs. It has required schools to educate minority students alongside white children. It has forced districts to provide a free, appropriate education for special-needs students and to give girls the same academic and athletic opportunities as boys.

But the uneasy truce between states and districts and the federal government in these areas has not meant that state and local officials were willing to permit Washington to trespass onto such sensitive turf as what is taught in the schools.

So it was a radical departure when President George Bush and the nation's governors met in Charlottesville, Va., in September 1989 and agreed to set national education goals. "It was a major breakthrough," says Cross, who was an assistant secretary of education under Bush. "It was inspired by a sense of crisis about the performance of schools and what was happening. We had to put aside our traditional beliefs and positions and come together around a new way to look at things, a new way to do things."

A Mathematical Model

None of the national goals eventually adopted by Congress specifically mentions academic standards.

One, however, calls for "all students [to] leave grades 4, 8, and 12 having demonstrated competency over challenging subject matter including English, mathematics, science, foreign languages, civics and government, economics, arts, history, and geography" by 2000.

Another calls for students to be "first in the world in mathematics and science achievement."

But without some way to define and measure terms like "competency" and "world class," educators asked, how could the nation ever determine if the goals had been met?

The National Council of Teachers of Mathematics had a ready-made answer. Shortly before the historic goals-setting, the NCTM published a 258-page book of curriculum and student-evaluation standards. It re-

defined the study of math so that topics and concepts would be introduced at an earlier age, and students would view math as a relevant problem-solving discipline rather than as a set of obscure formulas to be memorized.

Meanwhile, other education groups issued critical reports calling for changes in curriculum. The National Science Teachers Association and the American Association for the Advancement of Science, among others, launched their own curriculum projects.

And the nation's most populous state, California, began a massive restructuring of its curriculum frameworks that incorporated the latest research about how children learn.

"We were converging on this notion from many different directions," says Shirley M. Malcom, the head of education for the AAAS.

Diane Ravitch, then an assistant secretary of education, recalls that officials of the National Academy

---

State and local officials have not been willing to permit Washington to trespass onto such sensitive turf as what is taught in the schools.

---

of Sciences used the math standards in urging Secretary of Education Lamar Alexander to underwrite national standards-setting projects. The Secretary bankrolled the projects out of his office's discretionary budget.

Shortly thereafter, the National Council on Educational Standards and Testing, a Congressionally chartered bipartisan panel, recommended that content and performance standards be developed along with a system of national assessments based on the standards. It also recommended that states establish "school delivery standards" so that students have the necessary resources available to provide them with the "opportunity to learn."

Educational Apartheid

To be sure, critics quickly emerged. Some argued that national standards diverted attention from more pressing issues. They also feared that a government imprimatur might lead to the dangerous precedent of establishing a body of official knowledge.

Some of those same arguments reverberate today. "Some kids [are] going to schools which are barely habitable," says Theodore R. Sizer, a professor of education at Brown University and the founder of the Coalition of Essential Schools. "The maps on the wall [of classrooms] still call it the Belgian Congo. Those are the things that just cry out for attention."

Writing about the national history standards, historian Hanna Holborn Gray, a former president of the University of Chicago, questioned why national standards were needed at all.

"However respectable the motive, a nationally certified, federally funded, consensus-laden version of history can only be seen as a kind of mandated interpretation of the past, an official regulation of its lessons—and a sure invitation to political misuse," she wrote in a column in *The Washington Post* in January.

Broad-Based Support

Despite these concerns, many polls show the public overwhelmingly supports the idea of high standards.

One of the most in-depth gauges of public sentiment was undertaken in the fall of 1991. A series of focus groups, made up predominantly of parents, was conducted in 10 cities for the New Standards project, a consortium of states and school districts that is creating a national system of standards and assessments.

High standards were more important to working- and middle-class parents who worried that their children might not succeed because the schools did not expect or demand as much of them.

The focus groups were wary about "Big Brother" setting the standards and said it would be imperative for parents and teachers to be involved. They were also skeptical about applying the same standards to all children—a central tenet of the movement.

The poor performance of U.S. students, as measured by such tests as the National Assessment of Educational Progress, also brought the business community on board. Heightening employers' anxiety was the realization that the workforce of the future had to be far better skilled and knowledgeable than previous generations because of the changing world economy.

A uniform system of standards and assessments would also help employers judge prospective workers. A recent federal survey of managers from more than 3,000 companies found that employers were reluctant to base their hiring decisions on grades, teacher recommendations, and school reputations because of a lack of confidence in their reliability.

"We would ultimately like to see national standards and national assessments," says Sandra Kessler Hamburg, the vice president and director of education for the Committee for Economic Development. "You have to have an assessment system to go with it. Just to

have standards is meaningless."

The notion of academic standards is really not a new one. Whether they know it or not, every school already has standards. Schools that send large proportions of their students on to the most selective universities year in and year out clearly maintain rigorous standards. In schools where students ordinarily don't perform well, individual teachers may have high expectations. Even in schools in which the administrators, teachers, and students don't know about standards, they exist in the form of tests and textbooks. But the likelihood that those standards are rigorous is slim.

The differing standards, advocates of a national approach believe, sharpen the inequities within and between schools.

Although the United States, in theory, has 15,000 sets of curricula for its 15,000 districts, many educators believe there exists a de facto national curriculum established by the textbook and test publishers. And it's not a good one.

"What do these guys think is going on out there now?" Bill Honig, the former superintendent of public

> # The notion of academic standards is really not a new one. Whether they know it or not, every school already has standards in the form of tests and textbooks.

instruction who initiated standards-based reform in California, asks of opponents of national standards. Right now, Honig says, there are too many trivial, superficial lessons derived in large part from watered-down textbooks.

Federal Involvement

In 1991, science and history became the first standards projects to receive funding from the Education Department. Then, in summer 1992, the arts, civics, and geography projects were funded, later to be joined by English/language arts and foreign languages. Recently, the Education Department decided against funding the economics project.

Other federal agencies and philanthropic foundations also contributed to the projects.

There was no competition for the grants. "It was

never really the desire of the federal agencies that there be competing proposals," says one insider. Federal officials wanted all the key players working together to build consensus documents rather than fighting each other over federal funds.

Essentially, groups interested in developing standards in a given discipline simply approached the Education Department for funding. In some cases, such as English/language arts, professional teachers' organizations headed up the projects. In others, such as geography, it was a collective of interested parties. A nonprofit educational center took the lead in history and civics.

Meanwhile, other groups started writing standards in physical education, health, and social studies without the benefit of federal monies.

Most project leaders quickly discarded the notion of developing performance standards, which basically describe what students must do and how well they must do it to meet the standards—or how good is good enough. They decided there was neither the time nor the money. They had only two or three years to meet their deadlines—a relatively short time for the amount of work required and the number of constituencies involved.

History, for example, received funding in December 1991 and had to complete three documents by fall 1994. In addition to its 29-member oversight council, it had to satisfy 33 constituency groups.

Each project was also supposed to develop standards for all students, but bilingual and special educators, in particular, question whether they satisfied that requirement.

.

Confusion Reigns

In the beginning, policymakers and educators had hoped to see concise standards documents that had common definitions and symmetry. "We begged them to use the same terminology and definitions of their work lest there be total confusion," recalls Malcom, who was chairwoman of a committee for the National Education Goals Panel.

Malcom says she feared the projects would not be taken seriously if they did not keep a tight rein on their list of standards. "If you say everything is equally important, you run a risk of saying nothing is of importance," she says. "None has met the parsimony test."

Finn is less gracious in his critique. "The professional associations, without exception, lacked discipline. They all demonstrated gluttonous and imperialistic tendencies."

Some cover content standards only; some include performance standards, and some list "opportunity to learn" standards that describe the resources students need to meet the standards. Some even have assessment recommendations. Some include teaching activities; others don't.

And they clearly speak to different audiences. For example, the history standards' teaching activities speak to classroom teachers. Civics standards, on the other hand, have no activities and are described as a technical document to be used for planning frameworks.

Only in one area are they nearly uniform. Except for physical education and health, they have set their benchmarks at three levels: grades K-4, 5-8, and 9-12.

At least four organizations—the Alliance for Curriculum Reform, the College Board's Forum on Standards and Learning, the Council for Basic Education, and the Mid-Continent Regional Educational Laboratory—are looking at ways to reconcile the standards documents.

Walking a Tightrope

The standards-setters acknowledge that their documents are voluminous. But they maintain that they are realistic if schools approach them as guides, picking and choosing what is appropriate for their students. They also say the material is cumulative and practical if schools start offering core courses earlier and more often.

Moreover, they believe that some topics can be taught across the curriculum. History and geography, for instance, have standards related to migration; geography and science both address the environment. And, they note, they are in a no-win situation. They've been criticized for their omissions and commissions alike. Gagnon, who served in the U.S. Education Department when the projects were first funded, compiled a list of criteria for the groups to follow. But in the end, other officials chose a less formal approach.

"What I emphasized was brevity," says Ravitch. She says she also told the groups to avoid "pedagogical imperialism—to say there was only one way to do things. Some of them at any rate did what they wanted to do."

Both Ravitch, who worked for Bush, and Marshall S. Smith, the current undersecretary of education, say department officials have always walked a tightrope where the standards projects were concerned: Take too strong a position and the federal government is accused of dictating standards. Be too lenient and be accused of lackadaisical oversight.

"If I had it all to do over again," says Ravitch, "I would hope to have more time. I would have told all of these projects they had to be deliverable in under 100 pages."

Had it been his call, Smith says he would have liked to have seen the standards developed over a seven- to eight-year period, using the same voluntary collaborative and reflective model the NCTM followed.

Lynne V. Cheney, a fellow at the American Enterprise Institute, says the whole affair illustrates the pitfalls of government entanglement. "As long as you have an instrument of the state involved, any effort to control content is problematic," she says. "It's a perfect argument for why the government shouldn't be involved in these."

A Public Lashing

The first public sign that the national standards were in trouble came in March 1994, when the Education Department refused to continue funding the English/language arts project. Department officials complained that the project hadn't made sufficient progress. In addition, its draft standards were vague and dwelt too much on opportunity-to-learn standards. Cheney says that an early version of the document defined literacy as the creation of meaning. "Come on," she scoffs. "We have kids who can't read bus schedules and we're going to say [that]? Literacy is figuring out when it says the bus is going to come."

But the controversy over English/language arts was nothing compared to what was to come.

A few weeks before the completed versions of the history standards were released, Cheney unleashed a blistering attack on the U.S. history standards.

She accused the document of portraying the United States and its white, male-dominated power structure as an oppressive society that victimizes minorities and women. She also argued that it downplayed—or outright ignored—such traditional historical figures as George Washington and Robert E. Lee to placate advocates of multicultural education.

Suddenly, the relatively parochial issue of education standards burst into the public consciousness via a flood of newspaper, radio, and television coverage.

Cheney's views won such exceptionally wide exposure because, as chairwoman of the National Endowment for the Humanities, she had lobbied for history standards, funded the project, and selected its leaders and many of the people on its 29-member board.

Soon it became evident that the criticism was not about to subside—even though there were far more supporters than detractors.

Gordon Cawelti, for one, thinks it's a shame that a few people could destroy all the hard work that has gone into the history standards, and he cautions not to write off the entire movement because of it. "The large majority of standards haven't been rejected. They simply haven't had exposure yet," says Cawelti, the former director of the Association for Supervision and Curriculum Development and a founder of the Alliance for Curriculum Reform.

Since the assault on the history standards, the back-to-basics movement has gained momentum. Fresh assaults have been made on math. Educators are bracing for an attack when the science standards are more widely circulated because of continuing turmoil over "creationism" and evolution. And the English and language arts standards are still likely to raise hackles in some quarters.

Fifty Experiments

Even though many educators and policymakers believe a wholesale adoption of national standards is doomed, they are equally certain that many schools will adopt higher standards in some shape or form.

"I have always thought of this as 50 experiments, but 50 experiments carried out around the notion of improving quality and improving equity," says the Education Department's Smith.

In Romer's view, the controversy won't kill off the concept because it is too logical. "Standards are simply that process that says, school year by school year, this is the content of what you should know and how good is good enough in terms of good performance. And if you're in the 6th grade and you want to be employed by MCI, you'd better know if you're on a track to being employable. And if a school can't tell you that, the school has failed you." ∎

From Education Week, *April 12, 1995*

21.

The True Road to Equity

Standards and assessments are worthless—a cruel hoax—unless schools are able to help all students meet them.

Commentary by David W. Hornbeck

We have a miserable performance record in educating low-income, racial- and language-minority students. Given the changing demographics of our nation, we cannot succeed economically or in sustaining our democracy unless we succeed educationally with those students whom we have historically failed. We need to create the policies and structures that result in high achievement by those students as well.

The most important question facing the nation today is whether America is really serious about pursuing educational equity. Or is it enough these days to only embrace the rhetoric that all children can learn? Many of us tend to be more delicate with the question, but for those who truly care about equity, perhaps the time has come to be blunt.

To be sure, equity will require extraordinary systemic change in the way education is delivered and governed. Different and greater capacities within the system are necessary. But those who go beyond the rhetorical must make sure that two of the essential components included in our comprehensive efforts to ensure high student achievement by all students are high national standards and a rigorous national assessment system.

Standards and assessments provide us with new arguments—moral, political, and legal—that can give us the leverage we need to change the system to respond to the needs of all of America's children.

Advocating strong standards and assessments now is in sharp contrast to the traditional posture of those, including many whose first priority is the equity agenda, who come at these issues saying, "No standards and assessments until or unless ... " It also contrasts with others who argue for standards and assessments and "then we'll consider other features of the system."

We should be insisting instead on quality standards and assessments now as part of building the capacity to help every child reach high levels of achievement. This, for example, is the kind of "social compact" that the New Standards Project has promised with its partners, 17 states and six urban school districts.

It is not enough to have standards and examinations. They must be "done" right. To do so, the standards must first be challenging. They must be national—not federal—adopted voluntarily by states. They must be developed from the best thinking of leaders in the professional discipline areas and must include structured, significant consultation with a diverse community of perspectives, including those reflecting the interests of low-income and racial- and language-minority students.

Second, examinations should be embedded in a system of multiple exams of different types—not a single national test.

Third, these examinations must be validated for particular uses and populations. This has powerful, positive equity implications since validity criteria should revolve around students' access to good instruction and curriculum that is relevant.

Fourth, attaching high stakes such as promotion or graduation for students should be permitted only after the school and its support system demonstrate success with a sufficient proportion of students, including those who are low-income, racial- or language-minority, to make clear "the system" knows how to educate all students.

Fifth, the primary indicator of school performance would be the proportion of successful students, broken out by income, race, and language. Success should be defined in terms of the increasing proportion of a school's successful students measured against that school's previous performance. Success should not be defined through simplistic interschool or interjurisdictional comparisons.

Standards would be worthless without assessments permitting us to know whether they are being met. Similarly, standards and assessments are equally worthless—a cruel hoax— unless schools are able to succeed in helping all students meet them. Thus, the imperative of a system of standards and examinations must be accompanied by complete systemic change to provide new capacities to serve all children well. These changes include:

● Time, not achievement, as the primary variable in the organization of each child's instructional program. High achievement as reflected by the standards must be the constant. Additional time can include instruction before and after school, on weekends, during the summer, and better use of the existing school day.

● A profound commitment to professional development that reflects school-level needs. This is analogous to the kind of commitment America's most successful corporations make to the continuous training and education of their employees.

● Support for school-based staff members so they can identify or develop curriculum and practice instructional strategies that result in all students meeting the new high standards.

● School staff and parents having more authority over decisions affecting the instruction of their children.

● Quality early-childhood programs for all disadvantaged students.

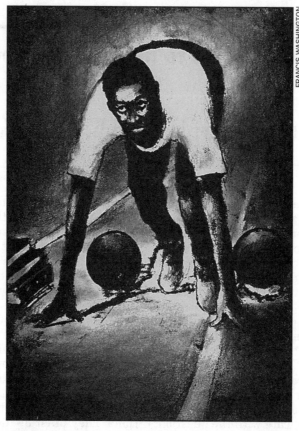

FRANCIS WASHINGTON

● Expanded, improved, and integrated services to eliminate the health and social barriers to learning.

● Technologies that enhance and individualize instruction and that offer teachers and students access to the best practice and people in the world. These technologies must be equitably available throughout the nation and within each state.

These are the elements of a change agenda that a number of us have been pursuing for some time. There even seems to be widespread agreement around them. So why are national standards and examinations so crucial to change and to the equity agenda? Because they provide the leverage to make it happen. They offer the leverage to affect every level of the system, from the classroom to the courtroom, from the student's house to the statehouse.

The single greatest obstacle faced by poor and minority students is the low expectations most adults have for their performance. Expectations are powerful, self-fulfilling prophecies. A highly visible national process of creating high standards and a rigorous examination system would create expectations for disadvantaged students that are not lower than those held for others. States and communities would be less likely to maintain today's system of expecting and asking less of poor and minority students and, consequently, offering them less. We must fundamentally change the present expectation framework that holds out only failure to far too many poor and minority students.

Standards and examinations that have been developed by a diverse community of interests will be a strong aid to teachers in fixing goals and testing what they need to do at the student and classroom levels.

There are more points of leverage. The proposed system would permit fair incentive systems for teachers and other school and district staff. Rewards, assistance, and penalties could be based on students' performance, with the school as the unit of measurement. It would be wholly unfair to work toward a system of high stakes for students if there were none for the adults responsible for their education.

A system rooted in high standards and rigorous examinations could provide the political basis for significantly higher funding. The public, as shown by poll after poll, is willing to pay more taxes if it can be certain that the extra money would result in improved education results. Legislators, following that line of thinking, often say they will not "throw good money after bad." They believe that more funding for "the same old things" will not produce results. In addition, there is a widespread view that, even after large increases in funding, educators are never held accountable. Educators, on the other hand, insist that more money must precede results. A new approach is necessary. If, for example, the public were assured that either the results would be forthcoming or that educators would face penalties, including possible job loss, the stage would be set for significant increases in funding.

Where the political remedy to insufficient funding was not forthcoming, the proposed system could offer a significant new legal strategy. If schools and districts don't bring students up to the new standards, the state could be held constitutionally accountable for providing the resources districts and schools need to have their students meet the standards. Moreover, student outcomes, not just the equal distribution of money, could play a more prominent role in remedies arising from such a legal strategy. The objective would become results, not just process and inputs.

There is at least one more compelling lever that a strong national standards and examinations system would provide. It could break the widespread complacency that now inhibits deep change. The prevalent view is that the country's schools are failing but "my school" is OK.

The fact is that a small percentage—some say as little as 5 percent—of our students perform at the levels required of an effective citizenry and an internationally competitive economy. But we now have no way of routinely sending an accurate message based on believable data. The common view arising from standardized, normed testing practice is that most students are performing at or above the "average." Many feel that is "good enough." High standards and rigorous examinations can change this perception. It will be clear that all students are at risk. Systemic change is more likely if the entire public knows that all children, including "my children," are in trouble.

The question we face is not standards and exams or no standards and exams. The actual choice is high standards and rich examinations in a system with enhanced capacity versus what we have now—a system of deeply embedded low standards, especially for disadvantaged students, and a heavy, sometimes exclusive, reliance on multiple-choice, normed tests. The proposed system is necessary to the equity agenda. The present system demonstrably undercuts that agenda.

Many believe that some form of national standards and testing is inevitable. If so, it becomes even more urgent that those who care most about those students we persistently fail become actively engaged. Only through such engagement can we help craft a system that helps all students succeed.

Some people come to this debate with an orientation toward the quality of the work force and America's economic competitiveness. Others come with a moral imperative to succeed with all students, including, for the first time in the nation's history, low-income, racial- and language-minority students. Neither will succeed without the other. The leadership of both groups must come at these issues affirmatively.

We must ensure that the system that arises from the debate includes high standards and rigorous examinations and the capacity to educate all students. Equity and excellence are within our grasp, but only if the Bush Administration, the Congress, educators, the business community, student and child advocates, and all others who care about children and the nation's future affirm a comprehensive change agenda. It is not an either-or choice. ∎

David W. Hornbeck is the superintendent of the Philadelphia School District.

From Education Week, *May 6, 1992*

22

Schools Are Not the Periphery

An accountability system that is rooted in local efforts would constitute a real national solution to our national problem.

Commentary by Joseph P. McDonald

All of the proposals to develop a national assessment system for the United States assert that we have a national problem. I agree. It concerns the fact that American schooling is out of sync with the needs of democracy and the emerging productivity demands in the workplace. By design, it aims some 30 percent of American kids toward college and ignores the prospects of the rest. Meanwhile, schooling insinuates through structures and attitudes that prospects are defined by native gifts, not effort.

Nearly everywhere, an industrial pedagogy, unapprized of the emergence of a postindustrial workplace, consigns school days to a regimen of decontextualized and decomposed knowledge, and measures "achievement" in hours of exposure to it. Overall, American schooling seems more concerned with sorting and labeling kids than with challenging them all to use their minds well. For want of resources especially, it is terribly resolute in diminishing the prospects of so-called minority kids, the parents of the American majority of the 21st century. All of this occurs against an ironic rhetorical backdrop that portrays the American school as the chief engine of equity and chief guarantor of citizenship.

A national problem demands a national solution. I agree again. That is, it demands a nationally concerted effort to ratchet up standards for all kids, to transform "common sense" attitudes about what intelligence is and about how intellectual interests and practical matters relate, to tune the intimate practices of hundreds of thousands of classrooms to new conceptions of knowledge and of learning, and to "rewire" tens of thousands of schools—that is, revamp how they go about the exchange of energy and information.

But how may we best pursue such a solution? Here's where I disagree. I think the current proposals for a national assessment system—those of the National Council on Education Standards and Testing, the America 2000 strategy, the latest SCANS Report, the New Standards Project, and Educate America Inc.—represent exactly the wrong approach. That is because these proposals pursue a national solution by means of a spuriously central mechanism. They mean to drive innovation from where they are—which they take to be the center of the American educational system—to where schools are—which they take to be the periphery. In fact, in the lives of teachers and kids—and of parents and communities—schools are at the center of American education. And at this center, they filter all policies through complex cultures. Ultimately, they are responsive only in perverse ways to incentives which discount their complexity and their centrality. A national examination—even elegantly realized in regional variations and alternative formats—may well drive schools toward mindless accountability.

As George Madaus has warned, no exam, however "authentic," can be considered immune from corruption when stakes rise. And as Linda Darling-Hammond has argued, an accountability system that only assesses kids, but that fails to assess the quality of the school's efforts to teach these kids, will be corrupted. Scores will rise as teachers reduce what they teach to just what the assessments assess and as principals manage to push out the kids whom they perceive as drags on their school's average. There is abundant evidence that in this fashion well-intentioned assessment hurts many kids now. Well-intentioned national assessment may enormously increase the extent of such injury.

This is not to argue that there is no good role for the National Assessment of Educational Progress, for nationally focused research and development efforts in assessment, or for nationally articulated goals and curriculum frameworks in the pursuit of higher standards for all kids. On the contrary, sensible accountability policy for the 1990s and beyond requires these initiatives. It is just that they must take care to avoid diminishing actual accountability by aiming too far and by inadvertently squelching local efforts. This will happen especially if they preempt the painstaking and difficult work of building local commitment and local capacity.

I want to see an accountability system that is rooted in local efforts to take stock—efforts that are networked with others, that are supported and audited by the states, and that are fed by perspectives on achievement and equity developed and refined on the national level. To my mind, such a system would constitute a real national solution to our national problem. It would require of each school that it open itself to inspection by stakeholders near and far; disclose what all its indicators of achievement reveal—including longitudinal and other locally constructed indicators; report annually to its community like a corporation to its stockholders; and equip itself with whatever internal systems it needs to take continuously corrective action in

the interests of ensuring all its kids' achievement at genuinely higher levels. It would also require, of course, a revolution at the center of American education—that is, in each American school's sense of purpose and in each one's design.

Advocates of national assessment schemes may well regard what I call a real national solution as a romantic and unattainable one. But I hurl the charge back at them. I think it is their vision that is romantic and unattainable—a kind of Napoleonic vision, whereby an authoritarian focus blurs out a historic opportunity for democracy. Their vision presumes that most Americans cannot be trusted to discern what is good—or bad—for their own children.

Chester Finn, for example, cites the evidence of polls that document most Americans' satisfaction with their own children's schools (urban parents notably excepted). You obviously cannot trust bottom-up reform schemes if people's taste is that bad, he argues.

But his argument—particularly curious coming from an advocate of school choice—lacks empathy for the polls' respondents. When faced with the stark question—"What do you think about the quality of your school?"—people closest to kids will color their response with an intuition: namely that kids derive much of the energy they bring to learning in school from their parents' and their teachers' investment in the value of that learning. To doubt one's own school is thus to seem to put one's own children at risk.

Yet I think most parents and teachers do harbor doubts, which then surface in their responses to the easier question: "What do you think of the quality of other people's schools?" That's when the fears tumble out—fears that are well warranted. That is also when the opportunity presents itself: Perhaps, after all, local commitment to genuine school reform is conceivable.

In fact, I believe that many local American communities yearn for a 21st century version of the Hoosier spelling bees, when whole prairie villages of the 19th century turned up at the schoolhouse once a year to verify that the year's school funds had been well spent. Of course, it is undeniable that many of these same communities have at best an inchoate sense of what achievement standards may be worthy of the 21st century. Some still seem to care more that their kids memorize the list of state capitals than that they acquire intellectually powerful habits of mind. It will

> # Whole prairie villages of the 19th century turned up at the schoolhouse once a year to verify that the year's school funds had been well spent.

be an exceedingly difficult task to awaken them to worthier standards than this, but to drive them there will be virtually impossible.

Meanwhile, I take heart from the recent revolution in the standards of American cuisine. Fairly recently, we had only two choices in American dining: either narrowly ethnic—red-sauce Italian, fried-rice Chinese—or else pot roast with salt and pepper. Today, however, our cuisine is among the most varied, the most inventive, the most dynamic in the world. We owe this result not to any effort to drive us toward the consumption of croissants and arugula—certainly not to the influence of a national gustatory exam—but, rather, to the confluence of several diverse factors, all of them with potential analogues in the effort to improve schools. First, there was an unprecedented opportunity—product of simultaneous surges in the nation's ethnic diversity, in its health consciousness, and in its media-based connectedness. Second, there was and is national leadership—Julia Child, Craig Claiborne, the Silver Palate ladies, even C. Everett Koop. Next, a national cadre of chefs trained by a handful of restaurants and cooking schools, patronized by in-

creasingly dispersed cosmopolitan taste, cultivated in turn by good writing and television. Finally—and perhaps most importantly—a great growth in appreciation of the value of local cuisines and of the freshness of locally available ingredients.

Like better tastes in dining, higher expectations for kids' achievement are inevitably entangled with values, and values legitimately vary somewhat from one American community to another. To ignore this preeminence of local interest in the overall effort to create change is to take a great ethical and political risk—and so to endanger a crucial mission.

In the matter of transforming our tastes in schooling, I think we have no choice but to tolerate each community's painstaking effort to cultivate taste. We outsiders can play a vital role in this valuable process—though not a decisive one—through the provision of national expectations, the provocation of richly constructed assessment models, the enhancement of communication among schools (for example, by means of the electronic network that the National Science Foundation is working on), and, of course, an insistence on the entitlement of every American child to a good education.

Happily, there is plenty of innovation in assessment and accountability that has been launched and is now proceeding well without benefit of national driving—in Vermont, California, Kentucky, San Diego, Pittsburgh, the Center for Collaborative Education in New York City, Sullivan High School in Chicago, Thayer High School in New Hampshire, English High School in Boston, to single out only a few state and local examples. In order to build a national solution to the national problem in American education, I think we need much experimentation with new accountability schemes and new kinds of assessment, and we need it at all levels of educational policy—from NAEP to Jefferson County, Ky., to Rancho San Joaquin Middle School in Southern California. We need it in such diversity and breadth as to match the enormous enterprise it seeks to serve, but we need it especially at the center of that enterprise. If we don't have it there, then all the scholarly and political talent we now have working at the periphery will be worth little. In fact, it is likely to cause a lot of trouble. ■

Joseph P. McDonald is senior researcher at the Coalition of Essential Schools, Brown University.

From Education Week, *May 20, 1992*

23.

The Changing Forgotten Half

It's less than half, and it's two-thirds male.

By Clifford Adelman

You remember "the forgotten half," of course. The phrase was propelled onto the editorial pages and into public consciousness by the 1988 reports of the William T. Grant Foundation Commission on Work, Family, and Citizenship. Despite the complexity of the commission's analysis of the interactions of education, family formation, and income dynamics, the phrase has become a sloganistic shorthand for "non-college-bound youths," and is applied to those between the ages of 16 and 20.

The Grant Commission warned us about misusing the phrase, but we have insisted. The shorthand makes three dubious statements. First, that those who complete high school and continue their education have enough attention paid to them, thank you. They are well taken care of, and will succeed as participating members of our society and economy. Second, and conversely, that nobody cares about people who do not meet these criteria, and they, in turn, will not succeed. The slogan thus labels and predicts winners and losers. Lastly, the slogan relies on a convenient benchmark, "half." Sounds neat.

How accurate are these assumptions? The best way to find out is not to look prospectively from the position of a 16-year-old, but rather retrospectively from the position of a 30-year-old. Determine what actually happens to people by the time they establish themselves as adults, and only then classify them on the basis of what they were doing when they were 15 or 18 or 20. Having done so, we can determine precisely whom we are talking about, how large a group they constitute, and hence where—and in what quanti-

ties—we should be aiming policy.

The best place to find out who winds up in "the forgotten half" lies in the U.S. Education Department's longitudinal studies. Longitudinal studies are like movies. We watch the same people over a long period of time. Longitudinal studies are slow and frustrating, but very accurate, particularly when the archive of information includes school and college records.

The studies began in 1972 (with 12th graders), 1980 (with 10th graders), and 1988 (with 8th graders). Each was designed to follow its group for 12 to 15 years. In 1993, we know a good deal about the first two groups.

What happened to the Class of '72 by "thirtysomething"? Since this group was set up in the spring of its senior year in high school, we miss the 20 percent of the cohort that the U.S. Census tells us never made it to commencement. Of the high school graduates (three million people), 40 percent neither continued their formal education nor received training in the military. Another 15 percent continued their education, but earned fewer than a semester's worth of credits by the time they were 30.

Notice that this description already includes two other retrospective groups: folks who pursued military careers (in which there is a good deal of care and training), and folks who went to college, community college, or vocational school but who wound up as incidental students. Were these people "forgotten"? I don't think so.

For the entire cohort that might have been in the Class of '72, "the forgotten half" is nonetheless an understatement: It's more than 55 percent. And if you look back from the status of these individuals at age 32 to their status as teenagers and young adults, what you see is no surprise: very little math or science in high school, low scores on basic-skills/learned-ability tests, no attempt to return to school at any time, higher degrees of unemployment, lower satisfaction with jobs and career paths.

The Class of '82 is already showing us a somewhat different pattern, starting with a high school graduation rate 8 percent higher than that for the Class of '72. And preliminary indications suggest an increase of 4 percent to 5 percent in the proportion of those who had some postsecondary education by the time they were in their late 20s. Based on what I've observed of the college transcripts coded so far, we should also see a drop in the percentage of incidental students. I don't know whether the final data (due in the fall) will support these estimates precisely, or how much of the class received its postsecondary training in the military, but it looks like "the forgotten half" is now less than 45 percent.

What's happened? First, it was a lot easier for people to attend college, community college, or vocational school in the 1980s than it was in the 1970s. We did not have Pell Grants or massive Guaranteed Student Loan programs in 1972 for people who might otherwise have been "forgotten," but by 1982 we did.

Second—and more importantly—while college enrollment rates rose by 10 percent between 1972 and 1989, the enrollment rate for women rose twice as much as that for men. Women now account for 55 percent of all postsecondary students. This trend is part of a larger story of the spectacular rise in women's educational attainment, and of changes in attitudes of parents toward their daughters' futures.

If "the forgotten half" is now somewhat less than "half," it is also heavily male. Unless we do something different than we're currently doing (or thinking about doing), it will continue to be that way. For what national longitudinal studies consistently demonstrate is that men are less frequent and enthusiastic participants in education or training than are women. In addition, the most conservative estimates of cutbacks in military "accessions" mean that from 85,000 to 100,000 people a year will no longer have this option for further education and training open to them, and will thus fall into "the forgotten half." The vast majority of this group is male.

Our current educational response to "the forgotten half" focuses on some well-intentioned alternatives to traditional vocational and cooperative education. Nearly all these new forms of school-to-work transition programs involve combinations of academic and vocational education, roles for community colleges, occupational (or career-path) "majors," participation of local businesses, and on-the-job mentoring.

But from limited data available on these experimental school-to-work programs directed at "the for-gotten half," men again appear to be a minority of participants. For example, the ProTech program in Boston, a creation of Jobs for the Future, is 64 percent female. The model apprenticeship program run by the Maine Center for Youth Apprenticeship out of Maine Technical College in South Portland is 67 percent female. The most recent estimate from the demonstration Tech-Prep program at Mt. Hood Community College in Oregon is that of the 252 students who transferred credits from their high schools, nearly 70 percent were female.

To be sure, some of this has to do with the way labor market segmentation drives demand-side education. That is, the health-service fields dominate the ProTech program, for example, and health services are traditionally female occupations. But even when new modes of school-to-work transition programs are established with a balance of "traditionally male" and "traditionally female" occupations, the curriculum and training pathways in the female fields attract larger

> # The challenge is to change young men's attitudes toward what will make a difference in individual lives and the life of the community.

populations. Why?

These programs are all small in scope: 115 students here, 15 there, and 40 somewhere else. Even when you add them up, double or triple their capacity, and assume that the capacity will be filled, their total coverage is still marginal. Expansions at the margin are worthy, but selective. When programs are selective, they "cream." That is, they take the best, the most motivated, the most likely to persist. In matters of education, whether academic, vocational, or some combination of the two, women meet those criteria far more than men, and are likely to dominate the selected.

This is a serious issue, one that is little marked in discussions of youth policy. As is the case with most education issues, we are obsessed with race and socioeconomic status. We rarely think about gender. But look within every ethnic or socioeconomic group, and you will see that men have fallen off the mark.

How do we bring them back to the mark? While the challenge involves family, community, and broader cultural trends, it is fair to ask what education and training programs can do. I don't have a full plate of answers, but a guiding principle in these efforts should be to nurture and not disconnect. Small study and work groups or networks have proven to be productive in this regard. As long as the networks are task-driven, members will feel more valued than if they worked alone, and, as a consequence, should develop more confidence in their ability to learn.

Study and work groups yield involvement, and I am less worried than the lawyers if all the members of a group are of the same gender. As a parent, I am also not disturbed if networking of male adolescents ties up telephone lines or shares family tools and books (as long as I get them back). These connections work against the doubt and discontinuity that adolescent men seek to cover with behaviors (braggadocio and hot air being among the least harmful, though most common) that close them off from future productivity.

Other occasions for male involvement in task-oriented teams, from athletics to drama to youth/church groups, should be utilized as much as possible. Don't sneer: The histories of the classes of 1972 and 1982 clearly demonstrate that those who were involved in these activities were more likely to persist in school and continue their education than those who were not involved.

Researchers at Pennsylvania State University have also reported these activities to be "validating" experiences for entering college and community-college students who were otherwise doubtful of their place in a learning community. Reading through transcripts of interviews with these students, I found the men consistently more uncertain than women.

Jack Miller, who directs the demonstration Tech-Prep program at Mt. Hood Community College and its eight feeder high schools, adds another dimension to our understanding of this phenomenon when he notes that "by age 17 or 18, men are more likely to give up on schooling; but the community college sees them again when they are 29 or so, coming back and struggling with basic skills so that they can make it into high-tech training programs." A decade is lost in there; and while the community colleges (unlike other educational institutions) are flexible enough to help, there is a lot of territory for them to cover.

This lost time and territory cry out for a changing of young men's attitudes toward what will make a difference in individual lives and the life of the community. That's a responsibility we all share. Let's start by not labeling people as "forgotten," or giving them the false security of thinking they belong to a large group, even if it isn't quite "half." ∎

Clifford Adelman is a senior research analyst at the U.S. Education Department. The opinions in this essay are his own, and no endorsement of the U.S. Education Department should be inferred.

From Education Week, *Sept. 8, 1993*

24.

A Sense of Ownership

When it came time to set demanding academic standards, folks in Beaufort, S.C., decided they'd rather do the job themselves.

By Debra Viadero

In November 1861, months before most of the great battles of the Civil War had even begun, 30,000 Union troops arrived by sea at this picturesque town on the South Carolina coast.

The soldiers in blue swarmed over the stately pillared homes left behind by fleeing cotton and rice planters. They transformed what was once known as the "Newport of the South" into a Southern headquarters for the Union army and occupied the town until the war ended four years later.

Beaufort County hasn't been the same since.

That is partly why, as national education leaders and policymakers are seeking for the first time to set common, voluntary standards that describe what all students across the nation should know and be able to do, people in Beaufort County have decided they'd rather do it themselves. It's not that the people here don't want to hold their children to the same academic expectations that students elsewhere are being asked to meet. They do.

But the achievement benchmarks that this community outlines for its own schools cannot appear to be imposed or handed down by someone else—especially not someone connected with the federal government. Beaufortonians have had enough of that. The standards that determine what Beaufort County's children learn in school must come from Beaufort County itself.

"It's ownership," says Kathleen D. Rundquist, the district's curriculum supervisor. "If you're given standards and told, 'do it,' you're doing someone else's standards," she says. "If you're given a chance to massage those standards, they become yours."

As suited as they are to a place like Beaufort, these sentiments are not unusual for districts looking to set academic expectations for students, according to some of the experts and consultants who advise them. From Red Clay, Del., to Corpus Christi, Tex., school districts that want to raise educational standards for their children are forging similar paths.

They are reviewing the subject-matter standards that have been developed by national panels of experts and educators, but they are also looking at their own state's curriculum goals and guidelines. They are borrowing standards developed by other school districts. They are looking at standards set by the College Board's Advanced Placement courses, and they are asking their citizens what they think.

In the end, many of these efforts, like Beaufort's, may encompass much of the same content that makes up the national standards. But they will also belong uniquely to the communities that shape them.

"National standards are already being used and will come to be used as reference manuals," says Ruth Mitchell, a consultant who has worked with the Council for Basic Education to help at least three districts craft their own academic standards. "The issue is not so much the content standards themselves but who

96

gets to talk about them."

Having communities reinvent their work may—or may not—have been what national standards-setters had in mind when they set to work in the late 1980s. However, had those meetings taken place in a setting like Beaufort—rather than in Washington—they might have anticipated that outcome.

Made up entirely of islands and water, Beaufort County can arguably stake a claim to being one of the most unusual places in the country. Of the more than 91 islands that make up this part of South Carolina's "low country," only 19 are inhabited. And many of the islands were not joined by bridges until well into the 20th century.

The county is also a place of socioeconomic extremes—a fact that facilitates and frustrates the job of implementing rigorous new academic standards.

One extreme can be found at the southern end of the county in such places as Hilton Head, which has become a haven for wealthy retirees, tennis players, and boaters. New waterfront homes in this part of the county may sell for $1 million or more. To the north lies another. Here, one can find poor, mostly black families living in abandoned trailers, one-room shacks, and homes with no indoor plumbing. The wealth of Hilton Head and other islands provides the county with a tax base substantial enough to allow the school system to spend an annual average of $4,300 on each pupil—more than most school districts in South Carolina do. But the poverty and isolation of many of the island communities to the north also means that the job of making sure that all 20,000 students in this system meet tougher standards will be that much more difficult.

Time To Raise the Bar

Like the rest of the state, Beaufort County schools had for years measured their success by their students' performance on state-required basic-skills tests.

It became apparent, however, that the tests had done little more than raise the scores of the district's lowest-achieving students. The performance of the district's top-achieving students, in the meantime, was stagnating.

Once Beaufort's students switched to taking national standardized tests it became even clearer that something was lacking in the schools. On one such test given in 1990, for example, 61 percent of students across the country were achieving at higher levels than Beaufort's students were.

In the late 1980s and early 1990s, educators in both South Carolina and at the national level were reaching similar conclusions about the need to set higher expectations for schools.

In the early 1990s, South Carolina took action.

Under the leadership of Barbara S. Nielsen, the state superintendent of schools, South Carolina set about the task of creating curriculum frameworks in eight subjects that would call for better-than-minimum academic performance from all students across the state.

At the national level, the movement to set higher academic standards began in earnest after 1989 when President George Bush and the nation's governors met in Charlottesville, Va., to set national education goals.

But those efforts would take time. Now, more than five years later, national standards have only just been completed in four of the five subjects originally specified in the national goals.

South Carolina has finished curriculum frameworks in four of eight targeted subject areas—mathematics, foreign language, English, and the arts. Beaufort County last year decided it couldn't afford to wait.

At the time, groups of angry citizens and parents were parading their concerns in front of the school board week after week.

Beginning in 1993, the district was also getting pressure of a more positive kind from a newly formed citizens' group on Hilton Head. The group, Beaufort 2000, was one of the thousands of community groups that sprang up across the nation to support the national education goals and President Bush's America 2000 plan for improving schools. Having academic standards was part of that group's vision.

But the discord within the district had also led to a movement to divide the county into two separate school systems, one north of the cultural and socioeconomic dividing line drawn by the Broad River and another south of it. And children were not getting any younger.

Beaufort's students are competing for jobs with students from school systems across the country and even around the world. Their education will have to be just as good. Or better. "What we want," says Richard Flynn, who became Beaufort's superintendent four years ago, "is to be the best."

Down to Work

At the urging of a local citizens' group, the district hired Denis P. Doyle, a nationally known education consultant, to assist in its standards-setting efforts.

With the help of Doyle and his colleagues, the district last fall put out the first call for volunteers to serve on standards-setting committees in some of the subject areas that Beaufort hoped to tackle. In all, the district will set standards in eight areas: mathematics, English, social studies, science, the arts, foreign language, health and wellness, and a broad area called community service that will also encompass vocational skills.

The 19 volunteers chosen for each committee included students as well as local business people, parents, and retirees. The director of a local orchestra sat on the arts panel, for example, and a retired Ford Motor Company telecommunications executive helped craft English standards.

"We find that the community people really tend to help push teachers out of their boxes," says Susan Pimentel, who is working with Doyle on Beaufort's standards-setting efforts.

"What I've suggested to my group is to periodically do a reality check," says Bonnie Smith, the retired Ford executive and chairwoman of Beaufort 2000. "They had a little bit of elitism in the beginning, and I would say, 'Wait a minute. Time out. Tell me how this is going to help me in business, how it's going to help this person get a job.'"

But 10 of the 19 members on each committee were teachers.

"Teachers are the ones who get stuck doing it, so they should have the loudest voice," says Doyle, who recommended the panel's configuration. "At the same time, we wanted to send the message to the community that they're important, too."

Each committee was handed a range of standards documents. If national standards were available in their subject area, committee members looked at those. They reviewed standards set in the early 1990s by the Charlotte-Mecklenberg, N.C., school system—another client of Doyle's. They looked at Advanced Placement exam standards and standards for the International Baccalaureate program.

In science, for example, the committee read a set of benchmarks for teaching science set by the American Association for the Advancement of Science, standards drafted by the National Academy of Sciences, and curriculum guidelines from Connecticut and Japan.

"When the best minds in the nation get together in a particular field, it would be irresponsible of us as educators to not take a look at what they're saying," says Melissa Sheppard, an elementary school principal who sits on the social-studies committee.

'People Like Themselves'

By far, however, the most helpful documents were not the national standards, these educators and citizens say. They took most of their cues from the standards set by the Charlotte-Mecklenberg schools. At the time Charlotte-Mecklenberg put its documents together, national standards for teaching math had already been published by the National Council of Teachers of Mathematics. Educators in the district had already taken that 258-page document, boiled it down, and put it in a format that made sense to Beaufort's standards-setters.

Moreover, says Doyle, "they know people like themselves have done it and not some intellectuals off at a watering hole somewhere."

Beaufort's educators also liked the format their North Carolina colleagues had chosen. Rather than set standards for students at the 4th, 8th, and 12th grades, as most of the national standards documents do, Charlotte-Mecklenberg's standards specify five academic levels.

As they are represented in Beaufort's documents, these levels begin with the "readiness" level, which applies generally to students in pre-kindergarten and kindergarten but could also mean students at any grade level who are just starting out a particular course of study, such as foreign language.

The next level, "foundations," loosely applies to elementary school students. There are also "essentials" levels for middle school students and "proficient" levels for high school students. In addition, the Beaufort standards-setters created a level called "distinction," which is intended for the handful of students who are expected to do better than proficient work, perhaps by pursuing college-level coursework while still in high school. Only the national standards developed for the arts set out similarly high-level standards for high school students.

Other districts have approached the task slightly differently. Corpus Christi, for example, went to its citizens first, asking them what they wanted students to know and be able to do by the time they graduated from high school. Then, teachers were asked to come up with standards that would help meet that goal and that also would comport with national standards.

In Milwaukee, the school system had already set goals for students in such broad interdisciplinary areas as problem-solving and communications. Educators in that city are now drawing up standards in every subject that would reflect those goals.

"This business about top-down, bottom-up reform is really working," says Patte Barth, who is assisting in the Council for Basic Education's effort to guide standards-setting in Milwaukee, Chicago, and Jackson, Miss. "In those three examples of districts, their standards all look very different on the surface, but when you read them, you can see that you really have some national coherence."

"This is a process that has to happen in a community," she adds. "We would like to see it happen in every school."

In truth, however, no one knows how many districts across the country are developing their own standards and guidelines for student learning. Experts say it is a good bet, however, that many will not bother at all.

The Debates

In Beaufort, when teachers first looked at the national standards placed before them, some said they were too demanding. They pointed out that resources weren't available for teaching to such high standards, and they said there wasn't enough time in the school calendar to meet them.

"As a teacher, it's hard to sit there and not say 'I don't think we can do that,'" says Brenda McLeod, the high school math teacher who headed up the standards panel in that subject area.

To such concerns, school administrators had a set reply. "We would tell them that their job is to create world-class standards," says Rundquist, the curriculum supervisor. "Let us worry about implementing them."

One rule was to remain ironclad throughout the process: Standards-setters could not craft benchmarks any lower than those on which they were drawing.

'It's like turning a big ship. There's going to be this continuous process of refinement.'

But the groups also varied in how they approached their tasks. Some, such as the math group, adhered closely to national standards. Others, such as social studies, saw their job as one of picking and choosing.

"We have to practice what I call courageous deletion," says Roy Stehle, the district's social-studies supervisor. "We can't teach it all."

What's more, Beaufort's students must learn South Carolina history in 8th grade. Nationwide, most districts tend to teach local history in 4th grade.

"If you said to a teacher, 'Here are national standards in history, geography, and economics, and you've got to put all this in your course,' that teacher is going to panic," Stehle adds. "What I hope to do with this process is translate standards into what happens in the classroom."

Sometimes, the groups debated language they knew would be "hot buttons" in their own communities. Members of the arts panel, for example, argued over the use of the word "meditation," in their guidelines for theater instruction. Some educators pointed out that the term could bring on accusations that they were trying to teach so-called "New Age religion."

"Who wants to argue with a parent over that?" a teacher on the panel asked other committee members.

The word "evolution," which appears in the national science standards, was also carefully avoided in Beaufort's standards statements. Current drafts of that document say only that students at the "essentials" level should study "features and forces that shape the earth and the earth's relationship to the universe."

The committees also weeded out technical jargon,

with the exception of "terms of art" for which there were no simpler substitutes, such as "palindrome," which refers to a specific choreographic structure in dance.

"If I'm a parent, I don't know what a 'palindrome' is, but at least I have something I can ask the teacher about," Pimentel, Doyle's associate, says. Pimentel's job, in part, is to moderate the standards meetings. Then, she edits the draft documents and "references" them to national standards, sometimes penciling back in for reconsideration a concept that the local panels had dropped.

The object of all the work done by Beaufort's standards-setting committees early on was to create broad two- to three-page statements that outline, in lay terms, what students should know and be able to do in each of the eight subject areas.

Now, new committees made up entirely of teachers are looking at those statements and, in Pimentel's words, "blowing them out" to come up with more specific performance objectives. They will describe, for example, exactly what it means for high school students to "analyze and respond to complicated literature." These objectives, rather than any standards themselves, will be teachers' classroom bibles. Most teachers in this district, in fact, will never see national standards. Shorter, more plainly written pamphlets will also be put together in each subject area and distributed to parents.

Beaufort's standards-setters, however, only last month began the process of showcasing to the public the work they have done.

The risk of losing credibility with the community is a real one. Like the national standards, Beaufort County's emerging standards appear to be high.

As one teacher at a January meeting of the foreign language committee put it: "Do the words 'Dream on' mean anything to you?"

Getting It Done

To be sure, the district does have some tools to help make the standards common practice. This summer, for example, educators will begin work on assessments that will be based on the standards. The idea is to eventually use these as gateways through which students must pass before going on to the next level of schooling.

These exams would also be performance based, meaning that students would have to demonstrate what they know rather than fill in boxes on computerized testing forms.

"All I want is for everybody to take the same kind of test," says Superintendent Flynn, who has come under criticism from some teachers for overemphasizing testing.

Already, a principal's salary is determined, in part,

by how his or her school measures up on standardized achievement tests. And, if Flynn had his way, teachers would be paid in the same manner.

Other factors will likely work to ease the way for the standards. State law bars local teachers' unions from negotiating salary contracts. And many Beaufort teachers, although paid at rates above the state-mandated minimum, already work unpaid hours after school to plan lessons and staff remedial programs. Beaufort's administrators say this, too, will be an asset in their effort to raise educational quality with minimal cost.

In addition, the district's newly elected school board voted to require the district to begin accelerated efforts this summer to train kindergarten through 3rd grade teachers to teach to new reading and math standards. Among the lessons they will get are strategies for doing away with ability-based reading groups, like the "redbirds" and the "bluebirds," in favor of more flexible groups formed on the basis of the specific knowledge a student needs to acquire.

The idea is to have at least those standards in place by the start of the next school year. "People say 'How can you do this?'" says Rundquist. "We ask them to think in terms of those kindergarten students just starting out who are getting everything in these standards from the beginning. If you look at it that way, then, yes, we can do this."

Pimentel predicts, however, that it may be eight to 10 years before Beaufort's administrators can confidently say that most teachers, in all the district's 17 schools, are teaching to the new standards.

"It's like turning a big ship," she says. "There's going to be this continuous process of refinement."

Teachers can use interdisciplinary methods to tackle standards in several subjects at once. Even so, however, most educators here seem to agree that teaching to the standards will take more time than schools now allot for instruction.

"We obviously can't think about 8:30 to 3:30 anymore," says Catherine Spencer, the district's arts supervisor. "That time frame was set up for another day and place."

Flynn says his district has already taken some tentative steps in that direction as well. Two schools plan to add five days to their calendars over the next academic year. Others require students who get low scores on current standardized texts to attend special three-week sessions. More concrete plans in that regard, however, have yet to materialize.

As for money, district officials do not expect they will need a lot more of it. The school board last year approved a five-year improvement plan that Flynn says translates to a total of $1 million to $1.5 million in additional funds for the system. Some of that money will be used to train teachers to teach to the new standards.

In addition, the $168,000 the district has agreed to pay Doyle Associates covers training and strategizing sessions to assist the school system in delivering on the standards.

Beyond that, school officials are talking about ways to creatively infuse more resources into the schools. They talk about using volunteers from the community, hiring primary teachers who may already be bilingual, and making creative use of Title I money as ways to fulfill the standards. And, as Spencer points out, the standards' call to require students to play an instrument might not necessarily mean a trumpet; rhythm sticks could qualify, too. Additional money might not be forthcoming. Last May, the county turned down the school district's request for an $80 million-plus bond referendum to build schools and upgrade the technology in existing ones. Perhaps the biggest unanswered question, however, will be how all of Beaufort's students will fare under newer, more rigorous academic standards. "A lot of youngsters will have no problem at all," says Laura Bush, the school board's new chairwoman. "We have a lot of youngsters who are going to get caught."

"That's the question I always raise."

Looking for the Positives

In the end, the federal invasion of Beaufort more than a century ago turned out to have a positive side. While other Southern cities burned to the ground during the Civil War, Beaufort's handsome homes emerged from the war unscathed.

Thousands of local slaves were freed and given an opportunity to buy small parcels of former plantation lands. And one of them, Robert Smalls, went on to become the nation's first black congressman.

Beaufort's educators are hoping that many such positive results will one day flow from the subtler, nearly invisible, infusion of national academic standards here. ■

From Education Week, *April 12, 1995*

25.

Learning To Care

The Child Development Project helps schools take aim at students' intellectual, social, and ethical development.

By Debra Viadero

Heather and Larry, two upper-elementary students at Hazelwood Elementary School, are at the age when boys and girls don't pal around together. Today, though, both are working busily on a Venn diagram that shows how they are alike and how they are different. One circle is labeled "Heather" and the other "Larry." In the outer edges of those circles, the classmates have scribbled a few of their individual preferences. Heather has written that she likes cats. Larry's tastes run to sports. But the space where the circles intersect is crowded with entries—swimming, rap music, hot dogs, snakes, pizza, school, and the *Mighty Morphin Power Rangers* television program. There is no more room to write.

"Hey," Heather says with a look of surprise on her round face, "look at all the stuff we both like."

Making these kinds of discoveries happen is what the Child Development Project is all about. The project, a 14-year-long research-and-development effort, is in its final year of piloting here at Hazelwood and at 11 other primary schools across the country. And the educators and researchers taking part in the project say the results so far are encouraging.

Like a lot of school reform efforts, the aim of the project is to improve children's learning. It uses real and compelling selections of children's literature, for example, to interest pupils in reading and to spur them to think critically. It advocates teaching strategies designed to help students build their own knowl-

edge much in the way they create houses out of Lincoln logs, and it encourages them to work cooperatively in groups.

But the Children's Development Project also goes contemporary school improvement efforts one better: It seeks to teach children like Heather and Larry to care about one another. And it does that by creating "caring communities" like the one at Hazelwood, a school that serves some of this city's most disadvantaged children.

Seeking a Better Answer

There is not much research on how to teach children to care, according to Nel Noddings, a Stanford University professor who has written several books on the subject. Of the studies that do exist, some of the earliest produced dismal results. For example, one showed that children in such groups as the Boy Scouts would demonstrate more caring behaviors when adults were present, but they behaved no differently than other children their age after the adults went away.

Up until the 1990s, Noddings says, the dominant strategy for teaching moral behavior in classrooms was the so-called Kohlbergian model. Under this approach, named for the late Harvard psychologist Lawrence Kohlberg, students were given moral dilemmas to discuss. The trouble was that no one could prove that the ability to reason morally would lead to improved moral behavior.

Schools that didn't use that approach—if they taught values at all—did so as an add-on to the regular curriculum.

In 1981, the Menlo Park, Calif.-based William and Flora Hewlett Foundation began looking for a better answer.

What they had in mind was a program that could address the whole child. That meant nurturing children's ethical and social development as well as their intellectual growth. It also meant making character education an integral part of the curriculum and the climate of schools.

What's more, the program had to be backed by studies to show that it could improve the learning and behavior of real children in real schools.

To put it all together, the foundation chose a California-based research organization called the Pacific Institute for Research and Evaluation. At the time, the institute was developing and evaluating programs aimed at preventing delinquency and drug abuse among teenagers. However, the new project quickly became its major focus, and the institute was recast as the Developmental Studies Center.

"This seemed to us to be a much more meaningful and productive kind of work rather than working later with problems that arise from inadequate development," says Eric Schaps, the center's president.

The center's research scientists sifted through all the available literature on children's development to put together a program. From Jean Piaget and L.S. Vygotsky, they gathered developmental theory. Studies on cooperative learning provided strategies for helping children learn to work together. They borrowed from cognitive psychology, research on children's motivation, and psychological studies suggesting that children thrive when they're given a sense of having a say in their lives and a sense of belonging to a group.

Testing the Waters

The program was tested in three elementary schools in San Ramon, Calif., a suburb in the Bay Area.

"We wanted a district that was large enough to accommodate the research well but small enough that the project wouldn't get lost," Schaps recalls. "We also wanted a district that was not experiencing declining enrollment because that causes a lot of financial and political problems, and we wanted a district where there was considerable support to do this."

Teachers in San Ramon were given curricular materials and intensive training that took place in week-long summer sessions, in monthly workshops during the school year, and in individual coaching sessions.

To gauge the program's success, the researchers tracked children at the three schools from the time they entered kindergarten until they reached 6th grade. They then compared their progress with that of students the same age at three local control schools serving the same kinds of student populations.

Observers who had no idea what the program was about were sent to classrooms in all of the schools for eight two-hour periods to record what teachers and students were doing. Researchers also interviewed students annually, giving them hypothetical moral dilemmas to solve and analyzing their responses.

They found that children in the experimental classrooms behaved more considerately toward their classmates and worked better together. In interviews, they showed a better understanding of others' perspectives and a greater ability to solve interpersonal conflicts.

And, on questionnaires, they were more likely to report that they saw their classrooms as communities.

Academically, students in both the experimental and the control groups scored about the same on standardized achievement tests. But the program students scored higher on another measure designed to assess their higher-order thinking abilities.

Two years later, after they left the program and went on to junior high school, the students were still showing positive effects from the program. In comparison with their peers in the control group, for example, program students were more involved in extracurricular activities, and their teachers rated them as more assertive and popular.

The program was tested again in much the same way in nearby Hayward, a poorer, more ethnically diverse school district that at the time was undergoing considerable upheaval. Implementation of the program was spottier there and, although the effort produced similar positive effects, they were somewhat weaker. One point, however, was clear: Classrooms that observers judged to be implementing the program extensively had students who showed more prosocial behaviors.

"It wasn't the kind of kid that made the difference," Schaps says. "It was whether the program happened or not that made the difference."

Encouraged, project developers in 1991 raised more than $14 million from several foundations and expanded to six more districts. They targeted two program schools and two control schools in each one. Jefferson County, Ky., where Hazelwood is located, is one of those districts. Others are in Cupertino, Salinas, and San Francisco, Calif.; Dade County, Fla.; and White Plains, N.Y.

The center has not yet released the findings from the second-year evaluation of those districts, but Schaps says the program is showing promise.

"What we've seen are the kinds of changes happening that, in all our prior research, are correlated with positive student outcomes," he says. The organization is already making plans to disseminate parts of the program more widely. After 14 years, Schaps adds, "we think we're ready now."

Putting the Program in Place

Of the six districts involved in the effort, Jefferson County was the only one to produce positive changes in students in as little as a year.

That's the sort of thing that is not supposed to happen in a place like Hazelwood, the school that Heather and Larry attend. Only a rusted chain-link fence separates this school from the largest housing project in Kentucky. Three-quarters of Hazelwood's 600 students go home to those projects every afternoon. In all, 93 percent of the school's students come from families poor enough to qualify them for the federal subsidized-lunch program.

"I can tell you that teachers were lined up at the door trying to find other places to go," says Brenda Logan, who became the school's principal barely a year before the project started there. "You're in a high-risk area, and you're dealing with poverty and difficult parents."

For the most part, teachers say they kept order in their classes by using assertive-discipline techniques. They would, for example, put check marks on the board next to the names of students who were behaving well, or they handed out stickers and marbles. It didn't work.

"The first year I came, there were monumental numbers of students being referred to me from teachers—for everything from chewing gum to major fights," Logan says. "It was almost like in any of those situations where kids had to work with one another or play with one another they just didn't know how to do it."

When the Child Development Project arrived, teachers had mixed reactions. Some thought to themselves, "This is just what this school needs." Others were more skeptical.

"I thought of that red-hot word 'values.' Whose values?" recalls Marcia Davis, who teaches kindergarten and 1st grade at Hazelwood. "And I thought, 'They're from California. I wonder if I'm going to find out I lived another life or something.'"

What Davis soon discovered, however, was that the values the program stressed—fairness, helpfulness, responsibility, and concern and respect for others— were the same values that she wanted for her students.

The project also arrived at Hazelwood just as the state was embarking on what is probably the most sweeping education reform effort in the nation. But educators at Hazelwood say they found the parallel efforts had compatible goals.

"When the Kentucky Education Reform Act came we kept asking, 'When is the training going to take place? What does the primary program look like?' No one gave you any map to get to that point," Logan says. The Child Development Project provided the map.

In the training sessions, teachers were taught to reflect on their own practice, to ask the kinds of questions that elicit students' thinking, and to give students responsibility for their own learning. They learned ways to maintain order without using extrinsic rewards or punishments.

"People started thinking, 'What did I accomplish with the old classroom management approaches?'" says Sheila Koshewa, who coordinates the program for the district. "They realized, 'I want my students to be able to manage themselves, to learn to get along, to realize they make choices in how they behave.'"

Now, in many classrooms at Hazelwood, students set their own learning goals and rules for classroom behavior early in the year. And they hang them up on blackboards, walls, and doors throughout the school.

"How we want our classroom to be," the lists begin. Or, "What we want to learn this year."

Class meetings are held to resolve problems that come up on the playground or anywhere else. And cooperative learning lessons serve a twofold goal: They teach students both academic content and techniques for getting along.

Creating a 'Family'

"Does anyone have anything to say about the activity?" Shumate asks her 1st graders after one such session. Her class has been working in pairs, drawing pictures of things that once frightened them. They have just finished sharing their drawings with the class. This comes after they have read *Alfie Lends a Hand*, a book about a young child who overcomes shyness at a birthday party.

"Were there any problems, and what did you do to resolve them?" Shumate asks. "We had problems. I couldn't hear him say if he was scared of a shark or an airplane," one boy says of another boy at his table. He says he resolved the problem by asking his tablemates to talk quietly.

The character-building lessons are also reinforced in the literature students read. The center provides a list of more than 200 books chosen first for their literary quality and second for the values they address.

The Venn diagram activity Heather and Larry completed is what Hazelwood teachers call a "unity builder"—an exercise intended to promote the sense of caring and community at the school. Heather and Larry will be reading partners this month, taking turns to read aloud to one another and helping each other make sense of what they have read. The exercise is also designed to help smooth the way for that partnership.

Some teachers at the school have also arranged for their younger students to have older "buddies" in other classes who meet with them once a week to have lunch together or work on an activity.

Hazelwood also sends home "family activities" several times a year. The homework assignments are intended to involve the whole family. Students might be asked, for example, to interview their parents and ask them how their family came to settle in the area.

Grandparents are invited to visit the school and have lunch with the kids during grandparents' week, and families are invited to come to the school for supper and reading activities with their children on the school's annual "family night."

"You weren't allowed to come into the school before, and now you're encouraged to come in," says Doris Jeffries, a parent of three Hazelwood students who now works as a classroom aide there. "There's more caring and nurturing."

The school also abandoned its traditional practice of handing out ribbons on field day only to those students who jump the farthest and run the fastest. Now the event is decidedly less competitive, and all students can participate in every event.

Gradually, all of the changes began to add up and to make a difference. The number of discipline problems referred to the principal's office dropped from roughly 50 a year to 12. Teacher requests for transfers to other schools practically halted, and the school became one of only four schools in the district to meet its target achievement goals under the state's school reform law.

"Our class feels like our family, and the whole school is like a family," says Judy Vowels, an upper-elementary teacher. "It sounds corny, but it does."

Word of the success of the project at Hazelwood and at the other local pilot school, Auburndale Elementary School, has spread. Now, district officials plan to start disseminating pieces of the program to 26 other schools.

"I think we could replicate much of the process without all the intense connectedness we had with the Developmental Studies Center," says Freda E. Merriweather, who oversees the district's elementary schools.

Nationwide, the Child Development Project plans to try a similar strategy.

"I think we want to make it much more broadly useful to schools," Schaps says. "We want to open it up by making the work more widely available, and we want to write about the work for practitioners and policymakers."

"We also want to make linkages to other reform efforts," he adds.

There is some wariness, however, that conservative parents will see the program's emphasis on ethics as a threat to their authority over their own children—even though the values instilled through the program are presumably not much different than those parents would want for their youngsters. Should that happen, the educators in the program say they are ready with their defense.

"Maybe the best way is to use this example," Koshewa, the district coordinator, says. "We would tell them: 'If your child drops a box of crayons, wouldn't you want someone to care enough to help your child pick them up and not kick them away?' People are not going to argue with that." ∎

From Education Week, *October 26, 1994*

26.

Standards Times 50

**Despite all the talk about national standards,
each state must decide for itself what children should learn.**

By Lynn Olson

The U.S. Constitution makes it clear: States bear the responsibility for educating their citizens. They decide how long students continue their education and how the schools are financed. They control what is taught, what is tested, which textbooks are used, and how teachers are trained. Thus, despite all the talk about national education standards, it is the 50 individual states that ultimately will determine what students should know and be able to do.

States have heard the calls for improved student performance and are raising expectations for student learning. But what the states have done varies widely. While most view the national education standards as guides, few feel any obligation to use them.

"The national standards ought to serve as a mirror that we can hold our standards up to," says Fred Tempes, an associate superintendent in the California Department of Education. "I guess, like most states, we'd like to feel that we can set our own standards."

If national education standards survive, it will be because states find them useful. If states ignore the national models, they will fade into irrelevance. "People are presuming that the standards movement is falling apart," observes Marc S. Tucker, the co-founder of the New Standards project, a consortium of 17 states and six urban school districts that is creating a national system of standards and assessments. "It's a very great misunderstanding of the situation. The real action was never in Washington to begin with."

Nearly all the states claim they have or are developing standards for what students should know and be able to do in the core academic disciplines. Forty-six states have applied for federal grants under the Goals 2000: Educate America Act that require them to develop content standards and a related system of assessments. Based on our survey, 31 states began work on what they identify as content standards in 1991 or later. Of those, most are still drafting or reviewing their standards.

Since 1992, the U.S. Education Department has spent more than $24 million to support the development of curriculum frameworks and content standards in 30 states.

Standards-setting in the states "was not on the radar screen very strongly four or five years ago," says Lauren B. Resnick, the co-director of the New Standards project. "The enormous effort going into setting content standards state by state now was not foreseen when the national efforts began."

For years, states have had curriculum guidelines or vision statements about what students should learn. But these have ranged from exhaustive lists of objectives to vague exhortations for student performance.

In the mid-1980s, California became the first state to develop a new set of curriculum frameworks that described what students should learn in each subject at each grade level. The frameworks help guide the state's testing system, professional development efforts, and textbook selection.

In the early 1990s, states like Vermont and Maine

asked citizens to help draft a "common core of learning" for students. Neither as specific as a curriculum framework nor as sweeping as a vision statement, these documents spell out what students should know when they leave school and the skills and attitudes they should take with them. Typically, they list broad goals and objectives that are not specific to an academic discipline. In some states, however, such documents provide the foundation for today's standards-setting efforts.

In her book *National Standards in American Education: A Citizen's Guide,* historian Diane Ravitch identifies three features of the content standards that many states are now developing: They are clear and measurable; they focus on cognitive learning, not affective traits; and they are usually based on traditional academic disciplines.

Three other things distinguish the current spate of activity at the state level. One is the extensive consensus-building that some states have engaged in to set standards. The second is the attempt by states like California to use the standards to drive other parts of the system, commonly known as "standards-based reform." The third is the focus on what students should know and be able to do rather than on what teachers should teach.

There are, however, no widely accepted definitions of terms like "content standards" or "curriculum frameworks." States do not have common criteria for what a good standard looks like. As a result, states use the same words to mean very different things. This situation has led to immense confusion and miscommunication at the national, state, and local levels.

Today, state approaches to standards-setting range all over the map. States call their standards everything from "content standards" to "curriculum frameworks" to "essential learnings." Some state standards are remarkably succinct, fitting on two sides of a page. Others encompass volume upon volume of detail. In some states, legislators have required that standards be set. In others, the state board of education or the department of education began the process.

Some states have tied their standards to statewide tests, professional development, and graduation requirements; others have not. A surprising number of states are drafting standards without determining whether they will be voluntary or mandatory, how they will be used to measure student performance, or how they will be implemented.

"There is a lot of standards-development activity going on, but it's very unevenly distributed and highly related to the capacity of states to do it," says Richard F. Elmore, a professor at the Harvard graduate school of education. "You've got everything from very low-level, off-the-shelf stuff to very elaborate, very original, very well-thought-out standards. I see that as a predictable outcome of federalism. It's just American Government 101."

In this sea of activity, it's hard to weigh the influence of the national standards documents. But they have clearly churned the waters. Richard P. Mills, the state education commissioner in Vermont, recalls going to a local school board meeting in Montpelier. "As I looked down the table, as I was waiting to speak, there was a copy of the arts standards and a copy of the geography standards. And somebody else had the science standards. So they're very much in evidence in local discussions."

Virtually every state claims to be heeding the national standards as it develops its own documents. None is embracing them wholeheartedly.

Ellen Last, the director of a project to develop content standards for the state of Wisconsin, says, "The national standards are one resource of a number of resources that are available. I don't think we have too many teachers involved with our project who are just going to take something and say, 'Gee, these are national standards, and we'd better do everything that is on this paper.'"

In addition to perusing the national documents, states have swapped standards among themselves, dusted off their old curriculum guidelines for schools, turned to their state professional organizations and universities for help, asked citizens what they thought, scoured the best of their district standards, and looked to such national models as the Advanced Placement and International Baccalaureate programs and the curriculum frameworks developed for the National Assessment of Educational Progress.

"We'll audit our work against the national standards to see where there are gaps in degree or expectation or intent," says Edward T. Lalor, the assistant commissioner for curriculum and assessment in New York State. "And then we'll make our own decisions as to whether that gap should be closed, or whether there is a difference in philosophy or opinion."

Impossibly High Standards?

Making sense of the national standards at the state level can also feel like tangling with an octopus. There simply are too many documents and too many expectations within each document to be doable.

"My guess is it would take teachers well better than a summer to read them," complains Barbara Atkins, the supervisor of the curriculum unit in the Michigan Department of Education, "And even then, you don't know what to do with them."

"As they stand, there's no way they could all be implemented," agrees Joan M. Palmer, the deputy superintendent for school improvement in the Maryland Department of Education. "We'd have to have a 365-day year, at least a 12-hour school day, seven days a week."

"Each content area obviously saw this as an opportunity to identify those things they felt were very significant," she adds. "But there are too many things of significance to be useful in the classroom."

Given the lack of restraint at the national level, state officials say they will make the tough decisions about what students should reasonably be expected to know and do.

At the national level, there are 18 geography standards and five geographic skills that students must master. Early drafts of the national standards in English/language arts have contained anywhere from 11 to 16 standards. In contrast, states like Alaska, Colorado, and North Dakota have only five or six standards per subject.

"We believe that six standards are a teacher-manageable number," says Clarence Bina, the director of special projects in the North Dakota Department of Education. "If a teacher can't manage 16 standards, neither can the students."

Many states want to avoid setting content standards that are too detailed. They stress that school districts have the right to design the curriculum, using the state and national standards as models.

"In Florida, we're going to leave all the specific content decisions to districts and schools because those decisions are really too difficult to make at the national and state level," says Doug Tuthill, a teacher who chaired the Florida commission on student-performance standards. "Otherwise, you find yourself debating for 10,000 years how many pages to give to George Washington. You have to make those decisions locally and move them down as far as you possibly can."

Wayne Martin, the assessment director for the Colorado Department of Education, likes to tell a story about how out of touch he thinks some of the national documents are. A nine-member council, appointed by the governor, oversees the standards-setting process. One day, the council met to review the national geography standards. "We had to get an unabridged dictionary to figure out if those were real words they were using," he says. "I know Ph.D.'s in geography who couldn't meet those standards."

Differences Among Documents

State officials also complain about the inconsistencies from one national standards document to another. They vary so much in terminology, format, definitions, and level of detail that it's hard to know what to make of them.

Just getting some common definitions of terms and an agreed-upon level of detail among all of the standards documents would help, says Palmer of Maryland. "Right now," she laments, "you have to read each document very, very carefully."

State leaders typically reserve their highest praise for the curriculum standards adopted by the National Council of Teachers of Mathematics in 1989. The standards are widely recognized as the consensus document in the field. They have withstood the test of time, compared with those in other subjects that have recently been completed or are still under development. They elucidate a new way of teaching and thinking about math focused on problem-solving. Because of those features, many states readily identify their math standards as being modeled after the national ones.

In contrast, states such as North Dakota are quick to distance themselves from the model standards in U.S. and world history. The national standards have been criticized, chiefly by conservatives, as politically biased. North Dakota officials assert they have excised those supposed excesses.

The national education goals identify civics and government, economics, history, and geography as some of the core academic subjects in which students' performance should be measured. But at the state level, social studies continues to reign supreme. The vast majority of states already have or are drafting standards for social studies. Only a handful are drafting separate standards in each of the disciplines that typically fall under the social-studies umbrella. Whether states are increasing the amount of attention given to history, geography, or civics within their social-studies documents is impossible to tell without looking at the specific standards for each state.

"We've decided ... to be at all usable for local school district officials, we cannot treat social studies as five discrete disciplines," says Mitchell Chester, the chief of the bureau of curriculum and instructional programs in the Connecticut Department of Education.

In science, states must choose between at least two competing sets of national standards: the Draft National Science-Education Standards produced by the National Academy of Sciences, and the Benchmarks for Science Literacy, developed by the American Association for the Advancement of Science. "The fact that there are at least two groups fighting for dominance has caused a little concern in the field," observes Robert Silverman, the administrator of the office of standards and assessments in the Alaska Department of Education.

And in English and language arts, a bedrock of the academic curriculum, states have made do without a national model at all. The International Reading Association and the National Council of Teachers of English are forging ahead with model standards, even after the U.S. Education Department withdrew its funding. But those standards will not be out until late summer or early fall.

Some states have also found the national models too tightly linked to the traditional disciplines. Most include only a nod to the interdisciplinary work that teachers will have to do to cover everything.

The 'Localness' of Standards

Given the division of responsibilities between the federal and state governments, the loosely coupled relationship between state and national standards is probably inevitable. But it raises at least two questions for those who believe all children should reach a high, common standard. First, how do states know if their standards are good enough? Second, should there be 50 different sets of standards or do Americans want some consistency?

Do citizens care, for example, if what children learn about science in Iowa differs radically from what they would learn in Mississippi?

"We're one country," argues Resnick of New Standards. "We're very mobile. Kids move. Adults move. I think that what parents want for their kids is to know that they are being given opportunities to learn up to standards that are recognized throughout the country and that they're being held to it."

"But people also value the localness of their institutions," she cautions, "and what we're trying to figure out is how you can have both."

Most state officials say they want to compare what they are doing to the work in other states and nations. North Dakota has sent its English/language arts standards to the education departments in all 50 states for review. Delaware translated Japan's science standards into English.

"We want to be able to ensure that Maine students are challenged to a level where they can compete nationally and internationally," says Robert Kautz, the director of the division of instruction in that state's education department. "We can't do that in a vacuum." But while states want help developing their standards, they don't want a federal judgment about whether their standards are legitimate.

"We really believe that standards-setting should be done locally," says Gov. Terry E. Branstad of Iowa. "We object to the requirement that the state be mandated or forced by the federal government to do this." Governor Branstad has challenged the provisions in Goals 2000 that require states to set content and student-performance standards and to design a related system of assessments. Iowa will not participate in the program, he asserts, unless those requirements are dropped and the power of a national panel to certify state standards is withdrawn. Congress is currently debating changes in the law.

But even without a federal panel to review standards, many predict the content of state standards will converge naturally over time.

"There ought not to be 50 answers to what is good math for 6th graders," says Gov. Roy Romer of Colorado. "Therefore, it's not necessary for each of us to invent the wheel alone. We ought to share information. We ought to share approaches. But we also ought to share a judgment as to how good is good enough." The existence of model national standards is not the only force pushing toward such a convergence.

Over 10 years, predicts Elmore of Harvard, "the states that have standards will look more like each other out of necessity because it's hard to produce this stuff and you need to have economies of scale to do it." But Elmore remains concerned that the push for standards-based reform will result in two separate and unequal groups of states: those that are moving aggressively to set standards and have the capacity to do it well, and those that don't.

"Ironically," he argues, "after all this obsession with standards, we may end up with more variability out there than we had when we started. We could end up with a system in which kids in certain states are basically doing what they did 15 or 20 years ago, and kids in some other group of states are doing something completely different. And that, I think, should be cause for concern."

Despite the hurdles, many state officials insist that setting high and rigorous expectations for student learning is worth doing.

But setting content standards is only the first step in a long and arduous process of reform, acknowledges Pascal D. Forgione, the state superintendent of public instruction in Delaware.

In Delaware and elsewhere, communities and schools must still massage the standards and make them their own. "I think the challenge ahead of us is how to bring life to the standards," he says, "because this good thinking means nothing if it's only a document that sits on a shelf."

Too many educators are familiar with those thick missives from the central office that contain a school district's curriculum guidelines. Most are opened so rarely that teachers have trouble locating them. That's not what content standards are supposed to be about. In an ideal world, such standards would be so clear and compelling that teachers, students, and parents would all know about them and embrace them.

"I think that in the future, when we ask why is this school such a high performer, one of the things we'll find is clear standards plastered on the wall," predicts Mills, the state commissioner in Vermont. "I'm starting to see that many students have internalized pieces of the standards. And teachers have. And to the extent that happens, we've all won. And to the extent that the standards debate remains something arcane and at a policy level ... then we've lost. I think we're going to win." ■

From Education Week, *April 12, 1995*

27.

Enemy of Innovation

Standardized tests dominate curriculum, shape classroom practice, sort students for tracking, and consume scarce time and money.

By Elizabeth Schulz

In 1987, a team of teachers, administrators, university faculty members, and technology gurus, bound by no tradition, gathered in St. Paul, Minn., to design a public school from scratch. Gone would be classrooms with forward-facing desks, 50-minute class periods, report cards, required textbooks, grade levels, and lengthy summer vacations.

Instead, this new school would be a place where students, working with teachers and parents, would identify their strengths, needs, and goals and create their own learning plan. Through projects that could reach into the community, students would find, organize, and make sense of information on their own instead of just passively absorbing what the teacher and textbook presented to them. Home base for these real-world students would be nothing like the traditional school building: Instead of classrooms, students would work in labs, wired with video and computer networks, and in enormous cooperative learning spaces. Students would regularly demonstrate their progress in areas such as reading, writing, and problem solving through what they produce—written work, video presentations, speeches, and computer programs.

Dubbed the Saturn School, after General Motors' break-the-mold approach to making cars, the 4th-8th grade school opened its doors in 1989 exactly as the design team conceived it—except for one vestige of the school that it could not throw out: norm-referenced, standardized testing. As a result of that one holdover, the true Saturn vision may not survive.

Immersed in the exciting business of learning to use their minds, Saturn students have not fared well in the trivial-pursuit world of standardized testing. Their scores in spelling and math computation declined significantly in the first two years. So, despite a shower of accolades from students, parents, and the steady stream of visitors, including President Bush, the school has been given the educational equivalent of the ultimatum, shape up or ship out: Get test scores up, teachers have been told, or the Saturn project will be terminated.

Factory-Model Schools Endure

Standardized testing and the traditional factory-model school were made for each other. In the latter half of the 19th century, the primary purpose of schooling evolved from producing an educated elite to training for industrial America the masses of immigrants and rural poor flocking to the cities. To fulfill that mission, schools were organized like assembly lines. Students would pass through grades, acquiring the nuts and bolts of knowledge as they progressed. The most basic skills would be taught first through drill and practice; material of increasing complexity would be added as students moved through school. Relying heavily on textbooks and locked into carefully sequenced curricula, teachers would efficiently transmit prepackaged information to docile students.

The public schools, Harvard University President

Charles Elliot declared in 1908, should sort children according to their "evident and probable destinies." The standardized test was the scientific and effective tool for accomplishing that goal.

Both the factory-model school and the norm-referenced standardized test have proven remarkably durable, despite cognitive research that strongly suggests traditional schools don't teach the way children learn, and the tests don't effectively measure what students really know.

After years of study, researchers and psycholinguists have concluded that children constantly engage in a search for meaning, structure, and order and that schools should support their natural inclination to develop and test hypotheses about the world around them. The development of thinking skills does not have to wait until students have mastered the basics; in fact, higher-order thinking and the mastery of knowledge are inextricably linked and mutually supportive.

The new insights fostered by research in learning have nourished such grassroots initiatives as the whole-language movement and cooperative learning. These findings have begun, especially during the past decade, to transform classrooms in hundreds of schools across the nation.

But, these new and more sensible approaches to teaching and learning are not likely to spread rapidly or endure for long if they are evaluated on the basis of student performance on the norm-referenced standardized tests that are dominant in American schools. In fact, standardized tests may squelch such creativity altogether.

Lauren Resnick, a cognitive psychologist and director of the Learning Research and Development Center at the University of Pittsburgh, says the best way to ensure the success of reform "is to attack directly what is one of the most powerful dampers to the kind of change we need: the current testing system."

"Talk to teachers who have caught on to the idea that the kind of teaching required in a 'thinking curriculum' is possible," Resnick says, "and then ask them what is the biggest barrier to it. Their answer every time is, 'Those standardized tests are coming, and I'm afraid my kids won't pass them.'"

Tests Drive Instruction

Teachers are in a quandary: They are urged to take risks and be innovative, but they know that their students will be judged on how well they score on tests that do not measure innovative teaching and learning. Monty Neill and Noe Medina of FairTest, a national watchdog organization, make this point in an article in *Phi Delta Kappan.* Research shows, they argue, that "teaching behaviors that are effective in raising scores on tests of lower-level cognitive skills are

nearly the opposite of those behaviors that are effective in developing complex cognitive learning, problem-solving ability, and creativity."

It is not surprising that America's near obsession with standardized testing has had a chilling effect on education reform. In *Testing in American Schools,* a comprehensive 1992 report on the subject mandated by Congress, the Office of Technology and Assessment warns that standardized testing is an enemy of innovation and that it threatens to undermine many promising classroom reform efforts. "Many teachers, administrators, and others attempting to redesign curricula, reform instruction, and improve learning feel stymied by tests that do not accurately reflect new education goals," the study states.

Principal Pamela Clark is one such administrator. Over the past six years, Clark transformed the program at Sunnyslope Elementary School in Phoenix. Her campaign to educate the whole child has included making sure each youngster has enough to eat, adequate medical care, and appropriate social services. She has linked the school with community service agencies, recruited a social worker for her students, and drummed up parent support in a highly transient, poor white neighborhood. As a result of the efforts, students are spending more time reading, writing, and learning from each other.

Parents are almost unanimous in their support for the school. Visitors tell Clark that Sunnyslope is on the cutting edge of school reform. Still, the principal is on the hot seat and feeling the pressure: Her students are not showing significant improvement on standardized tests. "We've taken the heat," Clark says. "People visit and say what we are doing is wonderful and developmentally appropriate, but we're sitting here with blistering fannies."

Pressure to raise test scores in groundbreaking schools comes in nerve-racking waves, observes Carole Edelsky, professor of curriculum and instruction at Arizona State University. Every once in a while, she says, there is a "whole flurry of activity" during which teachers and principals have to defend themselves against accusations that they aren't really teaching anything because the test scores aren't going up. Things quiet down for a while, and then there is more turmoil, she says. "Then it's OK again."

This grip that standardized testing has on American education is bad enough, but what makes it even worse, many educators argue, is that the tests themselves are seriously flawed.

Neill and Medina of FairTest write: "The use of standardized test scores as the primary criteria for making decisions of any kind is reckless, given the erroneous assumptions that undergird standardized tests, the limited range of skills and knowledge that they measure, their limited reliability, their lack of validity, and the impact that race, ethnicity, family income, and gender exert on test results. Yet just such reckless decisions seriously damage student achievement, the curriculum, and education reform in many schools and districts."

The nation's roughly 44 million students take a total of 127 million tests a year, for an average of three standardized tests a year per student, according to a report by the National Commission on Testing and Public Policy. A student sitting down with a No. 2 pencil in hand is most likely to encounter one of the "big four": the California Achievement Test, the Iowa Test of Basic Skills, the Metropolitan Achievement Test, or the Stanford Achievement Test.

These four, and many other tests, share some characteristics. They are standardized; that is, they ask the same questions across different populations to permit comparisons. They are norm-referenced, which means the items are chosen not to establish how much students know of what they ought to know, but rather to highlight differences in students so they can be ranked against others in their age group. And the tests are primarily multiple-choice items.

Test Scores Treated as Magic Numbers

Standardized tests are marketed as scientifically developed instruments that objectively, inexpensively, and reliably measure students' skills. States and school districts are buying the pitch—and the tests. The national commission on testing estimates that test preparation and administration consumes some $100 million of tax money each year and that the nation's students spend a total of 20 million school days a year taking tests.

Although norm-referenced standardized tests came into use just after the turn of the century, they were not employed by a majority of the schools until the 1930s. And it was not until the 1960s and '70s that standardized tests began to be used widely. A position paper on the subject by the Association for Childhood Education International points out that few students who graduated before 1950 took more than three standardized tests in their entire school careers. But today's graduates will have taken up to 36 standardized tests during their 12 years of schooling.

The recent explosion in standardized testing was triggered during the 1980s by the reform movement's demand for greater accountability. To garner support for sweeping education initiatives and the budgets needed to pay for them, lawmakers had to promise constituents that reforms would pay concrete dividends. Test scores, they said, would provide the proof.

By 1985, two years after the publication of *A Nation at Risk,* new testing laws had been passed in 30 states. By the 1989-90 school year, 47 states had mandated standardized testing. And even in the three states that had not, many districts required standardized tests, according to the OTA report. In Pennsylvania, for example, 91 percent of districts used standardized tests though the state did not require their use.

"There has been a dramatic increase in the use of students' scores to hold school systems, administrators, and teachers accountable," the national commission on testing's report states. "Thus, not only has the volume of testing increased, but testing now looms more ominously in the lives of many educators and children, influencing what they teach and how, and what they learn and how."

Today, test scores are treated as if they were magic numbers. Newspapers rank schools and districts by their scores. Real-estate agents pitch test scores to sell houses. Some districts have even fired school administrators because of test results. The principal of the Dool School in Calexico, Calif., for instance, was fired when test scores fell the year after he implemented a whole language program.

"When you take a simple little number and elevate it to the status that it is elevated to in this particular culture, it is very destructive," says Peter Johnston, associate professor of education at State University of New York at Albany. "While people may say it's only one of a number of indicators, it happens to have a very privileged status."

One reason the public hold test results in such high esteem is that the government and education researchers routinely use them to evaluate the worth of schools and programs. Says Edelsky: "The prevailing wisdom—you have to search so hard to find someone who doesn't believe this—is that the way to evaluate the success of anything is via tests."

Tests with High Stakes

Federal funding—including funding for Title I—is often contingent on schools meeting and maintaining specified achievement levels. Eva Baker, co-director of the National Center on Research on Evaluation, Standards, and Student Testing, says this may be the main reason so many states require testing. But even this use of tests can wreak havoc on reform. One of Arizona's top 10 schools, Granado Primary School, which has been recognized as a "Lead School" by the National Council of Teachers of English, was forced to re-evaluate its program or lose its Title I funding, based on the result of standardized test scores.

The research community also puts a high value on standardized tests; in fact, the bulk of education research is based on test score data. When a researcher wants to know if a particular teaching method is effective, he or she usually compares test scores of students taught with the new method with those of a control group. If the students' test scores are higher, the researcher feels comfortable saying, unequivocally, that the approach is more effective.

"It's such a tradition in educational research and in education," Edelsky says. "It fits so well a cultural search for and acceptance of quick answers."

Even some key members of the testing community believe that standardized tests have been accorded too much power. Gregory Anrig, the president of the Educational Testing Service, for example, has decried the overuse and misuse of standardized testing. "When I was in the Army," he says, "the order was: 'If it moves, salute it. If it stands still, paint it.' Now if it stands still, we say, 'Test it.'"

He and others complain that tests are being used to make decisions they were never intended to make, determining the fates of students, teachers, principals, programs, and whole schools. Parents, researchers, policymakers, and the public have become almost totally reliant on test scores as a measure of achievement. Whether kids actually learn is less important than how well they do on tests.

"Do schools and policymakers ask too much of these tests?" asks H.D. Hoover, an author of the Iowa Test of Basic Skills for 25 years. "God, yes. I'm tired of seeing the tests ... used for things they were never intended to do. They are using them to make policy decisions that the tests are not good at making."

The primary purpose of these tests, Hoover says, is to give parents and teachers an external view of a child's performance. Having been educated in a one-room schoolhouse in the Ozarks, Hoover knows how isolated schools can be. "Kids may be knocking the socks off the local district," Hoover explains, "but compared with other kids in the rest of the United States, how are they doing?"

But many teachers argue that standardized tests cannot provide reliable comparative data; test scores, they say, do not always give an accurate picture of students' accomplishments. "Tests measure what they were designed to measure: what goes on in a school that delivers a traditional textbook curriculum, with kids in packages of 30," says Saturn School project director Tom King. "They have limited usefulness in a school where kids are involved in activity-oriented, cooperative learning, out in the community, doing things with their hands and minds."

Limitations of Tests

Saturn evaluator Hallie Preskill, a professor at nearby St. Thomas University, elaborates: "You can't test how students solve a problem with other people or by themselves, how they access resources, how they develop ideas, and so on."

Two students in Mark French's math class at Saturn illustrate the point King and Preskill are making. One, a learning-disabled student, didn't score well on standardized tests when she started with French two years ago and still doesn't. "But now," he says, "this

person thinks for herself. She works in groups, she takes initiative, she is motivated, she is prepared. She is not shy and meek and afraid anymore." What's more, she can demonstrate academic achievement. "She can stand up in front of the class and give a speech," he says. "She can explain and demonstrate a computer project on geography."

The other student tests poorly but is an incredibly bright, meticulous worker. He doesn't get very far on the tests, the teacher says, because he is so careful and has difficulty with fine motor skills; he always has to go back and clean up his answer sheet. "But," French says, "he constantly challenges me as a teacher by what he can do in class, the questions he asks, and his thought processes."

Although Hoover acknowledges that tests can't reflect everything that goes on in a school, he insists that tests like the ITBS are a valid measure of a child's achievement. "People who say that you can only measure facts and low-level thinking on tests like these are just plain wrong," he insists. To bolster his argument, Hoover notes that the ITBS reflects the National Council of Teachers of Mathematics' new standards, which encourage the use of calculators, computers, and other tools to help illuminate the intricacies of mathematics rather than simply focusing on the mechanics of computation.

But when George Madaus, director of the Center for the Study of Testing, Evaluation, and Educational Policy at Boston College, looked at the leading norm-referenced tests—including the ITBS—in light of the national council's new math standards, he found that a vast majority of the test items tap lower-level knowledge. "The leading tests are peas in a pod when it comes to the standards," he says. "They don't reflect them."

And a survey of 1,000 math teachers conducted by the NCTM shows that teachers sense the dichotomy between the new math standards and the tests. Roughly half of the teachers said they emphasize rote drill and practice over problem solving and reasoning because the testing program in their state or district "dictates what they teach."

Teachers in the Westwood School in Dalton, Ga., say trying to innovate within the test-driven system has worn them out. Five years ago, while restructuring the school's curriculum, the teachers discovered "Mathematics Their Way," a program that teaches math concepts through the use of manipulatives.

At the time, Georgia had the most intensive standardized testing program in the country—starting in kindergarten. "The whole system of testing was mind-boggling," says 1st grade teacher Jimmy Nations, in a sweet southern accent that doesn't mask his anger. "The pressure on people was enormous."

Nations says he and his colleagues were operating in a schizophrenic world. "We were trying to do things that we believed as professionals were appropriate for our students," he says. "At the same time, we were being held to the very rigid state test, knowing our school's scores were going to be published and compared with other schools' scores."

Math Their Way teaches students math symbols only after they understand the concepts. Teachers at Westwood knew this approach made sense, but they didn't always use it because of the testing requirement. Nations vividly remembers one class where he drilled students on place value before they understood the concept because he knew they would need the lesson to answer questions on the test. "The little kids sat there with their eyes absolutely glazed over," he recounts. "I felt like a puppet."

The pressures Nations describes are common among teachers. A study cited in the OTA report sought to describe the effects of high-stakes testing on teaching and learning across the country. Seventy-nine percent of teachers surveyed said they felt "great" or "substantial" pressure by district administration and the media to improve test scores. Half of these teachers reported spending four or more weeks each year giving students practice exercises to prepare them for tests.

Teaching and Testing the Basics

There is some evidence that tests most strongly influence the academic program in urban and predominantly minority districts. Johnston, who has been studying assessment—including standardized testing—for a number of years, has noticed that testing is most benign in the suburbs, where, by and large, the students do pretty well. "Tests in this case keep the public somewhat off teachers' backs," he says. But in urban districts, he says, the tests continually point out how things aren't going very well, so teachers feel more pressure to "teach the basics."

The same sort of thing happens within schools. Students placed in the lowest tracks are most apt to experience instruction geared only to multiple-choice tests, according to Linda Darling-Hammond, a professor of education at Teachers College at Columbia University. These students are rarely given the chance to talk about what they know, to read real books, to write, and to construct and solve problems in math. "In short," Darling-Hammond writes in an article in *The Chronicle of Higher Education*, "they are denied the opportunity to develop thinking skills that most reformers claim they will need for jobs of the future, in large part because our tests are so firmly pointed at education goals of the past."

The limitations of what standardized tests can measure in math have their parallels in language arts. For example, the advanced spelling skills of students in a whole language program in Washingtonville (N.Y.) Central School District didn't show up at all in their Stanford Achievement Test scores. Last year, students in six whole language classrooms and six traditional classrooms scored below the 50th percentile. Yet when the children's spelling was assessed from their writing samples, three-quarters of the whole language students, but only half of the students in the traditional classes, spelled well. Many more whole language students than traditional students tried to spell words above their grade level, and they were more successful than the others when they did.

Tests can miss the mark in measuring reading ability, as well. Vivian Wallace, a teacher at Central Park East in New York City, was involved in a study with researchers at the Educational Testing Service. She says they wanted to see if students' scores on the state mandated test, Degrees of Reading, correlated with teachers' assessments of the children's reading ability. Students who read very well do very well on the test, they found. But if a student does not do extraordinarily well there is almost no correlation between the student's score and his or her actual reading ability.

Biases in Testing

Ruth Mitchell, associate director of the Council for Basic Education, takes multiple-choice tests head on in her recent book, *Testing For Learning*. The only place multiple choice is found in the real world, she writes, is at the race track and on the driver's license test. The format promotes passivity, she argues; it asks students to recognize, not construct, the correct answer. And tests tend to measure what is easy to test rather than what is important for students to learn.

Not all educators agree with her analysis. Education professor Bob Linn of the University of Colorado has been doing research on assessment issues for more than a decade. Although he acknowledges that tests have been misused, he insists that multiple-choice questions can assess more than basic skills.

To a large extent, he says, the multiple-choice questions are fair and revealing. "If you look at the kinds of paragraphs kids are asked to read on the tests or glance through the math problems," says Linn, "you'll see that most questions are things that parents think their kids should be able to answer."

But many of the teachers who administer the tests year after year have become outraged with some of the items. Too many questions, they say, are divorced from meaning and context, unnecessarily tricky, and targeted toward the white, middle-class experience. They insist that the test items are not good examples of what a literate person can do.

Nations of Dalton, Ga., complains that the tests aren't in sync with the culture of his children and offers an example. A passage on the state-mandated test is about baking muffins—but his students don't even know what they are. So, every year he teaches an impromptu lesson on muffins. "Somewhere along the line, when I'm talking about cookies, I throw out the word 'muffin,'" he says. "When kids ask what that means, I act surprised and bring a muffin pan to school and bake muffins so that they know what muffins are when they see it on the test."

Cultural bias aside, one of the things that gall teachers most about standardized tests is the fundamental structure of norm-referencing. When creating a test, test companies choose items that will spread students out the most because that will enable them to assign percentile ranks most reliably. In effect, says Resnick, the most interesting items, the ones that everybody can do and ones almost no one can do, are thrown out.

"The worst you can imagine is throwing out those parts of the test that show kids and teachers that they can succeed," says Resnick. "You also don't want to throw out the ones that are making trouble because in a way those are setting the stars to reach for."

The end product of this sifting of multiple-choice items is a norm-referenced test on which half of the students score above the norm and half of the students perform below.

Educators say that norm-referencing is incompatible with the belief that all students can learn. Even if all students learned everything we wanted them to, the tests assure that half the students will score below the mean. "That's an assumption that I could never accept as a teacher," says King of the Saturn School. "Why would I want to devise a test where half my students were below average, condemned to failure status? Especially when the point is to teach all students; you want everyone to learn everything."

An Accident Waiting To Happen

As part of an ongoing reform project, teachers in the Hilton (N.Y.) School District defined what it means to be a good reader and writer. Good readers, they said, are people who enjoy reading, know what strategies to employ if they aren't successful, understand that the purpose of reading is for meaning, can relate things they read in different areas, know how to respond to what they read, communicate what they read, and share their perspective on what they read.

When they compared their list to the state-mandated test, they discovered that the test measures comprehension of texts, but none of the other things that they believe characterize a good reader.

They went through a similar process for writing, and only three out of their nine attributes for a good writer were even minimally addressed by the test.

When a school community comes together to decide what it values, and the test doesn't look at any of these things, it is an accident waiting to happen, says Artis Tucker, language coordinator for the district.

The gap is likely to be most pronounced in schools that are heading toward reform. "Where change is being implemented," Tucker says, "often one set of values operates for instruction and another set of values operates for evaluation."

For many teachers struggling to improve their schools, this is the crux of the matter: Schools and society should decide what they value, find a way to truly assess students' progress in those areas, and then make that the criteria for whether a program is allowed to live or die.

At Saturn, these issues have not been resolved, and standardized tests are holding the program hostage. The staff has backed off from its bold vision and has devised a plan to raise test scores.

As King explains: "It's important that the school survive and become a model for change. To do that, it has to have a political base of acceptance. The community believes that standardized testing is critical, so it would be foolish not to make sure your kids do well—or the program disappears."

The Saturn staff has begun a program to familiarize students with test taking—a practice so widespread in this country that it has been given a name, "testwiseness." Students are told the test is important, given practice items, and instructed in the art of filling out bubble sheets.

The faculty is also reshaping the curriculum to match the standardized tests. For example, the school has abandoned the practice of teaching math through projects in other disciplines; now students are required to take traditional math classes that include drill and practice.

And an innovative plan to create mentorships and internships that link students with members of the community has been pushed to the back burner. What's more, teachers say that the pressure to raise test scores has discouraged them from taking their students out of the school building; they had hoped to structure their courses around the cultural, political, and business resources of St. Paul and Minneapolis.

"We've had to stifle our creativity," says one teacher, who asked not to be identified. "We haven't been able to focus on creating new and exciting learning opportunities for our students. What has taken precedence are classes that address facts and content that are going to be tested."

Saturn teachers are confident that the accommodations made to standardized testing will result in higher student scores. But some think the cost will be too high. The pity, says the teacher who asked for anonymity, is that "we are starting to look not so much like the school of the future; we are starting to look like a traditional school." ■

From Teacher Magazine, *September 1992*

28.

Basal 'Conspiracy'

Basal readers, along with their accompanying workbooks and worksheets, rob the nation's schools of quality education.

Commentary by Susan Harman

The publishers of elementary school reading textbooks are engaged in what amounts to a conspiracy to deprive the nation's schools of quality education. The K-8 reading-instruction market—which is essentially the heavy, several-hundred-page textbooks (known as "basal readers") and their workbooks, worksheets, and other paraphernalia—is worth half a billion dollars a year.

The big five sharers of this lucrative market are Macmillan/McGraw-Hill School Publishing Company (which owns Merrill, SRA, and Barnell Loft, who all publish basals); Harcourt Brace Jovanovich Inc. (which owns Holt Rinehart & Winston and The Psychological Corporation); Silver Burdett/Ginn; Houghton Mifflin (which owns Riverside); and Scholastic Inc. Though Scholastic is the fourth largest of these suppliers of elementary school materials, it does not publish a basal. Scholastic, however, has one foot in that market with a teachers' guide that "basalizes" the children's literature—real books—the company is famous for publishing, and its other foot is rumored to be poised over a basal of its own.

Whole city and county school districts, and even some states, adopt basal series for their entire districts and keep them for many years, because having once invested in a particular series, it makes fiscal sense to keep on buying the workbooks and other "consumables" that come with that series, year after

year. So the choice of a basal program has a serious financial impact on both the school district and the publisher. Districts are notoriously conservative. No publisher can afford to introduce much innovation in its series because the risk of being too different from the other series and losing a large-city district or even a whole state (Texas, for instance) is too great. Therefore, each company's basals and workbooks look like every other company's basals and workbooks.

All the series offer thick booklets containing end-of-unit tests of children's mastery of the vocabulary and skills covered in that unit. In some series, these tests are planned to be given as frequently as every two weeks. The tests are indistinguishable from the workbook exercises the children do all day as "seatwork" to keep them busy while their teacher listens to a group of seven or eight children take turns reading a paragraph each from the basal text (known as "round robin" reading).

Then, blighting the springtime of children, parents, teachers, and administrators alike, come the real tests, which are usually the sole means of holding schools "accountable" to the public. These machine-scored, norm-referenced, multiple-choice, indirect, standardized tests are held up as the "objective" check on teachers' "subjective," "soft" evaluations of their students. Teachers are said not to have the detachment necessary to make these important judgments.

The tests, however, are all made by the very same

people who make the texts. The California Achievement Test (CAW), the Comprehensive Test of Basic Skills (CTBS), and the SRA are published by Macmillan/McGraw-Hill; the Metropolitan Achievement Test (MAT) and the Stanford Achievement Test (SAT) are published by Psych Corp, which is owned by Harcourt Brace; and the Iowa Test of Basic Skills is published by Riverside, which is owned by Houghton Mifflin. Of the big four basal publishers, only Silver Burdett does not publish a test. Where is the distance that supposedly sets these tests apart from the mere judgment of teachers?

Next, since the stakes riding on these tests are very high, teachers and parents naturally are under great pressure to prepare children to take them, and the publishers have come to their aid. Children as young as 3 years old are in test-preparation courses, and Macmillan/McGraw-Hill offers the two best-selling test-practice series: *Learning Materials* and *Scoring High*.

The company hasn't made the sales figures available, but 10 million *Scoring High* booklets have been sold during the last 10 years, and about 2 million students have used *Learning Materials* over the last four years. Not surprisingly, these practice workbooks resemble the tests in both format and content, up to and including some identical questions. Isn't this cheating?

Lately, of course, the publishers have read the blood on the wall, and are scrambling to stay alive by providing schools with "authentic" evaluation instruments. Both Riverside and Psych Corp have begun producing *New Tests*. Riverside's are structured like traditional reading lessons, and are scripted, like the basal teachers' guides. This shouldn't surprise us, since Houghton Mifflin owns Riverside. Psych Corp's Integrated Assessment System is just as teacher-proof as any basal reader. The company has provided us with hardware (cardboard portfolios, storage boxes, teachers' manual, training tape, and trainers' kit) and has done all the thinking for us. It has picked a few passages from real books and composed the rest; it has written the prompts; it has decided what to score and how; and—for a few dollars more—Psych Corp will score these "untests" for us. The scoring rubric reminds me of the "scoring criteria" for the family of Wechsler IQ tests, which are also published by Psych Corp, which is owned by Harcourt Brace.

As the publishers are aware, these *New Tests* contain no items that the average teacher couldn't dream up on a slow day. They can't be machine-scored, and it is at least as easy to train teachers to score them reliably as it is to train publishing-company clerks.

But the *New Tests* are worse than just unnecessary. If the process of thinking up prompts that catch and hold students' attention, of deciding what is valuable enough to be taught and scored, and of establishing a "library of exemplars" has any relevance to teaching,

then it should be done by teachers. If we pay the publishers to make these important decisions for us, we will not only have forfeited the opportunity for exemplary and efficient staff development. We also will have paid in the loss of improved instruction.

So, whether the stuff that our children and their teachers spend time on is called "readers," "workbooks," "unit tests," "test preparation," "standardized tests," or "untests," it is really all the same thing, controlled essentially by three publishing companies.

This immensely profitable enterprise is based on a model of literacy acquisition that is pedagogically bankrupt. The result of decades of the basals' "controlled vocabulary," lists of words to be memorized out of context, artificial language, idiotic plots, trivial "comprehension" exercises, and scripted teachers' guides is generations of children who can bark at print, but don't know that what they read is supposed to sound like language and make sense.

We now know that children learn to read and write the way they learn to talk: They each invent the rules of grammar and usage; they do this in a systematic and predictable order; they do it from the top down—beginning with intention and then discovering syntax and vocabulary; and they do it within the embrace of a supportive community that responds to the meaning, rather than to the form, of their utterances.

It is the same with reading. The reading authority Frank Smith adapted the British adage "Take care of the pence and the pounds will take care of themselves" to describe literacy acquisition. His version is, "Take care of the sense and the sounds will take care of themselves." This news has been slow to reach teachers, perhaps because their main source of new information (aside from the teachers' guides that accompany the basals) is the local reading conferences they attend by the thousands. Many of the major speakers at these conferences are the university professors who write the basals, and whose conference expenses and honoraria are paid by their publishers. The basal companies have our teachers surrounded.

The three companies hold captive our nation's reading instruction. And since children, teachers, schools, and districts are "held accountable" essentially on the basis of test scores in reading alone, "reading" has become the curriculum that counts; so these publishers control not just reading, but the overwhelming bulk of elementary-school curriculum. Perhaps we could tolerate a benevolent conspiracy, if its attitude toward teachers were more respectful and its reading theory were sound. Since neither is the case, this conspiracy is malevolent and must be confronted. ■

Susan Harman is director of evaluation for Community School District One, Lower East Side, in New York City.

From Education Week, *Nov. 13, 1991*

29.

Remapping Geography

**The goal of improving geographic education is
to turn on the MTV generation to the dramatic change
going on in the world around them.**

Commentary by William B. Wood

For several years, leaders in education, government, and business have bemoaned our students' geographic illiteracy. In international comparative tests, we routinely rank at the bottom, with some students unable to locate even their own country on a world map. In response to this poor showing, geography has been designated one of five core subjects in which U.S. students must prove their competence by the year 2000.

Toward this end, a sampling of students will take geography tests in the 4th, 8th, and 12th grades beginning in 1994 as part of the National Assessment of Educational Progress. In almost every state, geographers are actively working with elementary and secondary school teachers in Geographic Alliances to develop creative resources and teacher training programs in order to improve geography education. A National Geography Education Standards Project aims to set a high, but attainable, level of geography teaching at all grade levels across the country. Private organizations, such as the National Geographic Society and the American Express Company are sponsoring nationwide competitions designed to stimulate student interest in geography. And we have just celebrated an event called National Geography Awareness Week.

The success of this national full-court press to wipe out geographic ignorance, though, lies not with presidential proclamations, but with not-so-worldly students, their harried teachers, and their perplexed parents. Most parents remember geography as the boring recitation of state capitals; because they still remember that Pierre is the capital of South Dakota, they think they understand geography. So what is all the fuss about? We will just have a nationwide crash course on place names and country locations and, presto, we will no longer have to hang our collective heads in shame.

Unfortunately, many teachers went to the same schools as the parents and view geography with the same blinders. With many competing demands, there is little wonder that geography has tumbled down the list of daily teaching priorities. Some teachers may envision meeting the nation's geography education goals by handing out homework assignments in which a map of the United States is filled in or the resources of some distant country are listed. Such "teaching" will fail to meet the national geography education standards being promulgated and will assuredly condemn yet another generation of students to the scrap heap of geography.

Most students are probably unaware that a battery of geographic tests is in store for them. It's just as well; many could not care less how they compare with students in other countries. For them, a more pressing question is, "How is geography relevant to me?" If we cannot answer this reasonable question, we should resign ourselves to the bliss of geographic ignorance.

The goal of improving geographic teaching should not be to ratchet up future test scores; rather, it is to turn on the MTV generation to the dramatic change going on in the world around them. Place-location drills and country reports copied from an encyclopedia will never bring a sense of excitement, discovery, and relevance that geography can offer. Here is my list of four "don'ts" for a sound and meaningful geographic education:

● Don't confuse geography with location memorization. Yes, it is important to know where places are (especially your own home), but it is even more important to understand why places are located where they are and how they got there. Some of the questions geography students should be encouraged to think and write about would include: how their parents or grandparents came to reside where they do; where items purchased on the latest trip to the grocery or department store came from and how they were produced and transported; and how land uses in their neighborhood, city, and county have changed over the past several decades. Most of these studies will transcend city, state, and national boundaries and give insight into the economic and political forces that influence our daily lives.

● Don't limit geography to map-making and don't limit map-making to geography. I've never met a geographer who didn't like maps, but they usually use them as a tool to help explain some issue or process. Cartography, the art and science of map-making, is undergoing mind-boggling leaps with the assistance of computer-generated graphics. But more important than plugging into the latest mapping program is proper guidance on how to use a map to tell a story or solve a problem. Well-conceived and -designed maps enhance almost any social- or earth-science project, especially those dealing with environmental problems.

● Don't get hung up on defining geography. Like the blind men feeling their way around different parts of an elephant, geographers will each give a somewhat different account of what geography is or should be. Most would agree that one of geography's longstanding goals has been to bridge the schism between social and natural sciences. Long before ecology became a household word, geographers were studying the dynamic relationship between people and their environments. Geographers also tend to emphasize relationships between places and regions, which can be measured by flows of people, goods, and most important of all, ideas.

● Don't forget that geography is integrative. Of all social scientists, geographers are perhaps the most open to the theories and experiments of other disciplines. We geographers have to be more receptive because our curiosity about the world keeps leading us across the silly academic divisions that inhibit biologists from talking to historians. We'll talk to anybody who can help us better understand the complex interplay of people and places, particularly now when our world is faced with so many difficult challenges. More than any set of learned facts, this multidisciplinary perspective on issues that span from the local to the global is the most valuable geography lesson of all.

I am not a teacher, so these suggestions may be somewhat presumptuous, but as the geographer for the U.S. State Department I have a vested interest that the next generation of U.S. diplomats and businesspeople have a solid background in geography. Although improving the quality of geographic education will require a long-term commitment by parents, teachers, and students, they will find geography to be the most stimulating of subjects. And the most fun. ■

MARK ANDRESEN

William B. Wood is the director at the Office of the Geographer and Global Issues at the U.S. State Department.

From Education Week, *Nov. 25, 1992*

30.

The Meaning of 'First by 2000'

The science curriculum can no longer be isolated from the realities of our culture.

Commentary by Paul DeHart Hurd

'By the year 2000, U.S. students will be first in the world in science and mathematics achievement." This is the fourth national educational goal from Goals 2000: The Educate America Act. I hope to give a glimpse of what it means for the reform of science teaching.

What's wrong with science education that needs fixing? Scientists and laymen alike have described precollege science education as a "fraud," "obsolete," "archaic," "outmoded," "dead end," and "largely irrelevant." The present curriculum is perceived as placing students and the nation at risk.

Since 1980, there have been over 350 national reports by panels, commissions, and committees lamenting the condition of education in America and calling for changes. The repeated reference to the year 2000 and the 21st century in these reports suggests that we are at the end of something in our history and entering a new era. This period is characterized by a globalized economy, a world community, and a shift from an industrial to a knowledge-based society.

The issue is not whether schools are doing well with the programs they have now, but how well they are meeting the demands of social change in the future. The call is for a new contract between schooling and society, one that will benefit children living in the next century while serving the common good and assuring social progress. Schools are in bad shape only when compared to the new perspectives of schooling.

The educational reform movement has gotten off to a misdirected start. Much of what has happened so far consists of hundreds of legislative mandates calling for structural changes in schools. Examples are lengthening of class periods and the school year, more rigor and more testing, and reorganizing existing curricula. These are actions that serve to reinforce traditional practices and can do more harm than good in terms of modernizing science education. The "radical changes" called for in Goals 2000 have yet to be found.

Let me return now to my main focus: the reform of science teaching within the guidelines of Goals 2000 and the national educational reports. Science has been a subject in the school curriculum since Colonial days. No one knows just how the goals and curriculum framework first came into being. But for 200 years it has been assumed that science can be understood only in the way scientists understand science and should be taught as science is practiced. The choice of subject matter has been that best suited to illustrate the theoretical structure of selected disciplines, including basic facts, principles, and laws. In turn, this approach requires students to learn the technical language and symbols that scientists use to communicate research findings to other researchers. As the knowledge in each field grows so does the vocabulary students are expected to memorize. The result is their understanding of science becomes more and more diluted.

Those who seek the reform of science education see the prevailing science curriculum as isolated from the realities of our culture and the lives of citizens. The charge is that the 200-year-old science curriculum is largely irrelevant and should be replaced by modern concepts of science. Although there is not a consensus on the full meaning of "modern science," there are identifiable characteristics. Since the turn of this century the old boundaries that separated astronomy, biology, physics, geology, and chemistry have faded away. Replacing them are thousands of fields of specialized research represented by more than 70,000 journals, 29,000 of them new since 1979. Old disciplines have also become hybridized: for example, biochemistry, biophysics, and biogeochemistry. Science is a singular noun, but it stands for a wide range of research fields, thought processes, and investigative procedures.

During this century a marriage has taken place between science and technology. Robert Oppenheimer described the relationship as "two sides of a single coin." Today, science and technology operate as an integrated system for the production of new knowledge. Each fructifies the other. For example, research scientists conceived the laser, technologists used the discovery to develop a tool for bloodless surgery, the reading of bar codes on merchandise, and a hundred other uses. A technological achievement, the Hubble space telescope, is expected to make observations so extensive that temporarily our ignorance of astronomy will be increased by approximately 80 percent. It could take a century to determine what all the observations mean. Much of scientific research today is done by teams of scientists and technologists pooling their expertise and insights. Computers assist in recording and processing observations and in formulating interpretive models.

In this century, science and technology have become socialized. Research endeavors are now more socially than theory driven; witness the volume of research on finding ways of controlling the AIDS pandemic, improving agriculture, managing the natural environment, and maintaining a long and healthy life. Science and technology today lie at the center of our culture and economy, thus fostering enculturation as a goal of science teaching. The criticism of the present science curriculum is that it graduates students as foreigners in their own culture, unfamiliar with the influence of science/technology on social progress and public policy as well as on personal and cultural values. To meet the educational demands of a new century there is a growing conviction that the traditional purpose of school science, to educate students to be like professional scientists, is no longer tenable. The trend is to view science as public knowledge to be taught within a context of human affairs.

Although there has been little coherent progress in the reform of science teaching, new goals are being debated. One of these is the concept of scientific literacy. There are differences in how the concept is viewed. For some, scientific literacy is seen as a collection of facts everyone should know. But the essential character of science is not embedded in its facts. If one simply knew all the facts of the sciences, the person could only be rated intellectually sterile.

A different view of scientific literacy and one more in harmony with modern science relates to understanding the interactions of science and technology as they influence human experience, the quality of life, and social progress. A scientifically literate person recognizes the unique character of science knowledge and is aware of its values and limitations in cultural adaptation.

Scientific literacy is a cognitive perspective toward knowledge and includes the ability to distinguish science from pseudo-science, theory from dogma, fact from myth, folklore, and conjecture, probabilities from certainty, and data from assertions. Scientific literacy has become a cultural goal for living in a society characterized by achievements in science and technology. Goals 2000 describes a literate person as one possessing the knowledge and skills essential to exercising the rights and responsibilities of citizenship.

There has been a public outcry for schools to emphasize the development of higher-order thinking skills. The curriculum-reform movement of the 1960s stressed the teaching of inquiry or process skills. These are skills that have to do with how science/tech-

MARK ANDRESEN

nology information is generated, classified, quantified, expressed, and interpreted. These processes are seen as lower-order thinking skills.

The appeal for higher-order thinking skills is related to the proper use of science knowledge in human and social affairs. These skills are for the most part qualitative. When science and technology information is brought into contexts where it is of service to people and society, elements of ethics, values, morals, bias, politics, judgment, risks, ideals, trade-offs, and aspects of uncertainty enter the thinking process. As science courses are now organized and taught in schools, higher-order thinking in the context of human experience is not an educational goal. Goals 2000 views these skills as essential in an era "in which citizens must be able to think for a living" and demonstrate responsible citizenship.

"Learning to learn" through one's own efforts has emerged as a primary objective for the teaching of science. Goals 2000 describes this goal as transforming the United States into "a nation of students." UNESCO reports that of the 141 nations now in the process of upgrading their science-education programs, "learning to learn" is the one goal common to all.

This goal is particularly relevant to science education when we recognize that in the sciences all knowledge is forever tentative and new knowledge is being developed at an exponential rate. The present school science curriculum fails to recognize that science concepts have an organic quality, changing and developing as new insights and data are generated—an "endless frontier." Students are not taught how to access knowledge likely to be useful in their lives.

School science curricula as they now exist are oriented to the past, under the guise of basics. Goals 2000 and a host of national reports emphasize an education appropriate for the 21st century. To keep pace with changes taking place in our society as influenced by science and technology demands a future-oriented education. The purpose is not to predict but to help students shape the society where they will spend their lives. The National Committee on Education Reform in Japan states that all subject matter for schooling should be selected with the assumption that students will live to be 85 years old.

A future perspective to schooling entails providing students a sense of their place in the world and their responsibilities for human welfare and social progress. Goals 2000 speaks of this goal in terms of meeting the demands of living in the 21st century and assuming the obligations of responsible citizenship. It recognizes that an education viewed as preparation for the future calls for "revolutionary changes" in what is now taught and how.

A final note. Students were the first to recognize, in their own way, that the science they are learning is of little value for living and adapting in the modern world. The most common question students ask in science courses is, What good is all this going to do me? The usual answer is, You will need to know this for the next test, or in the next grade, or in college. Rare

> # The criticism of the present curriculum is that it graduates students as foreigners in their own culture, unfamiliar with science's influence on human affairs.

is the teacher who answers the question in terms of human experience.

Yes, the United States can be first in the world in 2000, but not by tinkering with existing curricula and trying harder with 200-year-old teaching procedures that fail to recognize recent developments in cognition. In Goals 2000, the first task recommended for change is "to set aside all traditional assumptions about schooling and all the constraints that conventional schools work under." The next step calls for a "reinvention of schooling."

The vision for science teaching is one of relating modern science and technology to the realities of our culture, to social progress, to life as lived, and to the values we hold. ∎

Paul DeHart Hurd is professor emeritus of science education at Stanford University.

From Education Week, *Sept. 16, 1992*

31.

Caught Between Two Worlds

An Indian father pleads with his son's teacher to recognize the boy's cultural tradition and personal accomplishments.

Commentary by Robert Lake (Medicine Grizzlybear)

Dear teacher, I would like to introduce you to my son, Wind-Wolf. He is probably what you would consider a typical Indian kid. He was born and raised on the reservation. He has black hair, dark brown eyes, and an olive complexion. And like so many Indian children his age, he is shy and quiet in the classroom. He is 5 years old, in kindergarten, and I can't understand why you have already labeled him a "slow learner."

At the age of 5, he has already been through quite an education compared with his peers in Western society. As his first introduction into this world, he was bonded to his mother and to the Mother Earth in a traditional native childbirth ceremony. And he has been continuously cared for by his mother, father, sisters, cousins, aunts, uncles, grandparents, and extended tribal family since this ceremony.

From his mother's warm and loving arms, Wind-Wolf was placed in a secure and specially designed Indian baby basket. His father and the medicine elders conducted another ceremony with him that served to bond him with the essence of his genetic father, the Great Spirit, the Grandfather Sun, and the Grandmother Moon. This was all done in order to introduce him properly into the new and natural world, not the world of artificiality, and to protect his sensitive and delicate soul. It is our people's way of showing the newborn respect, ensuring that he starts his life on the path of spirituality.

The traditional Indian baby basket became his "turtle's shell" and served as the first seat for his classroom. He was strapped in for safety, protected from injury by the willow roots and hazel wood construction. The basket was made by a tribal elder who had gathered her materials with prayer and in a ceremonial way. It is the same kind of basket that our people have used for thousands of years. It is specially designed to provide the child with the kind of knowledge and experience he will need in order to survive in his culture and environment.

Wind-Wolf was strapped in snugly with a deliberate restriction upon his arms and legs. Although you in Western society may argue that such a method serves to hinder motor-skill development and abstract reasoning, we believe it forces the child to first develop his intuitive faculties, rational intellect, symbolic thinking, and five senses. Wind-Wolf was with his mother constantly, closely bonded physically, as she carried him on her back or held him in front while breastfeeding. She carried him everywhere she went, and every night he slept with both parents. Because of this, Wind-Wolf's educational setting was not only a "secure" environment, but it was also very colorful, complicated, sensitive, and diverse. He has been with his mother at the ocean at daybreak when she made her prayers and gathered fresh seaweed from the rocks, he has sat with his uncles in a rowboat on the river while they fished with gill nets, and he has listened to elders as they told creation stories and animal legends and sang songs around the campfires.

He has attended the sacred and ancient White Deerskin Dance of his people and is well-acquainted with the cultures and languages of other tribes. He has been with his mother when she gathered herbs for healing and watched his tribal aunts and grandmothers gather and prepare traditional foods such as acorn, smoked salmon, eel, and deer meat. He has played with abalone shells, pine nuts, iris grass string, and leather while watching the women make beaded jewelry and traditional native regalia. He has had many opportunities to watch his father, uncles, and ceremonial leaders use different kinds of colorful feathers and sing different kinds of songs while preparing for the sacred dances and rituals.

As he grew older, Wind-Wolf began to crawl out of the baby basket, develop his motor skills, and explore the world around him. When frightened or sleepy, he could always return to the basket, as a turtle withdraws into its shell. Such an inward journey allows one to reflect in privacy on what he has learned and to carry the new knowledge deeply into the unconscious and the soul. Shapes, sizes, colors, texture, sound, smell, feeling, taste, and the learning process are therefore functionally integrated—the physical and spiritual, matter and energy, conscious and unconscious, individual and social.

This kind of learning goes beyond the basics of distinguishing the difference between rough and smooth, square and round, hard and soft, black and white, similarities and extremes.

For example, Wind-Wolf was with his mother in South Dakota while she danced for seven days straight in the hot sun, fasting, and piercing herself in the sacred Sun Dance Ceremony of a distant tribe. He has been doctored in a number of different healing ceremonies by medicine men and women from diverse places ranging from Alaska and Arizona to New York and California. He has been in more than 20 different sacred sweat-lodge rituals—used by native tribes to purify mind, body, and soul—since he was 3 years old, and he has already been exposed to many different religions of his racial brothers: Protestant, Catholic, Asian Buddhist, and Tibetan Lamaist.

It takes a long time to absorb and reflect on these kinds of experiences, so maybe that is why you think my Indian child is a slow learner. His aunts and grandmothers taught him to count and know his numbers while they sorted out the complex materials used to make the abstract designs in the native baskets. He listened to his mother count each and every bead and sort out numerically according to color while she painstakingly made complex beaded belts and necklaces. He learned his basic numbers by helping his father count and sort the rocks to be used in the sweat lodge—seven rocks for a medicine sweat, say, or 13 for the summer solstice ceremony. (The rocks are later heated and doused with water to create purifying steam.) And he was taught to learn mathematics by counting the sticks we use in our traditional native hand game. So I realize he may be slow in grasping the methods and tools that you are now using in your classroom, ones quite familiar to his white peers, but I hope you will be patient with him. It takes time to adjust to a new cultural system and learn new things.

He is not culturally "disadvantaged," but he is culturally "different." If you ask him how many months there are in a year, he will probably tell you 13. He will respond this way not because he doesn't know how to count properly, but because he has been taught by our traditional people that there are 13 full moons in a year according to the native tribal calendar and that there are really 13 planets in our solar system and 13 tail feathers on a perfectly balanced eagle, the most powerful kind of bird to use in ceremony and healing.

But he also knows that some eagles may only have 12 tail feathers, or seven, that they do not all have the same number. He knows that the flicker has exactly 10 tail feathers; that they are red and black, representing the directions of east and west, life and death; and that this bird is considered a "fire" bird, a power used in native doctoring and healing. He can probably count more than 40 different kinds of birds, tell you and his peers what kind of bird each is and where it lives, the seasons in which it appears, and how it is used in a sacred ceremony. He may have trouble writing his name on a piece of paper, but he knows how to say it and many other things in several different Indian languages. He is not fluent yet because he is only 5 years old and required by law to attend your educational system, learn your language, your values, your ways of thinking, and your methods of teaching and learning.

So you see, all of these influences together make him somewhat shy and quiet—and perhaps "slow" according to your standards. But if Wind-Wolf was not prepared for his first tentative foray into your world, neither were you appreciative of his culture. On the first day of class, you had difficulty with his name. You wanted to call him Wind, insisting that Wolf somehow must be his middle name. The students in the class laughed at him, causing further embarrassment.

While you are trying to teach him your new methods, helping him learn new tools for self-discovery and adapt to his new learning environment, he may be looking out the window as if daydreaming. Why? Because he has been taught to watch and study the changes in nature. It is hard for him to make the appropriate psychic switch from the right to the left hemisphere of the brain when he sees the leaves turning bright colors, the geese heading south, and the squirrels scurrying around for nuts to get ready for a harsh winter. In his heart, in his young mind, and almost by instinct, he knows that this is the time of year he is supposed to be with his people gathering and preparing fish, deer meat, and native plants and herbs, and learning his assigned tasks in this role. He is caught between two worlds, torn by two distinct cultural systems.

Yesterday, for the third time in two weeks, he came home crying and said he wanted to have his hair cut. He said he doesn't have any friends at school because they make fun of his long hair. I tried to explain to him that in our culture, long hair is a sign of masculinity and balance and is a source of power. But he remained adamant in his position.

To make matters worse, he recently encountered his first harsh case of racism. Wind-Wolf had managed to adopt at least one good school friend. On the way home from school one day, he asked his new pal if he wanted to come home to play with him until supper. That was OK with Wind-Wolf's mother, who was walking with them. When they all got to the little friend's house, the two boys ran inside to ask permission while Wind-Wolf's mother waited. But the other boy's mother lashed out: "It is OK if you have to play with him at school, but we don't allow those kind of people in our house!" When my wife asked why not, the other boy's mother answered, "Because you are Indians, and we are white, and I don't want my kids growing up with your kind of people."

So now my young Indian child does not want to go to school anymore (even though we cut his hair). He feels that he does not belong. He is the only Indian child in your class, and he is well aware of this fact. Instead of being proud of his race, heritage, and culture, he feels ashamed. When he watches television, he asks why the white people hate us so much and always kill our people in the movies and why they take everything away from us. He asks why the other kids in school are not taught about the power, beauty, and essence of nature or provided with an opportunity to experience the world around them firsthand. He says he hates living in the city and that he misses his Indian cousins and friends. He asks why one young white girl at school who is his friend always tells him, "I like you, Wind-Wolf, because you are a good Indian."

Now he refuses to sing his native songs, play with his Indian artifacts, learn his language, or participate in his sacred ceremonies. When I ask him to go to a powwow or help me with a sacred sweat-lodge ritual, he says no because "that's weird," and he doesn't want his friends at school to think he doesn't believe in God.

So, dear teacher, I want to introduce you to my son, Wind-Wolf, who is not really a "typical" little Indian kid after all. He stems from a long line of hereditary chiefs, medicine men and women, and ceremonial leaders whose accomplishments and unique forms of knowledge are still being studied and recorded in contemporary books. He has seven different tribal systems flowing through his blood; he is even part white. I want my child to succeed in school and in life. I don't want him to be a dropout or juvenile delinquent or to end up on drugs and alcohol because he is made to feel inferior or because of discrimination. I want him to be proud of his rich heritage and culture, and I would like him to develop the necessary capabilities to adapt to, and succeed in, both cultures. But I need your help.

What you say and what you do in the classroom, what you teach and how you teach it, and what you don't say and don't teach will have a significant effect on the potential success or failure of my child. Please remember that this is the primary year of his education and development. All I ask is that you work with me, not against me, to help educate my child in the best way. If you don't have the knowledge, preparation, experience, or training to effectively deal with culturally different children, I am willing to help you with the few resources I have, or direct you to such resources.

Millions of dollars have been appropriated by Congress and are being spent each year for "Indian Education." All you have to do is take advantage of it and encourage your school to make an effort to use it in the name of "equal education." My Indian child has a constitutional right to learn, retain, and maintain his heritage and culture. By the same token, I strongly believe that non-Indian children also have a constitutional right to learn about our Native American heritage and culture because Indians play a significant part in the history of Western society. Until this reality is equally understood and applied in education as a whole, there will be a lot more schoolchildren in grades K-2 identified as "slow learners."

My son is not an empty glass coming into your class to be filled. He is a full basket coming into a different environment and society with something special to share. Please let him share his knowledge, heritage, and culture with you and his peers. ∎

Robert Lake (Medicine Grizzlybear), a member of the Seneca and Cherokee Indian tribes, was an associate professor at Gonzaga University's School of Education in Spokane, Wash., when this was written.

From Teacher Magazine, *September 1990*

32.

Multicultural Perspectives I

Public schools should not struggle to represent every minority group in their curricula; they should reveal to students what they have in common.

Commentary by Willard L. Hogeboom

In June 1992, the New York State Department of Education made public a report by a panel of scholars and educators, calling for a revision of the state's public-school curriculum to better reflect racial and ethnic diversity. Although there were divisions among panel members, on the whole it went much better this time than it did last time.

It was in the summer of 1989 that a panel of minority educators and activists, also appointed by the state education department, issued "A Curriculum of Inclusion," which began with these words: "African-Americans, Asian-Americans, Puerto Ricans/Latinos, and Native Americans have all been the victims of an intellectual and educational oppression that has characterized the culture and institutions of the United States and the European-American world for centuries." This report was quickly denounced in newspaper editorials and columns and in television commentaries across the country.

"A Curriculum of Inclusion" was one of the opening salvos in the debate over multicultural education that has dominated the education scene in the ensuing two years. At first glance, multicultural education seems deceptively appealing: The curriculum, both at the secondary and college levels, is too "Eurocentric," too concerned with the European origins of American ideas, traditions, and people. Multiculturalists claim that the number of non-European Americans is in-creasing and that it is wrong to impose an alien European culture and heritage upon their children in the public schools. These children deserve a curriculum of their own culture and heritage.

Those who make these demands are ignoring some basic facts about American history and society. America has always been a multicultural society composed of diverse peoples who, willingly or not, left different cultures all over the world to come here. These people all made contributions to American history and culture. But the reality is that America has shaped its immigrants more than it has been shaped by them. The institution that has had the greatest role in that shaping has been the public school system. Public schools are the most common shared experience for most Americans, and the school system has been the key to the Americanization process. Its mission has been to preserve and transmit the common American culture to each generation of young Americans.

Many multiculturalists, historians, and educators reject the idea of a common American heritage. Yet, it is what has been taught to public-school students for generations—the story of how this country came to be; the people who came here willingly at great risk and sacrifice for a new life, and those who came here unwillingly as slaves; the people who made outstanding contributions to all areas of that society; the great domestic and foreign struggles and events.

Perhaps the most important part of that story is

the uniqueness of America. Unlike other countries, it was and still is an experiment; America and its institutions were deliberately "invented," and often "re-invented," in an effort to get it right. America has had its defects, its mistakes, and, some would even claim, its crimes, but being American means being committed to keep trying to "get it right." Public schools are traditionally where young people, native and immigrant, learn what it means to be an American.

The multiculturalists are mistaken when they refer to Eurocentric culture or the white man's culture in the public-school curriculum as something alien to them. All children in the public schools, white, black, brown, or whatever color, have an equal claim to the American heritage simply by virtue of the fact that they are Americans. Certainly most of the American heritage derives from Europe because that's where the majority of people who settled this country came from. The early leaders were either educated there or received an education here patterned upon European education. It was therefore no accident, but neither was it a conspiracy, that our ideas and institutions derive from Europe.

At the same time, in recent public school curricula and textbooks, no secret is made of the fact that early Europeans were influenced by cultures to the east and south. Multiculturalists also make a mistake with their concern about the sources of the American heritage from a quantitative point of view. Obviously, the many different groups in America have not all contributed equally, but that does not diminish their right to an equal claim to the heritage.

This is what the Mexican-American writer Richard Rodriguez meant when he said: "I read the writings of 18th century men who powdered their wigs and kept slaves because they were the men who shaped the country that shapes my life. I am brown and of Mexican ancestry. . . . I claim Thomas Jefferson as a cultural forefather."

This is what the African-American author Maya Angelou meant when she wrote of an incident when, as a young child, she had to give a recitation to her church congregation. She chose Portia's speech from "The Merchant of Venice" and later observed, "I know that William Shakespeare was a black woman. This is the role of art in life."

The fallacy of multicultural lists is that they do not separate an idea or a work from its creator. It has long been a truism that the finest of art and learning is that which transcends "race, class, and gender," so that it touches everyone, and they can identify with it regardless of their background.

We have already had experience with the direction the multiculturalists want to take. In the 1960s, as the civil-rights movement gathered momentum, one of the issues was the missing African-American presence in the school curricula and textbooks. Other groups quickly echoed this complaint. Bernard Gifford, former deputy schools chancellor of New York City, has described his experience in trying to develop a history curriculum for the New York City schools that would satisfy the demands from different groups for inclusion: "We got a chapter on how blacks were systematically exploited by whites, a chapter on how Puerto Ricans were systematically exploited by whites, a chapter on how the Irish were systematically exploited by Germans, and so on. What we could not get was a chapter that said what held us together."

The path toward anything resembling comprehensive multicultural representation in the school curriculum is a dead end. Once you embark in that direction, more and more groups demand inclusion and the enterprise is doomed to defeat. More important is the fact that this approach is looking at the problem through the wrong end of the microscope.

The various groups in America did not come here to bring and continue their old culture. America is not some gigantic Ellis Island in which a multitude of people are thrown together, each group to look out for itself and to carry on in its own way. Recent interracial and inter-ethnic strife in Eastern Europe, the Soviet Union, Canada, and the Third World should be lesson enough as to the consequences of the failure to get diverse people in a country to put national unity ahead of group interests.

Past experience has demonstrated that, too often, programs designed for racial, ethnic, or gender identity end up setting one group against another. Students should be in public school classrooms as Americans, not African-Americans, Irish-Americans, Anglo-Americans, or any other type of what Teddy Roosevelt denounced as "hyphenated Americans."

The proper function of the public schools should be to reveal to each student what he has in common with the other students in the classroom—that he is an American and that he is there to participate in the legacy of the common American heritage, as generations of students before him have. ∎

Willard L. Hogeboom is a freelance writer and a retired social-studies chairman from Babylon High School on Long Island, N.Y.

From Education Week, *Dec. 4, 1991*

33.

Multicultural Perspectives II

Multicultural education should focus not on whose canon to teach but on developing tools of inquiry in all children.

Commentary by Eleanor Armour-Thomas and William A. Proefriedt

The multicultural debate has generated bitter polemics within the educational community in which each side caricatures the positions taken by the other, or seizes on the most extreme formulations of the other in order to denigrate the wider position. With complex ideas, it's best to examine particular formulations and practices, rather than to argue with or blindly support slogans unhooked from any reality.

"One Nation, Many Peoples: A Declaration of Cultural Interdependence," a report of the New York State Social Studies Review and Development Committee, manages a formulation of the concept of multicultural education that is likely not only to find wide acceptance among educators but also to stimulate alterations in curriculum and teaching, and in the ways we assess students.

The committee, which included historians and practicing social studies teachers, has accomplished this in one brilliant stroke by shifting the discussion from a crassly political emphasis to a more sophisticated educational one. The committee's conception of multicultural social studies education is neither Afrocentric nor Eurocentric. It is learner-centric. The question is not "Whose canon to teach?" but "What competencies must students demonstrate in order to deal intelligently with the complexities of history and of contemporary society?" The committee wants to develop "multiple perspectives" in all students, helping them see historical and contemporary realities from a variety of viewpoints, helping them hear the voices of those who have previously been neglected in high-school history texts, helping them see that their own parochialism is not universal truth.

What critics such as Arthur Schlesinger and Diane Ravitch should take note of is that this particular conception of multiculturalism allies it with the best in the Western tradition of liberal education. John Stuart Mill gave, in his inaugural address at the University of St. Andrews, the quintessential 19th century formulation of the purposes of a liberal education:

"Look at a youth who has never been out of his family circle: He never dreams of any other opinions or ways of thinking than those he has been bred up in; or if he has heard of any such, attributes them to some moral defect or inferiority of nature or of education. What the notions and habits of a single family are to a boy who has had no intercourse beyond it, the notions and habits of his own country are to him who is ignorant of any other.... But since we cannot divest ourselves of preconceived notions, there is no known means of eliminating their influence but by frequently using different-colored glasses of other people: and those of other nations, as the most different are the best."

Instead of multicultural education being seen as a threat to the tradition of liberal education in the West, as it so often is, in the committee's formulation, it becomes an extension of that tradition. Defenders of liberal education over the years have offered different subjects as candidates for fulfilling its purposes. Mill, for example, in the argument quoted, was defending the teaching of ancient Greek language and of Greek culture for its capacities to free the individual from worshipping the idols of the tribe. The genius of a liberal education has resided not in its claims about the role of different subject areas, or texts within those subjects, but in its formulation of liberating educational purposes and in its insistence on the connection between those purposes and the ways in which subjects and texts are taught.

This document picks up on that tradition, insisting on the central role of the teacher and the approaches she takes to her subject matter. It identifies with John Dewey, with a number of current reform initiatives, and with more recent research on human cognition and learning. The report points out the need to seek organizing principles and to sacrifice coverage of outlandish amounts of information for in-depth analysis of exemplary issues, and it calls for attention to developing the tools of inquiry in all young people.

The writers of the report, as much as they reflect theoretical ideas about educational purpose that have been a part of the discourse about teaching and learning since before Dewey, also reflect recent changes in this country brought about by the civil-rights movement and by more inclusive immigration laws enacted in the 1960s. Contemporary events have created new perspectives affecting educational policy. The report is a particularly thoughtful expression of and response to the new climate created by these events. It will not come as an idea from out of the theoretical blue to wise teachers and curriculum makers who are already working within this kind of climate.

Attached to the report are papers by individual committee members that reflect the debate on the committee. Some of these criticisms miss the thrust of the main report. They argue, it seems to us, not with the report but with less sophisticated versions of multiculturalism. They fault the report for sacrificing the "unum" to the "pluribus."

We find in the report an effort to get beyond the oppositional context of one nation, many cultures by an emphasis on increasing the inquiry skills of the learner. We see a healthier society emerging from an educational approach that encourages critical reflection on the values we share in common, as well as on those that make different groups unique. We learn from an approach that allows students to hear the voices of previously silenced groups and to incorporate the voices into their understanding of the American

past from an approach that will allow them to critically examine the claims and counter-claims of textbooks of the past, and the political debates of the present. We see the need for a new understanding of American culture that recognizes its continuous reinvention and recognizes also the many contributors to its sometimes clashing ideals.

A fundamental assumption of multiculturalism is that the larger culture of the United States emerged from a synthesis of the experiences of diverse cultural groups. The report argues that the task of students learning about our society is to critically examine these experiences in their historical context.

While some of the comments on the report missed the mark, we found Nathan Glazer's balanced criticism particularly thought-provoking. He argues that we need to recognize that the various ethnic groups in this country are not "monolithic and unchanging realities." Different ethnic groups and individuals and classes within these groups have undergone different degrees of assimilation and intermarriage, taken different attitudes toward their own ethnicity and toward the American culture of which they are a part. Mr. Glazer points out that these groups are not something "hard and unchanging."

But he worries that both teachers and students will want something more definite. He worries that presenting ethnicity in this oversimplified fashion might have the effect of inhibiting the processes of change that have helped us create a common society. We feel that blatant racism has been the most serious inhibitor of the creation of a common society, but that Nathan Glazer's caveat is nonetheless helpful. The silliness surrounding the attribution of different learning styles to different ethnic groups with the admonition to teach each accordingly seems to us a product of this penchant for oversimplification.

Implicit in this new educational agenda is the notion that all students, regardless of economic and cultural backgrounds, can be inducted into the habits of critical thinking. The achievement of this lofty goal will depend not only on the commitment of individual teachers, but also on the availability of curriculum resources and on extensive opportunities for teacher education. We hope that budgetary constraints will not get in the way of local districts' and colleges' offering courses to teachers that will help them teach the culturally complex history of the United States to all their students. ■

Eleanor Armour-Thomas is an educational psychologist in the school of education at Queens College, City University of New York. William A. Proefriedt teaches philosophy of education at Queens College.

From Education Week, *Dec. 4, 1991*

Where We Will Teach

"The education system we have was designed to give most students only 'basic' skills. It produces a curriculum that sacrifices understanding to 'filling' in the blanks on the worksheet. It rewards those who follow rules rather than those who produce results, so it naturally generates bureaucratic behavior. Valuing efficiency more than quality, it operates by sorting students out rather than educating everyone to a high standard. Every feature of this system reinforces all the others. That is why it is so durable, so resistant to change. That is why successful schools succeed *despite* the system, not because of it. 'Breaking the mold' means breaking this system, root and branch."

—National Alliance for Restructuring Education

34.

Standing in the Winds of Change

Fraught with inequities and inefficiencies, America's education system is under assault.

The American public school system is vast and complex. In more than 80,000 schools in some 14,600 districts, more than three million teachers and administrators labor nine months a year to educate 44 million students. One out of every three Americans is directly involved in the educational system—as students, employees, parents, and policymakers. The rest of us are indirectly involved as taxpayers.

The states have the ultimate responsibility for education, and most of their constitutions guarantee children a thorough and efficient education. State departments of education, overseen by the chief state school officers and boards of education, set standards, provide funds, and regulate schools. How heavy-handed the state is in discharging its responsibility differs from place to place and from time to time.

The states delegate the day-to-day operation of schools to local boards of education, most of which are elected. There are some 97,000 local school board members—the nation's largest group of elected officials—and membership on the school board is often the entry point for a political career. The school boards hire superintendents to manage the districts, and the superintendents, in turn, appoint principals to run the schools. Because power flows from the top downward, teachers have organized into labor unions to bargain for rights and benefits.

The total operating budget for public precollegiate education totaled $252 billion for the 1992-93 school year, or about $5,800 per student. Most of the money—49 percent—comes from states; education is the largest single expenditure in state budgets. Another 45 percent comes from local communities, mostly from property tax assessments. The federal government's share of the bill comes to about 6 per-

cent—mostly in the form of categorical support for the poor and the handicapped.

Because the local funding for schools comes from property taxes, schools in affluent districts spend more money to educate a child than schools in poor school districts. In the state of Texas, for example, the annual per-pupil costs range from about $2,500 in the poorest districts to more than $19,000 in the wealthiest. To counter such gross inequities, states have developed complicated and arcane funding formulas, but the problem remains. Where a child lives determines, perhaps more than anything else, what quality of education she or he will get.

For the past quarter century, the war over equitable funding has been fought in courts throughout the land, from California to Kentucky, from Texas to New Jersey. In Kentucky, the state supreme court in 1989 took the ultimate step of declaring the entire educational system to be unconstitutional and ordered the legislature to rebuild it from scratch. And the battles rage on. In early 1993, school-finance litigation was under way or pending in 27 states.

Widespread funding inequities, the vastness of the public school system, and its uniquely American tradition of local governance assure that the system will be diverse and variegated. Schools meet the needs and reflect the standards of individual communities. The tiny, all-white rural school perched amid endless corn-fields of Iowa is utterly different from the predominantly minority school amid the slums of Los Angeles. And neither resembles the "shopping mall" high schools of the affluent suburbs of Baltimore.

But despite their apparent diversity, the nation's public schools are alike in profoundly important ways. Each is part of a system shaped early in this century to prepare the rising generations for their roles as workers and citizens. The way schools are organized and operated today still largely reflects the dominant theory of that period. Industrial managers, seeking ever greater productivity, created factories in which the work was divided into a series of simple tasks and workers were assigned, in assembly-line fashion, to those tasks. Well-trained managers and supervisors oversaw the process to make sure that each worker played his assigned role quickly and efficiently. Frederic W. Taylor, the inventor known as the father of scientific management, was the architect of this method, and Henry Ford made a fortune applying it to the production of his Model T's, boasting that one could buy any color one wanted as long as it was black.

The factory became the model for the school, which was expected to produce workers with the basic skills needed for the factory. The curriculum was divided into segments, the knowledge within courses was divided into components, the day was divided into periods. Students sat in rows, while teachers imparted information under the watchful eye of the principal.

That system has proved exceedingly durable in education, even as it falls from favor in corporate America. In most of the nation's schools, teachers still stand before rows of students dispensing information, often culled from textbooks and fed back to them in work sheets. The day is still divided into periods, and bells ring every 50 minutes or so signaling students that the time has come to leave geography and move on to algebra. Teachers remain essentially isolated from each other, with little influence over decisions affecting curriculum and instruction. With increasing frequency, students must take norm-referenced, multiple-choice tests that sort them by scores along a curve.

While the essence of schooling in America is much the same today as it was 70 years ago, the demands on schooling have changed to reflect the needs of a larger society in flux. To survive and succeed in the complex world of tomorrow, citizens will need higher-order thinking skills in addition to basic skills. Shopkeepers' arithmetic is not sufficient for today's high school graduate. High levels of literacy are virtually a prerequisite for success in the increasingly sophisticated workplaces of the nation. Factory assembly lines are increasingly manned by robots; tomorrow's front-line workers will need at least a high school education and will be expected to solve problems, make critical decisions, and perform at high levels.

Moreover, the society has begun to realize that it can no longer afford to waste its human resources—not if the United States is to succeed in the fierce competition of the global marketplace. We have long embraced the idea that all children have a right to all of the education they are capable of. But our definition of the pledge has evolved over the years. For a long time, "all children" did not really mean *all* children.

The schoolhouse door opened slowly to minorities, the poor, the non-English speaking, the handicapped. And though it surely was not intended to be, the concept of "all the education they are capable of" has been a rationale for limiting educational opportunity, particularly for the disadvantaged, according to some perception—often flawed—of ability. The current system is characterized by the perverse practice of tracking.

Today, we have nearly achieved the "universal" part of universal education. It is our success in bringing virtually all children into our schools, that exposes so painfully how far we have yet to go to fulfill the other half of the promise—the "education" part. Here, too, our definition has evolved: A central concept in the current reform movement is that almost all children have the capability to learn at a high level. That will require changes in schooling even greater than those that were necessary to open the doors to all children. And the years ahead will doubtlessly see protracted battles over quality and equality.

Launched in 1983 with the publication of the federal report *A Nation at Risk*, school reform has evolved into a concerted effort to overhaul the entire system of American education. Systemic reform involves changing every part of the educational enterprise essentially at the same time: teacher preparation and professional development, the use of time and space, the content and organization of the curriculum, student assessment, and the roles and relationships of educators and students. If systemic reformers succeed, schools will be substantially restructured, financed differently, and held accountable using a new system of rewards and penalties.

Reformers face a formidable challenge. The current system is well-entrenched; people, when surveyed, acknowledge that the system is troubled but generally believe that their own schools are doing OK. The vastness and complexity of the system pose an awesome barrier to change. The great majority of the teaching force has not been persuaded to accept, nor adequately prepared to implement, the sweeping and deep changes being proposed.

On the other hand, the reform movement has lasted longer than any in history. Much of the power structure has joined the cause: the White House, Congress, the governors, the chief state school officers, the national business leadership, and the heads of many of the nation's educational and professional associations. A number of states are well along in their efforts to reinvent their schools. And thousands of schools throughout the country are involved to one degree or another in piloting reform ideas.

The education question of the 1990s will be the outcome of the classic conflict between an irresistible force and an immovable object. ■

35.

Boards of Contention

The embodiment of democracy, school boards come under attack as defenders of the status quo.

By Lynn Olson and Ann Bradley

Last year, Massachusetts abolished the nation's first elected school board. After more than 200 years, Gov. William F. Weld replaced the popularly elected Boston School Committee with one appointed by the mayor. "The citizens of Boston will be disenfranchised by this legislation," Governor Weld acknowledged at the time. But, he said, Boston's schools are "in desperate need of fundamental change."

Rarely in American history have school boards been under such attack as they are today. A combination of forces—ranging from ever-increasing state mandates to rapidly changing demographics—is threatening an institution once considered synonymous with public education in the United States.

In districts throughout the country, radical governance ideas are taking hold. Parents can now choose from among public schools; schools have been empowered to decide whom to hire and how to spend their money; and the operation of entire school districts has been delegated to private management firms.

As the educational landscape shifts, most agree that the roles and responsibilities of school boards cannot possibly remain static. While some think the existing system of local lay governance of education is still viable, increasingly vocal critics are calling for major changes. Some would even scrap it for an entirely revamped infrastructure.

"Local school boards are not just superfluous; they are also dysfunctional," Chester E. Finn Jr., a former

professor of education and public policy at Vanderbilt University, has written, expressing one of the strongest views on the subject. "At a time when radical alterations are needed throughout elementary-secondary education," he argues, "school boards have become defenders of the status quo."

Far from contributing to education reform, those who agree with Finn contend, school boards have become part of the problem: mired in minutiae, prone to meddling, resistant to change, and victims of public apathy toward elected government in general. "I think a lot of school boards are taken in by the bureaucracy and fed the kind of information that would please them," says Herbert J. Walberg, professor of education at the University of Illinois at Chicago, who recently edited a book on school boards. "And since many of them are essentially amateurs and only stay on the board for two or three years, it's a way that the education establishment maintains the status quo."

Mandates from Above

School boards clearly are caught in the crossfire of rapidly changing ideas about who should control public education in America. The 1980s witnessed an unprecedented growth in state control of education, as one state after another passed comprehensive reform laws dealing with everything from who should teach to the content of the curriculum.

State financing for public education is also approaching local expenditures for the first time in history. According to the National Center for Education Statistics, the state share of K-12 schooling is now 46.4 percent; the local share is 47.6 percent.

In the midst of such changes, local school boards have been largely left out of the debate. "Local boards never, ever caught the big picture of what needs to be done in public education," says Howard M. O'Cull, the executive director of the West Virginia School Boards Association, "and because they haven't, states simply moved the policy arena to the state capital."

By 1986, a national poll of school board members revealed high levels of anxiety about the intrusiveness of state policymaking into local affairs. The potential creation of national standards and assessments in education could undermine local control still further.

Threats from Below

Hemmed in by mandates from above, boards have also found themselves challenged from below. If schools are empowered to make decisions about everything from budgets to curricula—as many reformers now advocate—then boards of education cannot continue to exercise the same kind of direct management they have in the past.

The rapid growth of parental-choice plans that enable youngsters to attend schools outside the district in which they live has also threatened the sovereignty of school boards.

Finally, the competing demands on boards from a host of special-interest groups have resulted in what some observers describe as "policy gridlock," in which boards cannot possibly satisfy all parties. Today, argues Michael W. Kirst, a professor of education at Stanford University, education is being pushed and pulled by a "fragmented, elevated oligopoly" in which no one group has central control of the schools.

Although every state but Hawaii delegates substantial authority to local boards of education, critics charge that their role is becoming irrelevant.

Worse yet is the sense that school boards have lost their internal compass: that clarity of vision and purpose needed to steer an organization. John Carver, an expert on private and nonprofit boards, describes local lay governance of education as a "vast wasteland."

Even if board members received the best training and acquired the discipline to fulfill their roles as defined by conventional wisdom, he argues, "they would simply have learned to do the wrong things better than before." As most currently operate, Carver and others assert, school boards are collections of misguided talent that have the potential to accomplish far more for children than they do.

"It's not that many people see school boards as being damaging to the system," says Sharon Brumbaugh, a former board member in Pennsylvania, "but that they are not using the powers they have to bring about change in the system."

With 97,000 members on more than 14,500 public-school boards in the United States, it is hard to generalize about their functioning. The diversity is astounding. They range from the seven-member New York City Board of Education, whose system has more students than there are residents in the state of Rhode Island, to the five-member school board in Big Cabin, Okla., whose entire 58-student population could fit into a few New York City classrooms.

In 1990-91, 54 percent of the nation's school districts enrolled fewer than 1,000 students each. But 4 percent had enrollments exceeding 10,000—accounting for nearly half of all students nationwide. "The danger," Theodore R. Sizer, a professor of education at Brown University, cautions, "would be for policymakers to generalize about anything as diverse as school boards and, on the basis of that generalization, suggest policy."

Most of the national media attention paid to school boards in the past couple of years has focused on the turmoil and dissension on big-city boards of education. In 1990, 20 of the 25 superintendencies in the largest urban districts were vacant. And media accounts blamed the problem, at least in part, on the personal agendas, daily meddling, and inappropriate behavior of board members.

"Constructive board-superintendent relationships have collapsed almost entirely in many large cities," contends a report on school boards released this month by the Twentieth Century Fund and the Danforth Foundation. Most big-city superintendents now last less than three years on the job.

> Mired in minutiae, prone to meddling, resistant to change, and victims of public apathy, school boards have become part of the problem.

Others attribute the turnover to the dwindling size and quality of the selection pool from which urban executives are chosen. They argue that some tension between school boards and their chief executive officers is inevitable, since lay boards must rely on these professionals for most of their information. When board members show any inclination to pursue data on their own, they are quickly accused of meddling. And the lack of trust on both sides can become explosive.

In some cities, evidence of patronage and the sheer inability of school boards to deliver a solid education to their charges has led to unprecedented measures. The Jersey City and Paterson districts were taken over by the state of New Jersey, and their existing school boards were disbanded. Boston University assumed operation of the Chelsea, Mass., schools.

And in Chicago, a coalition of advocacy groups pushed through a reform law that created popularly elected councils of citizens, parents, and teachers at each school, gave them the authority to choose principals and spend discretionary funds, and significantly curtailed the powers of the central board.

The vast size of many urban school systems—combined with the daunting social problems they face—has led some scholars to suggest they are simply ungovernable. "It's not that board members are malevo-

---

Education is being pushed and pulled by a 'fragmented, elevated oligopoly' in which no one group has central control of the schools, argues one professor.

---

lent," says John E. Chubb, a senior fellow at the Brookings Institution. "It's that they're responsible for a task that is basically impossible."

But the problems with school boards are not limited to urban areas. Governance changes in the Kentucky Education Reform Act of 1990 were directed mostly at the nepotism and political agendas that characterized the state's overwhelmingly rural boards of education.

And many of the nation's suburban school boards are struggling with the same societal dilemmas as their urban neighbors: a growing population of students from racial, ethnic, and language minorities; a rising incidence of drug, alcohol, and sexual abuse; and a split and fractious community.

In many parts of rural and small-town America, however, the perception remains that school boards still work. In these relatively homogeneous communities, where most people know their board members personally, the sense of crisis is far removed.

"I'm just as happy as I can be when I go back to the Dakotas that the school board is as it's always been," says William H. Kolberg, the president of the National

Alliance of Business and a vocal critic of urban boards of education.

But it is precisely the self-satisfaction of some of these suburban, rural, and small-town school boards that worries other observers. "The biggest problem in some of [these] districts is the complacency about the quality of the educational policies they have," Kirst of Stanford says.

In a 1989 survey of 1,217 school board presidents across the United States, the vast majority gave low marks to American public education as a whole. But four out of five awarded grades of A or B to the public schools in their own communities. Presidents in small districts and rural areas gave lower ratings to a variety of reform proposals than did their peers in urban and suburban areas.

"If our criteria are a need for risk-taking, moving away from the status quo, educating the public to understand that reform does not mean going back to what we think worked yesterday," says Jacqueline P. Danzberger, an expert on school boards at the Institute for Educational Leadership, "then I think that you find the problem in a lot of kinds of communities."

Despite such charges, there have been few systemic studies of school boards. Thomas A. Shannon, the executive director of the National School Boards Association, says that "there is absolutely no substantiation" that public school boards have stood in the way of reform. "That sort of statement is 'scapegoatism' at its ultimate."

And Susan Fuhrman, the director of the Center for Policy Research at Rutgers University, says, "I think there are many boards, maybe even a majority of boards, that function the way one would advise them to function, and that is to set general policy and delegate a great deal to the central administration."

But if school boards are supposed to focus on broad educational issues, they devote a surprising amount of time to detail. Critics charge that many boards have become so hopelessly enmeshed in the minutiae of running their districts that they fail to see the forest for the trees.

A study of board minutes from all 55 school systems in West Virginia between 1985 and 1990 found that boards spent only 3 percent of their time on decisions related to policy development and oversight. At least 54 percent was spent on administrative matters, according to Carver, who has been advising the state's legislature on governance issues. At most, 42 percent was spent on decisions that could legitimately be called "governance."

"There is no reason to expect the West Virginia data to differ substantially from that which would be obtained elsewhere in the country," Carver writes. "Recent articles in the literature suggest that the same disease afflicts all."

Carver argues that boards have become a "staff member one step removed," rather than the policymakers they claim to be. "The fact that you can't hire a janitor or a teacher without a board taking action is ludicrous," he says.

The report by the Twentieth Century Fund cites the "tendency for most boards to 'micro-manage'" as the biggest problem they face. A curriculum audit of the District of Columbia schools last year found that board members made 181 written requests for information in 1991—many of them "frivolous."

Another indication of how bogged down boards can become in trivia is the number of times they meet. The Tucson, Ariz., school board met 172 times in one year. In such instances, superintendents spend most of their time servicing the board.

"If boards continue to involve themselves in some of the day-to-day things that should be left to the administration," warns Edward Garner, the former president of the Denver Board of Education, "I don't think boards as we know them will exist in the future."

The tendency of boards to become immersed in fine print has also blurred the distinction between policy and administration and led to repeated charges of "meddling." In Seattle, recalls Reese Lindquist, the president of the local teachers' union, one board member decided to take the school system's budget home and analyze it in detail. "It was so large, she had to get a custodian to help carry it to her car," he laughs. "Any school board member who thinks that's their responsibility is in serious trouble."

Other observers charge that the focus on minutiae discourages corporate executives, university presidents, and other prominent citizens from serving on school boards. "If a body is legally responsible for everything that goes on in a school district, and if the majority of people who come on a board do not have strong, broad, and deep leadership backgrounds," Danzberger of the IEL says, "then the tendency is to get into everything."

'Dictated by the State'

In fairness to boards of education, much of the trivia on their agendas derives from state mandates. West Virginia requires local boards to approve all student field trips. The California education code requires boards to approve all student expulsions. "My own experience is that our board meetings are dictated almost entirely by the state," says Fuhrman, who recently completed a term as a public school board member in New Jersey.

Such dictates, she adds, take time away from discussions about education and prevent boards from focusing on long-range planning. "We don't have the freedom to spend as much time discussing education issues as I would like to," laments Leslie Q. Giering, an 18-year board member in the 1,100-student Bloomfield Central School District in New York State.

"When I was first elected, we met once a month," she says. "Then we began having two meetings a month, with the idea of discussing education at the second. But we find that other things take up our time."

In fact, if most citizens attended an average school board meeting, they would probably be underwhelmed by its content. But few bother. Turnouts in school board elections typically hover between 10 percent and 15 percent of registered voters. And most board meetings are sparsely attended.

Such visible citizen apathy about a purportedly valued institution bodes ill for the future. If school boards "embody everything that everybody says they love and want in citizen-based control of a major institution," notes Neil R. Peirce, a political writer, "why is it that scarcely any of us bother to vote for any of the people who sit on these committees?"

Board watchers also describe a steady decline in the number and quality of people willing to run for election. According to Danzberger, about one-third of board members turn over each year. And it is getting harder and harder to replace them. The most noticeable drop has been among corporate executives willing to devote energy to board business.

Ward Politics

In large cities, the practice of electing board members from discrete electoral districts—rather than from the city as a whole—has helped increase the representation of minority populations. But it has also encouraged board members to focus on neighborhood constituencies and on narrow interests, rather than on the system as a whole. In some instances, critics charge, boards function more as neighborhood employment agencies than as service providers.

A 1986 study by the Institute for Educational Leadership found that board members elected by subdistrict were subjected to greater constituent pressure and voted more frequently in response to specific interest groups than did members who were elected at-large.

The rise of special-interest politics and the number of socially explosive issues that boards face have further impaired their functioning. "School boards face a whole set of controversial decisions for which there is no satisfactory answer for at least half of the citizens," says Denis P. Doyle, a senior fellow at the Hudson Institute, an Indianapolis-based think tank. "Abortion and drugs and condom distribution and AIDS and alcohol and sex abuse and poor academic standards—the list is daunting. And school boards, understandably, feel some compulsion to try to step up to the plate and hit the ball. But it has produced a really dysfunctional system in many large cities."

In essence, critics assert, some boards have confused representation of the public with the public interest. "What we've really created," says Phillip C. Schlechty, the president of the Center for Leadership in School Reform, "is a situation in which the board thinks its job is to be responsive to the community." Whereas, he continues, "its job is to be accountable to the community and responsive to parents and kids."

Historically, school boards were made independent from local government to insulate education from the corrupting influence of politics. But critics argue that school boards in many instances have become conduits for political influence. And in contemporary society, the separation is often a disadvantage.

Today, many families have health, social, and emotional problems that cannot be solved by the schools

---

West Virginia requires local boards to approve all student field trips. The California education code requires boards to approve all student expulsions.

---

alone. Yet, the continued structural isolation of school boards has made it difficult to coordinate activities on behalf of youngsters and their families.

"School boards were not set up to deal with social services and linkages to outside agencies," notes Sandra Kessler Hamburg, the director of education studies at the Committee for Economic Development. "And, frankly, a lot of them just feel overwhelmed."

When school boards do try to meet their students' nonacademic needs, they can get burned. Sue Cummings, the former chairman of the Roseville, Minn., school board, was ousted by voters in the conservative,

heavily Catholic community outside the Twin Cities after she supported spending $10,000 of the district's money to help a health clinic locate in the town.

"It is so hard for me to describe the tenor of the community during that time," she says. "They went wild, they were so emotional. People who were my avid supporters called me and said the Catholic priest had condemned me to hell from the pulpit by name."

The reaction also stemmed, she says, from the community's refusal to acknowledge the circumstances of its children's lives, such as teenage pregnancy. "People kept saying, 'No, no, no, this doesn't happen here,'" she recalls. "The statistics clearly show that these are not inner-city problems, that small towns in Minnesota have every bit the same problems."

The ability of 92 percent of public school boards to raise taxes and spend money as they see fit has further strained the relationship between local boards of education and their municipalities. Some mayors and town council members charge that this fiscal independence has produced waste and inefficiency and decreased school boards' accountability to the public.

Despite such criticisms, few think that Americans will do away with school boards entirely. The notion that local schools are the public's to run is deeply ingrained in the American psyche. "The board really is the arm of the community," says Margaret Myers, a member of the Muscatine, Iowa, school board. "I truly believe, the longer I have been involved in this, that there is real value in this kind of openness, doing business in open meetings, so that everyone in the community has the opportunity, whether they take it or not, of knowing and understanding what is going on in their school district—which is funded by their tax dollars."

Without the help of school boards and their communities, adds Shannon of the NSBA, real reform will not occur. "School board members are the gatekeepers of reality," he argues. "It's one thing to have a good idea. It's quite another to take it and put it in a form that works and that can be paid for." ∎

From Education Week, *April 29, 1992*

36.

Blurring the Line

Unusual new arrangements are making it harder to tell the difference between public and private schools.

By Lynn Olson

It used to be so simple: The government paid for—and provided—public education. Today, though, new approaches are challenging the government's once-unquestioned role as the direct provider of school services. Public vouchers are being used to pay for private education, and private firms are operating public schools. Some corporations are underwriting design efforts to transform the public schools; others are investing in for-profit enterprises to compete with them. In Minnesota, a private school has even opted to become public. "The whole notion between public and private is being blurred," John Witte, a professor of political science at the University of Wisconsin at Madison, observes.

What all these new arrangements have in common is a belief that the entrenched public school bureaucracy will not change willingly or quickly. To crack it open, reformers are proposing a variety of private and quasi-private alternatives that rely on the use of market forces and competition to do what they say regulation and exhortation have not.

While such experiments are not in abundance, their acceptance is growing rapidly as policymakers become more desperate to fix the public schools. Given this more congenial climate, new twists on how to deliver public education are surfacing with increased regularity.

Looking to the private sector is hardly unique to education. One of the most popular books in policymaking circles this year is *Reinventing Government: How the Entrepreneurial Spirit Is Transforming the Public Sector*. The book, written by Ted Gaebler and David Osborne, advocates making government services leaner and more effective, in part by throwing them open to competition, funding outcomes rather than inputs, and giving employees an incentive to earn money, not just spend it.

Proposals to contract out the operation of state prisons or citywide garbage collection, for instance, reflect the belief that private firms can accomplish results more quickly and efficiently than public institutions can.

"People don't think government works," says Susan Fuhrman, the director of the Consortium for Policy Research in Education at Rutgers University, "so we have to reinvent it, which to many people means making the public more private or making government more market-driven."

Private School Choice

In education, the purest reflection of this view can be found in the growing popularity of school choice plans that employ vouchers. Vouchers would provide parents with a government subsidy to spend at public, private, or parochial institutions. Schools that failed to lure clients would shape up or lose funds.

The assumption is that competition and parental pressure—not government regulations—would spur public schools to improve. Advocates also portray vouchers as a way of empowering low-income families. "So these are our beliefs, then, that parents, not the government, should choose their children's schools," President Bush said last June in announcing a proposal to provide $1,000 scholarships to low- and moderate-income families to spend at public, private, or parochial schools.

The momentum behind vouchers has grown rapidly during the past year, in part because of the choice issue's prominence in the Presidential campaign. In addition, ballot initiatives to provide families with private school choice will go before voters in Colorado in November and in California in June 1994. And lawmakers in at least six other states are expected to consider voucher legislation this year that would include private and religious schools.

Individuals and corporations in at least half a dozen cities have forged ahead with privately funded voucher schemes of their own. The scholarships are available to a limited number of low-income families on a first-come, first-served basis.

Patricia A. Farnan, the director of education and empowerment policy for the American Legislative Exchange Council, a bipartisan organization of state lawmakers who advocate free-market principles, predicts that it is only a matter of time before a state passes a voucher law that encompasses private and parochial schools. "And when you see one go," she maintains, "you'll see four or five head right behind it."

A Common Mission?

Critics charge that vouchers would violate the constitutional separation of church and state (90 percent of private schools in the United States are religious); drain money from financially strapped public schools; and segregate children on the basis of race, ability, and income.

"What markets are best at are allocating scarce goods," argues Marc S. Tucker, the president of the National Center on Education and the Economy. "And they do it on the basis of ability to pay. Any way you look at it, the incentives for suppliers are to leave the kids with the greatest needs in the lurch."

But the more fundamental concern is that vouchers would destroy America's long-cherished notion of the "common school": a place where children from all walks of life come together to become productive, participating citizens. "The purpose of education in our schools is to get all kids in our country to learn to live with and respect each other, just as much as it is about learning algebra and Shakespeare," asserts Albert Shanker, the president of the American Federation of Teachers. "We're destroying something that is extremely important as the glue of the United States of America."

Opponents also contend that vouchers undermine the notion of education as a public good and the willingness of taxpayers to support it. In an article written for the conservative Heartland Institute, Myron Lieberman, a longtime critic of the public schools, advocates that government reconsider its role as both the funder and provider of education through a process known as "load shedding"—"or ending government's role as funder of most or all educational services."

Unhappy with drivers' education? Lieberman asks. Stop funding it. Perhaps, he suggests, high school

Seven out of 10 Americans said they would back a government-supported voucher system that included public, private, and parochial schools.

teachers could be offered 20 percent pay raises, contingent upon eliminating the 1st grade. If parents pay for education from their own pockets, Lieberman contends, they will be more likely to insist on performance from their children and from their schools.

Only those who cannot afford to pay should get government help. "Just saying that something's a public good," he says, "it doesn't follow that government should pay for it. That's just a non sequitur."

Despite the heated charges of critics—and the organized opposition of the education establishment—public support for private school choice appears to be mounting. In a Gallup Poll released by the National Catholic Educational Association last month, seven out of 10 Americans said they would back a voucher system that included public, private, and parochial schools. Sixty-one percent said they would support such a proposal even if "some of the tax money now going to public schools" was used to pay for it.

Minority and urban residents voice some of the strongest support. A poll released this summer by the Washington-based Joint Center for Political and Economic Studies found that two-thirds of black respondents were not familiar with the concept of school choice or vouchers. But, of those who were, 88 percent favored choice. "I think mobilization of the low-income community offers breathtaking possibilities," argues Clint Bolick, the litigation director of the Institute for Justice, a public-interest law firm that supports choice.

The only state-subsidized voucher program now in place is in Milwaukee, where scholarships are available to send up to 1,000 low-income children to private, nonsectarian schools. A coalition of conservative Republicans and inner-city parents, under the leadership of State Rep. Polly Williams, a black Democrat, pushed for the legislation.

The Institute for Justice has also filed lawsuits on behalf of low-income parents in Los Angeles and Chicago, who are demanding vouchers to send their youngsters to private schools on the grounds that their public schools are unsafe, inadequate, and lacking in parental control and involvement. Bolick said at least one other lawsuit will probably be filed this year.

Whether the marketplace would enable families to purchase something better for their money—or just something different—is open to debate, research on the differences between public and private schools indicates. Shanker maintains that differences between the academic performance of public and private school students are minimal, and that neither group performs well on international comparisons of achievement. "What we're going to do is allow kids to escape from one set of schools that are lemons to go to another set of schools that are lemons, solely on the basis of phony reputation," he complains.

In contrast, many scholars have concluded that, at least on several measures, private school students substantially outperform their public school peers, even once differences in family income are taken into account.

The continued debate highlights how little is known about how an educational market would actually work and what its benefits would be. In 1990-91, the first year of operation for the Milwaukee program, seven nonsectarian private schools enrolled 341 students from low-income families. Although attendance was higher among students participating in the program than the systemwide average—and parents reported greater satisfaction with and involvement in their children's education—little progress was shown in test scores. And many of the children who enrolled in the program the first year did not return. Witte, who evaluated the Milwaukee program for the state, advocates that the experiment be continued, but not expanded.

Other studies indicate that even modest competition may produce some results. Since 1985, when Minnesota began permitting high school students to take courses at local universities at taxpayer expense, the number of Advanced Placement courses offered by area high schools has increased dramatically.

'At the Margins'

The question, many agree, is how much competition is enough to spur the system to change, without bringing it crashing down. Few think that there would ever

be enough private sector alternatives to actually replace the public schools. "Even if you doubled the capacity of private schools," notes Sandra Kessler Hamburg, the director of education programs at the Committee for Economic Development, "you'd still have 80 percent of the kids going to the public schools."

"We really are talking about movement from public to private schools at the margins, at least in the short term," Bolick of the Institute for Justice agrees. "But that may be all that it takes to make dramatic changes in the public system."

Some think the voucher movement will fade as political power shifts in Washington. But others think the pressure for vouchers will continue. "We have tough economic times, and we're likely to have them for a while, so the public wants to save money," Shanker asserts. "And they're going to find these things very appealing." The union leader also worries about a powerful "education-industrial complex" getting behind the voucher movement.

Shanker's reference is to the Edison Project: a $2.5 billion undertaking designed to launch a nationwide chain of for-profit K-12 schools by the fall of 1995. The Edison Project is the brainchild of the media entrepreneur Christopher Whittle. And it is backed by Whittle Communications L.P., Time Warner Inc., Philips Electronics N.V., and Associated Newspapers Holdings Limited.

Whittle refers to the project as a "private mission with a public goal." The aim, he asserts, is to create schools so powerful and innovative that they will have a real influence on the structure of public education in America. As part of that pledge, he has promised to provide a significantly better education at no more than the nation's average per-pupil cost, or about $6,300 a year.

One appeal of approaches like Edison's, advocates say, is their ability to start from scratch, instead of trying to fix the schools that exist. "There are real benefits from wiping the slate clean and thinking fresh about education," says John E. Chubb, a member of the project's design team and a prominent choice advocate.

Similar thinking undergirds the work of the New American Schools Development Corporation. Business leaders launched the privately funded foundation in 1991, at Bush's request, to underwrite the development of "break the mold" schools that public educators could emulate. The 11 design teams that have received grants include both for-profit and nonprofit corporations, as well as public school systems. But one of the most striking differences between the two initiatives has been their ability to raise money.

NASDC, which relies primarily on corporate donations, has only raised $50 million of its $200 million target. The Edison Project, which its backers hope will yield a substantial return on their investment, began with $60 million just for research and development.

Market Not There?

Much of the distrust of Whittle's project centers on his motives, which many contend are chiefly pecuniary. The suspicion is that, when children's needs are weighed against the bottom line, students will suffer. The checkered history of many profit-making trade schools has fed such concerns.

Critics also allege that Whittle is counting on government vouchers to make his project financially viable. The average parochial school in the Milwaukee area, Witte of the University of Wisconsin notes, charges slightly less than $800 a year in tuition. In contrast, the Edison Project is banking on the willingness of parents to pay up to $6,300 per student. "If you're competing at the bottom," Witte says, "you can't charge that much, unless, of course, you get vouchers. Without the public subsidies, I don't think the market is really there."

If Whittle cannot take advantage of vouchers, others suggest, he could still make a profit by contracting out his services to public school districts and educating their students for them.

Public schools have habitually contracted out the operation of such ancillary services as food delivery, transportation, and maintenance. In recent years, however, the practice has widened to encompass the very heart of the educational enterprise: educational management and instruction. The most prominent example is Education Alternatives Inc. In July, the Minneapolis-based, for-profit management firm signed a $140 million contract with the Baltimore school district to operate nine public schools. And it is conducting a feasibility study to see if it can manage several more in Palm Beach, Fla.

Education Alternatives has promised to assume day-to-day management of the Baltimore schools, train their teachers in new instructional methods, and produce measurable gains in student achievement, all for the same amount of money normally alloted to the schools: about $5,550 per student.

In the Midwest and Southwest, Ombudsman Educational Services has contracts with more than 60 school districts in Arizona, Illinois, and Minnesota to provide alternative education for students who are having trouble in traditional school settings. James P. Boyle, the president of the for-profit firm, is a former public school teacher and administrator. But he argues that trying to change the system from inside is "harder than changing the Vatican."

The freedom to operate outside the school's bureaucracy, Boyle says, has enabled his firm to break the "course and content" gridlock in education, providing services both less expensively and more effectively. Students in Boyle's program attend school only three hours a day, enabling each teacher to work with several groups of youngsters. The program is computer-assisted, individualized, and outcome-based. The cost

is between $3,000 and $4,000.

According to Boyle, the trick to succeed has been to cut out the "frills." "We don't have baseball and football and cafeteria and band and art," he says. "Particularly now, as school systems are hitting the wall in terms of funding, a cost-effective alternative becomes more attractive."

Education Alternatives is also hoping to improve education—and make a profit—by trimming wasteful expenditures in some areas up to 25 percent.

'An Extension of the District'

Such private entrepreneurs claim that they are a part of the public school system, not a threat. "We've always thought of ourselves, and still do, as an extension of the district," Boyle says. "If the district doesn't like us, they can fire us."

"Our mission," a company brochure states, "is not to replace or compete with the public schools, but to be

> **'Just saying that something's a public good,' says author Myron Lieberman, 'it doesn't follow that government should pay for it. That's just a non sequitur.'**

the public schools—and to fundamentally change the dynamics of the learning environment."

In Miami Beach, where Education Alternatives is entering the third year of a contract to operate the South Pointe Elementary School, Principal Patricia Parham describes the experience as "100 percent totally positive." "People get so excited about somebody coming in that's a private group," she says. "But we buy textbooks from private companies; we have consulting services all the time from private companies. It's really no different."

That view is not shared by teachers and paraprofessionals in Baltimore, who last month boycotted the company's training sessions to protest its replacement of unionized workers with college-educated interns.

Critics warn that, as with vouchers, the cost savings from contracting out to private firms may be overstated. In its first five years, Education Alternatives has failed to turn a profit.

In 1990, Chelsea, Mass., turned over the operation of its school district to Boston University, a private institution. Three years later, Shanker notes, the system has lost its superintendent, the university official who was monitoring it, and many of its principals. And student performance has still not improved. "And they say, 'Well, we couldn't do much, because we haven't gotten enough money,' " he says. "They sound just like the public schools."

Others argue that, because the ultimate responsibility for contracts still rests with local school boards, the idea does not extend far enough. "If boards of education are the problem," says Phillip C. Schlechty, the president of the Center for Leadership in School Reform in Louisville, Ky., "then the fact that they contract out to someone else doesn't change the fact that you have a board of education."

In part because contracting out is less threatening, however, many predict that the practice will expand over the next few years. "Such experiments are going to become much more widespread than they are," forecasts Paul T. Hill, formerly with the RAND Corporation. "Still," he adds, "it would be big news if there were 3,000 such schools in five years."

To many reformers, the private sector's allure lies in the ability of an outside agent to challenge the status quo. But some suggest that the same dynamics could be produced wholly within the public system. They advocate a third course: a new kind of school that would reflect many of the principles of high-performance businesses but that would remain public.

Under these proposals, groups of teachers or others could operate their own schools under a "charter," or contract with a school district. Unlike traditional schools, charter schools would enjoy total autonomy in budget, staffing, curriculum, and teaching methods. And they would be exempt from nearly all state and local regulations.

In return for such freedom, charter schools would have to specify the goals they want students to achieve and how they would measure progress. "It's simple," says State Sen. Ember Reichgott of Minnesota, who last year sponsored a successful measure to enact the nation's first charter-schools law. "No re-

sults; no charter. Teachers trade away regulation for results, and bureaucracy for accountability."

Although Minnesota was the first state to pass such legislation, others are close behind. Gov. Pete Wilson of California signed a charter-schools bill last month that allows for the creation of up to 100 such schools. Similar bills have either been introduced or are being considered in Colorado, Connecticut, Florida, Massachusetts, Pennsylvania, and Tennessee.

Such schools, Reichgott argues, reward innovation, empower teachers and parents, and increase choices— all within the context of public education. "I view charter schools as an incentive to enhance public education," she says. "I view vouchers as an incentive to abandon the public schools."

'A Strong Consensus'

All the talk about privatization and other new arrangements has spurred educators to think more openly about less radical options. Public school choice, an anathema in education circles a decade ago, has become widely accepted.

But the real question, many school-improvement devotees argue, is how to free most public schools to become more efficient and effective. "I don't hear much talk out there about that side of things," complains Christopher T. Cross, a former director of education programs for the Business Roundtable.

Nonetheless, continued pressure from advocates of more radical approaches is forcing the public schools to diversify and to create a greater variety of options of their own. "I think over the next five or 10 years, you're going to see all these creative bursts of how you package public education," Bill Honig, a former superintendent of public instruction in California, predicts. "They'll still be public schools, and they'll still be subject to standards, but there'll be a lot more variety. I think that's a pretty strong consensus." ■

From Education Week, *Oct. 7, 1992*

37.

A Clean Slate

District officials chose a radical remedy for a troubled elementary school in Houston: They wiped the slate clean.

By Lynn Olson

To reach Thomas J. Rusk Elementary School from downtown Houston, you cross the railroad tracks and pass a string of run-down wooden bungalows and industrial warehouses. To the west, the city skyline floats above the rooftops like a distant vision of Oz. In front of the modest brick building, a row of saplings supported by wires struggles to take root: a mute testimony to the rebirth taking place within.

Two years ago, Rusk Elementary was a school in crisis. Children roamed the halls and fought in the cafeteria. Test scores ranked among the lowest in the district. Teachers and the principal were at war. Various school factions had twice marched down to the schoolboard demanding that something be done.

"It was terrible," recalls Jane Cardenas, the president of the school's parent-teacher organization. "The kids were running around the halls, and the teachers were not doing what they were supposed to do. Sometimes, I'd come to school, and my son would be the one to open the door."

In June 1993, then-Superintendent Frank R. Petruzielo announced that he would wipe the slate clean. Rusk would start over. He reassigned the school's principal, declared the teaching positions vacant, and told teachers they'd have to reapply for their jobs or transfer elsewhere in the district.

Today, only three of Rusk's 29 teachers remain from that spring. A new principal has recruited an almost entirely new staff. The floors and walls sparkle. Class-room doors are painted bright red. Students pass through the halls, accompanied by their teachers, in quiet, orderly lines. Plans are in the works for a school health clinic, with funding from the district and area hospitals. And all its progress has not gone unnoticed. Last year, Rusk was taken off the list of the state's low-achieving schools.

Rusk Elementary's story is one that could play out across the country in the coming years. Chronically low-achieving schools—and what to do about them—have been a problem that has plagued educators for decades. Few school systems have taken the drastic step of completely restaffing a school, a practice now known as "reconstitution." But as the demand for accountability grows, more and more policymakers are interested in starting fresh with schools that persistently fail to perform.

In San Francisco and Cleveland, the school boards have adopted policies as part of court-ordered desegregation plans that call for the systematic reconstitution of poorly performing schools after three years. In Kentucky, beginning in 1996, low-achieving schools could be designated "schools in crisis" and their principals and teachers replaced. In New York, a project is under way to phase out two large troubled high schools and replace them with up to six smaller schools run by directors who could select their own staffs. In 1993, Texas passed a law that allows the state to reconstitute any poorly performing school that fails to bring up its test scores and other academic indicators for several years in a row.

"We just did a 50-state survey on accountability," says Susan H. Fuhrman, a professor of educational policy at Rutgers University and the director of the Consortium for Policy Research in Education, "and 43 states say they're changing their accountability systems, and one of the main features is some type of sanction."

"It's a popular notion," she adds, "but a lot of this is still rhetoric. What we found is that these things are more in planning than on the books. And even when they're on the books, the ultimate interventions have yet to be applied."

Except in a few cases. Like Rusk.

No one denies that Rusk Elementary needed help. The tiny building is tucked away in the southeast corner of the 312-square-mile Houston Independent School District. It's in a poor neighborhood populated mostly by Hispanics, many of them recent immigrants. The majority of the school's 442 students come from homes where Spanish is the primary language spoken. Of the school's 20 pre-K-6 classrooms, half are designated for bilingual or English-as-a-second-language instruction. Many of the school's students read below grade level in either tongue.

About one-fifth of the school's population comes from two homeless shelters—the Star of Hope Women's and Family Shelter and the Salvation Army—contributing to a student mobility rate that climbed to 175 percent in 1991-92.

When Johana Briseno Thomas, a first-year principal, took over at Rusk that year, it was already a school in academic trouble. Its standardized test scores were among the lowest in the district. Fewer than 20 percent of students met the minimum expectations on the Texas Assessment of Academic Skills. Still, there was little to distinguish Rusk from the other struggling inner-city schools in the 201,000-student school system.

Soon, however, reports of problems began to reach the area superintendent and the central administration. Representatives from the area shelters complained that teachers were mistreating homeless children, many of whom were black. They alleged that the children were being unfairly scapegoated for the school's disciplinary problems. Parents charged that the principal refused to meet with them. Teachers reported that they were left out of the decisionmaking process. Thomas requested the transfer of several veteran teachers based, in part, on her contention that they were physically and emotionally abusing children from the shelters.

Area Assistant Superintendent Jos Hernandez says that by November 1992, he was receiving complaints almost daily. Several people described Thomas as a novice administrator who was put into an almost impossible situation. By her second year, almost half the teachers were new to the building, and many of its more experienced teachers had left.

Noemi Martinez, a stout Hispanic woman who works as the cashier in the school's cafeteria, crosses her arms and lets out a snort of disgust when asked about conditions at the school back then. "Huh," she says. "Very bad. Faculty and staff, you were either on the principal's side or against her. And the parents were fighting each other. And the kids were running wild, up to the point where we even had a teacher locked up in a closet. For two years, it was like chaos here."

In 1992, parents and teachers addressed HISD trustees twice concerning the school's curriculum and disciplinary problems. Hernandez says he sent in Chapter 1 and bilingual supervisors to work with the school, but nothing seemed to make a difference. Thomas alleges that she asked for more staff and help allocating $200,000 that the HISD had earmarked for Rusk, but that her pleas went unanswered.

In April 1993, the Texas Education Agency sent in an accreditation team to conduct a peer review of the school. It was a few months before Texas lawmakers passed Senate Bill 7, the new accountability measure that would enable the TEA to restaff low-performing schools.

"The campus was generally in turmoil," says Larry Garcia, who works in the accreditation division of the state education department. "There was just a lot of strife and divisiveness." TAAS scores—which already fell significantly below the state standard—had been steadily declining for three years. Although Rusk's primary goal was to improve student attendance, it had set no specific, measurable objectives. The school's shared-decisionmaking committee stood divided. Its other committees had been abandoned, leaving many teachers without needed workbooks and other materials all year.

"Basically, the peer-review team concluded, 'This campus just needs to start all over,'" recalls Garcia, "and that was placed in the report."

Petruzielo had already proposed a new accountability system for the school district called "Blueprint: Houston Schools of Excellence." It called for the total redesign of a school's staff or educational program as one option for low-achieving schools that did not improve over a reasonable period of time. But the district had never resorted to using the intervention. In fact, it didn't even have a detailed policy on the books that spelled out the specific steps leading up to intervention or the criteria that would make such a drastic measure appropriate.

In a closed board session in the spring of 1993, Petruzielo informed the HISD trustees that he planned to use his existing authority to transfer administrators and teachers out of Rusk Elementary School.

"There was considerable discussion," recalls Rod Paige, who was then a school board member and today is the superintendent of the Houston school district.

"It was not a unanimous issue."

"I was for reconstitution," he adds, "but I wanted some definite guidelines and rules set down for when we ran into this situation again."

In the end, Paige says, the accreditation report forced the school district to do something. Reconstitution, he adds, "was almost a spontaneous response. We couldn't think of anything short of this that was going to fix it."

On June 4, a Friday, Petruzielo made a surprise visit to the school to announce his plans, with the Houston press corps in tow. Everyone but the custodial and cafeteria employees would have to reapply for their jobs or move on. Thomas, the principal, was placed on "special assignment" with the school district. Area newspapers described reconstitution as the "death penalty" for schools.

"It was volatile," Paige says. "We were frightened by the way it was played."

Today, staff members at Rusk Elementary don't like to talk about the past.

Many of them came to the school because they liked the idea of starting fresh. A few didn't know much about the school's history when they applied for their jobs. A sizable group—eight of the school's 29 teachers and one teacher's aide—followed Principal Felipa Young from her former post at Andrew Briscoe Elementary School across town.

Robin Henry, a 1st grade teacher with a thick Southern accent, came to Rusk from elsewhere in the district. "My principal had left the school I was at. I was there for four years, and I just wanted a change," recalls Henry, who stands barely higher than her students. "I didn't even know what all had gone on here. I still don't know everything, and I don't even want to know."

Diane Smith, a kindergarten teacher, was ready to leave the district for work in the suburbs. "I was very frustrated and just thought I needed to have a change of pace," she says. But she knew Young, who had evaluated her teaching for the district. So when she heard the news on television, she decided to apply.

"When I got here it was filthy," Smith recalls. "I got a room that really looked like something had exploded. There were pencil shavings mixed in with blocks and toys and torn pieces of paper just everywhere. Somehow, we threw everything in containers and just put it away. And the children were very needy—a lot of tears, a lot of trouble adjusting. They needed love and happy surroundings."

Today, Smith's room is decorated with a brightly colored carpet, and artwork hangs from the ceilings. A few weeks before Halloween, she's wearing an orange apron decorated with bats, and witches dangle from her ears. Gathered on the rug at the front of the room, the kindergartners carve letters out of the air with their hands, then with their whole bodies. Last year, Smith says, she had two classes of 22 students and 80

different children over the course of the year. "You have to want to be here," she admits. "You have to want to be in this kind of atmosphere."

Principal Young positions herself in the hallway as the children pass by, a cross between a mother hen and a sentry guard. Warm brown eyes shine out from a square face surrounded by graying curls. A large chunky wooden necklace, with a schoolhouse swaying

---

Reconstitution has brought a much-needed sense of order and stability to Rusk, but the school program, for the most part, remains traditional.

---

from the end of it, is her only concession to fashion.

When Petruzielo decided to restaff Rusk Elementary School, he recruited Young because of her work at Briscoe Elementary, an inner-city school where she had successfully increased parent and community involvement. "He gave me no choice," Young claims. "I really wanted to stay at Briscoe a couple of more years and then, maybe, go to a middle school. I gave him some other names." But a few days later, Petruzielo came back and asked her again. She relented.

"When I came to Rusk," she recalls, "the park next door was dirty, run-down. The school was not kept. It was just—the way the building looked, the way the grounds looked—it was nothing like what I had left. It just didn't have a cheerful warm feel about it."

One of her first decisions was to install windows in the doors to every classroom so she could see what was going on inside. She painted the walls. The school's business partners, Arthur Andersen & Company and NationsBank, the latter of which followed her over from Briscoe, contributed to a beautification program at the school and at the park next door.

Thanks to the combined efforts of some 100 volunteers and neighborhood residents, more than 75 trees were planted around the school grounds. The fences, bleachers, and basketball courts at the park were painted and repaired. Glass and litter were removed and flowers planted.

Young sought—and received—a waiver from the school district to release students at 1:30 p.m. on Wednesdays so teachers could make time for grade-level and cross-grade-level meetings and professional development. She revived the school-based decisionmaking committee. And she began to reach out to the community.

A grassroots advocacy group, the Hispanic Family Education Support Center, agreed to help. So far, it's held about a dozen meetings at the school, during which it encourages parents to vent their feelings and become involved in school issues. Eventually, the group hopes to recruit local college students to work with youngsters after school.

"The Hispanic community, they're reluctant to come in, unless they really feel that they're a part of the school," Young explains. "I want my parents to feel that the school belongs to them."

On a Friday afternoon in October, more than 30 parents pour into Rusk for a meeting about the school's Chapter 1 remedial-education program. Before Young came, the parents say, there was no discipline. Speaking through a translator, they say the children were out of control, and the principal never communicated with them. Now, says Hada Flores, the mother of three children at the school, she can see that the children are working and the teachers are working.

The teachers are interested in the children, agrees Francisca Villalobos, who has a 2nd grader at Rusk. Sylvia Trevino, the parent of a 1st and a 5th grader, says before reconstitution, the situation got so bad that only one or two parents would come to meetings at the school. Now, she says, she tries to come to everything to show her support, to make up for the years when she didn't feel comfortable at Rusk.

"Everything has changed," says PTO President Cardenas. "The principal is always here. Her door is always opened to us. She'll put anything on hold to attend to the person who wants her right here and now."

"Everybody is nice," she adds. "Everybody treats you good. We can't believe it." In a small—but significant—gesture, Young required every teacher to wear a name tag on a daily basis so parents could identify them. The name tags have turned into tiny pieces of artwork decorated with apples, rulers, and other symbols of the teaching profession.

Young's goal—still unrealized—is to have every parent volunteer at least eight hours at the school, including those who live in the shelters.

Teachers at Rusk like to talk about the camaraderie that comes from having a strong leader and a sense of mission. "We're all really good friends, as well as colleagues, and we share ideas and philosophy," Henry, the 1st grade teacher, says.

"Teachers feel that there is a value to what they're doing," adds Juannie Kyriakides, the technology teacher who followed Young from Briscoe. "They feel that their opinion, their input, is valued. And they don't have a fear of expressing their disagreements."

Mary McMurtry, a 3rd grade English-as-a-second-language teacher who first taught at the school in 1962 and has now returned, admits that Young is strict. "She believes in discipline. But she gives us the freedom to want to do better," McMurtry says. "She gives you an opening where you feel like you can do more because of her high standards."

Dolores Alanis, a 5th grade teacher, grew up in the neighborhood and still attends church here. Her mother runs a local flower store. "Ms. Young believes in keeping everyone together like a family," she says. "She's willing to work with you—with professional help, with home, with anything."

The school still has problems, admits Alanis, but "they're normal ones." There's no gymnasium, for example. And teachers say they have too much work.

For children, the most obvious change comes with the sense of order and discipline at the school. There's no talking or running in the halls, no talking in the cafeteria. At the end of the day, their teachers accompany them to the front of the building. Some students even wear uniforms, an optional alternative to street clothes. Others compete for attendance awards. All of the classrooms have visibly posted classroom rules. And many sport signs like "Hard Work + Sacrifice = Success."

But the increase in discipline has been accompanied by plenty of added support, too. This year, the school has started an "adoption" program that makes every employee responsible for the well-being of a small group of students. A school drill team has also been created to keep campus spirits high. Students in the 5th and 6th grades can now look to single-sex support groups for guidance. And with money from a state program for homeless students, the school plans to launch an after-school arts program.

On a Friday morning, art teacher Perry O'Brien is holding down the front desk because the school is currently without a full-time secretary. As children come in late, he scolds them: "You need to get up earlier. It's your responsibility, not your parents'."

Over the public-address system, children listen to the Rusk Elementary learner's creed: "I believe in myself and my ability to do my best at all times."

A group of 5th graders discuss the changes at the school. "When you're in the halls, you're supposed to be quiet," says Gerardo. "We can do a lot more fun things, and we can learn at the same time," chimes in Edilma. There's no more trouble in the bathrooms, adds Fernando. "People used to just walk in the halls—go back and forth—and now they don't do that." It's not messy anymore, says another student, and they're encouraged to wear uniforms instead of baggy clothes. Do they mind? No, the children say. It's better.

Many of the teachers say when they first came to Rusk, students didn't expect to work hard, and they didn't do their homework. It took several months to make their expectations clear.

Now, there is 20 minutes of silent reading each day, and Young encourages frequent oral reading to perfect students' English. Last year, all teachers participated in a series of workshops on whole language instruction and using literature across the curriculum. As a group, the teachers have begun to set academic goals for each grade so continuity exists from one grade to the next.

But inside the classroom, every teacher does what he or she thinks best. As a result, some teachers arrange desks in rows and have students filling out worksheets. Others expect their students to write in journals and read literature. Some classrooms look fairly traditional; in others, children work in groups and tutor their peers. In one 6th-grade classroom, most students work with partners to solve math problems, while a few help classmates who are having difficulties.

In general, however, teacher talk appears to be the norm, with adults standing at the front of the room dispensing information or asking questions. And all Rusk teachers put a heavy emphasis on the basic skills students will need to pass the statewide test—the ultimate barometer of whether a school needs to be reconstituted.

"I want all the students to feel successful," Young says. "If you come to school every day, you're prompt, you're ready to work, you are going to get better."

Last year, student mobility at Rusk dropped to 134 percent, a decrease of nearly 24 percent from 1991-92. Surveys show that the level of parent and community involvement is up. But academic progress, as measured by test scores, is more uneven.

If there is any point of agreement on the overall issue, it is that reconstitution is painful. Nobody likes the process, but many like the results.

"It's very frustrating," says Susan K. Sclafani, Houston's associate superintendent for administration. "Some scores have gone up, and some have gone down." In the past four years, the state has changed its testing program so often—in terms of when students are tested and the grades in which they are tested—that there are no comparable year-to-year data.

Still, she says, signs do suggest that Rusk Elementary is headed in the right direction. The percentage of students meeting minimal expectations on the statewide test is highest in the upper grades, among students who have been at Rusk the longest. In 1993-94, for example, only 33 percent of 4th graders met the state's minimum expectations in reading, but 67 percent of 6th graders did. In mathematics, those figures were 30 percent and 79 percent, respectively.

Despite the encouraging signs in both academic performance and atmosphere, there are critics of reconstitution and particularly of the way it was handled at Rusk Elementary.

The teachers' unions complain that the practice casts all teachers in a bad light, including those who are doing their jobs. "It puts a permanent, negative mark on a teacher," charges Gayle Fallon, the president of the Houston Federation of Teachers. "They've done this in two schools, and I've watched the teachers go out and attempt to find jobs. And none of the other principals want them."

The federation offered to file a grievance on behalf of Rusk's teachers, but none was interested. Last spring, Houston partially reconstituted Mamie Sue Bastian Elementary School, moving out the principal and nine teachers. The union filed a grievance on behalf of four of those teachers. It was withdrawn after the district agreed to work with the teachers to help them find jobs.

The unions blame the problems at Rusk and Bastian on bad management. "Both lacked leadership," charges Lee Barnes, the president of the Houston Education Association. "The school district lacks competent principals. That's just the bottom line."

Irene Kerr, the executive director of the Houston Association of School Administrators, disagrees. But she says the experience at Rusk "reinforced, for my members, that every administrator is subject to reassignment."

"What was done at the time wasn't illegal," she adds, "but it was surely badly handled. And because it was badly handled, those teachers were basically lepers."

Johana Briseno Thomas, Rusk's principal who was reassigned, has filed a lawsuit against the school district, Petruzielo, two assistant superintendents, and five current and former school board members.

In her lawsuit, Thomas alleges that Petruzielo reassigned her "in direct retaliation" for speaking out about possible child abuse at the school and for trying to transfer "problem" teachers. She charges that the school system demoted her without any inquiry into the facts and punished her without establishing personal guilt.

The negative publicity, the lawsuit alleges, has damaged Thomas professionally and made it impossible for her to secure future employment as an administrator. The case is set for trial this spring in federal court because Thomas claims that her constitutional right to freedom of speech was violated.

To further confuse the issue, three months before

Petruzielo removed Thomas from her post and placed her on special assignment, her annual evaluation was upgraded. However, it is not clear why that upgrade occurred.

In her complaint, Thomas asserts that Area Assistant Superintendent Hernandez correctly upgraded her evaluation after discovering that it was based on an earlier one that had been discredited. Hernandez, who is reluctant to talk about Thomas's lawsuit, says he gave the former principal higher marks "just to give her a chance to succeed." Thomas is currently earning $56,392 a year while serving in one of the district's area offices.

Olga Gallegos, a school board member who is a friend of Thomas's, says she supports accountability but did not support the actions taken at Rusk. "Accountability did not apply there," she argues, "because the principal there had been having problems with part of the staff. She was a new principal and

> ## 'Here was a school that was not only low performing but also where morale was shot, where the community was unhappy, where the children were ill-served.'

usually the area superintendent has to support and help a new principal. And she was not getting that support."

Whether the school district could have avoided reconstitution at Rusk if officials had intervened earlier remains an open question. But many business people, parents, and teachers connected with the school allege that their cries for help went unanswered for at least a year.

"Rusk isn't terribly unusual," argues Jos Salazar, the president of the Hispanic Family Education Support Center, the advocacy group now working with the school. "It just rose to the forefront somehow. There is a very strong sentiment in the Hispanic community that most of the schools that are in areas like Rusk are probably having very similar problems and are probably being very ineffective."

According to Thomas's lawsuit, the year Rusk was reconstituted, 56 schools in Houston had fewer than 20 percent of students passing the TAAS exam.

"It wasn't any one factor that made this school the candidate for change," asserts Associate Superintendent Sclafani, "It was the combination of factors. It

was that the administrators and teachers and parents were not united in working for student improvement."

"These are very difficult situations, and they're never clear-cut," she adds. "What can be said is the resulting changes of both teachers and administrators have been positive for the school. And that was our goal: to improve the learning environment for kids."

In May 1994, the Houston school board adopted a new accountability system that formalizes the procedures used to reconstitute Rusk Elementary. The system places schools in five categories—from exemplary to low-performing—based primarily on state test scores. Principals at low-performing schools that are making no progress, with help from their shared-decisionmaking committee, must devise a plan to raise student achievement over two years. They can also request additional resources and authority. Each plan is negotiated with the school board.

If a school is placed in the targeted category for a second year, the principal can request adjustments in the agreement. At the end of that year, if the school still fails to improve, the principal will be removed unless he or she can win an extension from the school board.

The district can then select a new principal, identify a management team to run the school, or issue a request for public- or private-sector groups to operate the school.

Last June, six elementary schools, nine middle schools, and one high school were placed in the bottom category, meaning that fewer than 20 percent of their students had passed all sections of the TAAS exam. This fall, only three schools received the lowest rating, based on revisions in the accountability plan to reflect changes in the state's testing system.

Don McAdams was school board president when Rusk was reconstituted. "I was upset then—and remain upset—that the area superintendent was not on top of the situation," says McAdams, who still serves on the board. "Here was a school that was not only low performing, but where morale was shot, where the community was unhappy, where the children were ill-served, and neither the area superintendent nor the people at the central office had been doing anything about it."

"I don't think we're ever going to have a Rusk situation again," he adds, "because we're going to know how schools are performing and their intervention points."

Superintendent Rod Paige, who replaced Petruzielo when he became chief of the Broward County, Fla., schools, has also made it clear that he would like to avoid similar situations by handling them with more precision. "I support reconstitution," he explains, "but you really are stigmatizing—to some extent—everybody, including those in the building who might have been doing a good job."

"What we're saying is that the overall climate

didn't work, and we didn't have any way to decide those who were part of the problem and those who were not," he adds. "We'll try to do it as painlessly as possible because we're not in the business of trying to hurt people."

The solution, he believes, is the kind of partial reconstitution that took place at Bastian Elementary. There, the school system tried to pinpoint a small group of individuals and ask them to "voluntarily" relocate themselves. McAdams compares partial reconstitution to a "lumpectomy rather than a mastectomy."

"I think that's the way to go," he says, "and reconstitution is a last resort."

Paige also suggests that students—as well as teachers and administrators—should be subject to transfer if they consistently disrupt learning. At the same time that Bastian was partially reconstituted, he moved approximately 20 "of the most severe discipline problems" out of the Dick Dowling Middle School and placed them in an alternative school. "We're not going to allow a small portion of the student enrollment to disrupt the whole thing," he argues. "It doesn't just stop with the teachers."

But some are less optimistic about partial reconstitution. In fact, the teachers' unions say such a half-measure can be even more stigmatizing for those who are singled out.

Others say it just doesn't work. Robert L. Green, a professor of education at Cleveland State University and an expert on reconstitution, says: "There seems to be something systemic about failure. It's like having a fever or a virus. A virus affects your entire system. And to get at it, you should entirely clear the decks. In San Francisco, where we partially reconstituted some schools, we didn't get the results."

These days, many people look to San Francisco—not Houston—as the model for school reconstitution. Under a pilot effort, undertaken a decade ago as part of a court-ordered consent decree, the district created two new schools and replaced the staffs at four others in the Bayview-Hunter's Point section of the city.

Each of the six schools adopted a coherent education plan based on six components:
● 11 "philosophical tenets" that emphasized high expectations for students;
● Specific student outcomes for each subject at each grade level;
● A technology-rich environment;
● Flexible adult-student ratios so small-group instruction could take place at various times throughout the day;
● Heavy staff development focused on the above components; and
● New staff members who were committed to the vision for the school.

(In the late 1980s, under special circumstances, San Francisco reconstituted two other schools without replicating the Bayview-Hunter's Point plan.)

In July 1992, a report to the court by a committee of experts found significant improvements in the academic performance of African-American and Hispanic students at the original six schools. Black middle-school students, for example, surpassed the districtwide average in reading. In contrast, other low-achieving schools that received more money and staff members as part of the consent decree did not produce overall gains in student learning.

"Some schools," the report notes, "spent a million

> 'People say that we closed the school. We really didn't close the school. We started the school over. And I think there are situations where that remedy is appropriate.'

dollars or more in supplemental funds without showing improvements."

The committee recommended that the district reconstitute at least three low-achieving schools a year, until the academic achievement of Hispanic and African-American students substantially improves. Reconstitution would include everything done for the Bayview-Hunter's Point schools.

Since April 1993, the school district has developed and implemented a Comprehensive School Improvement Program to do just that. The plan targets schools based on a carefully developed set of quantitative and qualitative criteria. These include: changes in test scores; attendance, suspension, and dropout rates; student grades; a review of the school's portfolio; a visit to the school by a review panel; and an oral presentation to the panel and the superintendent about the school's efforts to improve minority-student achievement.

In 1993, nine schools were given extra resources to help bring up student learning. A central administrator was assigned to each school to help write and implement an education plan. The schools received discretionary funds. They were allowed to use their categorical monies flexibly and were guaranteed that those monies would not decline. And they could ask for help from a management expert.

This fall, three of the nine schools—Woodrow Wilson High School, Visitation Valley Middle School, and Bret Harte Elementary School—were reconstituted. They are currently putting in place a revised version of the Bayview-Hunter's Point plan, which was updated by a committee of administrators from the original six schools. Nine others have been put on notice that they may be reconstituted in the fall of 1995.

Roger Brindle, a program evaluator for the school district, contends that simply moving staff isn't enough. "The one thing that is absolutely critical," he argues, "is you have to have a coherent education plan. You have to create a coherent culture in the school. And then you hire people who agree with that culture. It isn't just: Fire all the staff and hire somebody new and you get change. It's not that simple.

"People get really enchanted with reconstitution," he adds, "and they miss that there is this other point."

Brindle also worries that reconstitution may have a theoretical upper limit, even in a large district such as San Francisco. Most teachers are tenured, he notes, and disillusioned and burned-out teachers who are moved out of one school may simply end up clustered somewhere else.

"One hopes," Brindle speculates, "that it's not only the schools that are reconstituted that this has an effect on. It's a very negative thing, but one hopes in the long run the fact that the program exists is going to do something to bring together schools that are marginal and might fall under the net. Whether or not that will happen is an ongoing question."

If there is any point of agreement, it is that recon-stitution is painful. Nobody likes the process. But many like the results.

"People say that we closed the school," Superintendent Paige of Houston says of Rusk Elementary. "We really didn't close the school. We started the school over. And I think there are situations where that remedy is appropriate."

"The bottom line," he adds, "is schools have got to work. Children have got to learn. And these other types of issues will have to take a back seat to that."

For Rusk Elementary, the pressure is on to move forward and not look back. There is so much to do. So much to prove.

"When I came to school here, it was very strict, very disciplined," says Noemi Martinez, the cafeteria cashier. "I like it now. I'm beginning to see the old Rusk—the Rusk I knew—with new teachers, new faces, but dedicated teachers."

Amanda Robertson, a young 1st grade teacher, began her career at Rusk before it was reconstituted. "Before, it was just negative, nothing but negative. It got to the point where you just did the bare minimum," she explains. "It's a positive environment now. You're excited to come to school. You're willing to put out the effort." ■

From Education Week, *Dec. 7, 1994*

38.

Does 'Public' Mean 'Good'?

Has public education kept its halo of moral superiority through nostalgia, wishful thinking, and shrewd public relations?

Commentary by Chester E. Finn Jr.

As the debate over school choice heats up once again, in the halls of Congress and in many state capitals, a favorite gambit of defenders of the status quo is to damn such changes as "sure to undermine public education" or "bad for the public schools." They always stress the word "public," for that adjective is believed to carry moral weight and political suasion. It is meant to evoke patriotism and decency, Thomas Jefferson and Horace Mann, goodness, virtue, and the American way. If "public" education is inherently good, it follows that anything apt to erode it must be bad.

The "choice" schemes that get tarred with this brush are usually designed to help poor and middle-class children attend non-government schools when their parents judge that this would result in better education. Or greater safety. Sounder values. Whatever.

Secretary of Education Lamar Alexander was savaged by the American Federation of Teachers' president Albert Shanker for suggesting that any school willing to embrace high standards, to enroll children on a nondiscriminatory basis, and to be held accountable for its results, might reasonably be deemed "public," no matter who owns and operates it. Mr. Shanker called this notion "Orwellian" and warned of schools "established by the likes of David Duke."

Other examples abound. We heard some on the floor of the U.S. Senate when Orrin Hatch sought to overturn the Kennedy bill's ban on private schools' participation in a new federal choice demonstration. But such talk is not confined to Washington. A "poison

pill" for the public schools is how California's proposed voucher plan was described by Bill Honig, the former state superintendent of public instruction. Some of his allies use terms like "fraud" and "evil" when discussing that initiative.

When Milwaukee's mayor, John Norquist, suggested replacing failed urban schools with a "choice or voucher system," he was sharply attacked by the press and the education establishment for disloyalty to public education.

And in the closing arguments of a recent nationally televised mock "trial" on whether the public schools are irreparably flawed, the Harvard law professor assigned to defend them asserted solemnly that our "traditions and ideals of quality public education" are responsible for the nation's evolution from a "third rate" country to a "great power." (Viewers, it seems, were not entirely persuaded. In the telephone tally that followed the show, 53 percent of callers agreed with the other attorney that the public schools are "beyond repair.")

What is it about this word "public" when it comes to schooling, and does the same moral and political alchemy occur when we meld that adjective with other nouns? Does "public" always wear a halo? Try some other combinations:

●Public welfare: Summons images of sloth, dependency, fraud, and irresponsibility. Anything but virtue.
●Public transportation: How you get around if you don't have a car, a bicycle, strong legs, or cab fare. Often unsafe, dirty, and unreliable.
●Public hospitals: Where you go if, besides ailing,

you're destitute. They cost the taxpayer a pretty penny and often provide mediocre care.

●Public housing: Such bad news that virtually none of it has been built in decades. The corridors reek, you take your life in your hands on the elevator, and the maintenance people are never around when the pipes burst.

●Public radio and television: Sources of boring shows, politicized documentaries, and leaks by the likes of Nina Totenberg.

●Public parks, beaches, swimming pools, tennis courts, and golf courses: Better than none.

●Public safety: Grand idea, honored mainly in the breach. When people talk about it, watch for rising crime rates, menacing streets, and bad guys who go unpunished. Hence the surge in private security services, bodyguards, etc.

●Public colleges and universities: Often OK, sometimes fine, but wouldn't you rather send your kid to Princeton?

●Public relations: Puts a nice face on bad situations and tries to persuade you of things that aren't entirely true.

●Public restrooms: Yuck.

The main exceptions that come to mind, places that may be enhanced (at least not diminished) by the adjective, are public libraries and—maybe—"public" utilities. As for "public" policy, it's largely responsible for all the preceding.

There are, to be sure, some domains where the only sensible way to get something done is through a single, government operated system. The armed forces. Highways. Printing money. Yellowstone National Park. These enterprises, however, have distinctive features: We seldom use the word "public" when describing them. There are fewer of them today than in the past, since many fields that once belonged to government monopolies—mail delivery, space satellites, trash collection, etc.—have privatized and diversified. Where this has occurred, moreover, the private versions usually operate more efficiently and reliably.

Elementary-secondary education is diversified, too, but not very. Its private sector consists of 27,000 schools, yet they enroll just 11 percent of all pupils. The hot policy issue, of course, is whether those numbers should be encouraged to grow. Private schools, by many measures, do a better job than government-run schools at imparting skills, knowledge, values, and character to their students. (That's not to say they do a good enough job!) They operate at lower per-pupil costs. And the vast majority of them welcome anyone who knocks on their door. They are far more open to poor and minority youngsters than the "public"

schools of Beverly Hills, Chappaqua, Wellesley, Evanston, and hundreds of other communities such as these.

How, then, has "public" education kept its halo of moral superiority? Mostly, I think, through nostalgia, wishful thinking, and shrewd public relations (see above). We want to believe that today's tax-supported schools are bastions of democracy and learning. That wish, however, has left us vulnerable to establishment propaganda and has helped perpetuators of the status quo lay claim to the adjective. Today they are squeezing every possible drop of political advantage from it, mostly by depicting alternatives to public schools as elitist and discriminatory.

The vast majority of private schools are far more open to poor and minority youngsters than the public schools of Beverly Hills, Chappaqua, and Wellesley.

The truth is that the emperor we know as public schooling, despite an expensive wardrobe, has worn his present garments so long that most of them need cleaning if not replacing. Our solemn obligation is not to dress him up in new finery, however, but to see that American children—all of them—get access to a world-class education, no matter who provides it. Educating the public is a part of the social contract; institutions called public schools are not. Occasionally we do well to recall that it's the consumers, not the suppliers, for whose benefit we have an education system. Most Americans agree that we need a quality revolution in that system. We're a lot more likely to get one, however, if we banish from this domain—as we've done from so many others—the shibboleth that goodness and legitimacy attach only to institutions that bear the "public" label. ■

Chester E. Finn Jr., a former assistant U.S. secretary of education, is a John M. Olin fellow at the Hudson Institute.

From Education Week, *Feb. 12, 1992*

39.

Schools Within Schools

A unique program may be the lever for radically restructuring high schools in one of the nation's largest urban districts.

By Ann Bradley

At 9:15 on a crisp, sunny fall morning, lines of students pour in through the doors of Simon Gratz High School in North Philadelphia, a formidable Gothic-style building with castle-like battlements. As the latecomers receive passes that will admit them to class, they file into the cavernous hallway of the school, built in 1927 in what has since become one of the city's poorest neighborhoods.

At one time, Gratz was considered one of the worst of the district's 22 neighborhood high schools. But that sad distinction meant that Gratz differed from the other schools only in degree, not in kind. By almost any measure—course passage, credit accumulation, dropout and graduation rates, performance on standardized tests, and students' experiences after high school—Philadelphia's comprehensive schools are troubled institutions.

These are the schools that serve the average child in Philadelphia, those for whom there is no spot in the city's 12 special-admissions high schools. Their students are likely to be disadvantaged members of minority groups, many overage for their grade and with poor academic records.

Staffed by aging teachers and hidebound in their allegiance to academic departments, this city's neighborhood high schools "tend to be almost like a little school district unto themselves," observes Robert B. Schwartz, the director of education programs for the Pew Charitable Trusts, which is based here. "If you're

looking for an entry point for structural changes," he adds, "that's typically the last place you look."

Nevertheless, the neighborhood high schools are the focus of one of the most comprehensive school improvement efforts in the nation. The Philadelphia Schools Collaborative, with more than $16 million in funding from Pew, has been working since 1988 to break down the anonymity of the neighborhood high schools by creating "charters," or semiautonomous schools, within their walls.

'We Cannot Go Back'

Each charter serves a heterogeneous mix of 200 to 400 students and is run by a team of 10 to 12 teachers. These teachers have common planning time and develop their own instructional methods and curricula, which are often interdisciplinary. Ideally, to forge a sense of connection and commitment to the charter, the teachers and students will remain together for four years.

These smaller units also have drawn parents back into the schools. Parents are invited to participate in many of the planning and staff development activities, and receive stipends for their attendance just as teachers do.

There are now 97 charters in the neighborhood high schools. Every school has at least two charters; 11 schools are "fully chartered," meaning that all students and faculty members are attached to a charter.

By the end of this school year, the collaborative estimates that there will be 120 charters.

Some charters have ties to universities and help to prepare new teachers. Some emphasize the humanities or multicultural studies, while others prepare students for careers in business or human services.

Despite its reputation for academic problems, Gratz is the home of what observers say is one of the most successful charters in the city. This writing-intensive program, called Crossroads, was the brainchild of veteran teachers who say that, with the collaborative's help, they were finally able to create a school that made sense to them.

Crossroads "has made a remarkable difference in the lives of some adults and children," says Marsha Pincus, an English teacher who founded the charter with two colleagues. Talking with a reporter, she and Bob Fecho, another English teacher and a co-founder of the program, interrupt each other in their eagerness to talk about Crossroads. "You're always cautious and cynical" about new programs, Fecho says. "We'd plan and then say, 'If it doesn't work out, we can go back in the room and close the door.'"

"Never having tasted this, we could do that," he continues, "but having tasted this autonomy, and sharing with other people, the continuity ... "

"Or that I could know these kids ... " Pincus quickly interjects.

"We cannot go back," he says.

"If this is taken away from me," she warns, "then, personally, I am out of here."

Aside from teachers' enthusiasm, there is evidence that the more personalized approach is paying off for students. The collaborative reports that students who are attached to charters have better attendance records and lower dropout rates, and pass more courses than students who are not. The number of students who repeat 9th grade has also increased, meaning that they are returning to school for another year instead of dropping out.

The concept of creating "schools within a school" is a familiar one in education, but the charters are not ends in themselves. Michelle Fine, a senior consultant to the collaborative and a professor of education at the City University of New York, makes no secret of her disdain for what she calls "precious" programs that serve only the "creamy slice" of the most able students.

Instead, the charters are seen as a lever for radically restructuring each high school and for decentralizing the district. "Decisions and money should be at the site of practice," Fine asserts. "Schools should become autonomous sites for teacher work, student work, and parent involvement."

In setting as its goal the realignment of the district's bureaucracy to support these small, personal units, the Philadelphia Schools Collaborative "has adopted a much more encompassing view of restructuring than that typically espoused by reform initiatives in other communities," concludes an assessment of the PSC's first three years.

Janis I. Somerville, the executive director of the collaborative, and Fine have designed a multifaceted approach to school reform. The collaborative has played a lead role in establishing shared decisionmaking and school-based management in the district. Nineteen of the comprehensive high schools have governance councils that are charged with developing educational plans for the schools that include provisions for planning charters. More than 60 parents serve on the councils. Teachers in 12 charters are exploring the use of performance assessments for their students, also under the PSC's guidance.

The collaborative encompasses a College Access project to help inner-city students continue their studies, and the Algebra Transition Program, which is working to improve students' access to and passage of higher-level mathematics courses.

One of the collaborative's most difficult challenges is to identify the administrative and procedural hurdles that interfere with high school restructuring and to work with district officials to remove them. The nonprofit organization occupies a prime spot for doing so: just down the hallway from then-Superintendent Constance E. Clayton's office in the district's massive art deco headquarters.

An $8.3 million grant from Pew paid for the PSC's first three years. In 1992, the foundation approved a $7.8 million grant for another three years. The gifts were the largest ever made to a district by a single philanthropy, Pew says.

Fine, explaining why she believes big-city school bureaucracies need to be broken down, compares the work here with the massive decentralization of the Chicago schools mandated by the Illinois legislature. "Chicago is the best test of what the law can do," she says, "and we're the best test of what money can do."

'Creeping Academics'

What Pew's money has purchased, collaborative officials say, is enriching professional opportunities for seasoned teachers who have spiced the charters with academically rich programs. The charters receive some discretionary money from the district for materials and "release time" for the charter coordinators to plan the program.

In the earliest days of the collaborative's work, Fine has written, teachers who were asked to dream about what schools "could be" envisioned very traditional improvements: more teachers and counselors, more tracking, and more special-education placements. The collaborative's task became to help teachers broaden their ideas, an approach she calls "neither top-down nor naively bottom-up." The result of the emphasis on including special-education students in charters and broadening all students' access to college-preparatory courses, she says, has been a phenomenon she calls "creeping academics."

Schools were given a set of broad guidelines for creating charters, specifying that they should have "substantive themes" to which teachers and students would commit for several years, teams of teachers, rigorous and integrated academic curricula, and varied instructional strategies.

The planning teams began their work by focusing on the 9th grade, a difficult transition year for many students. In Philadelphia, it is particularly so, because the district's promotion policies have resulted in as many as 25 percent of 9th graders being overage for their grade.

Through travel to national conferences, contact with teachers from around the nation who visited Philadelphia, and summer institutes and curriculum-planning seminars, the teachers began creating the

> The collaborative's task became to help teachers broaden their ideas, an approach one consultant calls 'neither top-down nor naively bottom-up.'

new charters. Last summer, 1,300 parents and teachers registered for the summer institute.

The charters have provided a fertile environment for teachers whose intellects have been stimulated by such professional opportunities. In the past, teachers who developed new approaches were "sent back into institutions that were defeating," notes Morris J. Vogel, a professor of history at Temple University who helps teachers develop interdisciplinary curricula. "In all of the charters, it's the same principle," he says. "You don't separate the person who designs the curriculum from the person who implements it."

Teachers have seen immediate results from their efforts. Zachary Rubin, a history teacher at Lincoln High, which has a charter with a professional-development emphasis that is affiliated with Temple University, says his students' grasp of the subject has increased markedly since teachers at his school organized their instruction around such themes as "creation." Before the charter began, he says, "there was absolutely no retention. I realized I was not getting the materials across."

Jacqueline Burton, a mathematics teacher who works with Rubin, recalls overhearing a student saying how he heard about nothing but creation in his math, English, and history classes. She knew then that the interdisciplinary message was getting through.

Working as a team with other teachers also has cut down on attendance and discipline problems, Burton adds, because students know that their teachers are in close contact with each other. "If something happens in Rubin's room, I will know about it," Burton says. "It helps a lot, it really does."

Ultimately, collaborative officials say, the success of the restructuring effort rests on the shoulders of teachers like Rubin and Burton. "We are trying," says Somerville of the collaborative, "to build a constituency for change from within the ranks of teachers."

In doing so, and in pursuing the kinds of policy changes at the district level that will support the charters, the collaborative and leaders of the charters have begun to run up against some of the formidable barriers to urban school reform. "A whole lot of dynamics are involved when it becomes a school full of charters, as opposed to an isolated program from the rest of the building," Somerville explained. "When the whole building is involved, there is this tremendous energy and questioning everything."

At Gratz, a "fully chartered" school, teachers in the Crossroads program have begun questioning some of the traditional high school staffing positions. They wonder, for example, whether it still makes sense to have a full-time "roster chairman" to schedule students and teachers, since charters are devising their own schedules. The role of department heads—who teach a reduced load, order supplies, discipline some students, and observe but do not formally evaluate teachers—also has come into question.

The average high school class size is 33, a number that many teachers would like to see reduced. "There are ways we could do it," Fecho says, "but not just with Crossroads. The whole school would have to buy in, and there are real turf problems. You don't talk about department heads teaching four classes."

At Kensington High, says Shirley Farmer, a teacher in a charter there, "we have charter meetings instead of departmental meetings. It's clear to me that [system] is pretty obsolete."

But these positions, the teachers note, have provided some of the few perquisites available to teachers and have spawned a number of union leaders who are loyal to the jobs. There has been a great deal of reluctance, in general, to rethinking the organization and mission of the high schools, Fine says. She calls the lack of faith in change and suspicion that has grown up in some schools "communitarian damage," and frankly admits that the collaborative had underestimated it when the restructuring work began.

Such attitudes have meant, not surprisingly, that the quality of the charters varies. Fine estimates that 15 are "really interesting," 30 to 40 are "pretty good and getting better," and that the rest are "not so good, but no worse than the high schools they came out of."

The wariness that has greeted the collaborative's initiatives is easy to understand, says Schwartz of Pew, because there has been so little new blood in the comprehensive high schools. Special education has been one of the few exceptions to that rule. "Particularly in high school English and social studies," he says, "there hasn't been anybody new hired for 20 years. You're dealing overwhelmingly with a veteran teaching force in these schools that has seen highly touted innovations come and go."

Even though few new teachers have been hired, teachers themselves are highly mobile. Fluctuations in the student population, caused by such factors as mobile families and dropouts, mean that teachers must be reassigned. The mobility of students and teachers, in fact, has emerged as one of the central challenges for the charters. Without finding a way to reduce it, teachers here warn, the goal of having teams of students and teachers stay together for more than a year will be impossible to attain.

Essie Abrahams, an English teacher at Lincoln High School and a charter coordinator, recalls the time during the end of her charter's first year when it was announced that the school could lose 17 teachers. "I walked into our charter meeting, and it meant that the only person who would be there was me," she says. "We certainly can't do everything they want us to do if they are constantly throwing away our people."

The losses at Lincoln were prevented, but teachers say they are mindful that teacher turnover could undermine their best efforts to create cooperative faculties. The problem is particularly acute given the fact that the charters began with the 9th grade, the level at which high school teachers with the least seniority are clustered, according to the evaluation of the PSC. "The collaborative, district, and Philadelphia Federation of Teachers must examine policies related to teacher assignment and staff allocation to ensure that

The Crossroads charter "has made a remarkable difference in the lives of some adults and children," says Marsha Pincus, center, an English teacher.

charters are not jeopardized," it warns.

The concern about teacher mobility was highlighted this fall, when the teachers' union and the district announced an agreement on a two-year contract that will move the district from a year-long schedule into a two-semester calendar. The motive for the switch was to give students who were failing courses the opportunity to have a fresh start during the second semester, explains Ted Kirsch, the president of the union.

But some teachers involved with charters express fear that the district will have to realign teacher assignments during the middle of the school year, which could disrupt their programs. The outcry of concern after the contract was signed was so loud that then-Superintendent Clayton sent teachers a letter noting that they could ask for a policy waiver if they believed transfers would harm their charters.

The new schedule "has nothing to do with breaking up the continuity of instruction in the charter or in any other school," Clayton says. "I tried to put that to rest."

The concern over how systemwide or schoolwide policies affect charters has raised a deeper question about whether charters might someday be completely autonomous units. Fine is enthusiastic about that possibility.

But Dick Clark, a consultant to the Pew Charitable Trusts, warned that a school cannot simply be a collection of charters because the overall environment must be a "healthy setting" for students and teachers. "The piece that hasn't been worked out," he says, "is what is the role of the schoolwide leadership? Is it a confederation or a republic?"

Over lunch with Kirsch and an associate, Somerville and Fine pose the question of whether teachers might be allowed to transfer into charters, rather than moving from school to school. They argue that the option would help create a better match between teachers' interests and the charters' themes. Some teachers say they would like to go a step further and have the authority to hire their colleagues into the charters. Others, however, adamantly oppose that idea, arguing that it would create an "elitist" system that would discriminate against some teachers.

The teachers' union, Kirsch says, takes a "firm and consistent" position that teachers should not start hiring other teachers. "I don't see the need to hire their own teachers," he says. Focusing on the teachers sends the message that the program would be more successful with different teachers, he explains, which means that teachers are to blame for the current conditions. "I don't believe that," he adds.

In schools where the topic has come up, says Jerald Hairston, a union official who assists restructuring schools, teachers have decided that "they shouldn't be about getting teachers to come in," but should concentrate on helping existing teachers "buy into it."

'In Constant Discourse'

The answers to some of the larger questions posed by restructuring the high schools ultimately will have to come from district officials and not classroom teachers. Some teachers remain skeptical of the extent of the administration's commitment to the charters. "The district hasn't moved much," Fecho of Gratz's Crossroads charter says. "We are like a big person in a small room. We have pushed this district as far as it has moved. Unless downtown changes, this whole school is going to be stuck."

At this point, observers say, the district and teachers' union are considered to be generally supportive of the high school restructuring, but each side appears to be keeping a close eye on the other to make the first move toward radical change. They note that the new teachers' contract was reached through traditional bargaining and contains little to advance the high school initiatives.

The problem of teacher mobility, Clayton asserted, is a "union issue." "We stay in constant discourse with the union on issues of that nature," she says. "I am trying to negotiate with the federation without having them feel that there's an erosion of what they worked so hard for and what they feel are the rights of their constituents. It doesn't happen overnight."

Kirsch believes that, while the superintendent is supportive, "middle management gets in the way."

The assessment of the collaborative's first three years concludes that its efforts to create an environment in the central administration that is "conducive to restructuring" have been "stymied."

But Clayton insisted that she has sent a strong message in favor of reform to her subordinates. "We have tangibly and honestly taken a much stronger position of being of service to the field rather than issuing directives."

Over the past 10 years under the superintendent's leadership, the district has achieved a remarkable degree of stability for an urban system, Schwartz of Pew noted. Clayton has balanced the budget, achieved labor peace, standardized the curriculum, and established a good working relationship with the board of education. "The flip side of that continuity and stability also means that when you're talking about change of the magnitude that is contemplated in this restructuring effort, it makes it more difficult," Schwartz observed. "The key players have been in place for a long time, and they are accustomed to a certain way of doing business."

As the larger questions raised by the reform effort are debated, hundreds of teachers throughout the city are pressing on with their programs. At Horace H. Furness High on the city's south end, the creation of charters has "bred nothing but professionalism," says Bill Tomasco, a department head. Before the charters were created, he says, the school was "languishing. It was a sleepy hollow with no direction." Now its students, many of whom are Southeast Asian immigrants, are using the city as their classroom to study immigration, planning trips abroad, and writing books about resettling in America.

The investment in their professionalism, says Valerie Nelsen, the coordinator of the school's multicultural charter, "makes teachers rise to the occasion." She adds: "Their creativity is at such a high; plus, there's the enthusiasm of the kids." ■

From Education Week, *Nov. 18, 1992*

40.

Who's in Charge?

The movement to decentralize and empower individual schools is colliding with the teacher unions' most cherished protections.

By Ann Bradley

As urban districts move to grant individual schools greater autonomy, teachers' unions are confronting challenges to some of collective bargaining's most cherished protections and procedures. In particular, the push to decentralize big-city school systems often calls into question the centralized personnel policies that were created when teachers were regarded as interchangeable laborers in a factory-like system.

In recent months, attempts to give schools greater control over their budgets, staffs, and programs in such cities as Boston and Detroit have run headlong into the desires of unions to protect the tenure and seniority policies, centralized hiring, and common work rules that have traditionally been key features of teaching contracts.

And at the same time that reformers are pushing for greater authority at the school site, the American Federation of Teachers, which once led the charge for schools to govern themselves, is downplaying school-based management as its primary reform strategy. Without clear curriculum goals, better assessments, and incentives for students and teachers, such initiatives often flounder, says Albert Shanker, the president of the AFT. "We're convinced that school-based management, in and of itself, does not lead anywhere."

Union leaders acknowledge that school autonomy calls traditional labor practices into question. Some union presidents, such as John Elliott, who heads the Detroit Federation of Teachers, insist that teachers should not and do not want to take on the responsibility of managing schools. Others, such as Adam Urbanski, the president of the Rochester (N.Y.) Teachers Association, contend that unions could give up some of their traditional roles and become "service centers" for their members. "It would mean a different kind of union," Urbanski says, "not lesser, just different."

Researchers have found that the most successful schools are those in which teachers, principals, and students feel a sense of ownership, have created a distinctive culture, and have the freedom to go about achieving their goals. Many reformers are now suggesting that principals and teachers be given greater control over who works in their buildings as a way to build such school cultures.

But in many big-city districts where such devolution of authority may seem most critical, teachers are hired and assigned to jobs in a centralized way that allows individual schools little leeway in choosing and managing their own teachers. These procedures, many experts now believe, eventually could undermine efforts across the nation to give schools more autonomy.

"If teachers continue to be assigned on the basis of seniority or other general criteria," says a RAND Corporation report on decentralization, "staff assignment could become a serious barrier to the continuation of healthy site-managed schools."

Decentralization efforts are under way in a number of urban school districts. Unlike the movement of the late 1960s and early 1970s that resulted in the creation of community school boards in New York City and subdistrict offices in Detroit, the focus of the current activity is on devolving power and authority to schools themselves.

The best example is Chicago, where local school councils that include administrators and teachers along with parents and community members now hire and fire school principals and make critical decisions about a school's budget and programs.

School reformers in other cities, while advocating a variety of approaches, also believe that the best strategy for addressing the problems that plague their schools lies with the people who work in them. In Los Angeles, a diverse civic coalition has drafted a plan for moving decisionmaking and budget authority to the schools. In Detroit, the school board has been locked in a struggle with the teachers' union over a proposal to "empower" schools to run their own affairs. In Philadelphia, the comprehensive high schools are being broken down into smaller units that are viewed as a step toward eventually decentralizing the district.

And in Boston, the school committee has proposed creating deregulated "demonstration schools" that would be free to hire and manage their own staffs. The committee and the Boston Teachers Union are now negotiating a new contract.

Whether these efforts will be successful is unclear. Three members of the Detroit Board of Education who were most closely associated with the empowerment effort there lost their bids for re-election last month, in large part because they had alienated the district's labor unions.

Because the historical trend has been toward more, not less, centralization, experts believe that these efforts face formidable obstacles. The issue of what to decentralize and what to maintain as the province of the central office is not a simple one, says Susan Moore Johnson, a professor of administration, planning, and social policy at Harvard University's graduate school of education. "People are totally unrealistic about how complicated these organizations are, how difficult it is to bring about change, and how long it takes," she says.

But the unmistakable trend toward breaking down the centralized administration of big districts has important implications for teachers' unions. As districts move decisions about what to teach and how to teach it, grading and attendance policies, and the like down to schools, observes Charles T. Kerchner, a professor at the Claremont Graduate School in California and the editor of a new book on urban school reform, "you tear big hunks out of the notion of the existing bureaucracy."

"We are talking about departures from industrial-style organizations that are strongly hierarchical, relatively formalized, and relatively differentiated between levels," he says, "where teachers are real different than managers." Kerchner adds, "Once you depart from that mode of operation, the existing mode of organizing teachers doesn't work very well."

Some union leaders have thought about new ways of serving their members that break with existing practices. "My whole thrust has been that the bargaining agent has to play a minimal role: Bargain and get the hell out of the way," says Patrick O'Rourke, the president of the Hammond (Ind.) Federation of Teachers. "Practitioner power, not bargaining-agent power."

"That is controversial within the AFT," he adds. "There has always been a minority who wants to really increase the role of practitioners at the expense of traditional roles for the unions."

The "logical consequence" of school-based management, write RAND researchers in their decentralization study, would be a "districtwide teacher labor market in which teachers and schools choose one another on the basis of affinity to school mission and culture."

How to create such a system—while still protecting teachers' rights and guarding against inequity—is a subject of intense debate. Union leaders insist that, for a number of reasons, it cannot and should not be done. For one thing, school-site hiring would create imbalances among experienced and inexperienced teachers, Shanker, the AFT president, argues.

"In New York City," Shanker says, "if you didn't have a central-assignment and central-transfer plan, then teachers would be distributed according to the racial composition of the school and the socioeconomic status."

"It's also true right now that when New York City teachers are centrally hired and sent to the school that probably about 30 percent of the teachers quit because they do not want to work at the school that they are sent to," he adds. "So this is not a simple issue."

In addition to concerns about equity, union leaders point out that districts have to guard against undue political pressures in teacher hiring. And some, most notably Boston, are under centrally administered school-desegregation orders that regulate the racial composition of their teaching forces.

"In the 1950s," recalls Jack Steinberg, the director of education issues for the Philadelphia Federation of Teachers, "we had ward schools, where a teacher had to go to a ward leader, pay the ward leader, and work for that person on election day [to get a job]. That's not so far back in our history."

The notion of schools choosing teachers on the basis of their adherence to a certain philosophy or approach to education also runs counter to the egalitarian norms that influence teachers' relationships with one another.

In Philadelphia, some of the teachers who have created "charter" schools in the comprehensive high schools have expressed interest in hiring the other teachers who will work with them. The teachers' union opposes the idea, arguing that it would create divisions in the ranks. Some teachers, Steinberg argues, tend to become "dictatorial" in their views.

"The thought of only having people in your school who agree with our philosophy is one that we reject," he says, "because the whole purpose of restructuring is to give an opportunity to all ideas to come out and be discussed."

In addition to personnel policies, the centralized work rules contained in teaching contracts have come under fire in some cities. Critics argue that it no longer makes sense to negotiate a specific set of regulations that apply to all teachers, because schools are being encouraged to find the practices that suit their communities and students best.

Steven F. Wilson, the co-director of the Pioneer Institute for Public Policy Research in Boston and the author of a book about reforming the Boston schools, writes that the detailed contract "overpowers" anyone who wants to undertake change.

"The teachers' union demeans its own membership by insisting that everything about the workplace be prescribed," he writes, "from the length of lunch breaks, to the length and schedule of the workday, to the maximum number of minutes per week that teachers are permitted to meet with one another." The rules in the Boston contract governing staffing, he reports, are spelled out in 221 single-spaced pages.

Edward Doherty, the president of the Boston Teachers Union, says it was unfair to criticize his union's contract as unduly restrictive, noting that with its clause on school-based management it is more "educationally flavored" than most such agreements.

Other union leaders point out that work rules have grown up over time to protect teachers from poor managers. "Most are in there because of some real or perceived abuse," says Edward McElroy, the secretary-treasurer of the American Federation of Teachers. "The unions also become a bureaucracy, because they are dealing with a bureaucracy."

The frustration with the Boston procedures is one reason the school committee wants to create demonstration schools, according to Robert Culver, the senior vice president and treasurer of Northeastern University and a member of the Boston school committee. "We've got to focus on outcomes," he says, "as opposed to processes."

In Chicago, a group of teachers, principals, and members of local school councils that convened to brainstorm about how to further decentralize the system proposed that teachers be hired and given annual contracts by individual schools. Teachers whose contracts were not renewed at a particular school, they suggested, could have their names returned to a city-wide eligibility list maintained by the central office.

Chicago principals now work directly for schools on four-year performance contracts. But in what is widely regarded as a political compromise to secure the support of the Chicago Teachers Union for the reform legislation, teachers continue to work for the school system under a central contract.

The reform law did give principals the authority to hire teachers for vacant or newly created positions without regard to seniority; it also shortened the remediation period for teachers who are judged to be performing below par. In addition, schools can ask for waivers from the teaching contract.

Paul T. Hill, formerly a senior social scientist at the RAND Corporation who was present during the Chicago brainstorming discussions, says the tone was not hostile to teachers. "The desire was to make it clear that the real employer of the teacher was the school," he says. "It isn't like the teachers become helpless pawns—they are involved in collaborative activities at the local level in ways that are not constrained by other loyalties they might have."

But the proposal for individual school contracts was denounced by the CTU as the equivalent of having "600 superintendents." "That would do more to destroy the profession in this city than anything else I've heard of," Jackie Gallagher, a spokeswoman for the union, says. "No one in their right mind would walk into a situation that you could be asked to walk out of in a year."

G. Alfred Hess Jr., the executive director of the Chicago Panel on Public School Policy and Finance, noted that the political power of Chicago's unions makes it highly unlikely that labor-protection laws there could be relaxed. "A lot of people are riding the anti-unionist wave at the moment," he says. "With the political structures bending over backward to make the unions happy, as has recently happened with the settling of the budget in Chicago, I don't see how anybody thinks there's going to be any relaxation of the labor-protection laws for Chicago."

Both Hill and Wilson have given some thought to how a teacher labor market could work. If teachers were hired by schools, those who did not make a good match with a school could have the right to a paid period to search for another position, Hill suggested in an interview. Teachers with more seniority could be given a longer job-hunting opportunity. At some point, however, teachers who were not hired by any school would no longer be employed in the system. The union contract would set salaries, qualifications for employment, and standards for promotion in such a system.

Wilson, in his book *Reinventing the Schools: A Radical Plan for Boston,* proposes that the teachers' union in that city "serve as a placement agency" for teachers contracting individually with schools. "The Boston Teachers Union could come to protect the right of teachers to enter into such contracts," he writes, "rather than constrain it through collective bargaining agreements that limit autonomy and choice for both teachers and principals."

Wilson's book, which has influenced the school committee in its negotiations with the union, outlines an "entrepreneurial model" that would allow any teacher or principal in Boston to come up with a plan for creating a school. These plans would be reviewed by several "sponsoring councils" whose members had been approved by the superintendent. The councils would decide which schools the system should "invest in."

The new schools would receive funds based solely on the number of students they enrolled, with special-needs students carrying greater amounts of money. But the schools would have great flexibility in spending that money.

Doherty, the president of the Boston Teachers Union, summarizes the proposal as: "Pick a principal, and let him operate in a union-free environment with no work rules."

"I think it's almost all political," he says of discussions of Wilson's proposals. The new, mayorally appointed school committee, Doherty charges, is "out to kill the union."

The Boston teaching contract that ushered in schoolbased management gave school councils the right to pick teachers transferring into their schools without regard to seniority, the union president notes. In schools that do not have councils that can serve that function, principals pick from any one of the three most senior teachers.

Giving schools their money on a per-pupil basis, Hill believes, is the key to creating a labor market for teachers. Most school systems now give schools resources, but not their own budgets to manage. Although the cost of teachers' salaries in a big-city high school might be between $4 million and $5 million, Hill points out, the school might only have about $85,000 to spend on its own.

If schools were given lump sums based on their enrollment and told to live within their means, a district could create a labor market. Schools with concentrations of highly paid teachers would find themselves over budget, while those with lesser-paid teachers would have a surplus, Hill says.

The teachers' union could then become a broker, recommending teachers to schools, Hill suggests. "In the old days, and still in a lot of trades," he says, "that's the brokerage role the union plays."

Although such a scenario might seem far-fetched, the Los Angeles Unified School District has entered into a consent decree requiring it to distribute money to schools for salaries and supplies on a per-pupil basis. Schools will be given broad discretion over how to spend the money. The agreement is intended to equalize the distribution of experienced teachers and resources throughout the district. The order comes in a lawsuit brought by advocates for disadvantaged, non-English-speaking children, who were found to be commonly and disproportionately taught by inexperienced teachers or those who were unlicensed.

The court order contains provisions sought by the United Teachers of Los Angeles to mitigate its effects on the current teaching force. In general, says McElroy, the AFT secretary-treasurer, a teacher labor market could drive down salaries. Schools would replace retiring senior teachers with lower-salaried teachers, he argues. Principals in other schools would want to transfer senior teachers to free up some salary money for other uses. "Then it becomes a business decision," he says, "not an educational one."

These debates go far beyond the celebrated teachers' contracts of the 1980s, when school-based management, peer-evaluation plans, and other reforms were negotiated. During that time, Kerchner of Claremont Graduate School observes, unions, management, and members of the public coalesced to bring about a "renaissance around the schools" in such places as Dade County, Fla.; Jefferson County, Ky.; Pittsburgh; and Rochester, N.Y.

As the cry for radical change in big-city districts has continued, he adds, "powerful external actors" have gotten involved in education, changing the terms of the debate. These actors include the Chicago reform coalition and Gov. Roy Romer of Colorado, who stepped into a labor stalemate in Denver to create a plan to give the city's schools more autonomy.

William Ayers, an associate professor of education at the University of Illinois at Chicago and the author of a chapter about that city's reforms in Kerchner's book, says he believes that the city's teachers' union is in "deep crisis, deep pain" about the implications of school reform. "This puts them in a situation of chaos and confusion, not because they're sitting on their hands," he says, "but because who knows how this will turn out? Teachers hiring teachers is the least of it. Where's my contract going to come from if the end of a big-city school system is also the end of negotiations and unionism as we've known it?"

Other observers say that it is simply unfair to focus too much attention on the unions, since management has a critical role to play in bringing about reforms. The administration often does not "courageously try to renegotiate things," Johnson of Harvard University says, "or really exercise the discretion that they have."

In the end, says John Kotsakis, the assistant to the president of the Chicago Teachers Union for educational issues, the teachers' union represents the only stability urban districts have. "Future contracts will reflect flexibility for local-site initiatives more and more," Kotsakis says. "Wouldn't it be much better to have the union driving the change, being significant partners in it, accepting accountability, and identifying with success or failure, than having them simply sitting on the side?" ∎

From Education Week, *Dec. 9, 1992*

41.

A Welcome Change

Los Angeles' Elizabeth Street Learning Center offers teachers a supportive environment for education reform.

By Ann Bradley

There was a time, not too long ago, when professional development at Elizabeth Street School amounted to briefing teachers on how to use a new set of textbooks. The school, in this tiny town southeast of Los Angeles, hadn't caught the wave of education reform. Teachers handed out worksheets and lectured to students seated in carefully aligned rows. Quiet was a prized commodity.

The staff spent most of its energy coping with the nearly overwhelming conditions at Elizabeth Street. With 1,600 students, it was one of the Los Angeles Unified School District's first year-round schools. More than three-quarters of its students weren't fluent in English. Most came from low-income, immigrant Latino families that were constantly moving.

Today, the school is no longer on its own. Rechristened the Elizabeth Street Learning Center, the school is in its third year of an ambitious project funded by the New American Schools Development Corporation. The corporation—a private, nonprofit organization founded by business leaders during the Bush Administration—is backing nine "break the mold" schools across the nation.

The designers who put together the learning-center concept hope it can serve as a model for urban education. The plan calls for rethinking instruction, school management, and social services for students and their families at two schools: Elizabeth Street and Foshay Middle School in South Central Los Angeles, which began implementing the design this fall.

In the summer of 1992, the Los Angeles Educational Partnership, a nonprofit organization that administers several programs to improve schooling in the city, won a $2.5 million grant from NASDC to spend a year fleshing out its reform ideas. Initially, the designers hoped to open the first learning center in a new school, perhaps in a commercial space.

When it became clear that starting from scratch would take too much time, they began scouting existing Los Angeles sites to find a school big enough to expand to house kindergartners through 12th graders.

Elizabeth Street won by default. The elementary school, on 16 acres in a residential neighborhood, was already scheduled to add middle grades and had enough land to accommodate senior high students.

What's more, the district offered no better testing ground for change: Elizabeth Street was struggling to educate a difficult population with traditional approaches that didn't seem to be working.

"It was the best learning laboratory we could have asked for," recalls Judy Johnson, the program director at the Los Angeles Educational Partnership. "And it's also the toughest work in the whole world."

Teacher Appreciation

The key to success at Elizabeth Street, the managers of the project say, is providing its teachers with rich and varied professional development to help them change their instructional approaches.

The teachers at the school, briefed about the learning-center design, voted nearly unanimously to participate. In doing so, they were buying into a package of reforms designed by knowledgeable outsiders.

"Everyone voted eagerly, but to say that they fully understood what they were voting for is a misnomer," says Peggy Funkhouser, the president of the Los Angeles Educational Partnership. "This was a very traditional faculty with not a whole lot of dreamers."

In addition to helping teachers dream—and giving them the tools to make their dreams come true—the project must cope with the sheer size of the schools. Creating a true learning community, the designers felt, would be best accomplished by having children of all ages on the same campus.

This year, Elizabeth Street has more than 90 teachers and 2,600 students in prekindergarten through 10th grade. In two years, it will add 11th and 12th graders to the rolls. Foshay Learning Center has 115 teachers and 2,700 kindergarten through 10th grade students; it's also scheduled to add two more grades.

The logistics involved with such large schools are complicated because they are on year-round calendars, with one-third of the teachers and students off campus at any one time. The high schools will never enroll more than 300 to 400 students at a time. Elizabeth Street high schoolers will attend its health academy, while Foshay students go to its finance academy. Both programs are designed to prepare graduates for work or further education after high school.

When the project began, the faculty at Elizabeth Street included many veteran teachers and some novices with emergency credentials. The atmosphere, many teachers said, was stifling.

"This school needed uplifting," recalls Linda Stewart, who has taught at Elizabeth Street for 14 years. "We were all dying. You just did your own thing."

The opportunity to introduce a cutting-edge educational design was an unexpected boon for teachers, adds Mary View-Schneider, another veteran teacher. "We would not have gone out and sought it with this staff and principal," she says bluntly.

Beginning in the spring of 1993, with $3.5 million from NASDC, teachers were barraged with professional development opportunities. The school also used the money to buy instructional technology and notebook computers for every teacher on the staff.

The contrast with past attitudes toward teachers' development couldn't have been starker. It used to be "find it yourself, pay for it yourself, and do it on your own time," View-Schneider recalls.

Peer-to-Peer Training

The designers of the learning-center concept had a clear idea of the kind of teaching and learning they wanted to see at the school. Teachers were to work together to devise an interdisciplinary, thematic curriculum. Children would be combined in multi-age groups of two or three grade levels. Clusters of four or five teachers would work together to plan and teach lessons.

Instead of lecturing and assigning work from textbooks, teachers would be encouraged to try cooperative learning, to give students more hands-on experiences, and to infuse reading and writing throughout the school day.

Although by now these concepts are quite familiar, at first they were a dramatic departure for most Elizabeth Street teachers. Many prided themselves on running well-controlled, quiet classrooms where they—not students—played the starring role.

To ease the transition, the Los Angeles Educational Partnership devised a plan for exposing the teachers to the concepts over 20 full, paid days. First, groups of teachers attended a retreat at a comfortable hotel to discuss the components of the learning-center design.

There, they heard from teachers who had been trying some of the same techniques at other Los Angeles schools. At a workshop on multi-age classrooms, for example, Elizabeth Street teachers could ask their colleagues detailed questions about how the educational theory actually worked in a real classroom.

Encouraging teachers to learn from each other was the most frequently used training strategy, says Johnson of the educational partnership. That philosophy also sent Elizabeth Street teachers into other schools across the district—schools serving children similar to theirs—to see teachers in action. The visits made the new ideas and approaches concrete, Johnson says.

"The usual excuse for not doing something new is the lack of belief that your kids would really benefit," she explains. "When you see children like the ones that you work with really being successful, it's much more convincing and makes it worthwhile to try."

After observing lessons, the Elizabeth Street teachers again had time to question the demonstration teachers. In this way, groups of about 25 teachers were exposed to new kinds of assessments, whole language approaches, and new strategies for teaching mathematics and science.

To provide support back at Elizabeth Street, the educational partnership also selected four lead teachers to help their colleagues find information, present demonstration lessons, plan curricula, and connect teachers with resources. The school also now has a "curriculum toolbox" of materials and information for teachers.

A cadre of teachers with expertise in such areas as the national math standards or bilingual instruction is available to visit Elizabeth Street teachers. Lead teachers help faculty members set up such visits.

Teachers from another elementary school also trained Elizabeth Street teachers to use the technology purchased for the school. The school's Product Development Center—a room jammed with computers, videocassette recorders, videocameras, and videotape editing machines—provides Elizabeth Street teachers with a variety of high-tech tools for learning.

Eventually, after teachers have built a solid foundation of knowledge and have developed their capacity to perform, they're expected to become expert in a particular area. In this way, the school's teaching teams will include, for example, faculty members who are knowledgeable about teaching mathematics or social studies. Some teachers might also be experts in assessment or in strategies for helping students acquire a new language.

For Stewart, who describes herself as "a teacher who wanted to hear myself talking," observing other teachers and classrooms convinced her of the need for change at Elizabeth Street. "I saw organized movement and learning taking place," she recalls. "The children knew everything that was going on in the classroom."

At this point, Johnson says, it's too soon to see much impact on students. "What we have," she says, "are nice stories of change worth patting ourselves and the teachers on the back for."

Now, the project's managers estimate that clusters of teachers are using thematic instruction 40 percent of the instructional day. They're most likely to do so in language arts and social studies.

The infusion of technology also has gone smoothly. Parents can visit the Product Development Center to learn to use computers alongside their children. And some teachers say that having a computer in their classroom helps motivate children who once seemed indifferent to schooling.

Of course, the project designers have hit some rocky points, too. Not every teacher has participated in the training, and some are clinging to traditional ways. But the number of such teachers is small.

Principal John Kershaw, who has been at the school for seven years, says he believes everyone at Elizabeth Street has changed. "Some have been quantum leaps and others have been a little bit," he explains. "I don't think you can push, but you can encourage and support the best you can. Hopefully, the other folks will come along."

In July 1993, the start of the new school year for Elizabeth Street, teachers felt ready to plunge into what they had learned. They decided to begin multiage classrooms, even though the project managers did not believe they were ready.

In retrospect, that might have been a mistake, says Anola Hubbert, a lead teacher. Teachers hadn't had enough time to absorb all the components of the learning-center model, she explains. "So many things were being put before us," she recalls. "We got so excited, we probably entered into a lot of things more quickly than we should have."

Teachers of 7th and 8th graders also complained that they didn't have enough common planning time to devise interdisciplinary lessons and adjust to teaching more than one grade of students.

Burt Snyder, a social-studies and history teacher, says his team did "a little bit" of interdisciplinary teaching last year. "We were gung ho at first," he says. "We went whole hog the first semester, and things went pretty well for four to six weeks. Then it had run its course."

Interactive Lessons

In the side-by-side classrooms of Bette Stephens and Jan Miracle, who teach together as part of a cluster, a visitor can begin to see the type of education that the learning center is trying to foster.

Their students are studying immigration—a potent topic in the lives of children whose families are immigrants themselves. The lessons began with discussions of the children's own experiences. Teachers helped students see parallels between the reasons their own parents left Mexico and Central America and the reasons that people immigrated to settle the British colonies.

Then the students began studying the westward movement, mapping the routes pioneers took across the Plains.

On this day, groups of students are making butter, writing their own stories on computers, and reading books about the settlement of the West.

Some of the students' work, gathered into portfolios, can be stored on teachers' lap-top computers—including reading logs, computer-generated illustrations, and science lessons. One eager student quickly calls up her personal portfolio on a classroom computer. It includes a short autobiography titled *All About Me*, by Sandra Cobos. For the lesson about pioneers, she's written and illustrated *Sandra's Story of the West*.

Miracle, who has taught at Elizabeth Street for 15 years, says she has adjusted to the many instructional changes. Before the school became a learning center, she says, the only professional development she had was when the school's curriculum committee picked a new textbook that teachers were taught to use.

At first, she says, she wanted the "experts" to tell her how to teach. But as she's grown more confident, Miracle and her colleagues have realized they have a lot to offer. "We're still good teachers," she says. "We're not totally changing the way we're teaching."

Stephens, a 20-year veteran, says she was more hesitant about change than some of her colleagues. Some of the schools she visited, she says, were "idealistic settings" not relevant to life at Elizabeth Street. "We still have our certain beliefs that we will always keep," she asserts. "I require a certain amount of quiet at times."

Feature Attractions

The learning-center design has attracted new teachers to Elizabeth Street, many of whom said they were frustrated with conditions at their previous schools.

"I see myself as a teacher-researcher here," said Eduardo Munoz, a 10th grade English teacher hired from another Los Angeles high school. "That means constantly reading, being innovative, searching, evaluating, and sharing with other colleagues what I'm doing in the classroom. I see myself as part of a larger community."

For Monique Lopez, coming to Elizabeth Street meant finding support for the teaching methods she'd been trying alone at another school. "It was like fighting an uphill battle. I felt I wasn't being supported by my peers," she explains. "Here, it's a given that you're doing what the latest strategies and studies are saying to do."

Teachers also can take comfort in knowing that the learning center is actively addressing some of the daunting conditions that make it difficult for their students to learn.

Cudahy, a community of 23,200 people packed into 1.1 square miles eight miles southeast of downtown Los Angeles, was founded as a rural ranch area. Its large lots, once home to livestock, are now jammed with modest stucco homes and apartment buildings. Still, many families face a housing shortage and can pay $500 a month to live in a motel room or garage.

The city also is relatively cut off from the social services that its young, low-income, Spanish-speaking population desperately needs. The Elizabeth Street Learning Center is expected to play a crucial role in linking students and their families with helping agencies. The school also is considering opening a clinic in partnership with a local hospital.

Eventually, all of the students at the two learning centers will be linked with people who will monitor their school progress and help them through difficult times. The plan calls for groups of about 30 students of all ages to be linked with three adults, who might be teachers, community members, or businesspeople. Within each group, students will be paired with older "buddies," says View-Schneider, who is coordinating the support system.

The groups, which will meet on a regular basis, will work on school-related projects as well as make time for dabbling in arts and crafts, playing games, and reading in pairs. Over time, the groups are expected to stay together, providing a sense of responsibility and stability for students.

Already, Elizabeth Street Learning Center has begun to serve as a hub for the Cudahy community. On any given day, about 150 parents can be found at the sprawling campus, a mixture of 1920s-era stucco buildings, 1960s additions, and new two-story buildings built around a vast concrete courtyard. Parents can take English as a second language, study computers, learn to sew or paint, and help with the many after-school programs offered for students.

Maintaining Momentum

For this school year, the learning-center project has received $4 million from NASDC. The bulk of the money goes for buying technology and paying for staff development at the two sites.

In the future, though, Elizabeth Street will have to figure out how to keep the momentum going without huge infusions of money. Last spring, teachers and parents were involved in the budget process, making decisions about spending more than $1 million.

View-Schneider, who is a lead teacher, says she's confident that the school can write grant proposals and make innovative use of the money it already receives. It's unlikely that Elizabeth Street's teachers will accept anything less.

"Students are relaxed and learning and having fun at school, and it's not recess time," Stewart says. "That said it all for me." ■

From Education Week, *Sept. 21, 1994*

42.

Crossing the Tracks

Massachusetts leads a nationwide charge against ability grouping, but the resistance is formidable.

By Peter Schmidt

When school districts in this state group students according to their academic ability, Daniel V. French in turn groups the districts, separating those that agree to abandon the practice from those that face losing some state funds for declining to do so. As the Massachusetts Department of Education's director for student development, French is leading his agency's effort to discourage public schools from putting children in different classrooms based on their perceived ability.

The agency lacks the authority to forbid ability grouping outright. But it uses the award or denial of state dropout-prevention and remedial-education money as leverage to get schools to "rethink traditional notions of grouping students," in the words of a 1990 department advisory statement that strongly criticized the use of homogeneous grouping.

With the backing of Gov. William F. Weld and Commissioner of Education Robert V. Antonucci, the department has put Massachusetts in the forefront of a growing offensive against ability grouping and tracking in public schools. Here and elsewhere around the nation, increasing numbers of educators, educational researchers, and civil-rights advocates are aggressively promoting an end to such practices.

Many of these critics base their efforts on a long-held conviction that ability grouping contributes to segregation of students by race, ethnic group, economic background, and other nonacademic characteristics. Just last December, the Amherst, Mass.-area chapter of the National Association for the Advancement of Colored People filed a federal lawsuit charging that the Amherst-Pelham Regional School District had violated the civil rights of minority students by grouping them disproportionately in low-ability classes.

But many of the newest attacks on ability grouping are based not only on concerns for ensuring integration and equity. Advocates of heterogeneous grouping have also begun to frame their arguments in terms of a broader movement for education reform. They argue that it is not enough simply to mix together students of different ability levels; a commitment to a stimulating curriculum and to methods such as cooperative learning, they say, is central to ensuring that heterogeneously grouped classrooms succeed.

"If you just implement heterogeneous grouping without any thought, it doesn't help," French acknowledges. "It does not help high-achieving kids and it does not help low-achieving kids."

Unless its proponents can demonstrate that heterogeneous grouping improves the education of all students, including the brightest, it is likely to continue to meet staunch resistance, especially from many parents and advocates for children deemed high-achieving or gifted and talented, experts from both sides of the debate say.

"By totally doing away with ability grouping, you are clearly preventing children from reaching their full potential," argues Peter D. Rosenstein, the executive director of the National Association for Gifted Children. Educators of the gifted have increasingly seen their programs under attack by both budget cutters and education reformers. Rosenstein contends that the elimination of higher-ability classes has been inspired by a desire to trim budgets and is being carried out by "politically misguided educators who are looking not at what is good for children, but what is politically correct."

In Massachusetts, 21 percent of all public middle schools now group all students heterogeneously, compared with only a handful a decade ago, and an additional 69 percent have adopted more heterogeneous grouping during the past three years, according to the Massachusetts education department.

Some schools and school districts in the state undertook heterogeneous grouping well before the state began promoting it, and are seen as models for others that are considering such a change. Among the districts is the Pioneer Valley Regional School District in northwestern Massachusetts. Kevin J. Courtney, the superintendent of the rural, virtually all-white district, says pedagogic concerns, rather than civil-rights considerations, inspired the heterogeneous grouping effort that they undertook eight years ago.

The so-called "detracking" effort there was initiated by teachers who questioned the educational value of ability grouping, Courtney says. The move probably would have been "doomed" if it had been imposed on teachers by school officials or the state, he says.

John D'Auria, the principal of the Wellesley (Mass.) Middle School in the suburbs of Boston, credits a long list of experiences for his decision to push for mixed-ability grouping soon after taking his school's helm in 1988.

He notes his stint as a teacher in a heterogeneously grouped Catholic school, which impressed him with its "sense of community." And he cites his experience as a guidance counselor in public schools, where he came to see young adolescents as "molting," or experiencing a key formative stage, during which they are especially vulnerable to negative messages that may be conveyed by grouping practices.

Thus, D'Auria says, he was distressed when he came to Wellesley and found the 7th and 8th grades divided into three levels each. "We really had some hidden belief that kids who learned things the first time and quickly were the bright ones," he says.

D'Auria set out to heterogeneously group the school's classrooms and to have all children taught the honors-level curriculum. He endeavored to create a culture within the school that constantly reminds all children they can succeed, and he established an after-school study center for students who got low marks for effort.

At about the same time that D'Auria was undertaking his changes in Wellesley, officials at the Massachusetts education department were attempting to identify the obstacles that seemed to be limiting the impact of its discretionary grants for dropout prevention and remedial education.

State officials were frustrated because, although dropout rates had dropped slightly, grade retention and in-school suspensions apparently were rising in a number of districts where the state-funded programs were in place, French says.

The state began to encourage systemic change in schools to improve student achievement and, in 1990, targeted ability grouping as one of the biggest obstacles to improvement for low achievers. The education department's statement issued that year is one of the most strongly worded state advisories on ability grouping to date.

"There is little evidence that ability grouping or tracking improves academic achievement," it says, "while overwhelming evidence exists that ability grouping retards the academic progress of students in low- and middle-ability groupings."

The advisory blamed ability grouping for widening the gap between high and low achievers and for segregating students by race, income, language background, and disability. Gender also skewed the grouping process, it says, with girls being more likely than boys to be placed in low-level science and mathematics classes.

The education department offered schools technical assistance and training to implement heterogeneous grouping. Agency leaders asked the department's staff to work with educators, other state agencies, and various child-advocacy groups to promote an end to ability grouping and tracking.

Lacking authority under the Massachusetts constitution to require heterogeneous grouping, the department opted to use as its "carrot and stick" the awarding or denial of grants for dropout prevention and remedial education. For example, one school that embraced heterogeneous grouping, the Bartlett School in Lowell, received an additional $150,000 in state money over a year, which it used to fund professional development to prepare teachers for heterogeneous classrooms. Other districts had state grants revoked if they refused after a year to abandon ability grouping, French says.

Depriving the Gifted?

Some local newspapers responded to the state's initiative with editorials charging that the education department was trying to water down the curriculum used in public schools. And some educators criticized the state advisory as ignoring the fact that the research appears inconclusive on the value of ability grouping for high achievers, especially those deemed gifted and talented.

Many parents of gifted and talented children, meanwhile, have continued to oppose some districts' efforts to act on the state advisory. Some parents have removed their children from public schools over the issue, according to Joseph F. Harrington, the president of the Massachusetts Association for the Advancement of Individual Potential. "The bottom line," Harrington says, "is that bright kids, while they can learn cooperatively, at the same time learn better with other bright kids."

Although a small minority, the parents of gifted and talented and other higher-track children tend to be among the most well-to-do, influential, and heavily involved parents in schools. Such parents have proved to be formidable opponents when they feel the welfare of their children is threatened, according to many educators and administrators who have tried to implement mixed-ability grouping.

Many educators also have reservations about heterogeneous grouping, and getting them to implement such programs remains "an enormous struggle," says Maria Garza-Lubeck, the director of the Middle Grade State Policy Initiative. That program, with the oversight of the Council of Chief State School Officers and funding from the Carnegie Corporation of New York, has targeted grouping by achievement level as a practice it wishes to eliminate.

Many teacher training programs continue to prepare their graduates only for ability-grouped classrooms, and the use of ability grouping and tracking remains "deeply entrenched in the junior high model," Garza-Lubeck says.

Elizabeth J. Bryant, the principal of the Bartlett School in Lowell, says teachers there "still have some serious concerns" about the heterogeneous grouping undertaken by the school five years ago. Bartlett's enrollment is about 40 percent white, 30 percent Cambodian, 25 percent Hispanic, and 2 percent black; 77 percent are economically disadvantaged.

"Teachers still are wondering if the brightest kids are getting sufficient attention," Bryant says. "They worry sometimes about whether to gear their instruction to the top or the middle."

Nevertheless, Bryant says, most teachers in her school have given an "overwhelmingly positive" response to heterogeneous grouping, largely because they still remember the "horror show" each had encountered in teaching the lowest of four tracks in the school's 7th and 8th grades.

The students who had been in Bartlett's lowest tracks "had no role models" under that system, Bryant says. In contrast, she says, their behavior improved dramatically once they were placed with higher achievers.

Although Wellesley Middle School did not face the same disciplinary problems as Bartlett, teachers there had been uncomfortable with ability grouping because they felt it encouraged students to focus on grades rather than learning, or discouraged them from taking risks out of fear their placement would be questioned, D'Auria says.

In her book *Crossing the Tracks,* Anne Wheelock, a former policy analyst for the Massachusetts Advocacy Center, a child advocacy group, examines dozens of efforts to heterogeneously group students undertaken by schools in Massachusetts and in other states across the country.

Heterogeneous grouping, Wheelock concludes, requires a profound shift in a school's basic mission and culture. Existing emphases on quantifying intelligence, defining ability, and identifying weaknesses must give way to releasing intelligence, nurturing effort, and building on strengths, she writes.

D'Auria of Wellesley Middle School echoes that view. "What people believe really, truly influences the outcomes that you see," he says. To help reinforce that message, D'Auria has decorated his school's hallways with street signs bearing the names of triumphant underdogs, such as Jim Abbott, a professional baseball player who was born with one hand.

Schools that undertake heterogeneous grouping, Wheelock writes, also need to provide their teachers with staff development so they can learn to use mastery learning, cooperative learning, curriculum-embedded assessment strategies, and other pedagogic tools that have proved useful in working with diverse groups of students.

Phasing in Changes

An updated version of the Massachusetts education department's advisory on ability grouping maintains that all students, including the gifted and talented, benefit from a change to mixed-ability grouping as long as it is accompanied by appropriate changes in curriculum, instruction, and testing. The updated advisory cautions, however, that such changes should be phased in. It recommends that schools spend a year on staff development and planning before they implement heterogeneous grouping.

"I have to really think about the concepts I want to teach, and I have to think: What is a really student-centered way for them to learn this?" observes John C. Lepore, who teaches science at Pioneer Valley High School.

One recent morning, Lepore was teaching a class of heterogeneously grouped 7th graders, some of whom had special needs. Working cooperatively in groups of four, the students dipped thermometers into various-sized containers of water to determine which would lose heat faster—a mountain lion or a mouse.

Watching the class, one could not tell the brightest children from those with special needs. Working in one of the groups was a child with autism, a beneficiary of the complementary relationship between heterogeneous grouping and the mainstreaming of students with disabilities.

Lepore says his task of teaching a mixed classroom

was being helped by "an explosion of new textbooks that are using an integrated approach to science education," as well as interactive laser disks and hands-on activities. Noting that he had taught in both homogeneously and heterogeneously grouped classrooms, he calls teaching the latter "more fun."

Largely due to the efforts of the state education department, only about 10 percent of public middle schools in Massachusetts continue to separate their students into at least two groups based on ability, French says. However, he adds, ability grouping remains prevalent at the high school level, which the state so far has given a lower priority in its campaign to promote heterogeneous grouping.

"If you are really going to talk about all kids graduating from high school with a high-quality academic preparation, then you need to look at some of the rigid tracking that goes on in the high schools," French says. He plans to give high schools "a bit more of a friendly push" to reconsider their grouping practices.

Heterogeneous grouping appears, ironically, to meet the most acceptance and success in schools that are relatively homogeneous to begin with. In such schools, proponents of mixed-ability classes acknowledge, the prospect of lumping all children together appears less threatening to parents and faculty members.

Bryant of the Bartlett School in Lowell says that she received virtually no unfavorable reaction from parents when she implemented heterogeneous grouping. But she says she probably would have run into more resistance if more of her students were from wealthier socioeconomic backgrounds.

"There is no question that it is easier if you are more homogeneous to start with," Wheelock says. "But I don't think it is fair to say it is impossible when you are extremely diverse."

School leaders in the Amherst-Pelham district strongly defend their ability-grouping policy, which is the target of the federal suit filed last month. John E. Heffley, the principal of Amherst-Pelham Regional High School, argued that grouping students by ability is a necessity in his district, which serves both the children of recent Southeast Asian refugees and of University of Massachusetts faculty members. The enrollment is 72 percent white, 10 percent Asian, 9 percent Hispanic, and 9 percent black, and it is disproportionately limited-English-proficient.

Heffley says the vast majority of parents and staff members at his school endorses its grouping system, which provides three tiers of instruction in most courses and involves parents by asking them to approve or reject a teacher's recommendation about where their children should be placed. "I believe that school systems should develop their institutional pattern of grouping students to fit their own system," Heffley says.

The Amherst-Pelham grouping system, Heffley says, produces large crops of National Merit Scholar-ship finalists and college-bound students, as well as low dropout rates among limited-English-proficient students who get the extra help they need.

William A. Norris, a lawyer for the Amherst-area chapter of the NAACP, believes otherwise. He contends that the chief product of the Amherst-Pelham grouping system is "permanent, irrevocable scarring, low self-esteem, underperformance, and boredom" inflicted on minority students who are disproportionately represented in the lower tiers.

"This is a racial issue," Norris says. "Within the same schoolhouse, we have two groups being treated differently. We have in-house segregation." The district's policy of involving parents in the grouping process "is no defense," Norris adds. Many parents may be unwilling, unable, or afraid to challenge a teacher's recommendation, he says.

The suit Norris filed in U.S. District Court argues that Amherst-Pelham should be denied federal funds because its grouping system deprives minority students of full access to the school curriculum, and thus violates their rights under the 14th Amendment to the U.S. Constitution and various federal civil-rights laws. "We want to choke off funds," Norris says. "That is the ultimate sanction."

On a recent Friday afternoon in Lowell, meanwhile, Bryant celebrated the success of the Bartlett School's heterogeneous grouping efforts by treating her faculty to ice cream. Last year's 8th graders surpassed those in comparable schools in all four areas of the Massachusetts Assessment Test, Bryant points out, and "we celebrate when we can."

Bryant concedes, however, that she puts little stock in standardized-test scores and that she probably would have barely mentioned the test results if they had not been good. Courtney, the superintendent of the Pioneer Valley district, takes an even dimmer view of the state's standardized tests, which he describes as "so full of holes they are not worth talking about." The tests, he asserts, are incapable of measuring the positive impact of heterogeneous grouping on higher-level thinking skills and in other areas.

Unless educators in Massachusetts and elsewhere can agree on valid measurements of student achievement, the debate over the relative merits of homogeneous and heterogeneous grouping appears unlikely to be resolved. In the meantime, many proponents of heterogeneous grouping base their arguments on personal observations, ideals, and faith.

"When kids are forced to explain and answer questions, they are learning that material in much greater depth," Courtney declares as he gives a tour of Pioneer Valley High School.

Lepore, the science teacher, says, "I have never had a parent come back to me and say their son or daughter is not challenged." ∎

From Education Week, *Jan. 13, 1993*

43.

Under the Surface

An unusual study looks at schools from the inside and finds a deeper set of problems that reformers aren't dealing with.

By Robert Rothman

An unusual study that examined schools "from the inside" has concluded that the policy remedies offered by most education reformers bear little relation to the problems identified by students, teachers, and parents. The study, based on 18 months of in-depth conversations in four Southern California schools, found that such issues as low student achievement and problems in the teaching profession, which many reforms are aimed at addressing, are in fact consequences of what the authors see as the real problems in schools.

These underlying issues include unsatisfactory relationships between and among students and staff members, differences of race and class, and deep concerns about school safety. Perhaps as a result of such factors, the schools studied exhibited a "pervasive sense of despair," the authors write.

"If the relationships are wrong between teachers and students, for whatever reason," John Maguire, the president of the Claremont University Center and Graduate School, which conducted the study, said at a New York City press briefing late last November, "you can restructure until the cows come home, but transformation won't take place."

"If that is right, the national conversation about restructuring schools has to change," he said. "You can't get the answer right if you don't ask the right questions."

Marc S. Tucker, the president of the National Center on Education and the Economy and a prominent leader in national school reform efforts, noted that the Claremont report is consistent with his group's analysis of the need for reform. "Any effort to restructure schools for high performance has got to take into account the realities they report on," Tucker said.

The report does not offer specific recommendations for change. But the authors said that the participatory process they undertook in conducting the study could serve as a way of allowing schools to change themselves. They also said that they plan to spend the next few years identifying policies and practices that impede schools from addressing the problems identified in the study, with an eye toward dismantling them.

"We can't afford to spend any more money or time trying to enact changes that will not increase the ability of practitioners to relate and spend their energies and talents with students," said Mary Poplin, the director of Claremont's Institute for Education in Transformation and the study's director.

'Surprising' Findings

The study differs markedly from most of the 300 or more reports on school reform issued in the past decade, according to Maguire. Unlike most such studies, which examined schools "from the outside in or from the top down," he said, the new study went inside schools to find out what the problems are.

The John W. Kluge Foundation funded the study by Claremont, an independent, exclusively graduate-level institution in Claremont, Calif. The research team chose four schools in the area surrounding Claremont, which is 35 miles east of Los Angeles. The schools—two elementary schools, one middle school, and one high school—are made up of low-income urban populations as well as affluent suburban students. They are representative of the schools of California and the nation, according to the study directors.

The researchers spent over a year in the schools, held more than 160 meetings with members of the school communities, and received written comments from them. In all, they heard from 4,000 students, 1,000 parents, and 200 teachers, administrators, and other employees. The meetings generated 24,000 pages of transcriptions, essays, drawings, journal entries, and notes, as well as 18 hours of videotapes and 80 hours of audio tapes.

Culling through the data, the researchers—along with members of the school communities, who contributed as part of an unusual "participatory" form of research—found a surprising amount of agreement around a set of themes that differed sharply from those that usually pervade reports on schooling.

"No one was more surprised by the results of this report than those of us on the outside," the authors write. "We, like the authors of previous reports on schooling and teacher education, would have predicted issues such as what to teach, how to measure it, how much a teacher knows, and choice of school would have surfaced; they did not."

Rather, the report states, the most commonly cited problem identified by the people in the four schools was the issue of "relationships." "The typical school day is nothing more than a series of relationships," said William Bertrand, the principal of Montclair High School, one of the participating schools.

But the study found that most relationships within schools leave something to be desired. Students reported that, although one of the best aspects of school for them was "seeing their friends," they often had a very narrow circle of friends. They also said that they liked teachers who cared about them, but they complained that they were often ignored or received negative treatment. These attitudes had a direct effect on how well they performed in the classroom, Poplin noted. "Kids said, 'I do well in classes where the teacher respects me, and I do poorly where the teachers don't like me,'" she said.

Teachers, for their part, said that they often did not understand students who were ethnically different from themselves. They also complained that they were isolated from other teachers and that their relationships with administrators were often strained. "We have to put relationships at the core of what we're doing," one middle school teacher is quoted in the report as saying.

In addition to relationships, questions of race, culture, and class ran through every other issue, the report says. Many students, both white and minority, perceive schools to be racist, it states. These perceptions, it says, reflect incidents of racism on campus as well as a curriculum that they say is heavily weighted toward white Europeans.

"Students from various races and occasionally young women doubt the very veracity of the content of the curriculum," the report says. "Students of color rarely see their histories or their literatures adequately addressed in schools." One high school student is quoted in the report: "One thing that should be done is to change the history books. Our history books show Hannibal, a man coming from Africa on elephants, as white. It shows Egyptians as tan, and we don't even teach about the Zulu Nation, but we teach about the Roman Empire—what's the difference?"

These problems are exacerbated by the fact that most teachers are white, Poplin said. She noted that several schools issued edicts not to talk about the controversial verdicts last spring in the Rodney King police brutality case, despite students' strong interest in it.

In a more encouraging finding, the study contradicts the popular view that members of different cultures hold different values. "Different groups and people may express particular values in different ways," the report states. "However, in our data, participants across race and class express values of honesty, hard work, beauty, justice, democracy, freedom, decency, and the need and desire for a good education."

The study also found that many teachers and students held strong views on teaching and learning, and their concerns echo those found in other reform reports. Many students, it found, consider schoolwork boring and irrelevant to their lives, and teachers find themselves under pressure to cover mandated material so that students can pass tests.

It also found, like previous studies, that students and teachers consider schools unsafe and complain about the physical environment. But such concerns go beyond the surface-level threats of physical harm and crumbling buildings, noted Bertrand, the high school principal. "When students speak of safety, they are talking about psychological safety more than physical safety," he said. "That's more at risk."

It may be due to all of these factors, the report suggests, that there is a "pervasive sense of despair" in the schools included in the study. "Teachers and staff have a sense that some students do not perform because they feel hopeless," it states.

But it also says that the study itself offered hope by allowing students and teachers to discuss issues of mutual concern. Said Patricia Ortiz, a 6th grade teacher at Vejar Elementary School and one of the study's participants, "All of us agree change is absolutely necessary." ■

From Education Week, *Dec. 2, 1992*

44.

'A Model of Strength'

Schools in rural areas have long embraced the kinds of education reforms that are now finding their way into larger urban school systems.

By Drew Lindsay

In overcoming rugged conditions to boost their students' academic performance, rural schools have become a model for national education reform, a new federal report concludes. Rural schools have seen their students' test scores climb in the past decade, to the point where they generally match or top national averages, the report notes. The gains came despite the geographic isolation and dwindling financial resources of rural areas and schools. The schools "have achieved so much with so little," the report says. It says they can provide "a model of strength" for other schools.

Rural students have recorded gains on several nationwide assessments. Between 1984 and 1990, for example, rural 4th graders raised their writing proficiency scores on the National Assessment of Educational Progress from 25 points below the national mean to three points above it. Similarly, rural 9-year-olds lifted their scores on the NAEP mathematics assessment by nine points, to one point above the national mean, in 1990.

But the report also makes clear that the improvements had little to do with the national education-reform movement of the 1980s. "The focus on reform has not really found its way into rural communities," said David P. Mack, who headed the report project for the U.S. Education Department's office of educational research and improvement. The report suggests that more study is needed to determine what did spark the improvement.

Particularly helpful, the report says, would be examinations of how rural schools compensate for their fiscal woes with creativity and a "supportive ethos."

"Many so-called 'innovations' being championed today were born of necessity long ago in the rural schoolhouse," the report says, pointing to such ideas as cooperative learning, multigrade classrooms, peer tutoring, and close community ties. "This is the question that I'm interested in," said Theodore Coladarci, the editor of *The Journal of Research in Rural Education* at the University of Maine and a peer reviewer of the report. "How is it that rural schools are able to do what they do?"

'New Sensitivity' Seen

Experts on rural development and education praised the report for avoiding the scornful tone that had characterized previous federal rural-education surveys. "Every Department of Education report on rural education in the past was an indictment," said Thomas W. Bonnett, the author of *Strategies for Rural Competitiveness*. "They would just beat up on rural schools, rural teachers, and rural administrators."

Bonnett noted "a new sensitivity" in the report to the role of the school in the community. But some analysts said the report should have put more emphasis on the need for schools to become a force in rural renewal. "We've decided that in rural areas, schools have to look just like urban schools," said Paul G. Theobald, a rural historian and the head of teacher education at South Dakota State University. "There's no reason why you can't use the community as a curriculum source."

Consolidation Gains Slight

The report, which encompasses more than four years of research and preparation, pulls together dozens of published studies. While breaking little new ground, it does present for the first time a state-by-state breakdown of the nation's 6.9 million rural students. The report bases its count of rural students on the U.S. Census Bureau standard, which defines rural communities as those with fewer than 2,500 resi-

dents. Ohio has the most rural students—379,764.

But Kansas has the highest concentration, with more than half of its enrollment attending rural schools. Rural students make up more than 30 percent of the enrollment in a total of 12 states, and less than 10 percent in seven states.

While the notion of the one-room schoolhouse is fading, rural schools remain predominantly small. More than 40 percent of rural schools serve fewer than 200 children, while less than 5 percent serve 800 or more. Rural schools are also financially strapped, according to the report. School consolidation—the chief policy tool used by many states to drive down costs and improve education in rural areas—has not paid off as expected. ■

From Education Week, *Aug. 3, 1994*

45.

Bridging the Divide

What the public is telling educators could help resuscitate school reform. If reformers will listen.

By Deborah Wadsworth

These are not the best of times for educators or education reformers. Educators are frustrated by an apparent paucity of understanding and support, as evidenced by rising criticisms and a wave of failing referendums. Reformers see their grand designs unraveling in communities from Colorado to Connecticut as parents and taxpayers join more traditional advocates of the status quo.

It's a particularly good time, then, to stand back and re-examine goals and strategies. We at the Public Agenda Foundation in New York City have very current information on how Americans feel about education reform, information we believe is essential to resuscitating reform that otherwise may be drowning.

Reviewing the situation recently, we realized that despite all our previous intensive research with multiple constituencies across the nation, we still had fundamental questions. Why, we asked, is there so much opposition to reform, not only from educators who might feel threatened but also from parents? And why is there so little support from the citizenry at large? Why are referenda and legislative initiatives going down in flames, often ignited by a bizarre coalition of left-leaning advocates of "political correctness" and right-leaning adherents of "values"?

Convinced there was more to learn, in the summer of 1994 we conducted focus groups in Birmingham, Ala.; Philadelphia; Minneapolis; and Des Moines, along with a national, random-sample survey of 1,100 Americans. We included an oversampling of parents with children in school, African-American parents, and parents identified as traditional Christians. The resulting report, released in early October, was titled *First Things First: What Americans Expect From the Public Schools.*

Analyzing that research, along with our other recent studies in several individual states, we discovered something old and something new.

The "something old" was further evidence of what we had found in previous research: extraordinarily strong support among Americans for higher educational standards and expectations. They strongly favor clear guidelines on what children should learn and what teachers should teach. Eighty-seven percent believe students should not graduate from high school without writing and speaking English well, and seven in 10 favor raising standards of promotion from grade school to junior high.

People believe that by asking more, you get more. They don't believe in passing kids from grade to grade, or in letting them graduate without evidence of achievement. They oppose giving "A's for effort."

We also found that African-American parents and traditional Christian parents share most of the same concerns about the public schools, and they support most of the same solutions. In fact, African-American parents are by any measure even more dissatisfied than others with their children's schools and more concerned that standards in their communities' schools are too low. They neither want nor expect the schools to make allowances for their children.

The "something new" we discovered may explain why this broad base of potential support has not been translated into positive public engagement, for we found fundamental differences between how educators and the public view the schools and school reform. Our conclusion: Until the views of the public and of society's leaders, including educators, are better aligned, and until these groups start listening meaningfully to one another, progress is unlikely.

First, educators and the public hold fundamentally different views about how the schools are doing. Educators generally believe the schools are doing pretty well under the circumstances, while the public finds their local schools better than schools elsewhere, but nowhere near as good as they should be.

An indication of the gulf between these groups is exemplified by findings from a study we conducted in Connecticut, where 68 percent of the educators said they believe schools today are better than when they were in school, while just 16 percent of the public share that optimistic view.

The differences in how these groups analyze the problem are equally dramatic. Educators often perceive a breakdown of the social contract whereby each generation supports the education of the next, a breakdown they sometimes attribute to public complacency, taxpayer selfishness, and, in the case of inner cities, even to racism. They often see the solution in terms of more money, smaller classes, and extra help for students with various special needs.

Public Disconnect

Contrary to what many educators believe, the public values education as much as ever. It also strongly supports the goal of racial integration and believes that every child deserves an equal education. But it also believes intensely that while the schools haven't created today's problems, they are badly off track in addressing them. People suspect that many of these problems have little to do with money, and that until they are addressed, more money will be wasted.

But the disconnects aren't only between educators and the public; there are equally wide gaps between the public's priorities and the reform agenda. Such differences may well explain why the public's overwhelming support for higher standards has not translated into support for school reform.

We found three major reasons for this lack of support. One is that the public's chief concern about our schools—making them safe, orderly, and purposeful enough for learning to take place—is not being addressed by today's reform agenda or by today's reform leaders.

People see and read about schools in chaos—schools with little sense of order, respect, or discipline; schools where teachers appear to dress or act unprofessionally; schools in which discussions take place that people consider inappropriate for the classroom; and schools increasingly infested with drugs and violence.

How, people ask, can learning take place in such a disaster zone? And shouldn't this problem be fixed before any academic reform agenda is tackled?

It's difficult to overstate the force of public opinion on this issue. Almost nine Americans in 10 believe that dependability and discipline make a great deal of difference in how students learn, versus about half who believe that learning will improve by, for example, replacing multiple-choice tests with essay tests. Three-quarters of the population supports the permanent removal from school of students caught with weapons or drugs and the removal from the classroom of persistent troublemakers.

It's people's chief interest, and they fail to find it covered in most discussions of school reform.

Some people will respond that the media have overemphasized the problems of order and discipline or that certain proposed reforms will help address them. But the public is convinced that the learning environment is seriously deficient, and reformers need to deal with that fact, whether it be perception or reality.

The second public view that is threatening support for reform is captured in responses to the question "Which student is more likely to succeed?" Sixty-one percent of the public responded that the student from a stable and supportive family who goes to a poor school is more likely to succeed. Only 26 percent believe a good school can compensate for a troubled family. Moreover, 55 percent of the public say parents are doing a worse job than in the past. And if that's the case, some people reason, will it really do any good to pour more money into the schools or reform the curriculum? Americans across all racial and demographic categories support this concept.

The third factor at work is a strong suspicion among the public that reformers are promoting fuzzy and experimental teaching techniques at the expense of the basics. People believe that children should learn grammar and spelling before creative writing; that they should learn to add, subtract, multiply, and divide by hand before depending on electronic devices to do it for them. And for most people, it doesn't seem cruel or wasteful for students to memorize the 50 state capitals and where they're located.

What's happening, we believe, is that people are discovering through their own interactions and experiences with young people that those basic skills are not there. When someone observes a supermarket checkout person who cannot make change, that to them is authentic assessment. It convinces people that the basic skills are not being taught or learned, and they regard those basics not only as important in themselves but also as the foundation for more advanced learning. To promote "higher-order thinking skills" when kids can't make change seems to the public wrongheaded if not absurd.

Public views on teaching techniques remain pretty traditional, and people are concerned about what they see as educational "fads." They tend to reject extremes of any kind; for example, they support neither corporal punishment nor the use of street language in teaching inner-city kids.

So when we talk about math reform, for example, we face a dichotomy. Over 80 percent of our math professionals favor the early use of calculators; only one in 10 Americans agrees.

In contrast to their concern about teaching techniques, the public is less preoccupied with debates of such issues as sex and AIDS education, multicultural experiences and stereotyping, and school prayer. They also go beyond what I have space to cover here. For purposes of this exposition, let me say only that people are far less concerned about these issues than they are about safety, order, and the basics.

It's also worth adding that while teachers remain generally well regarded, we found what seems to be some diminution of public support. We think that people's doubts grow out of a perceived lack of discipline and order in the classroom, and a perception that some teachers are more anxious to be pals with kids than to be role models. People cite good teachers and an orderly learning environment as the most important factors needed for children to learn. But 54 percent say teachers are doing only a "fair" or "poor" job dealing with discipline, while only 36 percent question teacher performance on academic matters.

Using the Research

The key issue, of course, is what to do with this information, which seems to me to be practical, commonsensical, non-ideological, and intellectually consistent.

In fact, whether we believe people are correct in their views is beside the point. These are strongly held views by the people who pay the taxes, pass or defeat the referendums, and elect members of schools boards and state legislatures. If we want to improve our schools, we had better be prepared to take their views into account.

Educators and education reformers need to consider at least three possible alternative responses.

Any one of these choices, or a combination, could be appropriate in any particular situation.

One option is to decide that the public's concerns require genuine change in the leadership agenda. This might mean expanding that agenda to incorporate such items as safety and discipline and programs in parenting skills. It might mean a more overt emphasis on basics and possibly re-examining or delaying some of the more innovative teaching techniques until a successful foundation has been laid and the public is more receptive.

Another option is for leaders to determine after an honest and candid soul-searching that the public's views stem from serious misunderstanding about what is really taking place in the schools and to respond, therefore, with better, more effective communications that correct these misperceptions. That does not mean a new slogan or marginal repackaging; that approach has been tried in many communities and found wanting. It means real, thoughtful, and ongoing communication that acknowledges and addresses the public's concerns and priorities and explains clearly how schools are addressing them.

A third approach is for leaders to conclude that the public's point of view is in whole or in part mistaken, a conclusion that requires the exercise of true leadership—the slow, exacting process of building a constituency for ideas that are worthwhile but not popular. This is the most difficult path but the only honest one if leaders conclude that their approach, and not the public's, is the one that will best help children and their families.

We at Public Agenda present this research in the hope that educators and reform leaders will read it carefully, thoughtfully, and objectively in an honest effort to understand what the public is saying.

Is the public right or wrong? Perceptive or wrongheaded? Whatever one concludes, and whichever course of action is adopted, the public's perceptions should not be dismissed lightly.

Educators and reformers must listen to and respect what the public is saying. For change will not occur until the public becomes an equal and valued partner in the effort. ■

Deborah Wadsworth is the executive director of the Public Agenda Foundation.

From Education Week, *November 30, 1994*

46.

Does Money Matter?

Some experts claim that more money won't help schools. Others say it will. Both are right, depending on how the numbers are analyzed.

By Debra Viadero

When the Brookings Institution this month unveiled a book calling for schools to adopt more disciplined spending practices, it waded into an academic and political morass that has been growing in recent months.

The central question at issue is this: Does spending more money on schools improve students' academic achievement? The Brookings report, called *Making Schools Work: Improving Performance and Controlling Costs,* concludes that more money makes no difference—that is, at least, if it is spent in the ways schools have typically used it.

The panel of economists that put together the report based its concluions in part on studies done in the 1980s by Eric A. Hanushek, the lead author of the new book.

Hanushek, a professor of economics and political science at the University of Rochester, analyzed all existing studies that looked for relationships between additional resources and student learning. He determined that, in most cases, those resources had had no effect.

Conservative critics of schools, such as former U.S. Secretary of Education William J. Bennett, over the years have championed those findings.

But, in another study published earlier this year, a different group of researchers looked at the same data and came to the opposite conclusion. Writing in the April 1994 issue of the journal *Educational Researcher,* Larry V. Hedges, Richard D. Laine, and Rob Greenwald said higher spending on schools had produced higher student achievement.

Who is right?

The answer, according to some experts, is that maybe both sides are.

Counting and Synthesizing

Each study used markedly different approaches to analyze the data. Hanushek, using a common method known as "vote counting," essentially calculated the proportion of studies that found significant correlations between increased spending and improved student achievement.

Of the several dozen previous studies he examined, only 20 percent showed a strong positive effect.

The method used by Hedges, who is a statistician and education professor at the University of Chicago, is known as a "meta analysis." It took into account the magnitude of the effects that were found. In other words, if students' standardized-test scores rose, by how much?

By that method, he and his colleagues found strong ties between student achievement and both per-pupil funding levels and teacher experience. Other factors, such as class size, teacher education, teacher salary, administrative staffing, and facilities, showed less connection to achievement.

"If in the majority of places money is not used wisely and, if in the minority of places where it is used in economic ways, that money could make a large difference, that could compensate for the large number that aren't using it wisely," said Richard J. Murnane, an economist and professor at the Harvard Graduate School of Education. Murnane contributed to the Brookings study and is also writing a book on the subject.

"They both are telling you useful information," he said.

Even Hanushek, who in the May *Educational Researcher* gave a pointed response to the Chicago researchers, now says the two studies are "in complete agreement."

"There are some places that use money ineffectively and some that use it effectively," he said. "If you throw money at schools, you get at about the rough average."

He pointed out that his study found no systematic links between money and results—not a complete absence of links. But those links, he concluded, were not enough of a foundation on which to build policy.

But neither are Hanushek's findings, Hedges countered last week in an interview.

"To the extent that any of them are finding relationships, the relationships are positive and some are quite positive," he said.

A Matter of Method

To some extent, the debate is as much about research methodology as it is about whether giving schools more money improves student achievement.

Meta-analyses, like the one Hedges and his colleagues carried out, have been used increasingly over the past 15 years or so in psychology, medicine, and social-science research. But, said Hedges, they are still relatively rare in the realm of economics, Hanushek's world.

Betsy J. Becker, a professor of statistics and quantitative analysis in Michigan State University's college of education, said she prefers the meta-analysis.

"Magnitudes are always more interesting," Becker explained. "But if you don't believe in looking at magnitude of effects you're not going to believe the numbers anyway."

Hedges said the vote-counting method is flawed in part because errors in the studies can compound.

"If the individual studies are relatively weak, which is the norm, there is a good chance the results won't be there," he said.

Discounted or Discarded

In truth, both studies leave something out. In Hanushek's work, for instance, studies that have small positive—but statistically insignificant—effects would have been discounted.

In the Chicago findings, the researchers had to discard studies that did not include enough information.

Typically, those were studies in which researchers may have said there was "no significant effect" without indicating whether that tiny effect was positive or negative.

Hanushek, in his written response to Hedges's study, contends that practice reduced the pool of studies the Chicago researchers used by 20 percent to 30 percent.

The researchers also differed over technical matters. For instance, if several findings from the same study were used in the larger analysis, could those findings have been influenced by some other factor that is unique to the study from which they were taken?

Becker said the task of researchers now is to go beyond the age-old question of whether money makes a difference.

"If we didn't think it made a difference, we would not have been spending it all these years," she said. "When you find an effect, the next question ought to be: Why?" ∎

From Education Week, *Oct. 19, 1994*

47.

Why Charter Schools?

If leaders are serious about change, they must give charter schools the time and resources to reinvent schools.

By Tony Wagner

While doing research for a book on school reform in three different communities, I came to understand more clearly the difficulties of working for systemic change within large educational bureaucracies. Many of the best principals and teachers practice what they jokingly call "creative noncompliance" in order to initiate new programs. When attempting something new, they never ask for permission and they keep a low profile. Others take a more head-on approach and deliberately confront central-office and local-union practices that prevent them from creating better schools for all children—but sometimes at great personal cost.

Ruben Cabral was for 10 years a housemaster within the 2,400-student Cambridge Rindge and Latin High School in Cambridge, Mass. In his last two years there, he led the planning and implementation of a school-within-a-school—called The Academy—which features interdisciplinary team teaching, cooperative learning, and other innovations. He succeeded in launching the new program, but the struggles with the local union and school administrators exhausted him and prompted him finally to accept another job.

Shortly before he left, Ruben confided: "The truth of the matter is I'm glad to be getting out. I'm tired of fighting the bureaucracy. There's more and more of it. Why do we need a business office when we do all the purchasing and payroll here? Why do we need a personnel office, when we are the ones who should be doing the hiring anyway? What do the assistant superintendent and the superintendent's cabinet [a group of central-office middle managers] contribute to improving schools? Most of our energy goes to fighting the system instead of changing it. We need schools that are completely outside the system. How do you dismantle a bureaucracy?"

The possibility of creating new charter schools completely outside the confines of existing district and union bureaucracies promises one answer to Cabral's question. Charter schools offer the opportunity to create from scratch small, autonomous units which are much more like independent schools than traditional public schools in their size and governance. Susan Moore Johnson's recent book *Teachers at Work* documents the greater degree of professionalism, collaboration, and esprit de corps that she found among teachers in private schools.

Many believe that these are reasons enough for supporting the concept of charter schools. However, without a broader vision of the social need and value of charter schools, there is a serious danger that many will simply replicate the worst side of private schools—elitism and the accompanying educational conservatism. The answer to this country's education crisis is not to create more Andovers and Exeters at public expense. The education these schools offer, while of high quality, is as obsolete in curriculum and pedagogy as that offered in many public schools.

Circumventing bureaucracy, then, is a necessary but insufficient mission for charter schools. In my view, freedom from bureaucratic constraints simply provides the opportunity to do the real work of charter schools—educational research and development.

I have recently had the opportunity to work with

two very talented and committed high school teachers in Chelsea, Mass.—Sarah Kass and Ann Connolly Tolkoff. Tired of trying to change curriculum, teaching, and administrative practices that they felt were damaging to their students, they decided to apply for one of the first Massachusetts charters for public schools, created with the passage of new legislation in 1993.

The existence of this opportunity gave these two risk-taking entrepreneurs the incentive to plan a very different kind of school—to be called City on a Hill. Their goal is to "teach urban youth to lead ... to rekindle the passion for democracy, the commitment to public service, and the hunger for learning."

City on a Hill—like many of the better alternative schools of the 1970s—will require all students to perform community service, do independent research, and participate in weekly school "town" meetings. Learning from some of the mistakes of the past, these two teachers are also determined to create an academically rigorous program. Students will have to demonstrate mastery of specified competencies in order to earn a high school diploma.

Tolkoff and Kass have spent long hours thinking about what those competencies should be. They have consulted examples of best practices in other schools, like Central Park East in New York City, and have now begun to plan with the teachers they have hired for their summer program. Being able to get "out of the box" of serving seat time and amassing Carnegie units for a diploma has enabled these educators to completely rethink what all students need to know and be able to do for productive work, citizenship, and personal lives, as well as how to involve parents more actively and how to assess teachers. It is an extraordinary intellectual and creative challenge.

The approaches City on a Hill is developing promise to provide a better education for a representative cross-section of urban adolescents—but, more importantly to its co-founders, it will also be an open laboratory for educational innovation. Tolkoff and Kass hope to locate their new school within an existing Boston high school so that educators, academics, community leaders, and parents from around the city can benefit from what they are learning. They are even planning to involve representatives from all these groups in assessing the quality of their graduates' work. Their commitment, then, is to create highly visible and replicable models for change.

Even if charter schools are wildly successful in Massachusetts and elsewhere, I do not believe they will drive other public schools out of business—which is the marketplace argument for charter schools and public school choice that many conservatives and business leaders use. Seeing how hard Tolkoff, Kass, and their colleagues must work to raise $150,000 in private "venture capital" or start-up funds is sobering and makes clear that these schools will not be created

in large numbers. (Thus far, the state has not provided any start-up money.)

Leaving aside the problem of start-up funding for a moment, providing a high-quality education has never been a highly profitable endeavor—not with motivated, affluent students, and especially not with students who need a great deal of remediation.

Even in well-run private schools, tuition usually only covers about 85 percent of the operating cost—the "deficit" being made up with income from endowment and annual fund drives among parents and alumni. And most private schools keep costs down by refusing admission to students who have special needs or learning disabilities. In my view, it is highly unlikely that any national chain of for-profit schools will ever turn a profit. If they do, it will be at the expense of students' real learning.

In another way, business practices do have a lesson for educators, however. There is much that schools might learn from corporations about how to stimulate innovation. First, research and development must be funded. Businesses that need new products have large research-and-development budgets. School districts have no such budgets. Second, corporations identify the risk-takers and provide them with the opportunities to create new approaches—and they leave them alone! When Compaq needed to develop a better method for manufacturing computers, rather than try to change existing plant practices, they spun off an entirely new small plant to pilot and perfect new approaches. General Motors is trying the same strategy quite successfully with the Saturn project. Such efforts—often called "skunkworks"—are given the resources and independence they need to create improved products and methods. If successful, the pioneers teach others how to replicate the work.

I believe that publicly supported charter schools can and must be our "skunkworks" for educational research and development, but they must be given the time that is needed to do the job. We are too impatient for a quick educational fix in America. It's worth noting that it took Ford more than 10 years of research and development to come up with the better products and quality that finally enabled them to regain the number-one car-sales slot over Honda.

I don't think it will take City on a Hill quite that long to develop much better approaches to education. But their charter is only for five years—as are all the other charters in Massachusetts. If business and political leaders are serious about change, then they must give charter schools the time and resources needed to do the vital work of creating laboratories to reinvent American schools. Nothing else will suffice. ■

Tony Wagner is the president of the Institute for Responsive Education in Boston.

From Education Week, *June 22, 1994*

48.

Savage Inequalities

Jonathan Kozol's slashing book goes beyond arcane finance formulas to put a human face on fiscal inequalities.

By Lynn Olson

'We have a school in East St. Louis named for Dr. King," the author Jonathan Kozol quotes a 14-year-old girl saying toward the beginning of his new book, *Savage Inequalities: Children in America's Schools*. "The school is full of sewer water and the doors are locked with chains. Every student in that school is black. It's like a terrible joke on history."

Such humor is bitter indeed, according to Kozol. He places most of the blame for such conditions on the "arcane machinery," based heavily on local property taxes, that is used to finance public education in East St. Louis and throughout the country.

Drawing on visits to inner-city and suburban classrooms in some 30 neighborhoods around the country, the prominent social activist and former teacher concludes that American schools are more racially and economically segregated today than they were at the height of the civil-rights era.

This "dual society seems in general to be unquestioned," he writes in the book, released by Crown Publishers. "The nation, for all practice and intent, has turned its back upon the moral implications, if not yet the legal ramifications, of the *Brown* v. *Board of Education* decision."

Kozol established his reputation as an impassioned commentator on inequities in education with his first book, *Death at an Early Age,* published in 1967. That book was a first-person account of his experience as a 4th grade teacher in inner-city Boston. Since then, he has written about school desegregation, illiterate Americans, and, most recently, the plight of homeless Americans.

Savage Inequalities marks a return to the classroom for the 55-year-old writer. His latest, highly personalized reportage comes at a time when school finance has re-emerged as one of the central issues in education. More than 20 suits seeking reform of state systems of financing K-12 education are now pending.

The author's firsthand account describes schools that are 95 percent to 99 percent nonwhite—where "desegregation," as one principal told him, "means combining black kids and Hispanics."

Kozol depicts buildings that are literally collapsing around children's heads; teachers who only bother to attend school three days a week; principals forced to ration books, crayons, and toilet paper; and programs where little effort is made to teach failing students.

The insult, he maintains, is that such paucity exists within shouting distance of richly endowed public schools attended almost exclusively by the children of the prosperous.

One school the author visited in the South Bronx in New York City operates in a former ice-skating rink, where four kindergarten classes and a 6th grade class of Spanish-speaking students share a windowless room. The school does not have a playground; the library contains a meager 700 books in its collection.

Minutes away, in Riverdale, a more affluent part of the Bronx, a public school—surrounded by dogwoods, two playing fields, and a playground—houses a planetarium and a library of almost 8,000 volumes.

'On Their Side'?

In many ways, Kozol says in an interview, the situation has become worse since he left teaching 25 years ago. "I think it was better in 1965," he said, "because at that point, although the schools were, of course, segregated and unequal, there was at least the conviction among poor black kids that the government was on their side ... and the vast majority of white people were on their side."

"I don't think they feel that any longer," he adds. "I think they're correct."

Kozol attributes the shift he sees in the attitudes of the public and the federal government toward disadvantaged students to the "powerful effectiveness of Ronald Reagan" and conservative think tanks. He identifies the property-tax-based system of paying for schooling as the leading culprit in perpetuating inequalities.

The system enables wealthier districts to raise more money for their schools at a lower tax rate, he points out. At the same time, the richest homeowners get back a substantial portion of their money in the form of federal income-tax deductions that, in effect, promote and subsidize inequality.

In cities like Chicago, such disparities are made worse by the disproportionate number of tax-free institutions that reside in urban areas, and by the large portion of tax revenues that must be spent on such needs as law enforcement.

Total yearly spending in Illinois, Kozol reports, ranges from $2,100 for a child in the poorest district to above $10,000 in the richest. When the relative needs of students are factored in, he contends, the disparities in funding are "enormous."

"Equity, after all, does not mean simply equal funding," Kozol argues. "Equal funding for unequal needs is not equality."

In the long run, the author maintains, if Americans are serious about providing a level playing field in education, "we will abolish the property tax altogether as the primary, initial source of school funding in America."

Instead, Kozol pro-poses that three-quarters of public-school funding come from the state in the form of a steeply graduated income tax. The remaining one-quarter would come from the federal government. "That should be our peace dividend, at long last, at the end of the Cold War," he adds.

Jonathan Kozol

THOMAS VICTOR

But the book is not primarily about public policy, according to Kozol. "I was never a political person," he says. "I went to Harvard in the 1950s; I studied English literature. It was about as apolitical as it could be. ... I went into the Boston schools because I liked children."

Rather, the book is a stark depiction of the lives of children affected by what public policy has wrought. "The problem is that [most people] don't see that child," Kozol says. "I want to put that child in front of them and say to them, 'Look, this child is as precious as your child. And if you believe that, then fight for some decent policies.'"

"[W]hat struck me most, apart from the inequity and racial isolation [in inner-city schools]," he says, "is that most of these kids are having such rotten lives in these schools, that schools are so unhappy."

Kozol suggests that a special kind of despair characterizes the education of inner-city youngsters. The proximity of urban districts to some of the wealthiest school systems, he writes, "adds a heightened bitterness to the experience of children. The ugliness of racial segregation adds its special injuries as well."

"It is this killing combination, I believe," Kozol continues, "that renders life within these urban schools not merely grim but also desperate and often pathological."

"Kids see an unmistakable message in the degree that white people and affluent people have fled their school systems," he adds. "In the inner city, the children suffer not only the injury of caste, which is primarily an economic injury, but they also have the visceral experience of being shunned, of feeling themselves the object of despisal."

In such bleak environments, Kozol maintains, it is not surprising that so many students drop out. What is frightening, he argues, is that so many black school administrators appear to have accepted the idea of a separate and not-quite-equal education.

"It is the promise of American public education that no matter what other factors exist in a child's life, the school can make a difference," Kozol says. But, he writes, "[d]enial of the 'means of competition' is perhaps the single most consistent outcome of the education offered to poor children in the schools of our large cities."

'Two Separate Schools'

Even in "integrated" schools, the author found, there was little integration in classrooms. At P.S. 24, the school in Riverdale, for example, the vast majority of black and Hispanic students were in classes for the educable or trainable mentally retarded.

There were, in effect, "two separate schools," he writes, "one of about 130 children, most of whom are poor, Hispanic, black, assigned to one of the 12 special classes; the other of some 700 mainstream students, almost all of whom are white or Asian." Rooms for the former group were half the size of mainstream classrooms and equipped with far fewer materials.

Kozol disputes the argument that money makes no difference in education. "There is no doubt in my mind that a good teacher with 20 children is twice as good as a good teacher with 40 children," he says. "There's absolutely no question that, regardless of what happens in the home or in the streets, a school that has a French teacher teaches more French than a school that can't afford a French teacher."

The author is also highly critical of school-choice proposals, which he maintains will widen the gap between the haves and the have-nots. People "can only choose the things they think they have a right to and the things they have some reason to believe they will receive," he writes. "What reason have the black and poor to lend their credence to a market system that has proved so obdurate and so resistant to their pleas at every turn?"

And while Kozol is not against "restructuring" public education, he questions the efficacy of such efforts. "What are they trying to do?" he asks in an interview. "A restructured ghetto school? A ghetto school with more participation by ghetto parents?"

What is saddest, Kozol argues, is that America has the wealth to "give a wonderful childhood to every child, and the great pity is that we don't believe this."

"It was a despairing experience for me to find that all those years of work had come to nothing," he says about researching the book. "I do feel that this book was written less in anger than in sorrow," he says. "There's a very black feeling in the book, and it does not end with any real hope. It ends with longing." ∎

From Education Week, *Sept. 25, 1991*

49.

Girls Will Be Girls

Two researchers say that girls face gender bias in the classroom—from kindergarten to graduate school—just for behaving like girls.

By Millicent Lawton

It was back in the late 1960s when Myra Sadker and David Sadker first began thinking about gender bias against women and girls in the classroom. They were both doctoral students in education then, and Myra had experienced bias firsthand in her own academic program. In fact, those encounters gave Myra the idea for her first textbook, *Sexism in School and Society*. Written with Nancy Frazier and published in 1973, the text, designed for teachers, was the first to explore the nature of sexism in school.

Unlike others who have since left the study of gender equity, the Sadkers have not wavered from their work. Over the years, they have directed more than a dozen federal equity-research grants, written six books, and published more than 75 articles on the subject. They are still at it today, a quarter of a century later.

Now professors of education at American University in Washington and veterans of hundreds of workshops and lectures, the married couple have just published their first book for a popular audience, *Failing at Fairness: How America's Schools Cheat Girls*. The book has gained wide notice—thanks in part to a splashy publicity campaign and book tour orchestrated by their publisher, Charles Scribner's Sons.

USA Weekend featured a cover story by the Sadkers. And the couple has taken to the road to make appearances on local television and radio programs across the country. They've even discussed their work on the "Dateline NBC" television news magazine and "The Oprah Winfrey Show." And newspaper columnists and reviewers have seized the opportunity to comment—both favorably and unfavorably—on the Sadkers' anecdote-filled book.

In her book review in *The Wall Street Journal*, Rita Kramer, the author of *Ed School Follies: The Miseducation of America's Teachers,* called the Sadkers' conclusions "questionable" and their book "a work of advocacy rather than scholarship." A review in *The Nation* magazine charged that the Sadkers were "terrifyingly simplistic when it comes to analyzing what they report."

And the reviews from their colleagues have been somewhat mixed, too. Although most gender researchers hail the Sadkers as pioneers in the field, the couple have encountered their share of detractors as well. But the Sadkers don't shrink from the dissension—among academics or average citizens—that their work has engendered. "We're trying to draw people in," Myra Sadker says, "get them talking, arguing if they want—at least paying attention."

Judging by the media attention *Failing at Fairness* has already received, the Sadkers have succeeded on that front, at least. How America's schools really do—or don't—cheat girls is on people's lips from coast to coast.

Writing a book for a popular audience, the Sadkers say, was the one thing they felt they hadn't done. "We'd done research, we'd done grants, we'd done speaking and interviewing," Myra Sadker explains. "We've lived it with our own [two] daughters, and we just felt that we had to put it together."

It was after an early examination of textbooks, they write in *Failing at Fairness,* that they decided to look at "an even more powerful hidden curriculum that surfaced in the way teachers treat children and the way children treat one another." So, over the course of three years, the Sadkers sent trained "raters" to observe 4th, 6th, and 8th graders and their teachers in more than 100 classrooms in four Eastern states and the District of Columbia. Schools represented inner cities, rural areas, and affluent suburbs.

During their site visits, raters tallied interactions on observation sheets according to a methodology the Sadkers developed. It took the couple about a year of trial and error to design a rating sheet that they were satisfied with. Eventually, the Sadkers say, they gave up trying to record many aspects of classroom interaction because they were just too hard to document reliably.

What they discovered raters could dependably record were questions such as: Whom did the teacher call on? How did the student get the teacher's attention? By raising a hand? By calling out? Did the teacher designate the student? What did the teacher say after she or he called on students? What level of help or feedback were students getting? If the teacher praised a student, what was the praise for?

In a later study, the Sadkers analyzed classroom communication at the college level.

Based on the Sadkers' own research and that of others, *Failing at Fairness* tallies the myriad ways in which they see girls and young women treated differently from boys and young men—from kindergarten through graduate school. The Sadkers detail how "schoolgirls face subtle and insidious gender lessons, micro-inequities that appear seemingly insignificant when looked at individually but that have a powerful cumulative impact."

These "hidden lessons," as the Sadkers call them, take many forms—from less attention and praise from teachers to sexual harassment, and from sex stereotyping in course enrollment to biased standardized tests. The end result, they say, is clear: Girls often receive lesser educational experiences and opportunities than boys do.

Starting at an Early Age

Gender bias in the classroom begins in elementary school, according to the Sadkers, where girls get short-changed in class discussion, on the playground, and in the curriculum.

●Calling out in class, for example, is an "open invitation for male dominance," the Sadkers write. Their research shows that boys call out in class eight times

more often than girls call out.

●In the more than 100 classrooms the Sadkers studied, they found boys received more of four reactions from teachers: praise, correction, help, criticism—"all reactions that foster student achievement," they write. "Girls received the more superficial 'OK' reaction," the Sadkers continue, "the one that packs far less educational punch."

●Male dominance continues on the playground, the Sadkers note. In a "typical" schoolyard, they write, the area where boys play is 10 times larger than the play area for girls. "Girls huddle along the sidelines, on the fringe.... Recess becomes a spectator sport."

●When the Sadkers asked 4th, 5th, and 6th graders in 1992 to name 10 women and 10 men from history who lived anywhere in the world but were not entertainers or athletes, the children, on average, could name 11 men but only three women.

●In 1989 elementary school textbooks in mathematics, language arts, and history, the Sadkers discovered that mentions of boys outnumbered those of girls two to one or three to one. In one 631-page textbook covering the history of the world, only seven pages related to women.

In their book, the Sadkers acknowledge that girls get better grades in school and receive fewer punishments than boys, calling girls "the elementary school's ideal pupils." But they don't view that as all positive. Girls receive less time, less help, and fewer challenges. "Reinforced for passivity," the Sadkers write, girls' "independence and self-esteem suffer."

Teachers claim, the Sadkers write, that boys get more attention both because they act out more and because "they need it more," that is, they're academically behind the girls. But the Sadkers argue that by middle school, girls are more needy than boys in math and science but aren't getting more attention.

Moreover, David Sadker says, it's not good teaching to reinforce with the boys the idea of "Act out, threaten to act out, and I will shower you with instructional time to keep you on task." To girls, he adds, teachers say silently: "Do what's expected, and I'll ignore you."

Building Up to Bias

As girls get older, the Sadkers argue, the cumulative effects of gender bias combine with social and developmental factors to create an even more complicated picture. In middle school, for example, evidence suggests that the self-esteem of adolescent girls plummets. In addition to citing a 1991 American Association of University Women poll showing a self-esteem gap between girls and boys, the Sadkers document other research studies showing that girls begin to censor themselves as they grow older, becoming more reticent and masking and denying their feelings.

By their high school years, the Sadkers write, girls face social pressures that foster a negative body image, such as the emphasis on fashion-model-like thinness. These pressures further threaten their self-esteem and can even prompt some girls to become teenage mothers and drop out of school.

Citing U.S. Census and other data, they add that although more boys than girls drop out initially, by age 25 slightly more males than females have earned their high school diplomas. Unlike boys, the Sadkers say, when girls leave school, they rarely return.

Despite recent improvement in girls' enrollment in math and science classes, the Sadkers say girls still don't persist in them—nor are they expected to—in the same way as boys. Even though the same numbers of girls and boys take algebra and geometry, for example, boys go on to take calculus while girls drop out of math. Physical science courses, too, are especially male-dominated, the Sadkers write. A 1991 survey by the Council of Chief State School Officers revealed that the enrollment of first-year physics courses was 60 percent male and that seven out of 10 second-year physics students were boys.

In sizing up the high school experience, the Sadkers repeated their exercise of checking textbooks for references to women and asking students to name famous women from history. Their results mirror those found in elementary school. Fewer than 3 percent of the more than 1,000 pages of *A History of the United States* are about women, the Sadkers write. Only eight women in the 1992 textbook merit as many as a couple of paragraphs. And, once again, few women made the students' lists of famous historical figures.

Standardized testing, too, draws the Sadkers' scrutiny for being biased against girls. On the SAT, required for admission to many colleges, boys typically score 50 to 60 points higher than girls. A high school girl with an A-plus grade-point average typically scores 83 points lower than a boy with the same GPA, the Sadkers say.

On the Achievement Tests, which evaluate knowledge in a single subject area, boys in 1992 outscored girls on 11 of the 14 different versions of the test—from physics to American history to Latin. Girls outdid boys only in the subjects of German, English composition, and literature.

Although the Sadkers acknowledge that gender bias does not occur in every school or with every teacher, they offer possible solutions to the gender inequities that they say do exist in many of America's classrooms. They outline strategies for teachers, for example, to use to keep boys from dominating the classroom: wait longer for answers after asking a question, monitor cooperative learning groups, and make sure comments to girls encourage academic progress.

In addition to describing the "miseducation of boys"—the stereotyped roles parents and schools foster for boys—the Sadkers make suggestions for how students, parents, and teachers can improve the experiences of girls. They urge parents to be involved at home in shaping nonsexist attitudes in their children in the way they speak to them, in the toys they provide, in joining girls in nontraditional activities. Parents, they write, should seek out real-life female role models, encourage their children's school to use nonsexist curricula, and urge their daughters to speak up in class and at home.

Hearing Out the Opposition

Although the Sadkers have long been prominent in their field, they are hardly the only scholars who have researched the experiences of girls in school. By and large, their colleagues praise the Sadkers for both the content of their work and for bringing gender equity to the attention of the general public.

But not all of their fellow researchers agree with the Sadkers' approach. And not all research finds precisely the kind of sex-biased situations the Sadkers have found. In fact, some critics charge that the picture the Sadkers paint is incomplete. They claim that many factors other than gender differences—namely age, race, native language—come into play when looking at classroom or playground interactions.

Although Barrie Thorne, a University of Southern California sociologist, lauds the Sadkers' research as important, she says, "I think in their work they don't say enough about the complexity of gender, and they make girls too much into victims."

"The Sadkers' approach to gender is actually quite out of date in terms of feminist scholarship and feminist theory because we have moved to such a complex way of thinking about gender," adds Thorne, the chairwoman of USC's Program for the Study of Women and Men in Society. "Nobody in women studies says women are just victims."

The Sadkers vehemently deny their book is about victims. Rather, they say in unison, it is about "empowerment."

"We're trying to share with people what happened," says David Sadker, "some of which was females were victims. But not in the sense of making them victims, but of explaining to them and to parents and to teachers what they need to do to insure equity and a successful future. The book is a road map for educators and others on the pitfalls that lie ahead for females, at every level."

Thorne, who is also the author of the book *Gender Play: Girls and Boys in School,* agrees that curriculum is centered too much on boys, leaving girls on the margins. And based on the two ethnographic studies of elementary school children in California and Michigan described in her book, she has also found that boys usually dominate play areas.

But, she says of the Sadkers, "what they're missing is the great variation from classroom to classroom—the way social class, race, and ethnicity intersect with gender, which is just extremely important."

In *Gender Play,* for example, Thorne points to the mixed-sex play group that developed on the California school's playground. The Spanish-speaking boys and girls who made up the group, she suggests, were probably more comfortable speaking Spanish with each other in an alien environment than observing traditional gender-based rules of play. Same-age groups—more prevalent in schools than in neighborhoods—also tend to foster same-sex grouping by children, Thorne writes.

Sometimes, girls conquer traditional male dominance and some teachers treat children of different races differently, Thorne adds. "I saw girls in elementary schools exercising power over boys sometimes," she says, as well as teachers who paid more attention to "white, middle-class, 'clean' girls and didn't come near black and Latino girls."

Thorne also takes into account differences in classroom behavior based on the individual, regardless of gender. "Gender-related patterns, such as boys participating more actively and receiving more teacher attention than girls in classroom settings, are, at the most, a matter of statistical difference," she writes. "There is wide individual variation in patterns like readiness to talk in class." Gender relations are not fixed but vary by context, she says.

Jacquelynne Eccles, a University of Michigan psychology professor, also found that factors other than gender come into play in classroom interactions. In her observations of junior and senior high mathematics and science classes in the Midwest, she found academics affects behavior. The teachers tended to pay more attention to the high-achieving students, whether they were boys or girls.

"I can tell you the much more significant thing is how the children are performing" academically, says Eccles, who is also chairwoman of Michigan's combined program in education and psychology.

In about one-third of the classrooms, according to Eccles, the teacher did treat boys better than girls of comparable ability levels. But, over all, she says, "we found that the biggest gender difference is that the boys get yelled at more than the girls. That swamps all other differences."

The Sadkers have also encountered a fair share of criticism about their methodology. Critics charge that because they are feminists, their rating sheet used to record observations can't be objective.

The Sadkers disagree. The 50-page manual that ac-

companies the rating sheet, they say, clearly defines such classroom interactions as "praise." What's more, raters had to agree 85 percent of the time on what they had seen. If they couldn't, the Sadkers didn't use those results.

"We developed the form," Myra Sadker explains, "but it's not exactly a high-inference form. ... Who got called on? Circle it. Count it. That, to me, is the most objective thing you can do—not gain an impression, but count."

Sharing the Spotlight

The attention the Sadkers' book has garnered—from critics and supporters alike—has helped maintain the momentum building around the gender-equity issue since the release of *How Schools Shortchange Girls* two years ago.

Commissioned by the American Association of University Women Educational Foundation and researched by the Wellesley College Center for Research on Women, the report reviewed the literature, including the Sadkers' work, suggesting that girls usually receive different, often worse, treatment in school than boys do.

Other events are fueling that momentum, too. Last month, the American Civil Liberties Union, on behalf of the testing watchdog group FairTest, filed a complaint with the U.S. Education Department's office for civil rights. It charged that the Educational Testing Service and the College Board had violated federal law by administering and sponsoring the Preliminary SAT as the sole criterion in awarding more than $25 million annually in National Merit Scholarships.

In 1989, FairTest won a lawsuit charging New York State with gender bias in its award of scholarships based solely on Scholastic Aptitude Test scores. Scholarship awards in that state were subsequently based also on grades before budget cuts eliminated them.

After 25 years of pushing for educational equity for girls and women, the Sadkers seem to look to the future with equal doses of optimism and caution.

We're at a "very critical juncture," Myra Sadker says. "Equity is an attainable goal in education." But, based on the "backlash" she says she and her husband have encountered during their book tour, she also warns: "We could go backward." ∎

Myra Sadker died March 18, 1995. Sadker, who was 52, suffered complications from a bone-marrow transplant to treat breast cancer.

From Education Week, *March 30, 1994*

50.

Forging Policy for Harassment

Sexual harassment of students by students is on the rise, and schools and teachers may be liable.

By Millicent Lawton

What happened to Johna Mennone in her environmental-science class in the fall of 1990 left her feeling "humiliated, terrorized, and distraught." In the presence of her teacher and a roomful of classmates, Mennone says, a male peer grabbed her hair, legs, breasts, and buttocks nearly every day. He repeatedly made remarks about her breasts and told her that he was going to rape her. The student allegedly continued the behavior in a later course.

In the past, what happened to Mennone might well have been chalked up to "high school" behavior or "boys being boys." Today, it is the subject of a federal lawsuit filed by Mennone against the district superintendent, the school board, and her teacher at Amity Regional High School in Woodbridge, Conn.

Like Mennone, students across the nation—together with their parents, teachers, and school officials—are beginning to deal with the thorny issues of how to define, prevent, and punish sexual harassment among students.

In recent months, experts in the field say, inquiries on the topic have increased markedly. In fact, the National School Boards Association has received so many requests for information that it created a "fax pack" of information to be sent out via facsimile machine, says Karen Powe, the director of policy services for the association.

Many factors appear to have contributed to the heightened interest, experts agree, including a chang-ing social climate that is less tolerant of sex discrimination of all kinds, the 1991 Clarence Thomas-Anita Hill hearings on Capitol Hill, and a U.S. Supreme Court decision nearly a year ago that says school districts could be held liable for sexual harassment in school.

Although sexual misconduct by teachers involving students seems to have garnered more attention and has been the subject of more school-district policies, sexual harassment exclusively involving students is actually much more prevalent, according to Nan D. Stein, who in 1980-81 conducted the first study of peer harassment in schools for the Massachusetts Department of Education.

Most of the harassment in schools is inflicted on girls by boys and often takes place in the classroom, as in Mennone's case, according to Stein, who now directs a project on school sexual harassment at the Center for Research on Women at Wellesley College.

But the subject remains an unfamiliar one full of gray areas for school districts that are trying to codify prohibited student behavior and educate pupils and staff members in how to handle harassment.

Most experts agree that sexual harassment is defined by the victim: If an individual finds the comments or physical contact to be unwelcome, then it is harassment. But others acknowledge that what might not feel like harassment to the victim might appear to be harassment to, say, an administrator—and vice versa. Then, too, what may be acceptable in a social setting or among some racial or ethnic groups— teasing, joking, or flirting in a sexual manner—is not acceptable in an educational setting, experts say.

Because sexual harassment is a continuum that can range from spoken or written comments and stares to physical assault and attempted rape, some of it may also be actionable as criminal activity, depending on local laws, Stein notes.

Policymakers also face a difficult task in wording guidelines banning such behavior, according to Robert Peck, the legislative counsel for the American Civil Liberties Union in Washington. "The key is that it cannot be regarded as harassment just because someone takes offense at an utterance," such as the word "bitch," Peck says.

However, a "personally directed threat that makes it impossible for a person" to learn is something that a school has a right to regulate, he says.

Notion of Trust Undermined

As the issue has grown in public prominence, students have begun seeking school policies, legislation, and court decisions to protect themselves from the unwelcome verbal taunts and jokes, bathroom graffiti, pinching, groping, and other assaults that girls and women have been subjected to for generations.

"I think this is a dirty little secret that's been around for a long time … something we've kind of accepted," State Sen. Gary Hart of California says of peer sexual harassment in school.

Senator Hart sponsored a state law that took effect last month that makes sexual harassment by students in grades 4 to 12 an offense punishable by suspension or expulsion. "We're just serving notice to the principals and teachers … that they need to pay attention to this," Hart says.

If sexual harassment is allowed to go unchecked, "the whole notion of trust or school as a safe and democratic place is vastly undermined," Stein, of the Wellesley center, says.

The issue is also receiving national attention. Nineteen of the 40 sexual harassment cases currently being investigated by the U.S. Education Department's office for civil rights involve elementary or secondary education. Of those, at least two involve harassment by students, a department official says.

Both of those cases—one in Eden Prairie, Minn., and the other in Sherman, Tex.—allege harassment on school buses of elementary-age girls by their male peers. In addition, two separate attempts are under way to document the prevalence and develop a profile of in-school sexual harassment.

This month, the results are expected from a national survey on sexual harassment in school designed by Stein and another researcher at the Wellesley center and printed in *Seventeen* magazine last fall. And

the American Association of University Women will try to find out from a national random survey this year what both girls and boys have to say about their experiences and thoughts about sexual harassment.

The survey, the results of which are expected in June, will "hopefully raise the level of debate beyond anecdotal evidence," says Pamela Hughes, a spokeswoman for the AAUW.

Sometimes it is a specific incident in a school district that prompts officials to address the issue. Ana Sol Gutierrez, a member of the Montgomery County, Md., school board, says she knew her district needed rules about sexual harassment after a high school girl harassed by a male peer finally turned around one day on the school bus and slapped him. The incident earned both students a suspension for fighting because that was the only policy that applied. The board has since enacted a sexual harassment policy for students to give them a better line of defense.

Educators often cite the October 1991 allegations of sexual harassment against then-Supreme Court nominee Clarence Thomas by Anita Hill, a law professor, and the High Court's February 1992 decision in *Franklin* v. *Gwinnett County Public Schools* allowing a student to sue a district for monetary damages in a sexual harassment case as helping shape their thinking on harassment.

In Indiana, for example, before the Thomas-Hill hearings, many school administrators were not willing to acknowledge that sexual harassment of any kind was a problem in their schools, says Beverly Peoples, an equity consultant with the state department of education. Only a tiny number of administrators attended the voluntary in-service awareness sessions on sexual harassment offered by the state, Peoples says. But in recent months, such sessions have drawn a total of about 50 administrators. Still, there are 296 school districts in Indiana, she says, and "systemic change is very slow."

In the High Court's unanimous decision in *Franklin,* the Justices ruled that victims of sexual harassment and other forms of sex discrimination in schools may sue for monetary damages under Title IX of the Education Amendments of 1972. The law bars sexual discrimination in federally funded schools and colleges. While the *Franklin* case concerned harassment and abuse of a student by a teacher, many observers attach great significance to the decision and its expansion of students' ability to obtain redress from school districts for discriminatory acts.

Others, however, say that it is not clear whether the protections of Title IX extend to sexual harassment by a student's peers. That issue, and the potential for damage awards against school districts, must still be decided in the federal courts, they say, although some expect that such guarantees will be extended to students.

On a related topic, the U.S. Supreme Court last

January refused to consider the issue of whether the U.S. Constitution obliges public school officials to protect students from sexual assaults by teachers or other students.

"An employer is responsible for the conduct of employees," says Gwendolyn H. Gregory, the deputy general counsel of the National School Boards Association. "Is [a school district] responsible for the conduct of students? I don't think you can necessarily say [that]," she says.

The lawyer for Mennone, the former Connecticut student who alleges harassment in class, says she did not think the case would have been filed if it had not been for the precedent set by *Franklin*.

That case "certainly opens the door to students enforcing their rights under Title IX," Maureen M. Murphy says. "I really think we're going to see a lot of litigation in this area."

Becoming Less Vulnerable

Lawyers and others say that school districts with established policies on sexual harassment may stand in better legal stead should a lawsuit arise. In two states, districts have no choice but to confront the issue.

In Minnesota, and now in California, schools are required by law to adopt sexual harassment policies that cover students. Unlike the new California law, Minnesota's statute also requires each school to develop a process for discussing the policy with students and employees.

And State Commissioner of Education Betty Castor of Florida last year "strongly" urged the state's 67 school districts to adopt procedures for dealing with sexual misconduct in school, including student-initiated sexual harassment, which she termed a "serious problem."

"The safest thing for a school district to do is to adopt policies that provide remedies for students who believe they are victims ... and to build an awareness of the problem," says David S. Tatel, a former head of the office for civil rights at the U.S. Education Department.

Stein at the Wellesley center agrees. "If we don't believe those kids, then get ready for a lawsuit," she says. "Because the kids that speak up and write and tell me about sexual harassment—the descriptions are parallel to the descriptions that come out in the lawsuits," she says.

But Stein says officials also need to think about how to resolve complaints through both formal and informal, nonlitigious procedures. One possible approach, she says, is to have the accuser—who may be satisfied simply to have the harassment cease—write a letter to the perpetrator, under the supervision of an adult trained in the procedure, asking him or her to stop the sexual harassment.

Other educators use parent conferences or even have a police officer present during a discussion with the harasser to strengthen the message.

Even punishment under harassment policies can be a learning experience if an offending student must, for example, write a report on the subject of sexual harassment, officials say.

Teachers and counselors must also be intensively trained beyond basic awareness to discuss these issues in the classroom, Stein says, so that they can "impart not just knowledge, but the subjectivity and difficulty of this subject to the kids."

Lesson plans and pamphlets exist for junior high and high school students, who are able to grasp the meaning of sexual harassment when it is compared with its benign counterpart, flirting, experts say. But conveying the concept to elementary age students is more of a challenge and calls for comparisons to bullying, they say.

And the youngest student should not be left out of policies or education, educators say. Susan F. Sattel, a sex-equity specialist for the Minnesota Department of

---

An employer is responsible for the conduct of employees. Does it follow, asks one official, that a school district is responsible for the conduct of students?

Education, speaks of an incident in which two 6-year-old boys who were 1st graders at a private school sexually assaulted another 6-year-old child at knifepoint.

"The earlier you intervene [with kids on sexual harassment], the better results you have in the long run," says Cynthia Chestnut, the director of student and community services for the Alachua County, Fla., schools who headed up the effort to draft that district's policy last year. "If you make them aware of this in schools," she says, "you break the cycle and they're not growing up to be sexually harassing adults."

Students Push for Policy

Efforts to educate students can pay off, school officials say. Central High School in St. Paul is planning to reinstate two-day awareness lessons with its students that were successful several years ago in addressing sexual harassment, says Franklin Wharton, a social worker at the school.

The presentations—which included typical harassment situations—provided a "real dramatic impact on redefining what some youngsters thought were fun and games," Wharton says. "Many of them don't even know what constitutes sexual harassment."

In one district, the students gave the educators a policy lesson. The Sequoia Union High School District in Redwood City, Calif., credits the existence of its peer sexual harassment policy to the activism of students. Prompted by the Thomas-Hill hearings as well as by an incident in the district, a 23-member student advisory council decided to draw up the policy as its annual project, says Susan Bendix, the administrative liaison to the student group.

The panel, about evenly divided between high school boys and girls who are appointed by school officials, got administrators as well as students in the 6,400-student, ethnically diverse district to sign on to the idea. They saw their efforts result in the adoption of the policy last April by the school board, which had one eye on the possibility that the legislature would mandate such policies, Bendix says.

Policy Road Problematic

For some districts, the road to drawing up and implementing a policy against peer sexual harassment has been full of controversy and legal potholes. The school board in Montgomery County, Md., of which Gutierrez is a member, had just adopted its policy on student harassment in November when it found itself threatened with legal action, in part because training and educational materials were not yet in place.

Superintendent Paul L. Vance determined that one school had handled poorly a harassment complaint brought under the new policy. In addition, the school's printed information on the policy, which students had assailed as "sexist," has also been withdrawn.

Last year, another district, the Petaluma Joint Union High School District in northern California, found itself on the losing end of a lawsuit even as it

was developing a peer sexual harassment policy. Displeased with the way the district handled her complaint about boys who "mooed" and commented on her breasts, Tawnya Brawdy, then a student at Kenilworth Junior High, and her mother filed suit. Last year, they settled out of court with the school district's insurance company for $20,000.

However, "the district feels that it did act appropriately," says Kim Jamieson, the deputy superintendent in Petaluma.

A committee, which includes Tawnya's mother, Louise, is expected to submit a "model, state-of-the-art" student harassment policy to the school board within a couple of months.

Yet, even when a school district has a policy in place, it may face legal challenges. In what is considered the first case of a student's winning monetary damages from a district because of a peer harassment case, Katherine Lyle, a former student at Central High School in Duluth, Minn., received a $15,000 settlement in September 1991 from the state human-rights department for "alleged mental anguish and suffering."

The award came after an investigation by the state office found that the district had failed to act appropriately after sexually offensive graffiti about Katy, as she is known, appeared in a boys' bathroom at the school in 1987 and was not removed despite repeated requests from the Lyles.

Duluth has had a sexual-harassment policy that covered students since 1982, officials say. Unfortunately, says Katy's mother, Carol Lyle—who is a teacher in the district—graffiti was not considered sexual harassment at the time.

As part of the settlement, custodians in the district must check daily for graffiti, remove it, and report its existence to officials. And the district now instructs students about sexual harassment in grade-level appropriate curriculum, and Katy herself has led lessons on the subject.

"It seems," Carol Lyle says of the policy change, "to be taken seriously." ■

From Education Week, *Feb. 10, 1993*

Who We Are

"We are close to a fundamental rethinking of the way teaching works in America. We are ready to build on the tough standards we have created in the past three years. With an expanded pool of talented teachers, we can explore ways to empower teachers to do their jobs better. We can get teachers more involved in professional decisions within the school. We can help teachers better share their talents and knowledge with their colleagues."

—Thomas H. Kean, President, Drew University

51.

A Profession Evolving

Reformers envision more demanding and more gratifying new roles for teachers in the restructured schools of the future.

For as long as anyone can remember, teaching has been more of an occupation than a profession. The emergence of teachers' unions in the 1960s was tacit acceptance of that fact. Traditionally, all important decisions affecting teachers' classrooms have been made by administrators and policymakers at the state and district levels. They largely have determined the content of the curriculum and how it should be taught, selected textbooks and teaching materials, and decided which standardized tests would be administered on what schedule. The objective, in part, was to make schools "teacher-proof." Only when the classroom door was closed could teachers exercise a modicum of autonomy—and then at some risk.

To some degree, this situation has prevailed because teaching has largely been women's work. Before the feminist movement of the 1960s, a woman aspiring to a career had essentially two choices: nursing or teaching. Public schools had no trouble staffing their classrooms with women who were willing to work in unappealing working conditions for low wages. It used to be called the "hidden subsidy of women's work." The situation has changed over the past three decades, and women have many more career options. But 8 out of 10 beginning teachers today are women. Working conditions haven't changed much, and the average beginning salary for teachers is just over $22,000—not much higher in 1960 dollars than it was 30 years ago. And minority teachers are in short supply. Despite the widening diversity of the student body, only 5 percent of beginning teachers are African-American and only 2 percent are Hispanic.

Although teaching is often referred to as a profession, teachers' working conditions and career patterns reflect the characteristics of a blue-collar occupation. Teachers rarely have their own offices, lack the services that professionals have access to (secretary, telephone, typewriter, fax machine, copier), and, in large urban districts, must punch in and out on time clocks. The teacher's workday is highly structured, with little or no time for reading, reflection, or intellectual interaction with colleagues. Salary schedules are so rigid and precise that teachers can see immediately where they will be on the salary scale at any given point in their careers. The labor contract spells out their rights and responsibilities, their rewards and punishments.

Not surprisingly, the current school reform movement's early initiatives reflected the view of teacher as laborer. Administrators and policymakers believed that student achievement could be increased by improving teaching—and that could be done by ratcheting up the present system. So in the early and mid-1980s, many states raised requirements and standards in schools of education, required teachers to pass minimum competency tests, provided highly structured curricula for them to follow, and increased teachers' salaries. These actions had no noticeable effect on classroom practice or on student learning.

As reformers probed more deeply into the structure and content of schooling in America during the late 1980s, they became convinced that the entire system of schooling had to be overhauled. The emphasis, they argued, should be on learning rather than on teaching, on understanding and thinking rather than on acquisition and memorization, on cooperation rather than on competition. In this scenario, reminiscent of

John Dewey, teachers would be mentors and coaches rather than dispensers of facts; students would take more responsibility for their own education, and teachers would collaborate with them in a search for knowledge and understanding. The school structure would be substantially changed: Within broad curricular frameworks, teachers would decide how best to meet content standards; they would participate in the development of new performance-based assessments; they would be empowered to make decisions that affect instruction, budget, personnel, practice, scheduling, and student-teacher assignments.

Such a radically changed system would drastically alter the role of teachers. As one major report put it: "Teachers must think for themselves if they are to help others think for themselves, be able to act independently and collaborate with others, and render critical judgments. They must be people whose knowledge is wide-ranging and whose understanding runs deep."

In short, "teaching for understanding" would require restructured schools and truly professional teachers.

Sociologists who have studied professions such as medicine, law, and architecture note that they share several common characteristics. A true profession:
● Possesses a body of specialized knowledge to be mastered by the practitioner;
● Recruits able people to its ranks, requires rigorous preparation for its members, and controls which candidates are admitted;
● Sets high standards for professional practice and holds its members to those standards; in return, the professional is freed of undue bureaucratic regulation and supervision;
● Recognizes its responsibility to those it serves and places their interests above its own.

Although it has a long way to go, the movement toward professionalization has been gaining momentum. In many "restructured schools," teachers are deeply involved in decisionmaking. States are waiving regulations for innovative schools. School schedules are being revised to provide teachers with more time for preparation and opportunities to work together. Teachers are playing central roles in national and state efforts to develop standards and assessments for students. There is growing recognition that teachers, like physicians, need continuing professional development—rich programs that go well beyond earning college credits in night-school courses.

A major step toward the professionalization of teaching was the establishment in 1987 of the National Board for Professional Teaching Standards. Dominated by teachers, the board seeks to define what expert teachers of a variety of academic subjects and grade levels should know and be able to do, to develop assessments to evaluate them, and to award national certification to those who meet these high standards. The approach is analogous to the medical profession's board-certification system. The hope is that board-certified teachers will be in demand and will be compensated accordingly, that districts will compete for their services and rely on them to be leaders among their colleagues in schools. The first teachers "took the boards" in 1993-94.

In addition to this effort, a newly established consortium of state policymakers and representatives of the teaching profession has developed a model set of standards for beginning teachers that identifies for the first time the "common core" of knowledge and skills that all new teachers should possess.

Defining what teachers should know and be able to do is an important step forward, but it will not automatically result in a supply of teachers who are capable of teaching for understanding. Nor is it likely that even the most rigorous teacher education programs will produce such teachers. At best, pre-service programs can help students acquire a deep understanding of their subject matter and of the pedagogies that are essential in this new kind of teaching.

If good professional practice is to spread through the nation's classrooms, it must be made visible to teachers. They must have opportunities to see it, reflect on it, and discuss it. They must have opportunities to connect with other teachers in professional communities or with networks of like-minded colleagues. One of the startling and important findings of a major study described in this chapter is that such connections have a powerful effect on how successful teachers are in adapting their instructional strategies to meet their students' needs.

Unfortunately, role models for teaching understanding are relatively rare in schools today. The present system discourages it; it is more difficult than conventional teaching because it is more improvisational and less planned. Only the most exceptional teachers (a few of whom are portrayed in the following pages) have mastered the practice. They have done so through years of observing, questioning, and researching how their students learn and how they learn different things differently. And they have experimented with their craft and modified their practice to meet changing circumstances. That is what professionals do.

It is hard to imagine any social endeavor more worthy of being a profession than teaching. Physicians, lawyers, and architects can leave tangible and lasting records of their important contributions—a pioneering new surgical procedure, a precedent-setting judicial decision, a soaring skyscraper. The contribution of the teacher is not so evident and breathtaking. It is intangible, immeasurable, invisible—given to children, one by one.

But, as Henry Adams wrote, it "affects eternity." ∎

52.

By the Numbers

Percentage of beginning teachers who are female: **81**

Percentage who are white: **92**   Black: **5**   Hispanic: **2**

Percentage who are married: **33**

Average college grade: **B plus**

Average combined SAT score: **955 out of 1600**

Proportion who attended college within 100 miles of home: **3 in 5**

Within 500 miles of home: **9 in 10**

Proportion who commuted daily: **Half**

Percentage who hope to teach in or near their hometown: **80**

Who would seek a job nationally: **30**

Percentage who grew up in rural areas or small towns: **50**

In suburbs: **28**   In cities: **20**

Percentage who plan to teach in suburbs or small towns: **76**

In rural areas: **9**   In cities: **15**

Percentage who plan to teach elementary grades: **58**

Secondary: **42**

Percentage who want to teach in middle-class schools: **75**

In culturally diverse schools: **14**

In low-income schools: **6**

Proportion who prefer to teach in traditional vs. experimental schools: **3 in 4**

Percentage who feel very positive about a teaching career: **90**

Who plan to teach five years or more: **90**   20 years or more: **34**

Percentage who would consider or seek principalship: **51**

Superintendency: **48**

Average public school teacher's salary in 1991-92: **$34,213**

In 1960: **$4,999**

Sources: American Association of Colleges for Teacher Education,
American Federation of Teachers, National Center for Education Statistics

53.

Teaching Professionals

Signs abound that reforms to transform the teaching profession are taking hold.

By Ann Bradley

Meet Samantha, who is beginning her teaching career in an urban, multiethnic elementary school. Unlike countless new teachers who have preceded her, Samantha is unlikely to quit her job in the next five years. Instead, she enters the classroom fully armed with the knowledge and skills she needs. She is a graduate of a nationally accredited preparation program, where she received a rigorous liberal arts education, studied research-based pedagogy, and worked with real students in real schools.

Samantha has passed a battery of exams focusing not only on what she knows but also on whether she can put that knowledge into action. She has completed a yearlong, supervised internship in a professional-development school—a requirement for licensure in her state.

This new teacher understands children and how they learn, can tailor lessons to meet their needs, and can explain, based on research and practices, how she makes decisions. In short, she is a professional.

Scrutiny Yields Action

This illustration, drawn from a portrait created by the National Council for the Accreditation of Teacher Education, may sound too good to be true. It contrasts sharply with existing standards for licensure in most states, which still look primarily at whether a candidate has completed certain course work and attended a state-approved teacher education program.

But a decade of sustained scrutiny of the occupation's shortcomings has generated a multitude of signs that teaching is on the road to becoming a true profession. Consider:

● The National Board for Professional Teaching Standards, created in 1987 to elevate teaching by codifying what expert teachers should know and be able to do, this year awarded its first certificates.

● Spurred by the national board's work, states are changing their licensing standards for new teachers.

A consortium of 38 states has drafted model standards for licensing teachers that describe the knowledge, skills, and dispositions beginning teachers should possess. Four states have adopted the standards outright, and 10 more have modified them.

In addition, 10 states involved in the Interstate New Teacher Assessment and Support Consortium, called INTASC, are creating assessments that examine how candidates for licensure fare in classrooms.

The assessments, through videotapes and portfolios, look at several weeks of teaching and include samples of students' work.

● The National Council for Accreditation of Teacher Education continues to strengthen its standards and press the case for education schools to subject their programs to professional scrutiny.

● A blue-ribbon National Commission on Teaching and

America's Future is examining how policymakers can capitalize on the momentum by overhauling the preparation, recruitment, selection, induction, and continuing professional development of teachers.

● With the active support of the National Education Association and the American Federation of Teachers, researchers at the University of Wisconsin at Madison are studying new ways to pay teachers. They seek to design and pilot-test a compensation structure that would pay teachers for showing they had developed specific skills and expertise.

Experts say the activity in teaching is reminiscent of the strides toward professionalism that doctors took some 80 years ago.

"If you think about how long it took to professionalize medicine, it was a generation," said Albert Shanker, the president of the AFT. "This is the beginning of the generation that will professionalize teaching."

'Taking Major Steps'

James A. Kelly, the president of the teaching-standards board, agreed.

"The teaching profession is taking major steps to take responsibility for its own standards, for defining expertise and codifying it and measuring it," he said. "Having said that, though, I don't pretend that we're there yet. We have a long way to go."

The current reforms were spurred, in large measure, by an influential 1986 report from a task force of the Carnegie Forum on Education and the Economy.

The report, "A Nation Prepared: Teachers for the 21st Century," called for the establishment of the National Board for Professional Teaching Standards and sought changes in schools that would make teaching a more attractive job.

Since then, the drumbeat for increased student achievement has strengthened policymakers' attention to teaching. After all, high standards for students cannot be met without highly skilled teachers.

"This is the most important initiative to transform schooling going on in the country today," said Linda Darling-Hammond, a professor at Teachers College, Columbia University, and the executive director of the national commission on teaching. "We cannot do any of the other reforms if we don't do this."

She acknowledged a heightened rhetorical commitment to the importance of good teaching, but noted that decades of emphasis on the routine and less-skilled aspects of teaching still heavily influence how teachers and schools are managed.

Darling-Hammond observed that contemporary calls for teaching students to think critically, synthesize information, and create knowledge mirror the suggestions of progressive educators for transforming schools around 1900, and again in the 1930s and 1960s.

Every time, reforms were "killed by an underinvestment in teacher knowledge and school capacity," she wrote in a recent paper for the commission.

These failures led, in turn, to a backlash in favor of standardizing teaching and learning.

Linking Standards

NCATE has taken a leading role in pulling together and making coherent much of the effort to professionalize teaching.

The council has launched a $2 million project to link the three quality-assurance mechanisms in the field—accreditation, licensing, and advanced-certification standards—and to tie them to emerging benchmarks for student learning.

One strand of this New Professional Teacher Project involves revamping NCATE's standards for preparing teachers in mathematics, English, and other subject areas.

The new standards, to be created in partnership with subject-area groups, will express the knowledge and skills teacher candidates should have, rather than the content of courses that education schools should offer.

They also will be compatible with INTASC's standards for state licensure, which already have been incorporated into the accrediting body's guidelines for education schools. Those guidelines are scheduled to take effect in the fall.

> 'This is the most important initiative to transform schooling going on in the country today. We cannot do any of the other reforms if we don't do this.'

Arthur E. Wise, the president of NCATE, envisions a variety of uses for the performance-based standards for preparing teachers: as a beacon for education schools as they redesign their programs, as guidelines for NCATE to use in accrediting education programs, and as directions for states as they design new licensing systems.

As part of the New Professional Teacher Project, the accrediting group plans to hold a series of forums in several states that will gather a wide range of stakeholders in education to discuss plans for improving teacher education and licensure.

"There has not been an educational process to help people see the benefits of a serious quality-assurance system," Wise said.

Teacher education and teaching have suffered from "a pale imitation" of such a system, he said, and it is up to the states to fix the problem.

"The state is where the action is," he said.

Critics have charged that low state standards have allowed too many poor teacher education programs to produce graduates who then receive licenses to teach. Low standards also have given the public the damaging idea, Darling-Hammond said, that teaching does not involve any particular knowledge and skills.

One key to making teaching a profession, proponents believe, is establishing autonomous state boards

Devising a New Pay Structure for Teachers

Despite widespread dissatisfaction with the way teachers are paid, attempts to change the entrenched system of compensation have been highly controversial and fraught with problems.

In the 1980s, districts and states experimented with merit pay, career ladders, and incentive pay. Most of those efforts were resisted by teachers and failed to spread widely.

Education researchers at the University of Wisconsin at Madison hope to reverse that trend of controversy. With a $600,000 grant from the Pew Charitable Trusts, they are drawing on lessons from the private sector to devise a new compensation structure for teachers.

In trying to succeed where many have failed, the project has a big advantage: cooperation from the National Education Association and the American Federation of Teachers.

"We've always wanted to see if there was a better way to pay teachers," said Allan Odden, a professor of educational administration who is the principal investigator for the project, "and we've always screwed it up."

The project, which now has funding for two years, will take about six years, Odden estimated. The final phase will be to find school districts willing to try out the new pay models.

The National Board for Professional Teaching Standards also is participating in the project. Though it has no say over teachers' pay, the board has an interest in seeing plans developed that will provide financial incentives for teachers to seek certification.

Another group has been formed with other influential organizations, including the American Association of School Administrators, the principals' associations, the national and state school boards' associations, and the Council of Chief State School Officers.

The groups are holding parallel seminars to study pay plans in so-called high-performance organizations: businesses that have pruned their headquarters' staffs and given decisionmaking power to self-managed work teams. The payoff: increased productivity and better results.

Education is moving—slowly—in the same direction, with calls for streamlining central offices and giving teachers, administrators, and parents a much larger say in how their schools are run.

If teachers can be financially rewarded for becoming board certified, teaching will take a step toward the skill-based pay or pay-for-knowledge approach that decentralized companies typically use.

A new pay model could create five or six levels of performance between licensure and advanced certification, Odden suggested. School districts and states would have to invest heavily in professional development, which he believes should be controlled by schools.

The Wisconsin researchers will study a variety of pay plans:
● Skill-based pay or pay-for-knowledge. These systems pay workers for acquiring—and showing they have mastered—a set of skills and expertise.

The current salary schedule includes a kind of skill-based pay because teachers are paid for accumulating academic credits and years of service. But course work and seniority do not guarantee knowledge and skill, said Albert Shanker, the president of the AFT.

"We ought to move to a system where people who have knowledge and the ability to use it would be compensated on a different basis," he said.

Keith B. Geiger, the president of the NEA, agreed. "It's going to be problematic," he said, "but I think we owe it to the profession to give it our best shot."
● Group performance incentives. These provide bonuses to a school's entire faculty when student performance improves.
● Gain-sharing. These systems reward employees for working more efficiently. Odden said this pay plan could be used in combination with skill-based pay and group incentives.

to set standards for teacher education and licensing. Similar bodies, for example, regulate who can practice medicine and law.

Eleven states now have such standards boards for teaching, according to the NEA. The union has lobbied that teachers should make up a majority of the members of these boards.

In a new book, *A License to Teach: Building a Profession for 21st Century Schools*, Wise and Darling-Hammond argue that state legislatures and agencies, which traditionally have controlled standards in teaching, have "a conflict of interest in enforcing rigorous standards for entry to teaching, since they must ensure a warm body in every classroom—and prefer to do so without boosting wages."

Growing Knowledge Base

One reason teaching has made progress toward becoming a profession is a shift in the focus of research, experts say.

Instead of just doing surveys and crunching numbers, Darling-Hammond said, more researchers are visiting schools and talking to teachers. The change has helped build the knowledge base about practices that increase learning.

Until recently, teaching has lacked a professional consensus about good standards of practice, which is why standards have been lax, Darling-Hammond said.

"We're taking what we know about teaching that supports kids' learning and saying, 'My goodness, you ought to master that knowledge in teacher education, demonstrate you have it before you're licensed, and continue to develop it throughout your career'" she explained. The capstone for teachers would be receiving national-board certification in their field.

At the same time, education schools—often criticized as a weak link in preparing better teachers—have launched dozens of professional-development schools. In these schools, often likened to teaching hospitals, professors and classroom teachers work side by side to train new teachers and conduct research.

They have come to symbolize the closer connections between education schools and K-12 schooling that many experts believe are essential.

NCATE has received a grant to write standards for professional-development schools, which will be used in its accreditation process.

The national commission on teaching has found that some education schools are changing rapidly to focus on classroom practice, Darling-Hammond says. Many are using new assessments, including portfolios, to see whether their students can meet new standards for beginning teachers.

Demographic changes also favor continued movement toward professionalizing teaching. During the next decade, Darling-Hammond projects, more than 200,000 teachers will be hired each year.

Faculty members in education schools also are expected to retire in large numbers, making way for people who are themselves master teachers to prepare the next generation of teachers.

In the meantime, observers say, there is tremendous work to be done, particularly in devising new ways to determine how well teachers are doing their jobs.

New Ways of Testing

The national board's system, which involves portfolios, videotaped lessons, journals, and assessment-center exercises, has demonstrated several new ways of finding out what teachers know and can do.

Teachers find these methods more palatable than the competency tests that many states have imposed on them, and the methods are more likely to ensure that new teachers are ready for the challenges ahead, said Keith B. Geiger, the president of the NEA.

"People who are going to teach 7th graders better know something about adolescence, or they'll die real quick in the classroom, no matter how smart they are in math," he warned. "We've got to raise standards in pedagogy and the academic areas." ∎

From Education Week, *April 5, 1995*

54

Assessing Teachers

The National Board for Professional Teaching Standards pilots a new kind of assessment for teachers.

By Ann Bradley

In an annex of a downtown Methodist church in Austin, Tex., across the street from the state Capitol, three teachers are comfortably seated at a table with piles of paperback books in front of them. Across from them sits an interviewer, ready with a stack of prepared questions to ask. A video camera is trained on the entire group.

This is the new face of teacher assessment. There are no paper-and-pencil tests in sight. In this exercise, the teachers are judged on their ability to hold a productive discussion about the books with their peers.

The activity is one of a series the National Board for Professional Teaching Standards has developed to assess middle school teachers of English/language arts. The board plans to launch its system of voluntary certification for accomplished teachers on a limited basis next fall.

All told, the NBPTS plans to set standards for excellence in about 30 subject areas for students of all ages and to spend $50 million developing its certification system. The developers of the first assessment have now created and field-tested three components: a written examination of candidates' knowledge of their field; a portfolio showing their own and students' work from their schools; and performance exercises completed at an "assessment center."

From the results, the national board will decide which exercises to administer to the first candidates for certification. In the two days the Texas teachers

spent at the assessment center, each completed four exercises. Before arriving, each teacher also had taken the written test and prepared a portfolio. The process proved to be draining for many teachers, who put in an estimated 150 hours of work to finish the three components.

During a round table discussion about the assessments, one woman joked that, by the time she had finished, she felt like she "deserved another degree." "It's been a great deal of work," Ivey Mossell, who teaches in San Angelo, Tex., acknowledged. "But it has been interesting and enlightening."

'Cooperative Discussion'

The developers of the assessments—who are based at the University of Pittsburgh and the Connecticut Department of Education—tried to capture the essence of teachers' work through a variety of exercises. While the written examination and the portfolio drew directly on teachers' knowledge and experiences in their own schools, the assessment-center exercises were designed to examine their broader understanding of teaching.

For the "cooperative group discussion" exercise, for example, the teachers were told to imagine that they had been named to a curriculum-development committee in a mythical school. They were told that the school was in a metropolitan area and served a diverse group of students. They were also given a specific grade level and a theme for the unit of instruction they were to plan.

Each teacher had received eight novels ahead of time to read. To begin the exercise, they were given about an hour to prepare to discuss the books with other teachers. Their task was to decide which four of the books would be most suitable for the students in the fictional school, to justify why they had chosen or rejected each book, and to talk about how the books fit together.

The teachers then came together to talk about their recommendations, with the help of questions from the interviewer. It was clear from the discussion, which had a relaxed and friendly tone, that some of the teachers were thinking of their own students and not necessarily those described in the assignment. One teacher said, for example, that she thought a book would appeal to her rural students because it was laced with Biblical language.

Diversity Issues a Challenge

Removing themselves from their own classrooms and drawing on their general knowledge of how to teach language arts to early adolescents proved to be a challenge for most of the teachers here, in fact. One of the qualities that the assessments seek to identify in teachers is their ability to take students' genders, races, ethnicities, cultures, and socioeconomic levels into consideration in designing instruction.

The developers of the assessments have found that teachers either have "a real command of those areas, or they don't," said Raymond Pecheone, a Connecticut education department official who is developing the assessment package. "There is not an even distribution across all of the candidates."

In the essays, "we found that those topics were very difficult to try to assess," he said, "because many teachers haven't had a lot of experience with those types of activities. The answers didn't go into great depth."

As troublesome as they may be, multicultural issues were included in the board's vision of accomplished teaching simply because teachers think they are important, Pecheone noted. Part of the rationale for creating the board was to improve teachers' preparation and continuing professional development, he explained. Therefore, information from the certification process could be used to provide a new focus for training.

One of the most difficult exercises that teachers were asked to do here was the "instructional planning" activity, which focused on teachers' knowledge of language diversity. The teachers were given time to review a variety of materials that could be used to teach the topic to 7th graders. With those materials,

they were directed to select a focus for instruction and to design three activities for the students.

The interview was designed to explore the teachers' reasoning and to examine such issues as what difficulties might arise for the students and how the teacher would adjust for them. Although the activity was designed to tap teachers' knowledge of diversity and how it could be used to enrich students' understanding of themselves and others, two teachers who were observed downplayed the role of diversity in their interviews.

Instead, they appeared to interpret the exercise as an opportunity to highlight the similarities among people and to teach students not to be "prejudiced," as one teacher said.

In a third exercise, the teachers were provided with batches of students' writing to analyze. They were told to assume that they were 8th grade teachers at the beginning of a school year, perusing the papers for clues about the students whom they would now be teaching writing skills.

In the interview, the teachers were asked to talk about how they would instruct these students and develop their writing skills. They were asked to identify patterns that were characteristic of the papers in their entirety and also patterns of specific language elements, such as grammar, usage, and spelling.

The interviewers then asked the teachers a series of questions about these patterns and how they would help the students improve. The wording used in the exercise to distinguish between features common to the entire paper and those specific to language usage appeared to confuse some teachers.

Most teachers he interviewed, said Cliff Coan, a high school English teacher in DeLeon, Tex., realized what was being asked of them during the interview. But, he noted, some confusion appeared to stem from different terms that educators around the nation use for the same concepts. "I had to spend a lot of time saying, 'Could you clarify that?' because the terms we use may not be used everywhere," he said.

Coan said he found the exercise interesting because it simulated what teachers have to do during the first few days of the school year to make decisions about what their students already know and what they still need to learn. "Different people keep coming up with different ideas to work on," he said of the teachers he had interviewed, "and most of them seem to have some validity."

The final activity required teachers to step outside their own experience perhaps more than the others. It was designed to gauge their ability to analyze instruction and offer solutions to a beginning teacher. For the exercise, the teachers were given a written commentary prepared by the new teacher that described what she was trying to accomplish in her classroom. They were then shown a videotape of a scene from her classroom and given time to prepare written feedback on her instructional approach, her performance in the classroom, and her ability to meet her stated goals.

In the essays, the teachers were instructed to make specific recommendations about what the teacher still needed to learn and how she could improve her classroom instruction.

In addition to completing the four exercises, each teacher who came to the assessment center here also participated in a round table discussion to talk about their experience with compiling portfolios and with the assessment process in general.

Although the teachers had spent dozens and dozens of hours working on the assessments, they still expressed skepticism about the concept of national teacher certification. Texas teachers are particularly leery of another type of test, they said, because they have been subjected to so many of them in their state.

One reading teacher in San Antonio praised the group-discussion exercise, noting that it "teaches the need for teachers to get together and plan."

But she cautioned that she has "mixed feelings" about national certification, worrying that teachers might price themselves out of jobs if they receive bonuses for becoming certified. Other teachers worried that, without a financial reward, teachers would be unlikely to subject themselves to the work required to obtain certification.

In Texas, the distinction between teaching reading and teaching English could be problematic, some teachers here said, because the assessments place a great deal of emphasis on student writing.

Judy Gasser, a language arts coordinator for a regional service center who acted as an interviewer, said the Texas curriculum "doesn't always lend itself to as much writing as is indicated" in the assessments. "It's a bit of a challenge for the ones who are straight reading teachers," she observed.

A Catalyst for Change

A 6th grade teacher also mentioned during the group discussion that her primary emphasis in class is grammar, while the assessments drew heavily on teaching literature.

Teachers of English as a second language and special education also expressed some concern that the other types of activities students do in their classrooms were not reflected in the assessments' emphasis on reading and writing. For some teachers, however, the assessments' emphasis on writing caused them to take a second look at what they expect of their students.

Mossell, the San Angelo teacher, said her participation with the assessment field test made her realize that many of her students, who have limited proficiency in English, were not writing at all. Compiling her portfolio, she said, "caused me to reassess the writing portion of my program. And I realized I did not have one."

Since that time, Mossell said she has been doing research to identify techniques to help her students understand the rudiments of sentence structure with an eye toward writing in the future.

That kind of realization and effort to improve is what the national board is looking for, Pecheone of the Connecticut education department said. "One of the major reasons why we do performance assessment is that it can really be a catalyst for professional development and a way in which teachers can share their practice," he said. "If all it was was getting a certificate of accomplishment, and we didn't inform the profession," he added, "I'm not sure whether the national board really would meet its goals. It has got to do both." ■

From Education Week, *Nov. 11, 1992*

55.

Test Pilots

When two teachers agreed to try out assessments developed by the National Board for Professional Teaching Standards, they didn't know they were in for a bumpy ride.

By Ann Bradley

I t is a cold, blustery day in late November, and teachers Rick Wormeli and Diane Hughart are perched on the tattered brown plaid couch that takes up one end of the paneled trailer that is Wormeli's classroom. Their laps are full of papers, folders, and cardboard boxes. They are feeling a bit overwhelmed. The two English teachers, colleagues at Herndon Middle School, located in a Virginia suburb of the nation's capital, have volunteered to take part in a project that is widely viewed as one of the most significant developments in the teaching profession in decades.

But just what that commitment means is only now becoming clear to them. On the strength of a little bit of information and a lot of curiosity, they and a handful of other teachers from around the nation have signed on to field-test new assessments developed by the National Board for Professional Teaching Standards. The board has spent the last seven years creating a system of voluntary national certification to recognize outstanding teachers. The assessments, which ultimately will determine who gets certified and who does not, are nothing like the paper-and-pencil tests so familiar to teachers. Instead, Wormeli, Hughart, and the other teachers participating in the pilot test will spend the next few months putting together portfolios of their best work in the classroom. These portfolios will include videotapes of exemplary lessons, samples of students' work, testimonies from col-

leagues, and the teachers' own written comments on their professional successes and failures.

Assembling the portfolios, Wormeli and Hughart are just beginning to realize, is going to involve a massive amount of work. And it must be done in a short time—the two months between mid-November and mid-January. But even that won't complete the process. In early March, Wormeli and Hughart—along with other participating teachers throughout the Washington, D.C., area—will sit for two days of assessments designed to simulate classroom and teaching situations. They won't find out whether they've made the grade until next fall.

But on this chilly day just after Thanksgiving, the eventual outcome of the long process is not something Wormeli and Hughart are worried about. They're still reading through what they are being asked to do, making sense of unfamiliar terminology, and creating filing systems to organize their work. Just knowing which tasks to tackle first requires much thought. Looking down at all the papers and his neatly labeled accordion file, Wormeli says, "Right now, we're feeling like we've sold our souls." Hughart nods in agreement.

Wormeli, Hughart, and four other teachers from the Fairfax County, Va., schools are getting started on their portfolios later than most of the national board candidates because the county was late in joining the field test. Hughart, half-jokingly, says she and Wormeli decided to take the plunge, despite the late timing, because they are both "overachievers" who like to test themselves against high standards. That's exactly what the assessments are all about: Teachers' work will be judged against standards—set by accomplished teachers—that reflect the best current wisdom about teaching and learning.

Establishing Standards for Teachers

The National Board for Professional Teaching Standards, in fact, was founded on the belief that teachers themselves should define what it means to be a professional. It was established in 1987, following recommendations made in a landmark report issued by a task force convened by the Carnegie Corporation of New York. Task-force members believed that in order for teaching to become a true profession, with the increased pay and responsibilities associated with professionalism, more rigorous standards for teaching had to be established.

The board, which has 63 members, the majority of whom are teachers, hopes that its certification system will strengthen teaching and improve student learning by creating standards that all teachers can strive to meet. National certification is seen not as an end in itself but as an opportunity for teachers to experience professional growth.

While the national board, as a private body, has no direct control over how school districts and states reward nationally certified teachers, it hopes that they will receive higher pay, new career opportunities that don't require them to leave the classroom, and increased flexibility in moving between states without having to take additional course work. A number of states and school districts are now beginning to discuss creating incentives and rewards for board-certified teachers.

The board plans to officially launch the certification system in 1995 with the two assessments that Wormeli and Hughart are helping test. One is for English language arts teachers, and the other is for generalists; both are for teachers of early adolescents. More than a dozen committees are currently working to set standards in other subject areas and grade levels; eventually, the national board plans to offer certification in more than 30 teaching specialties. The field test, board officials say, is designed to identify and smooth out the kinks involved in administering a nationwide assessment system. But if Wormeli and Hughart do well, they will be among the first teachers in the United States to receive national certification.

Hughart, an 8th grade teacher who made a mid-career switch to teaching four years ago at age 36, signed up for the project after reading in a newsletter for Fairfax teachers that the board was looking for volunteers. She'd been interested in national certification since first learning of the concept several years ago. "I'm more curious than anything," she says, "and I like the idea of trying something new and being involved." She also was attracted because the field test is free. (Next year, candidates for certification will pay $975 to undergo the assessments. The board hopes that eventually some or all of the fee will be subsidized by states or school districts.)

Wormeli, who is 33 and began teaching 7th grade this year after a decade in elementary school, was encouraged by the chairman of his school's English department to take part in the field test. He hopes that national certification will lead to a raise—although he knows there are no guarantees—and enable him to teach in any district without losing his pension contributions. The prospect of spending some time in "quiet introspection" about his work also appeals to him.

Neither of the teachers volunteered for lack of better things to do. Hughart, a single mother of two boys, ages 11 and 13, recently sold her house and is planning to move during the Christmas holidays. Because of renovations at school, she will have to move to a new classroom at about the same time. Wormeli is also anticipating life-altering events. His wife is expecting the couple's second child in the spring, and their house is on the market.

Hughart will be field-testing the assessment for English language arts teachers, Wormeli the one for generalists. For this, he will draw heavily on his years teaching at the elementary level. The national board process encourages candidates to collaborate. The process, after all, is designed to be a professional development exercise as well as a measure of expertise. Although they are pursuing different certifications, Hughart and Wormeli have decided to work together on their respective portfolios.

As they are about to find out, they'll need all the help and support they can get.

The Process Begins

In compiling their portfolios, teachers are expected to spend at least three weeks documenting their work with one class. So, one of the first decisions Wormeli and Hughart must make is which of their classes to focus on. Wormeli turns to Chuck Cascio, a Fairfax County teacher who works part time in the national board's Washington office, for advice. The Fairfax teachers volunteering for the field test will also receive some assistance from faculty members at George Washington University's school of education. The teachers aren't the only ones who stand to gain from these regular meetings. The academics hope to learn how they can make their teacher preparation programs more compatible with national certification and how they can best support teachers going through the process.

With Cascio's help, Wormeli decides to work with a class that includes a large number of students with learning disabilities. Although he knows it will be tough to document growth over a short time period with such students, he's aware that the assessment favors teachers who meet the needs of diverse kinds of learners. Hughart, searching for a diverse group of outgoing students, picks her sixth-period 8th graders.

Almost immediately, Wormeli and Hughart begin videotaping their classroom lessons, letting their students take turns with the cameras. They also start to write about their teaching. Through their collaboration, they quickly notice that the board expects different things from each of them. In general, Wormeli's assigned portfolio exercises are more open-ended than Hughart's. For example, Wormeli, the generalist, must complete a running written commentary on his work, while Hughart, the language arts specialist, is asked to fill in "activity charts" that describe her teaching. The teachers theorize that the difference stems from the subjects being assessed: The role of the English language arts teacher is much more defined than that of the generalist, who must teach all subjects.

Each night about 10, after bathing his toddler son and grading papers, Wormeli sits down at his home computer to write a two- to three-page commentary on the day's activities. It usually takes him about two hours to describe what he had planned to do and why and to reflect on whether it worked or not and why. The assignment seems to mesh perfectly with Wormeli's enthusiastic, effusive personality. He looks at every situation from a dozen angles and eagerly shares his material with the other participating teachers. He clearly wants to do well and quickly becomes known among his colleagues for overpreparing each exercise in the portfolio. "Am I doing what the assessors are looking for?" he wonders aloud at a meeting. "I would hate to go all the way through this and not have what I was supposed to have."

Hughart, on the other hand, only needs about 20 minutes a day to document her teaching. The charts she is using break the class period into segments and ask her to describe what she and her students are doing and why. Later, she'll write an eight-page commentary from notes. She's somewhat disappointed by the confines of the charts. They seem quite dull compared with the nightly writing that Wormeli finds so stimulating. She is currently enrolled in a graduate course on teachers as researchers and knows the value of reflection.

"The commentary provides a place for me to tell my story," Wormeli tells Hughart one day in his classroom. "I look forward to this."

At this point, Hughart doesn't share his enthusiasm. "This is really very bland to me," she complains. "It's humdrum. There's nothing in here about how I make my decisions. To me, reflection is what makes individual teachers different."

At first, videotaping is a novelty that adds an air of excitement to the teachers' classes. Students love taking turns operating the video cameras and being responsible for something they know is important. But the fun soon wears off. Hughart begins to feel stressed, knowing that she needs to capture a near-perfect lesson on tape. Her students, she notices, are not adjusting well to the camera; their discussions are inhibited or silly. And the portfolio-preparation process, sandwiched between Thanksgiving and the Christmas holidays, could not have come at a worse time. Students are restless, and their schedules are full. "These days," Hughart says in mid-December, "I have a sense of urgency with the camera. There are only so many days until the winter break, when I'd like to have it finished." It doesn't help that the taping of one particularly good lesson is interrupted by a fire drill.

Wormeli, who teaches in a narrow portable classroom, is having problems of his own. The dimensions of the room make videotaping difficult; there's no room for a tripod, so the camera is wedged onto a shelf. He decides to let students take turns taping sessions with the camera on their shoulders. This seems to work better.

As the teachers proceed with videotaping, writing, and gathering samples of students' work, they periodically take time to read the teaching standards that underlie the board's assessments. Hughart, especially, feels that the standards are in synch with Fairfax County's curricula. And the teachers read and reread the directions that describe what they're supposed to

> # The process encourages candidates to collaborate. It is designed to be a professional development exercise as well as a measure of expertise.

do with the enormous amounts of material they are collecting. At times, the requirements seem reasonable and doable. But other times, the directions seem too specific and demanding. Hughart wonders, "If you fail to do one little thing they were specific about, will you fail to be certified?"

Wormeli decides to videotape and write commentaries for four and a half weeks, even though the board only requires candidates to do it for three. During this time, he's preparing his students, in cooperation with their history teacher, for an independent research project. He teaches them how to pick a topic, narrow it down, conduct interviews, and use a narrative writing style. He also is teaching parts of speech and tries to work in time for free reading and journal writing.

One day, during a grammar lesson, he dresses up as "Adverb Man" and zips around modifying things. As he explains concepts and answers questions, he changes his voice. One day, he's a pirate; the next, a Frenchman.

Meanwhile, Hughart's 8th graders are beginning a drama unit, reading a play based on *The Diary of Anne Frank*. They keep their own diaries, read the play aloud, discuss the play's characters, and watch a documentary film called *The Life of Anne Frank*. They also write about their own families' traditions, since, in the play, the Franks celebrate Hanukkah. "I had to think of something that would show integration of reading, writing, speaking, listening, and viewing," says Hughart, who manages her classes with an easygoing, friendly style, encouraging but not dominating the discussions.

Because Hughart uses portfolios to help evaluate her students' writing, she feels sure that she won't have much trouble analyzing the work of three students, a national board requirement. But all the hours she has spent documenting her teaching have kept her from returning students' papers in a timely fashion. She realizes she may have to devote a little less time to the assessment project. "I am past the stage of trying for perfection," she confides to the other Fairfax teachers at a support meeting. "I am just trying to get it done."

A few days before Christmas vacation, the two teachers meet in Wormeli's crowded trailer for a quick catch-up session during their preparation periods. Hughart is feeling confident about completing the planning and teaching exercise. She has begun to collect students' writing to analyze.

Wormeli has been looking back at his career, trying to identify, as the assessment requires, two "transformative" experiences to write about. Today, though, he's bothered by something that happened recently, and he wants to know if he should mention it in some way in his portfolio. Borrowing a classroom exercise promoted by the Folger Shakespeare Library, he encouraged his students to compile a list of Shakespearian adjectives and then use them in some way to insult him. It was a big hit with the students, but it rubbed the mother of twin girls in his classes the wrong way. In fact, the parent was so bothered by the exercise that she requested a transfer for her daughters.

Hughart isn't sure that the episode is worth including. "You are trying to show a good side of you," she says. "And because it's unusual, I'm not sure it's a true picture of your teaching."

The Christmas holidays pass in a rush. Hughart and her children move during a snowstorm, which costs her four precious days of working time. And then she has to move out of her old classroom and into a new one, causing chaos at work as well as at home.

At the Wormeli household, there's not even time to put up a Christmas tree. Instead, the Wormelis tack up lights around their living room window and count the days until the portfolio must be mailed. "This vacation has been nonexistent," Kelly, Wormeli's wife, sighs. "After dinner every night, he disappears for the next five hours."

As the holiday break draws to a close, Wormeli is feeling pressure. Among other things, he's bothered because he has let his routine grading slide. Seated at his home computer one afternoon, surrounded by neat stacks of papers and professional journals, he reviews his progress. He has finished writing a description of the class he is monitoring, edited his first week of commentaries, and selected video vignettes to illustrate them. He has also decided what "transformative" experiences to describe—his graduate work in middle school philosophy and his efforts to integrate special education students into the "regular" classroom—and which service project to highlight: his work as a peer observer.

Seeing himself on videotape has been a strange experience. "When I come home and watch the tapes at night, I am horrified and worried and feeling disillusioned; I see all the problems," he explains. "But when I watch them two or three weeks later, it's not nearly as bad as I thought."

Reflecting on Teaching

Wormeli's next task is to select the three students whose work he will discuss. He stacks students' papers into groups—high, middle, and low achievers—hoping to pick one student from each to analyze. Although his hours are filled with gathering materials and making decisions about how to use them, Wormeli has already learned a few lessons about his teaching. He has discovered that the way he organizes reading discussion groups doesn't work. And he has decided to scrap his current vocabulary book, which teaches words out of context, and use instead words from students' other subjects. On a less specific level, he worries that he doesn't give students enough feedback. "I don't give them or myself the opportunity to think reflectively and let them know where they stand," he laments.

But he has also noticed strengths that he believes will work in his favor as he seeks certification as a generalist. Because of his elementary background, he integrates other subjects into his English class well. His students write about math, science, and history each quarter. And when his 7th graders caught Jurassic Park fever, Wormeli taught a lesson on DNA.

He is making good progress on his portfolio, but the Jan. 14 mailing deadline weighs heavily on him. He knows that the last weekend before the deadline is booked up; his church needs a new pastor, and he has agreed to spend those days helping in the search. "Some days," he sighs, "I feel so burdened down by the load."

The weekend before the Friday, Jan. 14, deadline, Hughart can see the light at the end of the tunnel. She's relieved to have finished documenting her work with her sixth-period class. Now, she's trying to select one taped class period to use as an illustration. She's leaning toward the lesson that was interrupted by the fire drill because it shows her students working well in groups on the Anne Frank project. Each group randomly drew the name of a character from the play, found what the author said about the character, wrote down the information and defined any new words, drew a picture of the person, and recorded something the character said that reflected his or her personality. The students worked productively together as Hughart circulated around the room answering their questions.

Hughart also has picked the three students whose writing she will analyze: a boy in her gifted-and-talented class, a girl from the Dominican Republic who speaks English in dialect, and a boy from a regular English class. The three students have all shown improvement since the beginning of the year. The gifted student learned to revise his written work. The Dominican girl developed greater fluency in her writing, learning to elaborate and to use correct verb tenses. And the remaining student began the year with nearly illegible handwriting, which is now substantially neater.

Looking closely at many students' work, she explains, has made her feel "more secure" about her teaching methods. Her favorite exercise was a discussion she had with a group of students after reading *Flowers for Algernon*, a science fiction story by Daniel Keyes. The fifth-period class is one of her most challenging: a group of lively, talkative adolescents with a wide range of academic abilities. Some have physical disabilities, and one girl can't sit next to boys because of her religion. With this group, Hughart says, she was able to elicit a genuine literary discussion of free-flowing ideas and responses. "Through this discussion," she writes in her portfolio, "the students were making connections between the character and their own experiences ... and were able to recognize the universality of the theme and the pertinence of it toward their lives."

On Jan. 11, four days before the portfolios must be mailed, Hughart, Wormeli, and three other Fairfax County teachers participating in the field test get together. The atmosphere is festive—they are almost giddy—because the end is so near. Four of the five have worked in pairs, an advantage they say has kept them going. "If I didn't have Diane, it would be very difficult for me," Wormeli acknowledges. "Both of us have the same mentality, and she could interpret things for me."

But there's also an underlying note of tension, especially as Wormeli and other generalist candidates compare their work. Because their directions were less specific than those for the English language arts teachers, there is more room for interpretation—and possibly error—in their portfolios. Wormeli's teaching and learning commentary is 66 pages long. One of the other teachers has written six pages; another, only one page. Wormeli is astonished. "I'm a little troubled that we could have such different interpretations of it, and yet it could still be acceptable," he says. "That's really subjective."

Wormeli has other things to worry about, as well. Buyers have just signed a contract to purchase his house, so he has to rush home to conduct final negotiations. And tomorrow, his son has to have tubes surgically placed in his ears. There's always Friday to look forward to, though. The Wormelis have lined up a babysitter and are dreaming about a quiet post-deadline dinner together.

At this point, Hughart is disappointed with her product. She doesn't have a letter-quality printer and worries that her work doesn't look polished enough. And the directions for putting together the materials are intimidating. "I thought I would be proud of it," she says, "but I'm not. I feel like it's not good enough." And then, she adds, "I don't know if I'd want to do this again." Both she and Wormeli believe that future candidates should have an entire school year to put their portfolios together.

Before breaking up, the Fairfax teachers share information about which local post offices stay open until midnight. The knowledge that they have until midnight on Friday to mail their portfolios seems to buoy everyone. They are all eager to send off the fruits of their labors.

The Finished Product

When Friday night finally comes, Hughart beats Wormeli to the post office—arriving at 11 p.m. The previous two nights, she turned in at 3 a.m. and 2 a.m., and she's exhausted. Her last few hours were spent labeling the materials and putting them together in the right order. She found herself constantly snacking on junk food. Driving through the winter night on her way to the post office, she kept thinking, "I can't believe I'm doing this. I can't believe I'm doing this."

Wormeli finally arrives at 11:30. His dreams of a night out with his wife are shot. The previous two days have passed in a blur of realtors, doctors, and substitute teachers. (Fairfax County arranged for each candidate to have subs for two days.) He's running on empty after a nearly sleepless week. Today, he spent hours making copies of materials on his father's copier—"having anxiety attacks every hour." He and his wife combed carefully through his 66-page teaching account, making sure that each reference to students' work was accurate. At the last minute, he realized he'd forgotten to copy an important document describing his work as a peer observer and had to rush back to his parents' house. Finally, at a quarter to 11, he left for the 25-minute drive to the post office. "The whole way there," he says, "I kept saying, 'Don't go fast and get in an accident. It's not worth it.'"

As Wormeli enters the post office, he sees two of the other Fairfax teachers, and they all burst out laughing. One of the teachers, worried that the portfolio might get lost, is trying unsuccessfully to persuade the postmaster to insure it for $600. Wormeli has a postal clerk securely tape his package closed, pays $7.45 for postage, and walks out—numb.

On the way home, he stops at McDonald's and celebrates quietly with a vanilla milkshake.

The Northern Virginia weather, typically mild in winter, takes pity on the tired teachers and delivers heaps of snow, forcing schools to shut down for several days the week following the deadline. Hughart makes home-cooked meals for her kids and curls up with them to watch videos. Wormeli can't rest; he and his wife have just purchased a new house, and there are details to wrap up. He spends the rest of his time grading student papers that have piled up.

After a few days' reflection, Hughart is feeling cheerier about her portfolio. She enjoyed meeting new people from George Washington University and her school district, and she learned some things about her students from looking closely at their work and gathering information on their backgrounds. "There is always more to know," she says.

For Wormeli, examining his own professional development was a worthwhile activity that helped him clarify who he is as a teacher. Exploring ways to integrate other subjects into his lessons was particularly exciting. "I can't turn it off," he says. And writing about his teaching, rather than just thinking about it on the way to work, proved a powerful experience. "Writing it out solidifies your own ideas," he says, "and gives you the vocabulary and the structure by which to analyze something."

But the time constraints, he notes, were too severe. In fact, he would not go through the process again unless he were given more time. Hughart admits that she considered giving up but feared disappointing the university professors who were so interested in her work.

The return to normalcy is short-lived for the two teachers. By mid-February, they are already gearing up for the assessment center activities, which will take place at George Washington University over two full weekend days in early March. After receiving information from the national board, they have homework to do.

Wormeli has received a copy of SimCity, an interactive computer software program that simulates community development. Users can build cities from scratch or resurrect San Francisco after the 1906 earthquake. Wormeli's task is to figure out how it could best be used by his students. The problem for Wormeli isn't a shortage of ideas—it's knowing that, to actually use SimCity, his students would need far more access to computers than they currently have. "It's hard to be motivated," he says, "when you know it's just a wisp of smoke."

Hughart, meanwhile, needs to read eight novels for young adolescents—among them *The Red Pony,* by

---

Examining his own professional development was a worthwhile activity that helped Wormeli clarify who he is as a teacher.

John Steinbeck, and *The Pigman,* by Paul Zindel—which she will be asked about at the assessment center. Although she is already familiar with some of the books, she plans to read each one. She simply wants to be able to do her best. At this point, Hughart says she's not thinking much about whether she will actually be certified, but she concedes that she may not handle it very well if she doesn't make it.

She knows that certification will not bring any immediate rewards—other than the sense of accomplishment from a job well-done. In fact, board certification doesn't really have much meaning yet. Fairfax County hasn't developed any rewards for board-certified teachers, although those who are participating in the field test will get credit toward the requirements they must fulfill to renew their teaching licenses. "It will be a long time before this has real importance," Hughart acknowledges, "and that's OK."

In his characteristic zealous style, Wormeli decides to study the textbooks for every core subject in the 5th through 8th grades to brush up on his subject knowledge. He also reviews the videotape he made for his portfolio because he has been told that he will have to answer questions about it at the assessment center.

Although he is concerned about whether he will have enough time to complete the exercises, Wormeli is excited at the prospect of meeting other certification candidates and trading "war stories." He has decided to spend $138 of his own money to stay at a hotel near the university so he can have peace and quiet before the big days.

Like Hughart, Wormeli knows the rewards for national certification are down the road. But he can think of things he'd like if he does get certified, and they are embarrassingly modest for a teacher of his caliber. He'd like, for example, to be paid to be an assessor for other board candidates next year. And he'd also like for his school system to foot the bill for him to attend professional conferences.

On Saturday, March 5, Hughart rides to the assessment center with another Fairfax County candidate. They arrive at 7 a.m. and are asked to show identification. This tickles them. "We said, 'Yeah, like you could pay someone to take this test for you,' " Hughart says, laughing.

After taking two, two-hour written examinations, Hughart finds a discussion with an assessor a refreshing change of pace. She answers questions about

Wormeli felt as if he had climbed a mountain: 'I have an exhausted ache all over, but I'm tingly with what I have done.'

samples of students' writing, pointing out their strengths and weaknesses and how she would help the students improve. The discussion is videotaped for later evaluation. Overall, Hughart feels comfortable about the assessments but a little rushed at times. Still, by the end of the day, she is dazed. "After a lot of concentration, I get to the point where I am staring at people," she says. Saturday night, she unwinds over dinner with a friend.

Sunday's assessments begin with a written analysis of a videotaped lesson taught by another teacher. "I was impressed with the fact that it really was an actual class videotape," Hughart says. "I don't know what I expected, but it was nice because it was the real thing and not a setup." After her final written examination, she participates in a small-group discussion of the novels she read. The discussion, she says, feels lifelike—actually, better than real life. The 45 minutes allotted for the exercise is more time than most teachers at Hughart's school generally have to plan together.

When she walks out of the center at the end of the second day, Hughart feels like the pioneer the national board says she is. "I really did finally feel a sense of achievement," she says.

Wormeli's weekend gets off to a rocky start. The day before the assessment activities begin, he receives a letter from the national board telling him that, due to lack of time, he won't be evaluated on the videotaped lesson that was in his portfolio. He's disappointed and a little angry to receive such late notice; his preparation for that part of the assessment has been a waste of time.

After checking into the hotel late Friday night, Wormeli spends a few hours reading civics and physics textbooks. He wakes up the next morning feeling nervous. The day begins with a curriculum exercise that has Wormeli and other candidates discussing how they would create a thematic unit. Then, he is asked to write an essay describing how he would develop the theme drawing on one of three topics—systems of government, ecosystems, and the influences of the media—that he was told in advance to brush up on. Next, he takes the first of three one-hour subject-matter examinations. The day ends with a three-and-a-half-hour analysis of a mathematics teacher. During the first hour, he watches a videotape of the teacher at work in the classroom and reads a narrative in which the teacher describes her instruction. Wormeli spends the rest of the time writing a response to her teaching, suggesting strategies that might be more effective and recommending ways to incorporate the arts into the lesson. The videotape and teacher's narrative are very much like the ones Wormeli submitted in his own portfolio.

When he finishes, Wormeli is so foggyheaded that he gets lost trying to find his hotel. He's thwarted in his attempt to buy dinner; the cheapest entree on the hotel restaurant menu costs $18.95, and he only has $15 in his wallet. Finally, he orders pizza, talks to his wife on the phone for an hour, and crashes at 9 p.m.

The next day is just as long, starting with an assessment of the candidates' writing proficiency. The one-hour time limit frustrates Wormeli. "We never, ever, ever teach kids to do things in one hour," he explains. "For a good writing piece, you would give kids at least a week." He finds it odd, at best, that the cutting-edge assessment would be "such a contrast to the standards."

The SimCity exercise, which Wormeli calls "the bane of his existence," comes next, followed by two content examinations. As he finishes, Wormeli feels the way he does after climbing a mountain. "I have an exhausted ache all over," he says, "but I'm tingly with what I have done." It's a good feeling, but it doesn't compare, he says, with how it felt to finish his master's degree. "It's not like I have rocketed ahead."

Looking back on the whole experience, Hughart feels that the assessments tied in naturally with her portfolio. For Wormeli, however, the two steps were totally different. And he preferred the portfolio over the assessment.

The national board will pay close attention to such

comments from teachers who participated in the field test. The goal of the trial run, after all, was to learn as much as possible about both the assessments themselves and the operation of the certification system. In general, says Valarie French, the board's vice president for assessment operations, the field test ran smoothly at 26 sites across the nation.

But there were some glitches, among them the last-minute decision not to conduct interviews with generalist candidates on their own videotapes. Including that exercise would have meant a 12-hour day at the assessment centers, French says, so the interviews will be done later. Board officials also have heard complaints about the strict rules enforced by the proctors monitoring the assessments. This was necessary, French says, to ensure test security and standardization across the sites. But, she adds, the policy most likely will be revised.

Wormeli's complaint that the timed writing assessments seemed to violate good teaching practice was also mentioned by other teachers. But French says the assessment center wasn't intended to be an instructional situation. The point of the written assessments was to see what teachers could do under time constraints, responding to a question they hadn't seen before. In the portfolios, she notes, teachers had plenty of opportunities to prepare drafts and rewrite their work.

"We have to do a better job of describing our expectations for the assessment center," she says, "so that at least the candidates will be better informed and acknowledge that we understand that if we were asking, 'How would you get the best performance out of students?' this isn't what you would do."

In the future, candidates likely will have more time to complete their portfolios—at least six months, French guesses. That would give them much more latitude in deciding which lessons to focus on. Until practicing teachers assembled the portfolios, the national board could only guess how long completing the exercises would take. Teachers reported spending about 100 hours on the portfolios, twice what the board had estimated.

In the end, 545 teachers—out of 1,500 who received materials—completed the portfolio, far fewer than the board had hoped. "We're certainly very proud of the people who stuck with this and completed it on time," French says.

The national board and its senior officials sent a couple of congratulatory letters to the teachers who took part in the field test, thanking them for their hard work. Although she knows that the intention of the letters was good, Hughart says she felt a little "degraded" by a suggestion in one that undergoing the national board's assessments should have changed her teaching. "It's like they think you need to change," she says, "or that their purpose is to change teachers." The process, she notes, taught her some things that she plans to incorporate into her teaching. But, she adds, it wasn't a "major, earth-shattering event" in her professional life.

Now that it's all over, though, both Hughart and Wormeli want very much to make the grade. They won't find out until next fall. "I will doubt myself if I don't pass," Wormeli confides. "This tested true abilities in teaching." ■

From Education Week, *April 20, 1994*

56

The Spoils of Success

Teachers of the Year are often lured from the classroom by more money and the chance to reach a wider audience.

By Joanna Richardson

Last summer, the syndicated columnist Colman McCarthy wrote an editorial imploring Rae Ellen McKee, the 1991 national Teacher of the Year, to shun corporate job offers—and a spot on the lecture circuit—and remain in the classroom. "Please, stay put," wrote McCarthy. "You're more needed by your children at Slanesville Elementary than in front of a microphone or behind a corporate desk."

Soon after the column was published, says McKee, she was bombarded with hundreds of letters of advice from across the country. Many of those with careers outside education agreed with the columnist and urged the West Virginia native to continue teaching. But "most of the letters I received from teachers," she says with surprise, "encouraged me not to stay in the classroom."

She says she believes the teachers, in a nod to the power of celebrity, thought McKee could "use her influence to make changes." And a few acknowledged that the six-digit salaries she had been offered would be a welcome fringe benefit. So despite McCarthy's pleas, McKee took the teachers' advice and accepted offers to speak on behalf of teachers and teaching.

She is not alone. Although most Teachers of the Year remain in the classroom, many decide to pursue other activities in administration, in higher education, and—like McKee—on the lecture circuit. "They go to other areas, perhaps, but they never leave education," says John Quam, the director of the Teacher of the

Year Program for the Council of Chief State School Officers. "They just broaden their activities."

McKee says that her new career has enabled her to make more of a difference in education by spreading her message beyond her students. But she acknowledges that the added income—a considerable boost over her $20,000 salary as a remedial-reading teacher in a rural school—has helped ease the pain of the transition.

"At the heart, I think [McCarthy] very much understood how I felt" about teaching, she says now. "But I don't think he realized how little money I've made. I've been the first one not afraid to admit that."

Like many Teachers of the Year, McKee says that her life began to change when she won her award in April 1991. The offers from educational associations, universities, state governments, and corporations were overwhelming.

But it was not the money or the fame that lured her away from Slanesville Elementary School, in the northwestern corner of West Virginia, she contends. "I wanted to be involved in changing instructional tactics," she says.

To that end, McKee has been traveling around the country speaking to groups about what she knows best: teaching. "I had always been kind of worldly, trying to bring ideas back into my school," she says. But now she is exporting her knowledge to the outside world.

McKee hopes to bring to teachers the message that their work is significant. And she says she aims to shatter stereotypes about the profession. "I think it's important for society to see me as articulate and professional ... not as a schoolmarm," she adds.

On leave from her teaching job since she won her award, McKee commands $2,000 an appearance for her speaking engagements. While she is still based in West Virginia, by all accounts the former teacher is leading a corporate life. Her community, in the heart of Appalachia and just 10 miles from where she was raised, is amazed that "I'm riding on airplanes and I have a fax machine," she remarks.

Now, she has two publishing contracts to develop stories she used as teaching tools. And a national book tour could be imminent.

Despite all the excitement, she says she has not considered leaving Slanesville. "My heart is in West Virginia, so I feel like I want to try to bring about change [here]," she says. "We need to retrain and reinvigorate our teachers."

McKee says she has considered looking for a county-level position in educational policy. And she has not ruled out going back to the classroom. "It's a shame I can't be paid more for what I like to do and what I do well," she observes. "But I think I will eventually go back to the classroom, or I'll run out of things to talk about."

Terry Weeks taught social studies at Central Middle School in Murfreesboro, Tenn., just south of Nashville, when he was named the 1988 Teacher of the Year. But he has since moved on to other education-related pursuits. Now, Weeks is "four or five blocks away" from the middle school, at the department of educational leadership at Middle Tennessee State University. He teaches a course in social studies methods there and is working toward a doctorate in curriculum and supervision.

"During my travels [as Teacher of the Year], I had the opportunity to speak to several college classes," Weeks says. "In my interaction with them, I saw their readiness to learn, and I came to the realization that maybe I had something to give" them. "Now the spark inside me burns a little brighter because of the freshness" of a new career, he adds.

Though Weeks says he was "desiring a challenge" even before he won the award, he says being Teacher of the Year "cast a light" on some hidden strengths. And "if you have talents that extend beyond the four walls of the classroom," Weeks says, "you might want more."

As a teacher, "you tend to think you have very little

to offer ... but the desire to reach for the stars and advance is always there," he adds.

In teacher education, there is the opportunity to create a "ripple effect," Weeks explains. "My influence extends out further than it did before. And if I have an impact on these teachers-in-training, then they will go out and make a difference with even more people," he reasons.

Donna Oliver has a similar philosophy toward education. She got involved in teacher training at a local college in 1988, the year after she was recognized as Teacher of the Year. "I was convinced that I had a greater effect there," says Oliver, who was a biology teacher at Hugh M. Cummings High School in Burlington, N.C., when she was tapped for the national award.

Now she is working on her doctorate in curriculum and teaching at the University of North Carolina at Greensboro and is directing the teacher education program at nearby Bennett College. She says she was reluctant to leave her classroom to accept a short-term post in higher education. But once the switch was complete, "I knew immediately this was the area I needed to be in," she says.

Bennett is "historically African-American and all female," adds Oliver, "so I had a unique opportunity to train this group as teachers." And "every time I touch one life there, I can multiply that by 20," she remarks.

Oliver, like her successors, says she did not look at the teaching honor as "a way out," but rather an "invigorating experience." "I'd say 99 percent of those [named Teacher of the Year] would stay in the classroom," she adds. "I think they just get into other areas of the field."

A handful of former Teachers of the Year have tackled careers as college instructors, educational consultants, or administrators, according to the Council of Chief State School Officers. And some choose to continue on a speaking circuit while they are teaching part time.

"I encourage the teachers the year after [the award] not to do anything drastic," says Quam, the program's director. But "what makes many of them so special is they can move among so many worlds." And, says Quam, there is no reason for the teachers to feel divided by that freedom. "They are not just teachers or administrators or trainers of teachers," he remarks. "They're educators." ∎

From Education Week, *Dec. 2, 1992*

57.

Dynamic Duo

Two teachers start a feisty newspaper, an experimental school, and a reform movement to change their schools.

By Karen Diegmueller

I t's a late winter day in Milwaukee, and a brilliant sun has elevated the temperature to a balmy 50 degrees—a rarity for these climes. All along Lake Drive, the road that hugs the Lake Michigan shoreline, people are bicycling, tossing Frisbees, walking, and celebrating the golden weather. But holed up inside a two-story red brick building several miles from the lake, a dozen men and women resist the promise of spring and concentrate on the task at hand.

They are volunteers, dressed in the uniform of the day—jeans, flannel shirts, sweatshirts, and sneakers. Some wear buttons touting a particular cause. A 3-month-old boy naps cozily atop a formica conference table while his mother works. In these cramped quarters, haphazardly decorated with mismatched furniture, posters, and plants suspended in macramé hangers, they pass the afternoon proofreading copy, writing, and typing corrections into a computer.

Were it two decades ago, this could easily be a conclave of anti-war activists. Despite the wrinkles and graying hair, these men and women are clearly agitators. But unlike their counterparts from the 1960s, the people gathered here are not outsiders. They agitate within the system. Their cause: to reform the Milwaukee public schools. They are the editors and publishers of a first-of-its-kind newspaper, a periodical produced by an independent group of educators. Collectively, they spend hundreds of hours each month

getting out their message of reform to colleagues and the community at large.

Two among them—Bob Peterson and Rita Tenorio—exemplify the passion and energy that has driven *Rethinking Schools* since the quarterly tabloid was started six years ago.

Peterson and Tenorio have been at the forefront of school reform in Milwaukee for nearly a decade. They co-founded *Rethinking Schools* in 1986 and a year later helped establish a nationwide organization for educators and parents seeking to change public education. Then in 1988, the two helped create the experimental Fratney Street School, where they are putting the principles and ideas they preach into practice. And last year, they headed a reform slate that gained control of the local teachers' union.

Says Anita Simansky, a volunteer proofreader for *Rethinking Schools* and a guidance counselor in the nearby Kenosha public school system: "These are people who, when they were very young, decided on a lifetime conviction of putting a lot of time and energy into trying to change the world."

People who have known Peterson for a long time say it's only natural that he grew up to be some sort of reformer. That he did so as a school teacher is another matter entirely.

Peterson was raised in Madison, Wis., in the late 1960s and early 1970s when it was the heartland's hotbed of student activism. At Madison West High

School, he worked for student rights and against the Vietnam War. Peterson thought of high school itself as an infringement of his rights, and he rebelled by participating in sit-ins and walkouts over the dress code and other issues. "For the most part," he says, "I really despised school."

Nonetheless, after high school, Peterson took a job as a teacher's aide in Milwaukee. His first day on the job did little to improve his opinion of public schools. It happened to coincide with the first day of busing to desegregate the school system. Black students were being bused to his predominantly white high school. The bus arrived late, and as the wary students emerged, a physical education teacher stood at the school door noisily demanding that they go get tardy slips. "I couldn't believe it," Peterson says. "Here are these kids, they're scared, and this gym teacher is yelling at them."

Surprising even himself, Peterson subsequently enrolled in the University of Wisconsin at Milwaukee, got a degree, and began teaching in a city school in 1980.

Like Peterson, Tenorio had not set her sights on a career in teaching while growing up in the Milwaukee suburbs. But as a young woman coming of age on the verge of the women's movement, it was one of three career options suggested by her high school counselors. "They told me I could be a teacher, a social worker, or a nurse," she recalls. She chose social work. But during her field experience at the University of Wisconsin in Milwaukee, she discovered how much she enjoyed children. So, Tenorio switched majors and, in the early 1970s, took her first full-time teaching job at an all-black, inner-city parochial school.

She liked the work. Her students' parents had high expectations for them and were actively involved in their education. But the pay was bad; after eight years at the school, she was only making $8,000 a year. To gain some financial security and to get involved in a new bilingual education program, Tenorio decided to move to the public schools.

The switch, however, was not all positive. She was surprised to find that parental expectations and involvement in her new school were both disappointingly low. And she was soon disenchanted with the curriculum and pedagogy the district imposed. At the parochial school, she had been free to use components of what is now known as the whole language approach

to instruction. But not at her new public school. It seemed that each year, the district added another basal reader to get through. "I really resisted having to do some of the things public schools said we had to do," says Tenorio, whose principal gave her some leeway. "At times, it really did feel like I was a subversive. If there was a choice between painting on an easel or [completing] two workbook pages, in my mind, there was no choice."

Peterson and Tenorio met in 1980 at a meeting of the city's human relations committee and quickly realized they shared many of the same educational

Rita Tenorio says *Rethinking Schools* was created to challenge every teacher in the school system, including the union leadership. In the publication, she says, "We try to offer a vision of what we think should take place in public schools."

philosophies and concerns, including an unhappiness with the city's public school system. "We sort of connected at that point," Tenorio says. Strengthened by their minialliance, both plunged into more civic and school activities.

In the mid-1980s, Peterson and Tenorio began meeting regularly with a group of educators who shared their frustrations—both with the school system and with the lack of leadership in the teachers' union. The Milwaukee school district was plagued with all the problems of major urban districts: rampant truancy; a severe dropout problem; declining test scores; low grade-point averages; and a growing minority enrollment coupled with a lack of minority teachers. The central office and the school board were formulating reform plans, but without much input from teachers or their union.

Peterson, Tenorio, and their colleagues decided they needed to find a way to stir up the waters and get more people involved—some sort of sustained way to promote their ideas. So, the idea for *Rethinking Schools* was born.

As one member of the group would later write: "*Rethinking Schools* is the child of our frustration with how little voice teachers are allowed in the debates over what is and what should be happening in the schools. In Milwaukee, as elsewhere, the public schools are in deep trouble. But most of the people authoritatively offering solutions to the public have been central office officials, legislators, and businesspeople. When the blue ribbon commissions are established to investigate the schools and offer reforms, they usually include only one or two classroom teachers, often invited as an afterthought. As pawns rather than respected colleagues in the search for school reform, teachers often feel isolated and powerless."

The newspaper was created to end the sense of isolation and impotence and make teachers central players in reform. "We no longer wanted to be on the defensive all the time on school issues," says Peterson. "We wanted to have a vehicle in which we could begin to address in a pro-active way issues that affect teachers and parents."

The first idea was to produce something like an academic journal. But that idea soon gave way to a newspaper format, which seemed more appropriate for their mission and more accessible to teachers and the community. Moreover, the availability of desktop publishing software would enable them to do much of the work themselves.

Once a format was established, the group developed a statement of purpose, which still appears in nearly its original form in every issue under the headline "Who We Are." The educators vigorously debated whether their publication would incorporate a cross section of viewpoints or speak with one voice. In the end, they decided that unity would be more powerful.

They chose not to shy away from confrontation. Tenorio's "Confessions of a Kindergarten Teacher," the lead article in the first issue, set the rebellious tone for the publication. In it, she revealed her pedagogical transgression—forsaking the basal reader.

In the early days, the editors didn't know if *Rethinking Schools* would survive. When the newspaper first went to press in the 1986-87 school year, the group didn't have enough money to pay the printer. What little they had was scrounged up from house parties, donations, and $10 voluntary subscriptions.

When most of the writing was completed for each issue, the educators, who had but a fleeting knowledge of journalism and the production process, would set up shop in one of the editors' apartments.

David Levine, a former Milwaukee teacher and a member of the original group, recalls one of the early deadline periods: "For the next four days, my small Milwaukee flat would cease being a home in any normal sense of the word. Every flat surface—kitchen table, study desk, borrowed card table—was covered with layout paper. Extra lamps had been imported to augment my dim lighting and an ugly brown filing cabinet had displaced my living room rocking chair. I would have no place to cook dinner, no privacy, and little rest. I was entering a temporary throwback to my early days of political activism, when we cheerfully let the greater cause jostle and shove personal life into the corner."

The lack of money and amenities were not the only obstacles. Initially, the teachers were also concerned about repercussions from administrators who might take umbrage at the hard-edged copy. After the second issue was published, Peterson was summoned to his principal's office. Although personally supportive of the endeavor, the principal warned him to be cautious. As Peterson recalls, the principal said: "It's like the McCarthy era down at central office. Just tell your people to be very careful."

But nothing untoward occurred. In fact, a member of the original group, Cynthia Ellwood, was later moved, under a new district administration, into the central office as coordinator of a K-12 curriculum reform project. She subsequently became the school system's curriculum director, resigning from the newspaper's staff to avoid any potential conflict of interest.

Many who know the teachers doubt that political repercussions would have quieted them anyway. Says Erin Krause, a newspaper volunteer who teaches with Peterson and Tenorio: "They aren't afraid to step on people's toes."

Nothing was immune from scrutiny. Even the Milwaukee Teachers' Education Association became the target of their criticism, which produced cries of alarm from within the union. According to Tenorio, many union officials were convinced that *Rethinking Schools* had been created as a vehicle to attack and undermine the MTEA. Some union members, Peterson says, even thought the newspaper was being underwritten by another union.

Undermining MTEA "certainly was not the purpose," Tenorio says. But, she adds, the publication was created to challenge every teacher in the school system, including the union leadership. "We can no longer run the union as we have in the past 25 years," she says.

In 1989, the teacher-editors' financial plight was eased temporarily thanks to the first of several small grants from the New World Foundation of New York City. Says Ann Bastian, a senior program officer at the foundation: "We became interested in *Rethinking Schools* not only because of the quality but also because we thought the paper provided a forum in a way that teachers could really connect to the community. *Rethinking Schools* was very crucial in getting teachers actively and independently thinking about school change themselves." And because the ideas were not being generated by outsiders, she adds, teachers "were not stuck in a defensive position and could help set the agenda, which they should be doing."

The content of *Rethinking Schools* focuses on many of the crucial issues facing urban educators and parents today, as well as societal issues and teaching methods. The editors pay particular attention to multicultural issues. The paper has run in-depth articles about tracking, whole language, school choice, standardized testing, and teacher evaluation, among other topics.

The front page of the March/April 1992 issue offers: "The Illusion of Choice" and "Examining Proposals for Improving [Milwaukee's Public Schools]: Reform vs. Scapegoating." Inside stories include: "Teachers Evaluating Teachers," "Recession Goes to the Head of the Class," "Experimenting with Assessment."

Most of the articles are written by the core group of editors, although a small stable of correspondents from school systems elsewhere in the country also contribute stories. The writing style is a blend of reportage, analysis, and advocacy. It is the rare article that leaves the reader wondering on what side of the issue the writer falls. The editors have a number of firmly held opinions. They oppose, for example, choice and the creation of charter schools. And they are critical of standardized testing.

The newspaper also excerpts articles and books by prominent education writers and researchers such as Jonathan Kozol and Linda Darling-Hammond, a professor of education at Teachers College, Columbia University. Parents and politicians occasionally contribute articles to *Rethinking Schools,* as well. The back page of the paper is reserved for the art, prose, and poetry of schoolchildren.

Linda Christensen, a high school teacher in Portland, Ore., is one of the regular contributors. "The thing that I really find exciting about *Rethinking Schools* is that it is a collection of teachers who are putting it together," Christensen says. "Most publications that I've seen are specific toward a content area or issues in education. But *Rethinking Schools* really combines all of those. It's about classroom practice, but also about the large issues and struggles in education. And it comes from a perspective that is both pro-teacher and pro-student and, at the same time, pro-parent and pro-community."

The paper has grown from a 6,000 circulation periodical to one nearing 40,000, with an audience as far-flung as New Jersey, Kentucky, and California. While the publication is free to Milwaukee teachers, it also has 2,000 paid subscribers, most from outside the metropolitan area. This latter group includes a number of teacher educators who use the newspaper in their classrooms. After seeing an issue for the first time, Joyce Penfield, an associate professor of education at Rutgers University, ordered back issues for her students. "It raises very important topics," says Penfield, noting that it tends to be ahead of most other educational journals. "It's very applicable to what I see as good teaching, good learning, and good education."

Even though its budget has nearly doubled over the past few years to about $64,000, the paper is by no means a flush operation. Its founders have been able to raise enough money to hire two part-time employees, including a managing editor, and rent modest office space, but it still is mainly produced by volunteers. Dozens show up to unload the printed copies

One observer describes Bob Peterson as having a strong behind-the-scenes leadership style. "He has a way of making things work and keeping things going," she says. "He can do five things at once and still be nice to everybody."

and sort them for distribution to schools, churches, libraries, and other area locales.

The editors have published a few advertisements but generally eschew them because of the potential conflict between the ads and the paper's rebellious philosophy. They also acknowledge that this same philosophy has hindered efforts to score additional foundation support. Consequently, they are putting their energies into expanding the paid subscriber list to 6,000. And the publishers have launched a fund-raising campaign, asking readers to make an annual pledge to the publication.

To help the newspaper broaden its outlook as its national audience widens, the editors recently established a national advisory board. Their hope is that it will help critique the newspaper, identify prospective writers with differing perspectives, and raise funds.

Although the focus of *Rethinking Schools* has been on Milwaukee, its tone and message clearly have struck a chord with teachers elsewhere. Christina Brinkley, a member of the advisory board, says the paper has had a serendipitous effect. About three years ago, letters started arriving from grateful teachers relieved to learn that they were not alone in their attempts to improve their schools. "The letters were almost heart wrenching," says Brinkley, an associate professor of sociology and women's studies at Bates College in Maine. Until they started reading the newspaper, she says, "those lone teachers had been isolated."

Adds Christensen of Portland: "*Rethinking Schools* enables us to look at our local issues in terms of a national picture."

But its editors intend to keep *Rethinking Schools'* emphasis on Milwaukee. "We pick articles that we think are going to move things ahead," Peterson says. If the overall perspective shifts to a national audience, Peterson and Tenorio fear the newspaper will become abstract.

What's more, many articles have a hometown political flavor that might be lost if the emphasis shifts. This past spring, for example, the paper ran a piece knocking various community and school leaders—school board members, the mayor, a mayoral aide, and a local radio and television station—for taking whacks at the schools. "Criticizing [Milwaukee Public Schools] is not the problem; this newspaper has never been shy about criticizing MPS," Peterson wrote. "What is disturbing is the lack of analysis behind many of the current criticisms and the potential dangers in several of the proposed 'solutions.'"

The periodical's Milwaukee focus has made it a must-read for local policymakers. Even those who are the occasional targets of criticism appreciate the paper's overall high quality. "The publication is well-written; its thinking is supported by background data, interviews, good writing," says Milwaukee Mayor John Norquist. "It's really an important part of Milwaukee's

political culture now."

The paper's main flaw, he says, is that it is too much a part of the establishment. "Their reform is within the system; they don't threaten the basic premise of the system," he says, citing the newspaper's opposition to parental choice. "If we are going to keep the basic system we have, then *Rethinking Schools* has all kinds of great ideas."

Because they want to be taken seriously by everyone from fellow teachers to inner-city parents and state lawmakers, the editors take great pains to produce a top-notch product. They reject roughly two-thirds of the articles submitted by outside writers. But they are equally tough, if not tougher, on their own work. They spiked their premier edition, slated for mid-1986 publication, because it did not meet the standards they had set for themselves.

Peterson and Tenorio's schedules are particularly dizzying. They both generally arrive at school at about

---

The paper has grown from a 6,000 circulation periodical to one nearing 40,000, with an audience as far-flung as New Jersey, Kentucky, and California.

7:15 a.m. and put in a full day there. After school, they attend union, newspaper, or district committee meetings about four days a week. And then there are the night meetings. Tenorio says she often doesn't get home until after 9:30 p.m.

Weekends, too, are frequently taken up with business. On one Saturday, for example, Tenorio spent the entire day in union meetings while Peterson revised several newspaper stories. They both worked on the newspaper on Sunday from 1 o'clock in the afternoon until 9:30 that night, and then they had to get up bright and early the next morning for a 6:30 meeting.

Their growing celebrity has made them hot commodities on the conference circuit. This is particularly true for Tenorio, who last year was named Wisconsin Teacher of the Year. One friend marvels that Tenorio is able to attend "30 meetings a day but still knows somehow about Bart Simpson or a [news] report."

But Peterson and Tenorio, neither of whom is married, insist that the long hours and the wrangling are necessary if they are to fulfill their mission. A quick glance at some of their recent accomplishments shows that their efforts aren't for naught.

A series the paper ran helped persuade former Milwaukee Superintendent Robert Peterkin to spend $100,000 that had been earmarked for basal textbooks on other materials instead. Articles convinced the district to form a council to help schools adopt the whole language approach. And the publication played a role in swaying the school board to block an outcome-based education approach and a consultant's studentassignment plan.

The district's assessment task force, which Peterson co-chairs, successfully persuaded the district to replace a 3rd grade standardized test with a 4th grade holistic assessment—a move that *Rethinking Schools* had advocated.

Says Mary Bills, a district school board member and former chair of the board's curriculum committee: "Many of [the newspaper's] board members were instrumental in helping us change our curriculum. They showed the same dedication to developing our curriculum process as they do to putting out a very timely and useful publication. I'm generally very supportive of the role they play. They make us think, they occasionally make us change what we do, and they bring something to the table."

Peterson and Tenorio attribute their successes to hard work, a proven track record in the classroom, and a tested political strategy. "We have been able to criticize and take issue with policy, but at the same time we have been willing to get involved in the traditional mode of things," Tenorio says.

Peterson and Tenorio's juggling act also includes the MTEA, the largest unaffiliated local teachers' union in the country. Both were elected to the executive board five years ago but, according to Peterson, they represented such a minority voice that they were virtually ineffective.

Last year, however, the two of them ran as part of a reform slate, and a majority of the progressive candidates were elected; Tenorio was elected vice president and Peterson was re-elected to the union's executive board.

Mayor Norquist believes the new leadership from *Rethinking Schools* has an opportunity to open up the union to fresh ideas. "The previous [leaders] felt threatened by their own elections," he says. "You had a lot of sclerosis of the arteries."

Says Peterson: "I want our union to be an advocate for, not a barrier to, reform." He notes that there are already signs of progress: The MTEA is promoting a mentor program and supporting curriculum reform.

But Tenorio says the election has not eliminated tensions within the MTEA. Tenorio, for example, wants the union to retreat from its traditional adversarial approach to doing business, a stance that some within the organization argue is the equivalent to "giving away the store." That assertion, she says, is untrue. "I am an advocate of teachers," she declares. "I think we have to look at new ways of interacting."

As a result of all their labor, Tenorio and Peterson have come to be seen by many as the leaders of school reform in Milwaukee. But Christensen describes them another way. "Organizers would be the term that I would use," she says. "They are really trying to organize the community around the school people in a way that is not around cookies and teas."

Tenorio agrees that organizer is the more accurate assessment. One of their main goals, she says, is to involve others in school reform. "Every person working on a small piece can accomplish something," she says. She points to Erin Krause, who volunteers for each issue of *Rethinking Schools* despite having a young child and a full-time job. "That is a big sacrifice for her," she says.

Besides, Tenorio declares, "I'm not going to be able to continue at this pace forever. There are days when I want it to all go away." She pauses for a moment, and then adds, almost as an afterthought: "I'm a driven person; I need to be challenged all the time."

Both Peterson and Tenorio have been urged to turn their leadership and organizational talents to a principalship or some other administrative post. But they believe the only people who can really turn schools around are teachers—working primarily through the union. "We can't do that once we become part of the administration," Peterson says. "Plus," he adds, a grin spreading across his face, "we love to teach." ■

From Teacher Magazine, *August 1992*

58.

Consummate Professional

Throughout her teaching career, Nancie Atwell has been the constant questioner, the constant learner.

By Elizabeth Schulz

Down a snowy lane in Edgecomb, Maine, a town with more steeples than stoplights, the blanket of white is interrupted only by spruce trees and the occasional house with a snake of smoke escaping from the chimney. Fences of stacked, weathered rails zigzag across the frozen New England countryside.

Just off the road stands a two-story, clapboard structure with an addition jutting off one side. It looks like any other house—except for the bell on the roof. Inside, a sea of children are seated on pillows in a large carpeted room. Facing them, with sun pouring through three windows behind her, is a woman with thick, dark hair pulled back in a headband. Dressed in a maroon sweater that covers a flower-print blouse and a long, gray-green skirt, she sits—legs crossed—in a rocking chair, leaning forward with elbows resting on her knee like a mother reading to her children.

The woman is Nancie Atwell, renowned teacher, author, and researcher. The building is the Center for Teaching and Learning, the K-6 private school she built with royalties from her popular book, *In the Middle*—and with her own sweat and blood.

In the back of the bookshelf-lined room, three women furiously take notes. Teachers at Fayette Central School, a little over an hour away, the visitors don't want to miss a thing. Atwell doesn't want them to miss anything either—they are, after all, the main reason she built this school.

The center represents Atwell's vision for school reform in the United States: give thoughtful teachers real and practical models of good classroom practice—what she calls "primary sources"—so they can go back to their schools and be agents for change. Atwell admits it's a "slow growth" model; only a handful of teachers at a time can visit her center. But those who do are able to immerse themselves in a school that's organized very differently from their own. They can watch as students do real-life work. They can see how the children talk to each other and interact with teachers, how parents are involved, and what the tools of teaching actually look like.

Atwell's own experience has taught her to be respectful of the time one needs to change. It was a long and painstaking journey that led her to this quaint New England building. Years of reading, thinking, talking, observing, and experimenting spurred her to reshape her classroom. Then she tried to entice other teachers to re-examine their teaching. The school was born of the frustration Atwell felt when earlier efforts—speeches, workshops, and classroom demonstrations—fell short. But she believes she may have hit on a solution.

"It's the problem of trying to imagine teaching in a different way," she explains. "How do you do that when you went to traditional school for 13 years, went to college for six more years, and then went into a school that's always been organized one way? The only way to break the lock step and mindset is to put people into a situation that is organized completely differently. Let them learn the rhythm and incorporate it into their heartbeat."

The only books that Nancie Atwell had easy access to as a child growing up in Clarence, N.Y., a semirural bedroom community near Buffalo, were a set of encyclopedias. Her parents, a mailman and a waitress, worked hard to make ends meet. "Books," she says, "were just not something people could afford."

In high school, Atwell was a tough kid who traveled with a tough crowd. "She was smart as hell but not necessarily playing the school game," says her longtime friend and well-known educator, Donald Graves.

"Education was really not where my ambitions lay at all," Atwell recalls. "I just wanted to get out of high school, marry my boyfriend, live in a trailer, and party."

Her school days may not have turned her on to education, but they had an impact. "I've always found her an enormous champion for the underdog," Graves says, "for kids who have known what it is to struggle—because she has known it, too."

Atwell and her brother were the first members of their extended family to attend college, but even that was mostly by happenstance. She won a New York Regents scholarship to the State University College at Buffalo. She remembers her mother saying: "This is too good to pass up. Go for a year; if you don't like it, you don't like it. At least give it a try."

She started out majoring in art, a subject she loved in high school. But after a year of taking only art courses, she realized that she missed reading and writing, so she signed up for some English classes. In the fall term of 1970, Atwell landed in a seminar taught by a professor named Toby McLeod. "It completely turned my head around," she says. "It was a course where people talked passionately about ideas that were represented in literature, argued, acted out scenes from plays, and debated. It wasn't just people flapping their gums; we had strong personal opinions that were rooted in text. I had never heard this kind of discourse, certainly never in an English class in high school."

After receiving her bachelor's degree in English, Atwell stayed in the area for another semester to get certified to teach. "Teaching was something to do until I figured out what I really wanted to do," she says.

But in the classroom, she understood for the first time what it means to have an aptitude for something. "What happened, even during my student-teaching, is that I discovered I loved it," she says. "I had never done anything that I loved as much as teaching.

"It just seemed to be miraculous that you could have this kind of dialogue with kids," she adds, with a note of incredulity in her voice. "That this would be a *job* and that you would be *paid* to do it. It gave me extraordinary pleasure." She pauses. "It still does."

Atwell says Tonawanda Middle School, where she did her student-teaching and later landed a full-time job, was an extraordinary place to begin her career. At the time, her methods were mostly traditional, but her principal, "an enlightened instructional leader," expected teachers to be learners, constantly questioning their practice.

The wild beauty of the Maine coast, however, lured her away just a year and a half later. While on vacation with her new husband, Toby McLeod, the professor who brought literature to life for her, Atwell interviewed for an opening as an English teacher at Boothbay Harbor Grammar School. The superintendent there asked her if she would focus on teaching grammar. She said no; she had trained to teach kids to write, and that would be her first priority. As she left, she was certain that she wouldn't get the job.

Days before the start of the school year, Atwell got a call from the Boothbay superintendent. The other job candidate had seen the classroom where she'd be teaching and backed out. The superintendent asked Atwell if she still wanted the job.

So the couple put a new muffler on their beat-up Valiant, tranquilized the dog, and headed back to Maine. The day before school was to start, Atwell saw for herself why the other candidate had jumped ship. The school building, a Civil War-era structure, should have been condemned. There were rats, and raw sewage was seeping into some of the classrooms. Her own classroom was half of a big room, separated from another class by massive sheets of plywood. The tile floor was half gone, and bare light bulbs hung from the ceiling.

Birth of a Writing Project

But it was in these shabby surroundings that Nancie Atwell gave birth to "thoughtfulness" in her classroom. The story of how she came out from behind her desk to sit with her students and understand better how they learn has reached more than 200,000 teachers through her book *In the Middle*. In it, Atwell describes how she puzzled over students' behavior, invited researchers to observe and comment on her class, and looked critically at her practice. Deep analysis of what she does when she writes spurred her to experiment with structures that would help, rather than hinder, students' writing. "I saw the choices I made as a writer—deciding how, when, what, and for whom I'd write—weren't options available to writers in my classroom," she recounts in the book.

In the process, she reached out to other teachers in her school—not with answers but with questions. With a two-year grant from the federal government, she launched the Boothbay Writing Project to study the writing process. The 23 teachers involved read research papers, attended professional conferences together, kept detailed logs of observations of students, and discussed their own writing.

The teachers met formally and informally. Many of the conversations took place at the Thistle Inn, a bar they frequented. "We were madly talking all of the time about what we were finding," she remembers, "thinking about how the whole system of writing instruction in the school needed to be changed based on what we were learning."

"The process worked," she writes in *In the Middle*. "It worked because it was so complex. Layer upon layer of experience accumulated to form a body of shared knowledge and expertise. No one handed us a program from on high; in intense and personally meaningful collaboration, we invented our own wheel. Together, we learned from ourselves, each other, and our students."

They created a model for a "writing workshop" for students that later spread throughout Boothbay Region Elementary School, the new consolidated school they taught at. Students were given regular chunks of time to write. They chose their own topics and genres and were given feedback during— not just after—the writing process. Teachers covered the mechanics of writing in mini-lessons and when issues came up during individual writing conferences. The teachers wrote themselves and talked to students about their own writing.

Donald Graves, then a professor at the University of New Hampshire, remembers his first encounter with Atwell's 8th graders' work. "We were just amazed at what her students wrote," he says. "It wasn't just single pieces; she showed us whole collections where you could see how students first started and what they could do toward the end. I've seen very few situations where students changed so dramatically." In 1985, her students scored the second highest in Maine's writing assessment; a fifth of her students were in the 99th percentile.

Atwell soon began to wonder how all she'd learned about writing applied to her reading program. Her talks with Toby around the dinner table became the yardstick by which she measured her reading class. "It is a literate environment," she says of her dinner table in *In the Middle*. "Around it, people talk in all the ways literate people discourse. We don't need assignments, lesson plans, teacher's manuals, or handbooks. We need only another literate person. And our talk isn't sterile or grudging or perfunctory. It's filled with jokes, arguments, exchanges of bits of information, descriptions of what we loved and hated and why. The way Toby and I chat most evenings at that table were ways that my kids and I could chat, entering literature together. Somehow, I had to get that table into my classroom and invite my 8th graders to pull up their chairs."

The "table" she developed for her classroom was the "reading workshop." The idea behind it was that students learn to read by reading. She let students choose what to read just as real readers do and gave them opportunities to discuss what they were reading. Atwell flooded her room with books—both recognized literature and popular novels, such as S.E. Hinton's *The Outsiders*. She required students to read all period long and regularly write letters about what they were reading to her and other students. Students who had never voluntarily read a book were reading an average of 35 a year.

Throughout *In the Middle*, Nancie Atwell shows in painstaking detail that thoughtful change happens only through careful observation of how kids learn to read and write. She became an avid data collector. Her students' writing stayed in school all year; she scoured the material, looking for growth and changes. Every day, she filled out a "status of the class" chart, so she could look for patterns over time. She did some number crunching, keeping track of how many books students read and what genres were represented, what punctuation they used in writing, and what students chose to write about and why. She even interviewed her students about their own learning. "My experience as a teacher who observed her students—as a teacher-researcher—has changed me forever. Everywhere I look I see data," Atwell writes in a later book, *Side by Side*. "As I filled my notebooks, my teaching became more patient and more sensible."

Still, she needed a structure for all this information. "*In the Middle* became a story of me and my students and our struggles to make sense of school," she writes, "and I became the rueful, insightful, cheerful first person that my husband sometimes wishes he were married to when he finishes reading a manuscript with my name on it."

In the Middle, which struck a chord among teachers because it presents teaching as an intellectual activity but in a practical way, won her a loyal following and critical acclaim. She was the first classroom teacher to receive the David H. Russell Award for outstanding research in the teaching of English from the National Council of Teachers of English and the prestigious Mina P. Shaughnessy Prize from the Modern Language Association.

The awards were a welcome affirmation but didn't really change how she felt about herself and her work. "I have such an ego," she says with a self-deprecating laugh, "that I really believed I had something to say." Still, the attention was not for naught. She believes that the recognition she received lends credibility to other teachers who want to conduct research in their own classrooms.

The acclaim also made her a hot commodity on the lecture and consulting circuit. Atwell had left the Boothbay school system after her daughter was born in 1986, the year before *In the Middle* was published. Over the next few years, she conducted independent research and directed a writing-across-the-curriculum project for elementary schools through the Breadloaf School of English in Middlebury, Vt. But between 1987 and 1990, she also accepted more than 30 speaking engagements. She welcomed the opportunities, hoping she would be able to reach other teachers with her discoveries and challenge them to re-envision their classrooms.

She found the process of writing speeches rewarding because it forced her again to sit down and think about the things that went on in her classroom. "I've never written anything where I wasn't surprised in the act of writing," she says. "I'm always amazed by what turns up."

She remembers one speech-writing epiphany in particular. She was writing about two very different students who had been lagging but gradually became successful in her class.

"I can remember almost falling off my chair when, as I was sitting there with my data in my dining room, I figured out what was going on with these two kids," she says. "There is no other feeling like that, finding the connection and then trying to find the language for it before you lose it." Many of these speeches later evolved into articles for publication.

Limitations of Being a 'Guru'

Although she enjoyed preparing the speeches, Atwell found that giving them wasn't a very effective way to reach teachers. She felt like "a talking head." And delivering them, she remembers, was often a letdown. "The unfortunate thing about speaking is that the learning part was over by the time I left my house," she says. "Then I had to go deliver the speech. By then, it was dead on the page."

She was further dismayed to see that a kind of cult movement had formed around her work. After giving a speech, she would find herself hounded by teachers, who said things like: "Your book is my bible, and you're my guide."

"It's one thing to have people say in a letter, 'I admire your work,' but it's another for people to take work that is serious and intellectual and turn it into a charismatic movement," she says. "*In the Middle* offers a model of a teacher who found her own problems and used every resource available, especially her own students, to solve the problems. I want teachers to be professional enough to respect the genesis of the story."

Traveling around the country, leading teachers in inservice training, Atwell saw some other trends that disturbed her. "Everywhere I went, I would be sandwiched between the Madeline Hunter person and the thinking-skills person," she says. The programs these people were touting seemed to force artificial frameworks on teaching and learning and missed the crux of the problem and the solution: the relationship between teacher and student. "There was always some obstacle between us and kids, some prism through which you have to look at kids, something that will make teaching more efficient, easier, cleaner, neater, less emotional."

To break through this barrier, Atwell began looking for opportunities to teach teachers in situations where they could witness and experience a different kind of interaction between teacher and students. In graduate courses she taught through Northeastern University, she ran half of each class as a writing workshop, treating the student teachers like her 8th graders, so they could feel how it worked. And she took up demonstration teaching, where she would take on a class and invite other teachers to observe. Atwell's friend Graves watched her teach a class of students in Atlanta that she had never seen before.

"She has that knack of making almost instant contact at a student's level," he says. "She doesn't do it by coming down to the student. She is able to produce this incredible invitation to the student to go where she is going."

Atwell recalls those experiences with mixed feelings. "That was closer to what I wanted because at least teachers could see it happening with real kids," she says. "But in some ways it was still artificial because they weren't my students. I had no idea what had happened before I came in; I had no idea what was going to happen after. So the context was strange."

Atwell was ready for the next step. She wanted to continue teaching and working with teachers, but she wanted to do it right, without staying in a Holiday Inn every weekend. She also wanted to remain in Maine, an area that she and her husband love. And she needed a place for her daughter, Anne, to go to school.

So on Aug. 2, 1990, a grueling year after Atwell decided to start her own school, builders broke ground on the Center for Teaching and Learning in nearby Edgecomb. By Aug. 29, they had fit together two pieces of the prefab house and secured the roof. On Sept. 10, Nancie Atwell cried; the movers had brought the furniture, and, for the first time, the center looked like a real school. On Sept. 12, she and four other teachers opened their doors to 30 students.

In a part of the country that is run by town meetings, the students at the Center for Teaching and Learning have a distinct advantage: They are learning to speak out. When they are taken on field trips, the guide inevitably asks: "Who *are* these kids?" It's not because they are brilliant or particularly articulate; it's because they have a voice. They ask questions and want to know things.

One reason is that the school day starts and ends with a meeting attended by all 58 students, kindergartners to 6th graders, who sit side by side with their teachers in one room. On this bright winter's morning, Nancie Atwell leads the group from her rocking chair, peppering the talk with Spanish phrases the students have learned.

The meeting starts simply enough, with children raising hands to tell their news from the weekend. One describes a ride on a snowmobile sled; another tells how she spotted a fox. Atwell asks if anyone has heard any national news. "Arthur Ashe died of AIDS," one offers. Teachers and students alike talk about who this man was, the disease, and the loss.

Then Atwell leads them in reciting a poem; students clap and snap their fingers in rhythm. After that, Atwell reads aloud an excerpt from an interview with Eloise Greenfield, a poet they have read. According to the article, Greenfield does her best writing from about midnight to 4 a.m. The children gasp. Greenfield's advice to young writers: If you read a book you like, read it again to see how the author puts the words together.

Atwell then reads from a book about the Underground Railroad, and the group discusses it. Following the discussion, the students sing a song that they wrote about the work of the school.

This rich exchange takes about 15 minutes.

The only people who remain silent through the meeting are the three teachers from Fayette Central School. One of eight teams of teachers invited to spend a week at the school this year, the "interns" are asked not to speak to the children or teachers during class. This way, Atwell says, they can concentrate on observing and reflecting without interfering with the dynamics of the school. In fact, to minimize the disruption, no other visitors are allowed in the school.

"The great thing about the center is that these are real kids in a real school," Atwell explains. "We have a stake in what happens to them."

The interns are encouraged to take detailed notes and jot down questions to ask the teachers during meetings that are scheduled throughout their stay. As the week progresses, these women sometimes sit shoulder to shoulder with a teacher as she confers with a student; they scrawl notes but say nothing.

The application process for the intern program is rigorous. The teachers in each team must write essays about their professional development and their educational philosophy. The team application must include a letter from the school administrator stating that the teachers will be allowed to make changes based on what they learn during the visit. Each team leaves at the end of the week with a long- and short-term plan and three graduate credits.

When the morning meeting adjourns, most of the students scramble off to their work; a few stay behind to put the pillows back into an oversized closet.

Unlike at most schools, the students at the center don't have assigned desks. Instead, they move among four major rooms—the reading room, writing room, math and science room, and projects room. The rooms are plentifully stocked with the tools that real readers, writers, scientists, mathematicians, and artists would use. Students are broken into four groups by grade levels—kindergarten, 1-2, 3-4, 5-6—so most students stay with the same teacher for two years.

This morning, Atwell joins teacher Susan Benedict and her 5th and 6th graders in the writing room, an open space with wooden tables of different sizes to accommodate different-sized children. Strategically placed around the room are folders, papers, pencils, pens, scissors, books on writing, a dictionary, and a thesaurus. Atwell joins the students in a circle of chairs. A quotation by the poet Rainer Maria Rilke posted on the wall behind her captures the essence of the mini-lesson Atwell is about to teach: "Be patient toward all that is unsolved in your heart, and try to love the questions themselves."

Atwell tells them about an experience that Graves had recently on a flight to Atlanta. Graves found himself sitting next to someone from Boothbay, a man named Barry Sherman, whose 23-year-old son, B.J., had died in a car accident a few weeks earlier. Graves asked Sherman if he knew Nancie Atwell. "Yes," he replied, "She was the best teacher B.J. ever had." Sherman went on to tell Graves how he cherishes the piece of B.J.'s writing that Atwell excerpted in her book. When he reads it, Sherman says, he can hear B.J.'s voice and understand his feelings.

Atwell hands out copies of B.J.'s story about moving out of his mother's house to live with his dad. "We've been talking about narrative voice," she says. "This is in the third person. I call this fiction. Some of it is real; some is made up."

As she reads aloud, the students follow along, gripped by the tale. She finishes, and, after a long period of silence, she asks quietly, "Why did Barry Sherman remember this piece of writing?"

"Because it was an important incident," one student offers.

"Because B.J. was trying to work out his feelings in it," another adds.

Atwell lets other ideas emerge before she adds her own: "Because it was something that *mattered* to B.J. I call it *authentic* fiction. These are the things that last. When you sit down to write, ask yourself: Is it a real need I have? Is there some tension or problem I want to work out? Otherwise, all you're doing is an exercise to fill time."

She ends with a quotation from playwright Neil Simon: "I can't write anything unless my character wants something *dearly*."

Although Atwell does not have a class of her own in the center, she thinks of herself as the instructional leader. When Atwell and Benedict noticed that students in Benedict's class were turning out a lot of beautiful but voiceless writing, Atwell offered to teach a series of mini-lessons on the purpose of writing. Donna Maxim, a teacher at the center who knows Atwell from Boothbay Writing Project days, says: "To watch her do a mini-lesson is one of the greatest plea-sures in my life. She's such a great writer, and she can just talk to kids and make them aspire to be great writers, too."

As the writer's workshop continues, the students move off to tables to work. Some meet with Benedict for a writing conference during which they pose ques-tions about their work in progress, read the piece aloud, and ask for comments and suggestions.

(Even the kindergartners at the center learn this process; they, for example, have written a parody of the popular children's book *Bread and Jam for Fran-cis*, a piece called *Bagels and Salsa for Nancy*, about how their teacher eats bagels and salsa for lunch every day.)

Later in the day, Benedict's students gather, sprawled comfortably on the floor of the reading room, to hear her read aloud from *Roll of Thunder, Hear My Cry*, a book by Mildred Taylor set in the 1930s. In the chapter, a black man who has gone into town with his son is attacked by white men on his way home. After the reading, Benedict asks the students what they think. The conversation that ensues is easygoing but firmly rooted in the text.

"She describes too much ... that part about the cracking bones," one girl says with a shudder.

"I predict Papa's going to die," a boy adds.

"What does Mildred Taylor care about?" asks the teacher.

After a moment, Curt, who is reclined on the floor, says: "She wants to tell us what really went on at that time, to really feel it. Not like the history books. She wants to show us the human side of history."

Nathaniel, obviously troubled by the events in the book, asks, "Could a white person get arrested for shooting a black person?"

In virtual unison, the kids say: "No. Now, but not back then."

Kristin expounds on the idea: "I think she's against racism. She's showing how wrong it is for a white per-son to shoot a black person."

Benedict pushes: "Is she promoting integration?"

When the students answer no, she asks, "What in the book leads you to believe that?"

They point out that the blacks and whites in the book live separately and that one of the most promi-nent characters, a black gentleman whom readers grow to respect, is against his son's becoming friends with a white boy.

All of the students at the center spend half an hour to an hour reading independently each day, but there is also ample opportunity to hear good literature read aloud. Like most teaching at the center, the decision to read aloud to the students was based on research. It has been shown, Atwell points out, that listening to someone read builds students' long-term memory. "Reading aloud isn't just charming," Maxim tells one of the Fayette teachers. "It is essential."

Writing About Science

Since the opening of the Center for Teaching and Learning, the dinner-table talk at the Atwell-McLeod house has not been confined to books. Recently, their daughter, Anne, who is now a 1st grader at the center, cleared off a space at the table after dinner to draw electronic circuits in series and in parallel on paper napkins. She wondered which kind of circuit would conduct more power. Anne was still thinking about her science class, where she'd learned about circuits by making them. Students at the center investigate science as real scientists do, by asking real questions and setting up small experiments to prove or disprove a theory.

Recently, when teachers at the center talked about how they were going to have children write formally about the work they were doing in science, Atwell dug up a series of papers that a rain forest biologist who visited the school had presented at a scholarly confer-ence. The teachers studied them and decided to use them as a model.

Today, in keeping with this real-world philosophy, Donna Maxim starts a conversation about magnets with her 3rd and 4th graders by passing out magnets and asking students what they know about them. On a piece of chart paper, she writes their ideas: "Mag-nets attract and repel." "They have poles."

A student named Meghan interrupts with a ques-tion: "Do magnets attract all metals?" Maxim writes down Meghan's question—it is, after all, the point of the lesson—and asks her what made her think of it. Meghan explains that she has a butterfly magnet at home that doesn't stick to all surfaces.

Maxim hands a nail to each student and poses a question: "What will happen to the nail if it is kept near the magnet for a while?" The students think out loud: "It will make the nail lighter?" "It will make it rust?" "The magnet will 'magnetify' the nail."

"Is a nail a magnet?" Maxim asks. Most of the stu-dents say no, but one boy says yes. Maxim asks him: "Will this nail pick up a paper clip like our magnet?" The boy says no.

"Is it a magnet?" she pushes.

The boy doesn't budge; he says yes. Another stu-dent postulates that maybe all things are magnets, but in different degrees. With that, the class launches into a discussion about electricity, conductors, and in-sulators—all aspects of one of the school's themes this year, energy.

It is just this kind of rigorous exchange that Patri-cia Dickinson, one of the teachers from Fayette Cen-tral School, says really shakes up her thinking. "Everything they do is a meaningful learning experi-ence for the children," she says. "They never ask the students to do anything unless it is authentic and has a reason. This is something I will think about con-stantly now. Is this really an authentic activity? Could

I make it more so? How could I do it?"

The center's teachers and the interns probe the issues surrounding thoughtful teaching in a series of meetings, often held in the teachers' upstairs office. (The space is comfortable. The teachers each have their own desks, but they are grouped together to promote collegiality.) They first discuss some of the surface details the interns have noticed about the school. The way teachers and students remove their shoes when they enter the building, so the floors stay clean enough for students to sit and lie on. The way there are no chalkboards so there is less dust. The way students call their teachers by their first names so they realize the teachers are real people.

Then the talk turns to bigger issues. How to create a rigorous intellectual atmosphere in which students still feel safe enough to take risks. How to give students real choices in a structured way. As they get into the nitty gritty, the teachers quote liberally from research on teaching and from reading they've done in the subject areas.

As the week draws to a close, the conversation at these meetings focuses on the most pressing issue: How will these three teachers be able to go back to their public school and create a more thoughtful learning environment? Although their classrooms are housed in a trailer, the Fayette teachers hope to create a kind of ghetto for real learning next year. Among other things, they decide to meet weekly to talk about their practice, to make presentations to parents and administrators about their experience and ideas, to begin reshaping their classes, and to work to get doors installed between their classrooms.

But Atwell insists that this group will go away with something even more important. "They began to understand that they could be brave together," she says, "that there was real power in the coherence of their theory. There was a new sense of what was possible when teachers who shared beliefs got together and tried to forge some common ground."

Dreams and Nightmares

Nancie Atwell calls the time she spent preparing to open the Center for Teaching and Learning "the nightmare part" of her life. When she went looking for a place to house the school, the first three sites fell through. Her decision to build a new school gave her more control over its layout but also filled the following months with hundreds of details she had to work out. Even after the land was purchased and a blueprint drafted, it took four months to get approval from the local planning board. The application was roughly 100 pages long and cost more than $4,000 to compile.

"I have never worked so hard, so long, so consistently on anything in my life," she says. "They were 18-hour days—developing the plan, walking the site, taking measurements, digging holes, and meeting with groups of people about one thing or another."

Fund-raising was an enormous chore. Atwell knew that her teaching model would not hold water if she served only the typical private school clientele. To make sure her students represented the socioeconomic profile of rural Maine, she wanted to offer generous scholarships to offset the $3,350 tuition. So she sent a mass mailing to teachers she had come into contact with over the years, asking for donations. (She now receives about $10,000 a year in checks, ranging from $10 to $100.)

But she still needed more money to build the school. "It's been awful, the most humbling experience in my life," she says of her fund-raising effort. "I think I have this great professional reputation, and I go to foundations, and they have never heard of Nancie Atwell, they have never heard of *In the Middle*, and, after I explain my model for changing schools, they tell me they won't fund a local project."

Despite grants from the Bingham Trust, the Betterment Fund, and *The New York Times* Foundation, and a $50,000 no-strings-attached donation from veteran actor James Whitmore, she still had to collect her pension from Maine's teacher retirement fund to make a down payment on a mortgage. Some of her royalties from *In the Middle* go directly to the school. So far, she has received no pay from the center. Her husband keeps asking, half-jokingly, when she is going to draw a salary.

Despite her fiscal precariousness, Atwell is ready for a new challenge. She plans to open a secondary school by 1994. "If the model we have for the elementary school is powerful," she says, "the next level of work is going to be absolutely groundbreaking."

Others agree. Secondary education is her area of expertise, and there is a real paucity of models out there for middle and high school teachers. No matter what Atwell is doing, Donald Graves says, she provides a powerful example for others. "She expects so much of herself," he says, "that to hang around her you start to think, 'My god, am I carrying my weight?' She's not demanding that you do it, but you want to join her professionally."

The tough question is whether others can really follow in Atwell's footsteps. "You can't bypass the fact that she is one hell of a reader, writer, thinker, and learner," Graves says. "On the other hand, there are lots of teachers out there who are on the verge and who just need the chance to see a real pro at work." ∎

From Teacher Magazine, *May/June 1993*

59.

Hooked on Books

In Timothy Hamilton's 2nd grade class, everything begins and ends with children's literature.

By David Hill

Within the walls of Dodson Elementary School in Hermitage, Tenn., a Nashville suburb, is the Apple Classroom of Tomorrow (ACOT), a project funded by the computer company and the National Science Foundation. About 60 of the school's 3rd and 4th graders participate in the ACOT program, which attempts to infuse technology into every aspect of the curriculum.

But if ACOT is high-tech, Timothy Hamilton's 2nd grade classroom, just down the hall, is decidedly low-tech. Everywhere you look there are books, books, and more books. Big books. Little books. Hardcover books. Paperback books. Serious books. Silly books.

On one bulletin board is a banner that says, "Be Excited About Reading," or BEAR, which explains the abundance of stuffed bears in the classroom. Another board displays biographical information about James Marshall, the "author of the month." In the front of the room, above the blackboard, are these words: "Our Goal: 500. Books Read: 394." Like the old McDonald's signs that tallied the number of hamburgers sold, the "books read" figure is constantly growing.

For Hamilton, reading is everything. The 32-year-old Nashville native uses children's literature in every subject he teaches, including mathematics. "I just immerse my students in it all day long," he says. "And they get caught up in my excitement."

Hamilton isn't just boasting; visitors to his classroom are often astonished to find out just how much his students actually know about books. They understand the difference between a fairy tale and a folk tale, between a biography and an autobiography. They know who won last year's Newbery and Caldecott awards (the Oscars of children's books). They know detailed information about their favorite authors. They know what a copyright page is. They know that it was a 17th century Frenchman by the name of Charles Perrault who wrote *Tales of Mother Goose*.

But mainly, they have a love of reading that seems all the more remarkable in an age of Mighty Morphin Power Rangers and Super Mario Brothers. And if Hamilton has done his job, his students will carry that love with them for the rest of their lives. "If you can read," he says, "and you're real excited about it, then it's going to be something that can transform your life, something that you can use forever. I want them to be lifetime readers."

Monday, 8:50 a.m. Students are trickling into Hamilton's smallish classroom. As they enter, they put away their jackets, go to their desks, and look up at a white board on which Hamilton has written:
- List 20 things you would take to Grandma's.
- Read *Twits* pp. 15-23.
- Let's have a great week!

Hamilton, neatly dressed in khaki pants, a blue button-down oxford-cloth shirt, a red paisley tie, and brown penny loafers, has been at school since 8 a.m., so he's had time to place a paperback copy of *The Twits*, by Roald Dahl, on each child's desk. With little prodding from their teacher, the students take their seats and begin to read.

Hamilton's 25 students are heterogeneous in every sense of the word. Some are white, some are black. Some are fast learners, some are slow learners. Some are affluent, some are poor. Most of Dodson's 940 students come from the Hermitage area, which is both suburban and rural. But some are bused to the school from north Nashville, 45 minutes away.

By 9:15, all but one of the students have arrived. "OK," the teacher says, "I'd like everybody to close their *Twits* books. I'd like for you to put your index cards away, and I'd like to see you on the perimeter of the rug when I call you. I'm going to start with table three." One by one, Hamilton calls up the other tables, and the children take their places on the rug, a multi-colored affair decorated with letters and numbers. After the pledge of allegiance and the state-mandated "moment of silence," Hamilton sits down in a beautiful handpainted rocking chair, a gift from last year's class. Throughout the day, he will spend much time in this chair, sometimes reading books to his students, sometimes just chatting with them, creating a living-room atmosphere in an otherwise typical classroom. ("I let them know what I'm doing and what's going on in my life," he says later. "They need to know that I'm a real person.")

"Guess what Mr. Hamilton did on Saturday?" he asks, sounding like a younger, Southern version of Mr. Rogers. "I had a big test to take. A big test. I mean, it lasted forever, and I didn't know some of the answers. I had studied and studied for it."

Hamilton is referring to a state assessment that, if he passes, will place him higher up on the professional career ladder for teachers.

"The test was to help me be a better teacher and to help me make more money," he explains. "And I think I did pretty well on it."

"I hope you did," one girl offers.

Hamilton says that, after the test, he decided to give himself a treat by going to a bookstore. "And what bookstore do you think I went to?" he asks. In a flash, every hand in the room shoots up, and several students can hardly contain their excitement at knowing the answer.

Hamilton picks a student named Morgan to answer the question. "Davis-Kidd," she replies. The Nashville bookstore, which has a large children's literature section, is one of Hamilton's favorite haunts. He likes to take his students there whenever he can, especially if an author is on hand to sign books.

Hamilton holds up a copy of *The Horn Book Magazine*, a bimonthly journal that lists upcoming children's books. He says: "I was thumbing through it— and I always get so excited when I do this—and there was a book in here that looked good, and I thought, I sure hope Davis-Kidd has this book because if they don't, I'm not going to be very happy. So I got there, and, sure enough, they had it."

Next to Hamilton is an old wooden trunk, which he says he found in the classroom when he arrived this morning. "And when I opened the trunk up," he says, "I found an envelope with my name written in cursive. And I thought, This is my grandmother's handwriting. I opened the envelope up, and inside there was a little note. It said, 'Tim, here's everything you'll need to teach today. Love, Grandma.'"

Slowly, Hamilton opens up the lid of the trunk. The students strain their necks to get a peek inside, but the teacher quickly closes it. "Our focus today is going to be on grandmothers," he tells the children, and, in fact, the teacher will return to that motif often during the day. Hamilton may not be an author, but he creates his lessons in the same way that a writer conceives a book: by establishing an overarching theme. Even the trunk itself (which he, not his grandmother, actually filled up with goodies) has a certain literary flavor to it; if it were a book, today's lesson might well be titled Grandma's Trunk.

Hamilton allows his students to talk briefly about what they did over the weekend before he asks them to return to their seats. It's time for math, but there's not a textbook in sight. Instead, Hamilton reaches into the trunk and grabs a plastic bag full of Band-Aids. "I looked back in Grandma's trunk," he says, "and I found Shel Silverstein's book, *Where the Sidewalk Ends*. And I opened it up, and there was a poem called 'Band-Aids.'"

The teacher passes out a Band-Aid and a copy of the poem to each child. The students have no idea where this is leading, but they know enough about Mr. Hamilton to realize that, whatever happens, they're going to enjoy the ride.

Hamilton asks the students to follow along as he reads the poem out loud:

I have a Band-Aid on my finger,
One on my knee, and one on my nose,
One on my heel, and two on my shoulder,
Three on my elbow, and nine on my toes.
Two on my wrists, and one on my ankle,
One on my chin, and one on my thigh,
Four on my belly, and five on my bottom,
One on my forehead, and one on my eye.
One on my neck, and in case I might need 'em
I have a box full of thirty-five more.
But oh! I do think it's sort of a pity
I don't have a cut or a sore!

"Now, I'm going to close Grandma's trunk," Hamilton says. The lid drops with a loud crash. He asks, "What do you call the author of a poem?"

"A poet!" answers a student.

"Who's another famous poet you know besides Shel Silverstein? Who was that man who wrote 'Stopping by Woods on a Snowy Evening'? What was his name?"

Half the hands in the room reach into the air.

226

Hamilton calls on a boy, who has the correct answer: "Robert Frost."

Getting back to the poem, Hamilton asks the students to estimate the number of Band-Aids mentioned in it. After a moment, the answers come fast and furious:

"Thirty-two."

"Thirty-four."

"Thirty."

"Twenty-three."

"Thirty-five."

"Thirty-four."

"Eighty-nine."

(Most of the students giggle when they hear the last number, knowing that it's way off.)

To find the correct answer, Hamilton writes down all the numbers on the blackboard and then, with help from the students, adds them up. The answer, it turns out, is 35. "Who estimated 35?" he asks. Several students hold up their hands. "Good job."

Later, Hamilton will pass out a work sheet full of math problems, but right now it's time to have a little fun. On the front board is a drawing of a boy; Hamilton has his students go up to the drawing, in pairs, and stick Band-Aids on the boy's body parts, just like in Silverstein's poem. "I can't wait to see this guy when he's done," Hamilton says.

When all the kids have done their part, the boy is covered from head to toe in Band-Aids, which amuses the students to no end. Hamilton has combined math and poetry so seamlessly that the students are not even aware that the two subjects have been mixed. "You look around the room," Hamilton says later, "and it looks like a total mess. But we've been working. The children have been doing stuff. They haven't been mindlessly filling in the blanks all morning and staying in their seats. We can't teach like it's still 1952."

It comes as no surprise to learn that, when he was a boy, Hamilton knew he wanted to be a teacher when he grew up. And much of the inspiration came from his 2nd grade teacher, Eunice Bailey.

"She was a wonderful lady," Hamilton recalls. "She was the first black teacher at our school, and a lot of the parents were very apprehensive. This was back in 1969, 1970, when desegregation had first come about in Nashville. But she would probably stand out as the best teacher I had. She worked hard on getting kids to feel good about themselves, no matter what. And she was a very loving, grandmotherly type. So she always stands out.

"I can remember writing a story about wanting to be a teacher, way back in 2nd grade. And somehow I wound up teaching 2nd grade."

Hamilton's first teaching job was at a Nashville preschool, where he worked part time while attending Belmont College, a small, Baptist-affiliated liberal arts college. After graduating in 1984, he continued working at the preschool full time while seeking a job with the Metropolitan Nashville Public Schools. Although the district wasn't hiring a lot of teachers at the time, Hamilton was offered a job teaching 2nd grade at Dodson Elementary School. He jumped at the opportunity.

"If we traveled back to that class," Hamilton says of his first year at Dodson, "it would be very different. In those days, we did a lot of 'skill and drill,' with a lot of work sheets. It took me longer to run them off than it did for the children to complete them! And I knew that wasn't working. The kids may know it for that particular moment—you give them a test, and everyone gets an A—but it was not practical. They were not using the skills.

"So, the one thing that I saw that they did enjoy was the reading, even though the reading book that we used was not very good at all. And back in 1984, there wasn't much talk about whole language. It was unheard of unless you lived in Canada or Australia.

"That skill and drill—you never, ever remember one single work sheet that you did in your 12 years of schooling. However, you do remember those special activities, those special days, or that special book. We all do. Real literature—it touches you."

Slowly, Hamilton began to change the way he taught. First, during his second year, he stopped grouping his students by reading ability. "Every adult knows what reading group they were in," he says. "You still remember if you were in the bottom or in the top. And I think no child should have the stigma of being in a low reading group."

Second, he began to get away from using the basal reader. "I began to branch out and learn about authors. I had done a lot with books already, but not ... for enjoyment. I had used them more for teaching skills. I was not developing lifetime readers, where the child takes a book and has a personal relationship with it. And that's what I wanted to nurture."

The kicker came during the following summer, when Hamilton and some other Dodson teachers attended a whole language workshop. "We knew right then and there that we had to change some things," he says. "We had to get away totally from skill and drill." Hamilton's teaching hasn't been the same since.

He thinks of whole language more as a philosophy than a set method. "Whole language is a belief that reading and writing are something that you do naturally," he says. Hamilton has taken that basic tenet and created his own unique style of teaching. "A lot of what you do you have to investigate and find out on your own," he says. Now, Hamilton conducts his own workshops for teachers who want to incorporate children's literature into their lessons.

Clearly, Hamilton's love of children's literature comes from the heart. Over the years, he has amassed a collection of about 5,000 volumes, and he's read every single one of them. One reason he still lives with his parents is so that he can afford to keep buying books on his shamefully low teacher's salary. He even buys entire sets of books, like *The Twits*, so that his students can all read the same text at the same time. "If you look around here," he says, scanning the classroom, "basically everything but the furniture and the computers is mine." (The two computers are available primarily for writing and language "maintenance" exercises.)

Where does he keep all of his books? Wherever he can find room for them. "That entire cabinet is full," he says, pointing to the back of the room. "That's full. That's full. These three trunks are full. And I have three huge boxes at home."

"His books are his," says Dodson's principal, Nancy Coleman, "and he's sharing them with the children. That kind of personal commitment is what sets him apart."

Unlike many great teachers, Hamilton is fortunate to have been cited for his superior work. In 1991, his colleagues voted him Dodson Teacher of the Year, an honor that put Hamilton in the running for the districtwide Metro Teacher of the Year. For that, Hamilton submitted a portfolio in which he summarized his teaching philosophy: "I try to make each day special for each child. I want them to feel like they can't wait to get back tomorrow and learn some more."

The portfolio, which Hamilton keeps in his classroom, also contains glowing testimonials from colleagues, and parents. Typical is a letter from the Norvells, whose daughter was in Hamilton's class:

Rick and I feel privileged to write this letter of recommendation for Tim Hamilton as Teacher of the Year. Our daughter, Ellen, has acquired the confidence of a writer, the eloquence of a speaker, and the imagination of a poet under the influence of Mr. Hamilton's creative style. The positive reinforcement that Mr. Hamilton consistently displays provides an atmosphere that encourages the children to flourish and progress at a very rapid pace. . . .
   In our opinion, Mr. Hamilton is the most creative and innovative 2nd grade teacher we have ever known. We're very grateful that our daughter has had the opportunity to experience the very high caliber of Mr. Hamilton's expertise.

Hamilton became the youngest teacher ever to be named Metro Elementary Teacher of the Year, which put him in the running for the regional District Elementary Teacher of the Year award. (He was first runner-up for that particular honor.) Also in 1991, he received the Excellence in Teaching Award from the University of Tennessee. Not bad for someone who had only been teaching for six years.

The awards, Hamilton says, "made me feel like, 'Hey, somebody out there recognizes that I am doing a good job.' And a lot of times, as a teacher, you never hear that." He is quick to point out that his school is blessed with many excellent teachers; last year, a Dodson staff member won Metro Elementary Teacher of the Year, and this year one was a first runner-up.

Two years ago, as word of Hamilton's teaching began to spread, it reached Victoria Risko, a professor of education at Nashville's Vanderbilt University. She was looking for about 10 exemplary Nashville-area teachers whose classes she could videotape. Now, Hamilton's teaching is captured on two 30-minute videodiscs, which are used in two classes at Vanderbilt's Peabody College.

"We enjoyed being in his classroom," Risko says, "and he's had a real impact on our undergraduates. The students take away a lot of good ideas. We hold him in high regard."

In Hamilton's classroom, students don't just read books; they also write books, which they "publish" under the imprint of Cubblestone Publishing Co. Sometimes they even sell their works at school craft fairs. The proceeds, of course, are used to buy more books.

Following the Band-Aid exercise, the teacher again asks the children to come to the front of the classroom, this time so he can read from a book called The Doorbell Rang, by Pat Hutchins. The book, about a dozen cookies, will provide the students with a model for their own books about the number 12.

"It can be about absolutely anything," Hamilton tells his charges. "The only thing we can't do is Pat Hutchins' story. What if we do her story again? What have we done?"

"We're breaking the copyright law," a student responds.

"That's right," Hamilton says.

The teacher asks a boy named Robert to pass out two sheets of yellow construction paper to each student. Hamilton wants them to write first drafts, or "dummies," which he will then edit and give back to the students so they can create finished versions.

A hush comes over the room as the children begin writing. Hamilton moves from desk to desk, answering questions and offering suggestions.

A boy named Kevin has decided that his story will be about 12 brownies, so, on his book's title page, he carefully writes, "A Dosin Brownes." Then, on the copyright page, he inscribes, "Illscratid by Kevin. 1994." The story itself begins like this: "Ones upon ua time sum one nakt at the dore it was Sam he brot in tweve brownes." The next day, when Hamilton edits the book, he will correct the spelling mistakes and remind Kevin that sentences must end with periods.

Some of the other students create dummies that will require virtually no editing by Hamilton. One of the best is by Katie Lewis, a quiet, freckle-faced girl with a blond ponytail. Her book is called *The Twelve Books*:

I was on my way to the bookstore. When I got there, they had a sign up that said: Twelve new books! Buy them now before they're gone! Well, as you might know, I love it when bookstores sell new books. So, I went up to the cash register lady and asked: Excuse me, but can you tell me where the twelve new books are? Why yes my dear child, said the cash register lady. I will be glad to.

So, she tole me that they were in aisle four next to the Fairy Tales. Thank you, Miss Golder, I said. You're very welcome I'm sure. So, I went to aisle four, and I almost fell over my feet because there were not twelve new books. There was one new book with twelve new copies!

The End.

It's obvious that Katie reads a lot of books, for on the back page, she has written the following:

About The Author: Katie Lewis was born in 1985. She lives in Tennessee. Katie is eight, and in Mr. Hamilton's second grade class at Dodson Elementary School. Her favorite subject is spelling. Katie likes to read.

Last year, Hamilton took his students to Davis-Kidd to meet Aliki Brandenberg, a popular author of children's books who lives in London. "She was so impressed," Hamilton says. "I've got to tell you—my group last year could have told you everything about her. They knew every book she had written."

Brandenberg was so taken by the visit that she presented the students with a poster-size ink drawing of an "Alikisaurus" reading a book. On it, she wrote, "You are wonderful! Happy Reading Forever in Mr. Hamilton's Class!—Aliki."

Hamilton's dedication to his students has not gone unnoticed by parents. Former Dodson principal Carl Ross, who hired Hamilton back in 1985, says: "The parents were just crazy about having their kids in his class. There was always a waiting list to get in."

Such popularity created some problems. Until this year, parents could request which teachers they wanted for their children. But not all parents made such requests, and those who did tended to be the ones who were more actively involved in their children's education. Thus, the process resulted in some of the most popular teachers ending up with some of the best students.

"Last year," says principal Coleman, "we worked very hard to set up what might be a more equitable way of assigning children that still allowed for parental and teacher input." The goal was to have no teacher "overly burdened" by a high percentage of challenging students. Coleman says the new process seems to be working, but it doesn't mean that Hamil-

ton is any less popular. "He still is one of the most highly requested teachers," she says.

Coleman points out that Hamilton, who is Dodson's only male classroom teacher, is well-respected by his colleagues. "I think he's looked upon as a leader," she says. Teachers who want to learn more about using children's books in their classes see him as an important resource, and Hamilton has always been willing to share his expertise (not to mention his books) with others.

Finding the time, however, is another question. "I put in a very long day, every day," Hamilton says. "I'm always here before 8 a.m., and I usually leave at 5:30, sometimes later. And then I take things with me to do at home." Coming from someone else, such words might sound self-serving, but Hamilton is simply stating the facts.

At 3:30 p.m., after his students have gone home for the day, Hamilton likes to "close the door and collect my thoughts, think about the day and what I've done, what I could have done differently, and what I want to do tomorrow to improve myself. Because I'm a learner, too. And I'm not perfect."

Like most good teachers, particularly those who pour their heart and soul into their work, Hamilton worries about burnout. "I don't know how long I can continue to be enthusiastic in the classroom and stay fresh," he says, "coming up with new ideas year after year.

"I like to share my ideas, and a lot of folks here and at other schools use my ideas. But to say that I'm going to be a classroom teacher for another 30 years—I'm not really sure. I'm happy with it right now. But when you lose that edge ... We need folks right now who enjoy it. We need to be out there recruiting people to be teachers because it still is a very rewarding profession. It truly is, although maybe not monetarily.

"I'd like more materials," he continues, gathering steam. "I'd like fewer children. I'd like a larger classroom. I'd like a full-time educational assistant. I'd like to do whatever I want in my classroom regardless of the cost."

Sometimes Hamilton thinks he'd like to get into book publishing. Or maybe become a librarian. Or do more teacher training. But not just yet. "I know I'll be here next year," he says. "I can tell you that. But beyond that, I'm not sure."

Ultimately, what got Hamilton into teaching in the first place may be what keeps him in the profession. "There was a sense," he says, "that teaching was something that I could do and feel like I had accomplished something. So now, when I go home at the end of the day, exhausted from all the interactions I've had all day long, I can feel that what I've done with my life has been successful, that my little time on earth has meant something." ■

From Teacher Magazine, *May/June 1994*

60.

The Price of Isolation

A major study finds that the most successful and flexible teachers belong to 'professional learning communities.'

By Ann Bradley

When Milbrey McLaughlin and Joan Talbert launched their five-year study of the factors that influence high schools and teachers, they began, like most researchers, with a set of assumptions about what would be important to ask. But when they started interviewing teachers, the Stanford University researchers quickly learned that they were wrong. "What teachers taught me in the first year—much to my horror—was that we absolutely had to redo it," McLaughlin says.

Not surprisingly, the researchers had framed a set of questions that worked logically out from the classroom to touch on school, district, and state policies that might affect teachers' work. Teachers, they soon learned, "just don't see the world that way," McLaughlin says.

What the teachers wanted to talk about were the things that most directly influenced their work, like students and subject matter. So, the interviews were changed to let teachers tell their own stories, an approach the researchers call a "teacher's-eye view" of schooling.

In reframing their methods, the Stanford researchers moved to what observers call the cutting edge of social-science research. And their findings centered around the importance of relationships, organizations, and issues that are typically overlooked or taken for granted by traditional academic studies.

Most notably, the studies by the federally funded Center for Research on the Context of Secondary School Teaching, completed last year, revealed that teachers' participation in a "professional community"—whether through their academic department, school, or a network of like-minded colleagues—had a powerful effect on how successfully they were able to adapt their instructional strategies to meet their students' needs.

While other academicians have written about the importance of community for teachers, the center's studies were the first to look at communities as a specific context of teaching and to find a link between participation in a community and successful teaching, observers say.

Innovative Methodology

In using the term "context," the researchers refer to all of the variables that influence teaching: students, subject matter, academic departments, schools, parents, higher education, and the like. By examining how these contexts are embedded in one another, says Ann Lieberman, a professor of education at Teachers College, Columbia University, and member of the center's national advisory board, the center's work highlights the complexity of the environment that teachers and students work in.

"If we're serious about change and understanding

how it takes place," she notes, "we have to understand context in a far deeper fashion." The studies, she adds, also provide a "serious look at how teachers see change."

"That's a perspective that has long been absent" from education research, Lieberman continues. "I don't think it has ever been looked at in quite so thorough a fashion by people using an array of methods."

In fact, it was the innovative methodology used to conduct the research, Talbert says, that made some of the findings possible. To generate its primary database, the center conducted in-depth field research at 16 high schools in seven school districts in California and Michigan. Twelve of the schools were regular public schools, one was an alternative public school, and three were independent schools.

Almost 900 teachers in the high schools were interviewed each spring for three years. The center's researchers collected records from the sites and observed schools and classrooms. Various kinds of data also were collected for 48 students.

The studies generated voluminous data from the sites over the three years, including feedback from the teachers who were studied.

In an approach that the center's directors say is unique, the researchers built "bridges" between the field data and two national longitudinal studies: the 1984 High School and Beyond surveys of teachers and the National Education Longitudinal Study of 1988.

The marriage of these two kinds of data is reflected in the center leaders' backgrounds: McLaughlin, the director, is a field researcher and education-policy analyst, while Talbert, the associate director, is a sociologist who does large-scale quantitative analysis. The people who conducted the center's various research projects also hailed from a wide range of disciplines, including anthropology, curriculum theory, political science, and teacher education.

"We all saw something different," McLaughlin says. "We had multiple lenses of different disciplines and perspectives."

'Crest of a Wave'

The "bridges" were constructed by replicating some of the same questions used on the national surveys in the field interviews, Talbert explains. That way, the researchers could gauge how representative the schools, departments, and individual teachers in their 16 schools were.

The NELS:88 survey asked about such factors as collegiality, workplace climate, and leadership. So, for example, if the field data showed big differences between academic departments in terms of collegiality, the results could be checked against the yardstick of the national surveys to insure that all attitudes would be represented in the study.

Because the 16 schools that were selected for the field study were chosen for specific purposes—and were not intended to be a representative sample of U.S. schools—using the national survey data also "lets us have it both ways," McLaughlin says.

Gerald Sroufe, the director of government and professional liaison for the American Educational Research Association, calls the study's use of field data and national surveys "cutting edge." The research, he says, is "on the crest of the wave of combining qualitative and quantitative data to get a rich new perspective on things."

The center's findings will now have to be "tested through other measures to see how much you can generalize about it," he says.

The new methodology helped reveal the importance of "learning communities" for teachers. "It was really very much through the dialogue between the quanti-

> **Rather than adhering to rigorous standards and failing many students, successful teachers found ways to actively engage their students in learning.**

tative surveys and the interview data," Talbert says, "that we began to see a lot of variation among teachers in the sample and their access to or participation in collegial groups that could support them."

In conducting their interviews, the researchers used what they called a "student-decline scale" that was derived from comments they heard from teachers. The scale included such assertions as "students don't try as hard as they used to" and "students are not able to master the material."

Within a school, academic departments with different degrees of collegiality turned out to contain teachers with very different scores on the student-decline scale, Talbert says. Teachers in departments with low levels of collegiality, they found, tended to have more negative views of students.

Similarly, teachers who had made the most successful changes in their practice and had more positive views about their students' capabilities turned out to have one thing in common: belonging to an active professional community that encouraged and enabled them to transform their teaching.

Rather than adhering unswervingly to rigorous standards and failing many students, or resorting to "dumbing down" their instruction, these successful teachers found ways to actively engage their students in learning. "These healthy, positive professional communities have said, 'Hey, let's stop trying to fit the kid to this, and fit what we're doing to the kid,'" McLaughlin explains.

And, she says, "without support, many teachers fell back on their old practices or left the profession."

The importance of collegiality to a school's success was demonstrated vividly by comparing two schools in the same California district. Both served roughly the same student population and both lived under the same rules and regulations. The study found, however, that one school had high failure and dropout rates, while the other had among the highest test scores and sent 80 percent of its student to college.

The difference was reflected in the professional characteristics of the schools, Talbert says. In the school with the high failure rate, teachers complained frequently, came to work late and left early, and held meetings "at the mailboxes" if at all.

The successful school, she notes, held frequent schoolwide meetings to solve problems and develop innovative solutions, like an "adopt a student" program to provide more personal attention to students at risk of failure.

By adopting the perspectives of classroom teachers, the study also revealed some of the limitations of current education research, the center's directors say. Many studies look at an entire school, McLaughlin points out, which is too large a unit of analysis to pick up the differences among departments and classrooms that are central to the center's findings.

They also learned a number of things that contradict the way questions typically are framed in education research. Teachers are often asked about their sense of efficacy in their jobs, for example. But the center's work found that teachers' perspectives about themselves change depending upon what class period they are teaching: first period might be a breeze, but second period might be a constant struggle.

What those attitudes reveal, McLaughlin says, is that students are one of the most important contexts in teaching. As common-sensical as the notion sounds, she adds, "the policy world doesn't consider that at all."

Finding ways to help teachers deal with those contexts by creating professional communities may not be easy. "You can't command community," McLaughlin says, "and you can't concoct collegiality." ■

From Education Week, *March 31, 1993*

61.

Relax, Reflect, and Renew

The North Carolina Center for the Advancement of Teaching nourishes the mind, body, and spirit.

By Karen Diegmueller

Deep inside a dark, dank cavern the size of a football field, a guide illuminates a few discreet lamps to accentuate dazzling rock formations. At just the right moment, when the two dozen explorers have grown still, the leader presses a button on the boom box he has been hauling around, and strains from the chorale of Bach's Cantata No. 78 pierce the air. Suddenly, the pitch-black home of bats, lizards, and 40-foot drop-offs is transformed into a majestic cathedral, proffering solace to its visitors.

For these North Carolina teachers, this journey into Tennessee's Tuckalee Cavern is one of many singular moments they will experience during their week-long stay at the North Carolina Center for the Advancement of Teaching. The only center of its kind in the nation, the NCCAT is beginning its second academic year in a new $7 million retreat in the Smoky Mountains of western North Carolina. At the NCCAT, the emphasis is on reward rather than reform. Teachers can participate in stimulating, intellectual discussions, fish in mountain streams, enjoy the camaraderie of fellow teachers from across the state, conduct scientific experiments, write chapters of a novel, or be transported back in time to the Victorian age.

And, at the end of their week, if the teachers return to their classrooms eager to try out what they've experienced, so much the better, says the center's staff. But that is not the NCCAT's mission. "At the NCCAT, we turn our attention to the renewal of teachers rather than to their reform," R. Bruce McPherson, former director of the center, explained in a speech he delivered to the Minnesota Humanities Commission last year. "We do not seek to change people or their work environments, but rather to encourage them to rediscover and nourish their personal and professional strengths, the passion and the intellect that are their strongest allies in the daily business of teaching."

The NCCAT was the brainchild of Jean Powell, a North Carolina high school English teacher, who in November 1983 testified before the Governor's Commission on Education for Economic Growth about the need to instill pride, self-worth, and enthusiasm in teachers if the state wanted to retain and attract the best. "We have a governor's school for gifted students. Why not something similar for teachers?" she suggested. "We don't need any more educational methodology or the latest curriculum fads. We'd like to study the 'real stuff.' "

To Powell, that meant contemplating the Great Books, visiting art galleries, viewing plays, writing critical commentaries. "If that kind of learning experience doesn't turn on teachers, I don't know what will," she says. "That excitement will be communicated to students. Furthermore, being a student will give a teacher a renewed perspective of the student's role."

Her suggestion won the support of three of the state's most powerful forces: then Gov. James Hunt, the speaker of the House, and the president of the University of North Carolina. The trio shepherded the NCCAT through the state legislature, overcoming the opposition of the state National Education Association affiliate, which wanted the money to be used to increase teachers' salaries.

The center opened in the fall of 1986 and last year moved into its new quarters on 36 acres near the campus of Western Carolina University. The facility consists of three structures—two well-appointed residence halls, complete with fireplaces and full kitchens, and the main activities building. The latter houses seminar rooms, an amphitheater, a computer lab, a dining room, an exercise room, staff offices, and a combination lounge and library with a cathedral ceiling, skylights, a baby grand piano, and a spiral

---

At the NCCAT, the emphasis is on reward rather than freedom. Teachers can enjoy the camaraderie of fellow teachers from across the state.

---

staircase. Teachers are also encouraged to use the university's library, swimming pool, tennis courts, and other amenities.

Teachers' stays at the NCCAT are built around seminars led by academicians or other experts hired by the center. A typical seminar involves between 20 and 25 teachers who meet for discussions and various other activities throughout the week. But not every second of every day at the center is scheduled. Time is set aside for teachers to relax, reflect, and recreate.

The NCCAT now orchestrates about 55 seminars during the 10-month school year, generally offering two simultaneously. A sampling of titles from last school year's winter-spring catalog includes: "The Culture of Ancient Greece," "Personal Investing," "At the Movies," "Appalachian Spring: Wildflowers in the Big Spectrum," "Cowboy Culture and the American Psyche," and "Americans in Paris." This last seminar transported teachers to the Paris of the 1920s; they read Hemingway, fished for trout, and became actors

in a bistro—the dining room redecorated for a day.

Since the NCCAT began operating, some 3,000 teachers have gone through the center; it now accommodates about 1,200 a year. The state-funded center pays for both the teachers' travel expenses and a classroom substitute back home. Although North Carolina faces staggering budget problems, the center plans to continue operating its regular seminar schedule. Anticipating a cut of about 10 percent from their $3.4 million budget, the NCCAT officials say they will probably pare some of the center's various ancillary programs.

A week at the NCCAT is meant as a reward for exemplary service to those who have taught in the state's public schools for at least three years. Teachers must submit a fairly rigorous and comprehensive application that includes essay questions and references from their supervisor and a professional colleague. The program is popular; once a teacher is selected, it takes about a year before he or she actually arrives at the center. The lengthy wait is also a result of the NCCAT's attempts to pull together teachers from different regions of the state, grade levels, and areas of teaching expertise.

Despite the NCCAT's many attractions, it has had difficulty drawing men and minorities. Many male teachers in the state, McPherson says, double as athletic coaches. While principals may be willing to release teachers from their classrooms, getting them to replace coaches with substitutes isn't easy in a state that takes its sports more seriously than most.

Attracting African-American teachers outside of the large metropolitan areas also poses a challenge. Many African Americans in North Carolina live on the state's coastal plain, a good 10-hour drive from the mountain hideaway. Some, McPherson says, are wary of traveling to an area where few other African Americans live.

But most of the participants share the feelings of Lettie Polite, a middle school math and science teacher. Shortly before Polite's scheduled week at the NCCAT, she thought of canceling because she had so much to do. But her principal wouldn't hear of it, and Polite is now glad she didn't let anything get in her way. "It has given me so much insight," Polite says of her time at the NCCAT. "It just makes me feel like getting back in [the classroom]." ∎

From Teacher Magazine, *November/December 1991*

62.

For the Love of Books

Across the country, teachers are reading and discussing books—both for classroom use and their own enjoyment.

By Debra Viadero

It is a little after 4 p.m., and eight teachers, a librarian, and a principal are gathered around a large oak table in the library of Armel Elementary School in Frederick County, Va. It looks like the sort of after-school gathering that might be discussing a troublesome student, parking issues, or some other matter of school policy. The subject of discussion at this meeting, however, is books. "Good" books. Young-adult novels, adult fiction, professional-development books. Textbooks and readers are definitely not on this group's agenda. "Teachers can always find ways to use books in the classroom," says Anita Jenkins, the 4th grade teacher who leads this group. "But teachers almost never take the time to discuss books among themselves."

Teacher reading groups like this one, which meets monthly, are springing up in schools all over the nation this year. The groups are an outgrowth of a two-year-old program known as Teachers as Readers.

Initially begun by the Association of American Publishers' Reading Initiative and the Virginia State Reading Council, the program has an engagingly simple premise: Put books in the hands of teachers, encourage them to meet to discuss them, and, thus, rekindle in them a love of reading.

The hope is that the teachers' enthusiasm for literature will eventually spill over into their classrooms and schools, as well. "If you can really hook children into reading in the early grades," says Mary Sue Dillingofski, who directs the AAP's Reading Initiative,

"you hope that they become lifelong readers."

The Teachers as Readers program was launched in Virginia last year as an experiment involving 36 reading groups for elementary school teachers. The idea was loosely modeled on a project conducted in 1988 and 1989 by researchers at the Teachers College Writing Project at Columbia University. The researchers, Lucy Calkins and Shelley Harwayne, pulled together diverse groups of educators in New York City to read and discuss the works of Mary Gordon, Anne Tyler, and other contemporary authors. Five years later, Harwayne says, many of those groups are still meeting. "The intention was to give teachers an image of good 'book talk,' and, at some point later on, they begin to think about the implications for the classroom," Harwayne says. "How can we create this same experience for our students?"

The Teachers as Readers project, however, seeks a more direct link to the classroom. It specifies that the groups read at least four new children's books. The groups also can read one professional-development book. Dillingofski says the focus on children's books is important because so many are being published.

The growth of the whole language movement, which calls for extensive use of literature in teaching reading, has helped make children's publishing a $1 billion-a-year industry. "Five thousand new children's books are published each year," she says. "Teachers just can't keep up, so they tend to rely on the same old chestnuts."

Beyond that restriction, however, there are few guidelines. The sponsors require only that the reading groups include a principal or a district administrator and that they meet at least six times. It is also suggested that groups include no more than 10 members. New groups receive $500 or more to buy books for members.

The simplicity and flexibility of the program have contributed to its rapid growth. Virtually all of the groups started in Virginia last year are still meeting this year with no funding from the program, although some have found funding elsewhere. In addition, dozens of other groups have sprung up in school districts throughout the state.

This school year, the project has expanded nationwide and enlisted the aid of such major national groups as the National Council of Teachers of English, the International Reading Association, and the American Library Association, which use their resources and large memberships to advertise the idea to teachers. At least 6,000 school districts have received information kits on the program.

Jenkins' group, which draws educators from both Armel and Virginia Avenue Elementary School in nearby Winchester, was one of the pilot groups formed last year. The group received $850 and read a variety of books, including *The Wretched Stone* by Chris Van Allsburg and Carolyn Reeder's *Shades of Gray*.

Each member of the group also read a different professional-development book and shared it with the others. This year, the group solicited a $200 grant from a local chapter of the Veterans of Foreign Wars to keep going.

At today's meeting, the subject of discussion is *Nothing but the Truth*, a young-adult novel by Avi. The story centers on a teenager who is suspended from school for humming along with "The Star-Spangled Banner" in class. The incident takes on major proportions as the media begin to report on it and the matter comes before the school board. The brouhaha has devastating consequences for both the rebellious student and his teacher. The narrative is told through the use of memos, transcripts of conversations, newspaper articles, letters, and journal entries.

The book's familiar terrain sparks a lively discussion for the reading group. Over coffee and cake, the educators talk about how the experiences recounted in the book compare with their own. They refer to points in the story where a coach, a counselor, or a principal should have acted differently, and they express sympathy for the teacher and the pupil. "What I liked about this book," one teacher volunteers, "is that you could really see both sides."

It does not matter so much, these teachers say, that some of the books they read are aimed at readers older than their students, who range in grade level from 1st through 4th. "Now I enjoy reading books I'll never use in my classroom," says Mary Lou Gulosh, a 3rd grade teacher at Armel. "In fact, I like some of the young-adult books more."

More important, these teachers say, are the other benefits the group derives from their meetings. "I don't think there's any doubt teachers need contact with one another to have some intellectual stimulation," says one teacher. "Now, you have the time set aside, you know you're going to do it, and, suddenly, you feel, 'Gosh, I'm a professional.'"

Melvin Pearson, Armel's principal and the only man in the group, says the talks have given him a new perspective on his job. "I don't work in a classroom every day," he says. "Being involved with a group of teachers and hearing them talk about things they enjoy has helped my perspective and has helped me stay a little more open-minded about things."

The involvement of principals or other administrators is key, Dillingofski says, because they typically set school budgets for children's books. In a survey of the 36 pilot groups, 74 percent of the principals said they planned to increase their budgets for children's trade books as a result of participating in the project.

What surveys cannot adequately measure, however, is whether the discussions are affecting the teaching going on in the classrooms of the teachers involved. The teachers in this group say their book talks are making a difference, whether it is simply using more picture books in class or modeling their enthusiasm for literature to their students.

Jenkins, who teaches at Virginia Avenue Elementary, says she has come to understand that learning literature is not a matter of coming away with one "right" interpretation. Pupils can develop their own perspectives. "My children," she says, "are now doing literature groups that I don't really feel I have to be a part of." ■

From Teacher Magazine, *April 1993*

63.

Best-Kept Secret

A little known 'National Faculty' of college professors offers tailor-made staff-development programs to schools.

By Karen Diegmueller

Violet Anne Golden thinks she has discovered the secret to showing 7th graders how to do equivalent fractions. "They said, 'Miss Golden, that's not the way we learned it.'" she says. Undaunted, she explained to them, "That is the joy of mathematics. You learn it a lot of ways." On a more fundamental level, the teacher at Arthur Richards Junior High School in St. Croix in the U.S. Virgin Islands explains what her deepening knowledge of mathematics has enabled her to do in school: "It's to let the kids be creative, to reason in class."

Golden, to put it in terms that she most assuredly would appreciate, did not get from premise to conclusion on her own. She, along with other teachers in the Virgin Islands, had help from the National Faculty—a two-decades-old organization that links teachers and college faculty members to promote professional development. The group just might be one of the best-kept secrets in education. "We have worked very quietly," says Benjamin Ladner, the president of the Atlanta-based group. "We are not out to get people to pay attention to the National Faculty."

While the importance of preparing better teachers both before and after they get into the classroom has moved into the national forefront since the mid-1980's, the National Faculty has been working on-site with classroom teachers since the late 1960's. "We are radically committed to the centrality of teaching," says Ladner. "For so long, education reform focused on everything else, all of which is fine, but ... what about the teacher? Three days of in-service doesn't get it."

The National Faculty was the brainchild of Barnaby Keeney, the late president of Brown University, who, in the early to mid-1960's, conceived of a way to use university resources to benefit teachers. "The idea was very simple," says Ladner. "What if we establish a committee, simply take the best we have as college professionals, and approach schoolteachers as equals? By focusing on what we have in common as professionals, [we can] make our teaching better."

Funded primarily by the National Endowment for the Humanities and assisted by Phi Beta Kappa, the organization started on an experimental basis with a nucleus of 50 scholars. "What happened is, we touched a nerve that was quite remarkable," says Ladner. What makes it appealing, he says, is that the National Faculty offers teachers, who are largely isolated, the opportunity to talk about their work.

First, they form teacher teams, whose members decide what they need to shore up their teaching. If team members wanted to increase their knowledge of 19th century history, for instance, the National Faculty would match them, say, with an expert from Stanford University. "We will find you the leading people in the field and bring them into your school," Ladner explains.

Since its modest beginnings, the organization has boosted its network of scholars to nearly 600 and has worked on projects in all 50 states as well as in the

U.S. territories. It runs about 15 to 20 projects a year.

No two projects are alike, Ladner explains. They can range in scope from a single school to 60 sites within a district. No discipline is ruled out, but the focus clearly is on teaching content. "We think pedagogy arises out of content," says Ladner.

The length of time for each project varies from two to five years in order to ensure that it will leave a lasting mark. Typically, members of the National Faculty network hold week-long summer seminars; they are followed by two- to three-day monthly or bimonthly visits.

There are no curriculum guides, printed matter, or prescribed materials; each project is composed individually in collaboration with both the faculty and the local district. As Ladner explains, even though simultaneous history projects may be going on in Portland, Maine, and Tucson, Ariz., they will be different because the people involved are different. "In a way, the concept is scandalous," he says. "We feel you have to reinvent the wheel each time we have a project."

The network, however, tries to learn through trial and error. One crucial lesson it has learned is the importance of local "ownership" of a project. "We try to be a catalyst, a resource, a friend," Ladner says.

Schools and districts are selected in a variety of ways. In some instances, funding organizations come forward with a specific project; in others, the National Faculty elects to take on a project in response to what it perceives as a targeted goal. Most often, a phone call from a school or district begins the process.

Once a school or district is identified, the organization sends out a program officer to learn whether the prospective client meets accepted criteria. First, it has to define its own needs. Then, officials must commit to systematic teacher involvement, a significant amount of time, participant release time, administrative support, and funding.

The Virgin Islands project began two years ago with the long-range goal of helping children of limited English proficiency improve their mathematical skills. To do so, teachers and administrators who were identified as potential math leaders were trained by National Faculty scholars. These leaders are expected, eventually, to train other teachers.

Two summers ago, 27 designated math leaders from St. Croix came together for an institute; this summer, 38 from St. Croix and St. Thomas received training. The way the program was designed for the territory, scholars visit the islands every other month for two-day sessions. Funded by both the federal and territorial governments, the project cost about $52,000 the first year and $62,000 the second. "It is not a project that they picked up from California or New York. They tailor-made it for our specific needs," says Maria E. Sanes, the islands' coordinator for bilingual and English-as-a-second-language education. The scholars involved have included a National Science Foundation official, an Ohio State University mathematician, and John Firkins, a mathematics professor at Gonzaga University in Spokane, Wash.

Firkins has gone to the Virgin Islands three times now, conducting two-day workshops as well as participating in a summer institute. With teachers observing him, he taught in the schools to children who spoke Crucian or Spanish, not English. He broke through the language barrier via the language of mathematics. He measured the 1st graders' smiles with pieces of string and then showed the children their smiles were the length of four lima beans.

"Part of the work I saw myself doing as a person from the National Faculty was to change the teachers' attitudes and the kids' attitudes," says Firkins. "I wanted the teachers to see the kids' reactions. Then I think they bought into what we were doing much more easily."

The district will not have hard data on the project until the end of this year, the third year of the project. Meanwhile, educators have to rely on their observations to judge the results. "The enthusiasm they have engendered in our teachers has been nothing short of miraculous," says Marion Gallo Moore, the district coordinator of mathematics for St. Croix. "Math is fun, and [the teachers] are infecting students with it."

Gallo Moore says she has observed more activity in the classroom, more interaction between teachers and students, and more use of the pedagogical techniques that the National Council of Teachers of Mathematics advocates.

Geared to limited-English-proficient students, the project nonetheless has aided other students, says Lionel Sewpershad, the assistant principal at Charles H. Emanuel Elementary School. "Where we have mixed classes, the same technique is being used with all these kids," he says.

Not every National Faculty project has succeeded, Ladner acknowledges. Sometimes the fault has been the organization's, he says. Because of an error in judgment, the project may make a wrong match between scholar and site. Or a scheduling foul-up may sour the fragile beginnings of a new relationship.

At other times, he says, the fault lies with the school or district: Funding dries up, a new superintendent scotches the project, or the community gets in an uproar over a subject involving race or sex. Other projects have fallen to lengthy teacher strikes.

In the eyes of Violet Anne Golden, though, the project in the Virgin Islands is succeeding handsomely. Were it not for the scholars from the National Faculty, she says, she would not be where she is today. "Our teachers were inspired at those sessions," Golden says. "Language didn't mean anything for the first time in my life. The demonstrations were in our language— mathematics." ■

From Education Week, *Dec. 4, 1991*

64.

Somebody To Lean On

We can't work alone as teachers; we need to divide the pain and multiply the pleasure.

Commentary by John Morris

If you happen to walk past my classroom at about 7:30 a.m. on a school day, chances are good that you will hear coming from my record player Bill Withers' song, "Lean On Me." I often play this song when I arrive at school in the morning. It's message is simple and upbeat: Everybody needs a friend, from time to time— somebody to lean on. It has a great beat, so it helps me get moving as I start to prepare the room for the day. I do a bit of dancing as an antidote to the Oh-God-I'm-not-ready feeling.

Just as important as the dancing are the lyrics to the song. I need to get that idea of mutual need up on the front burner of my brain every day. I need to admit that I cannot work alone and that I won't get beyond all the inevitable failures if I only rely on myself. I need to look for partners with whom I can, as one of my colleagues says, "divide the pain and multiply the pleasure."

Several years ago, I began to feel that I was in a rut in terms of my teaching, and, as the saying goes, "The only difference between a rut and a grave is the depth of the hole." I realized that I had spent most of my career as a teacher in a self-contained classroom, which meant I had the freedom to create my own classroom environment and the opportunity to do spontaneous and crazy things if the moment seemed right. But the flip side of that kind of freedom and "self-containment" was a growing sense of isolation and loneliness. Feeling more and more buried in my classroom, I re-

alized I had to reach out and form some kind of partnership. I needed someone to lean on. I was fortunate to have a colleague right across the hall who was feeling the same way. After many informal conversations and brainstorming sessions, Judith and I decided to try doing a few things together, just to see how it might work. First, we scheduled storytime at the same time each day and gave the students a choice of listening to two different books. It worked. Suddenly, there was a new chemistry created in both classrooms. Each student had two teachers instead of one, and each teacher had a very different group of students to relate to for part of each day. It was a small step for us to take, but our dance had begun.

What began as a simple experiment blossomed into a much more ambitious attempt at team teaching. Judith and I tried all kinds of cross-grade groupings, multi-age activities, and interdisciplinary themes within the structure of our full-blown primary unit. As I reflect on the results of our four years of teaching together, the specific successes and failures are not the important things to recall.

The crucial thing for me to remember is that both Judith and I needed someone to share the work of teaching. It was like building a mobile: We started with one pair of balancing objects and then worked upward in order to construct something that became more and more complex.

Without that first effort, that first careful and tentative balancing act, the thing never would have existed, and I would have sunk further and further into the vast sands of "self-containment."

This notion of interdependence is at odds with much of what our culture tries to teach us, especially those of us who are male. All too often in this country, we are trained to be self-reliant and independent, to go it alone and make things happen all by ourselves, to trust no one and compete with everyone. It is this tradition that leads us to celebrate the heroic adventurer who strikes out alone to conquer the wilderness or make a new scientific discovery or battle against all odds to win some victory. It is this philosophy that produces cultural heroes who are "tough" and who can "make it on their own" and who "don't need any help from anybody." So, we are encouraged to be like the athletes, entertainers, business executives, military leaders, and politicians who have achieved fame and fortune in our society by relying on their own talents and hard work in order to "make it."

In this environment, when the concept of "teamwork" does appear, it is usually for the purpose of teaming up in order to beat someone else's team. It is not surprising that the language of football, business, and the military interpenetrate each other. In these endeavors, we are taught that it is "teamwork" that gets the job done and enables us to compete successfully against our opponent, competitor, or enemy. But what about the notion that teamwork has value in and of itself? What about the idea that cooperation is not a weakness but is at the core of who we are as humans? What about the fact that to be "self-contained" and "independent" is also to be isolated, disconnected, and ultimately alienated from other people? If admitting that we need to lean on someone is perceived in our culture as a sign of weakness, is it any wonder that we have such high rates of chemical dependencies and addictive behaviors?

Aren't they simply the end result of a philosophy that teaches us not to depend on anyone else? Our society produces a lot of rugged individuals, but it also produces a lot of lonely drinkers.

As I sit here in my study thinking about these things, I look at the poster hanging on the wall across from my desk. It is a poster a friend gave me after reading an essay I wrote comparing the work of teaching with the work of Sisyphus, the mythic Greek figure who endlessly pushes a rock up a hill. In one corner of the poster is a quotation from Albert Camus: "The struggle itself toward the heights is enough to fill one's heart." I agree with that idea, and I have felt in my teaching all of the strain and all of the exhaustion depicted in the beautiful line drawing of Sisyphus.

But I am now struck by the fact that the person pushing the huge boulder uphill is all alone. Sisyphus the self-reliant. Sisyphus the independent. But also, Sisyphus the lonely.

Next to this poster is a watercolor painting done by my wife. It is my favorite work of hers. Several years ago, I formally purchased it from her, just so it wouldn't be sold away from me. The painting is titled "Fred and Ginger," and it shows two lithe figures, against a background of muted blues and greens, dancing gracefully together. The effort of those two dancers is no less exhausting and will go on as endlessly as the effort of Sisyphus, but how much more wonderful it is to move and work and glide and turn and bend and push and balance together instead of all alone.

We all need somebody to lean on. ■

John Morris teaches 1st, 2nd, and 3rd graders at Marlboro (Va.) Elementary School.

From Teacher Magazine, *October 1992*

65.

'Stars' and 'Quitters'

Professor Martin Haberman has developed a controversial technique for choosing successful urban teachers.

By Daniel Gursky

Martin Haberman has been telling anyone who would listen for more than 30 years that not all teaching is the same. Urban teaching is different, he says, and successful urban teachers exhibit a distinct mixture of skills and beliefs. For almost as long, Haberman has been arguing that schools of education cannot prepare enough effective teachers for America's city schools because faculty members themselves have virtually no urban teaching experience.

Considering his position as a professor of education at the University of Wisconsin at Milwaukee, Haberman's solution to the nation's chronic shortage of qualified urban teachers is rather unusual.

He would break what he calls education schools' "cartel" on the preparation of teachers, and open the profession up to all college graduates. That alone is not enough, because there is no guarantee that arts and sciences graduates will make better teachers.

That is where Haberman's "urban-teacher selection interview" comes in. In three decades of using it to select candidates for nontraditional teacher-preparation programs that emphasize practical, on-the-job training, Haberman claims that the interview has proved almost flawless at predicting would-be teachers' professional potential in the classroom.

By interviewing hundreds of "star" teachers around the county, Haberman has come up with what he considers to be the central attributes of good urban teaching. And to get a better idea of what not to look for in

a teacher, he has talked to many self-described "quitters" who have left the profession.

The result is an interview process that looks more like a doctoral candidate's defense of a dissertation than a search for a teaching job. "Typical interview questions don't have any answers," Haberman complains. "For example, 'When did you decide to become a teacher?' That's like asking someone what their favorite color is. What are you going to do about the answer, and what does the answer mean?"

And, he argues, if the interviewer loves children and wanted to be a teacher from the time she was a little girl, she will look for similar answers from teacher candidates. "What you have are very stereotypical questions that reflect the background and experience and prejudice of the questioner," he says.

In contrast, Haberman and his colleagues—the interview usually is conducted by two people—start by asking the candidate what she would do if one of her students was not doing his homework. She might suggest talking to the student, for example. But the questioners do not just accept that answer and move on. They repeat the scenario, saying that the teacher's suggestion worked for a short time, but the student has reverted to not doing his homework.

"So what do you do then?" they ask. It is a relentless process in which the teaching candidate has to keep coming up with additional suggestions. The point of the persistent questioning is to test just that—the person's persistence in handling a tough problem.

Other questions in the 30-minute interview are just

as pointed and just as impossible to study for. Candidates are asked how they would deal with an authoritarian principal who wants them to discontinue an activity the children clearly love. They have to provide generalizations about teaching and apply them to themselves and other teachers. They are questioned about at-risk students, teacher burnout, and mistakes they might make in the classroom.

Perhaps the most unusual series of questions gets at a person's personal orientation toward teaching. "Is it possible to teach children you don't love?" the interviewer asks. And the converse, "Is it possible for children to learn from teachers they don't love?"

On each question or series of questions, Haberman has developed a continuum, with answers a star teacher would provide on one end and quitters' responses on the other. If the respondent provides the answer of a quitter on any question, he or she fails the interview. Successful candidates tend to provide answers that fall somewhere along the spectrum.

Haberman says he is trying to discover a prospective teacher's ideology and methods. "We get what a person thinks a teacher in a school serving poor kids is supposed to be doing and why, and also the behaviors they would engage in," he notes.

In his vision of a good urban teacher, what emerges is a persistent, flexible, intelligent, resourceful, energetic person willing to admit his or her own fallibility. (And no, Haberman is not looking for people who think they have to love all children and be loved by them in return.)

After the interview, Haberman and the other interviewer classify the candidate as a "star," "high potential," "average potential," or "no potential."

"We don't miss 'no's' and we don't miss 'stars,'" he asserts. Some teachers that he predicted would be great turn out to be merely good, and vice versa, but all the teachers he picks turn out to be successful in the classroom, he adds.

Haberman is currently interviewing Milwaukee paraprofessionals for a program that will train them to become elementary or middle school teachers for the city's public schools.

All three paraprofessionals interviewed this day express some surprise after they leave the room. "I expected the interview to focus a little bit more on me," Robert Tilden says. "But I guess that's what they're getting at by nailing you with difficult questions and seeing what you come up with." Tilden, who graduated from college almost 20 years ago with a degree in mechanical engineering, typifies the sort of older candidates with diverse experiences attracted to Haberman's training programs over the years.

After going through Haberman's interview as part of another recent program, Carolyn Ealy is a big fan of the process. "The beautiful part about this interview is that it knows no race, color, creed, or age," says Ealy, a math and science teacher at Milwaukee's Thomas Edison Middle School.

In interviews for other jobs with the city's school system, she found she could fudge her answers, says Ealy, who now helps Haberman conduct some interviews. "This really gets to the heart" of what urban teachers do, she says.

Haberman estimates that about two-thirds of the paraprofessionals he selects for the current program will be minorities. This, he says, proves that plenty of qualified minority candidates want to become teachers. "We can find all the good minority teachers we want, provided we don't look in undergraduate schools of education," Haberman says. "In undergraduate schools of education, we're going to find less than 5 percent of the students are minorities, and they're going to be less bright than the minorities in the other schools and colleges."

Milwaukee does not use the term "alternative certification"—the paraprofessionals are applying for the Metropolitan Multicultural Teacher-Education Program—but the similarities are unmistakable. Haberman has trained administrators of other alternative-route programs—most notably in Texas—to use his interview, and he has recently been working with the Chicago Teachers' Union because teachers and principals there now have the authority to select teachers for their own schools.

Despite his claims of success, however, people are not exactly scrambling to get their hands on the interview form. Part of the problem, Haberman maintains, is that many urban systems do not want to screen out any potential teachers. "They want anybody who shows up," he says. "There are a lot of cities that would like to use this, but they can't because they need enough day-to-day subs."

And Haberman acknowledges that some people do not believe the interview works as well as he says it does. Part of that skepticism may be a product of his blunt criticism of the education establishment, which does not endear Haberman to some of his colleagues. Some teacher educators, in particular, have said the interview eliminates candidates who could develop into good teachers, even if they fail to show that during the interview. Other critics have said that good teaching is a personal, subjective matter that cannot be distilled into essential elements and tested in a half-hour interview.

"I can't describe 100 percent of what good teachers do," Haberman responds. "But I can describe 60 percent, and I'm happy with that."

The fact that he does not charge people to use his interview process also makes it suspect to some, he says. "It's very hard for people to believe it's a quality product if they get it for nothing," Haberman says. "I would like to make a lot of money, but I just don't know how." ■

From Education Week, *April 1, 1992*